THE QUEEN'S FAVOURITES

Due to illness, Jean Plaidy was unable to go to school regularly and so taught herself to read. Very early on, she developed a passion for the 'past'. After doing a shorthand and typing course, she spent a couple of years doing various jobs, including sorting gems in Hatton Garden and translating for foreigners in a City café. She began writing in earnest following marriage and now has a large number of historical novels to her name. Inspiration for her books is drawn from odd sources – a picture gallery, a line from a book, Shakespeare's inconsistencies. She lives in London and loves music, secondhand bookshops and ancient buildings. Jean Plaidy also writes under the pseudonym of Victoria Holt.

CONDITIONS OF SALE

The Stuart Saga

THE QUEEN'S FAVOURITES

JEAN PLAIDY

UNABRIDGED

PAN BOOKS LTD : LONDON

First published 1966 by Robert Hale and Company
This edition published 1973 by Pan Books Ltd,
33 Tothill Street, London SW1

ISBN 0 330 23701 2

Text decorations by B. S. Biro

Printed in Great Britain by
Cox & Wyman Ltd, London, Reading and Fakenham

CONTENTS

Abigail Hill	9
In the Princess's Apartments	53
Queen Anne	95
A Death in the Family	108
King's Evil	140
Queen's Bounty	150
The Jealous Duchess	183
Blenheim	190
Intrigue in the Green Closet	200
The Sunderland Controversy	218
The Masham Marriage	254
After Oudenarde	280
Sarah in the Death Chamber	310
Marlborough's Request	317
Wine for a Laundress	329
Dr Sacheverel	337
The Last Meeting	355
The Fall of Godolphin	363
The Golden Keys	372
Disgrace and Departure	385
Queen Anne is Dead	396
The Exiles Return	423
At Langley Marsh	430
The End of the Favourites	432

BIBLIOGRAPHY

Memoirs of the Duke of Marlborough with his original correspondence. 3 vols. William Coxe.

An account of the Conduct of the Dowager Duchess of Marlborough.

Sarah, Duchess of Marlborough. Kathleen Campbell.

Duchess Sarah. The Social History of the times of Sarah Jennings. Mrs Arthur Colville.

John and Sarah. Duke and Duchess of Marlborough. Stuart J. Reid with introduction by the Duke of Marlborough.

Sarah Churchill. Frank Chancellor.

Marlborough's Duchess. Louis Kronenberger.

Robert Harley, Earl of Oxford. A study of Politics and Letters in the Reign of Queen Anne. E. S. Roscoe.

Lives of the Queens of England. Agnes Strickland.

Anne of England. M. R. Hopkinson.

That Enchantress. Doris Leslie.

Notes on British History. William Edwards.

Journal to Stella. Jonathan Swift, edited by Harold Williams.

Three Eighteenth Century Figures. Bonamy Dobrée.

Letters of Two Queens. Lt.-Col. The Hon. Benjamin Bathurst.

British History. John Wade.

Dictionary of National Biography. Edited by Sir Leslie Stephen and Sir Sidney Lee.

The National and Domestic History of England. William Hickman Smith Aubrey.

Bishop Burnet's *History of his Own Times.*

England Under the Stuarts. G. M. Trevelyan.

History of England. G. M. Trevelyan.

English Social History. G. M. Trevelyan.

England Under Queen Anne. G. M. Trevelyan.

Marlborough, His Life and Times. Winston S. Churchill.

Abigail Hill

When the attention of Lady Marlborough was called to her impecunious relations, the Hills, she looked upon the entire subject as a trivial inconvenience, although later – much later – she came to realize that it was one of the most – perhaps the most – important moments of her brilliant career.

In the first place it was meant to be an insult, but one which she had brushed aside as she would a tiresome gnat at a picnic party.

The occasion had been the birthday of the Princess Anne, and on that day Her Highness's complete attention had been given to her son, the young Duke of Gloucester. Anne's preoccupation with that boy, although understandable, for he was the only one of her children who had survived after countless pregnancies – at least Lady Marlborough had lost count, for there must have been a dozen to date – was a source of irritation. Before the boy's birth, Sarah Churchill, Lady Marlborough, had become accustomed to demanding the whole of the Princess's attention, and the friendship between them was the wonder and speculation of all at Court; when they were together Anne and Sarah were Mrs Morley and Mrs

Freeman respectively, because Anne wished there to be no formality to mar their absolute intimacy. But since the boy had been born, although the friendship had not diminished, Anne's first love was for her son, and when she went on and on about 'my boy' Sarah felt as though she could scream.

Thus it had been at the birthday celebrations; the boy was to have a formal introduction to the Court, and for the occasion Anne had ordered that a special costume be made for him; and she had had the absurd idea of decking him out in her own jewels. Anne herself did not greatly care for ceremonial occasions; she was far more comfortable reclining on her couch, with a cup of chocolate in her hand or a dish of sweetmeats beside her, entertaining herself with the cards or gossip. But she wanted 'my boy' as she, to Sarah's exasperation, constantly referred to him, to look magnificent.

Poor little wretch! thought Sarah, who delighted in applying terms of contempt to persons in high places. He needed to be adorned. When she compared him with her own handsome son – John after his father – who was a few years older than the young Duke, she wanted to crow with triumph. In fact it was all she could do to prevent herself calling Anne's attention to the difference in the two boys. When she brought young John to Court, as she intended to quite soon, Anne would see for herself what a difference there was between the two.

But young Gloucester, in spite of his infirmity, was a bright boy. He was alert, extremely intelligent, and the doctors said that the fact that he suffered from water on the brain, far from harming his mind, made it more alert; and so it seemed. He was old for his years; sharp of wits, and to see him drilling the ninety boys in the park whom he called his army, was one of the sights of the Court. All the same, his head was too big for his body and he could not walk straight unless two attendants were close beside him. He was the delight and terror of his parents' life – and no wonder.

There he was on this occasion in a coat of blue velvet, the button-holes of which were encrusted with diamonds; and about his small person were his mother's jewels. Over his shoulder was the blue ribbon of the Garter which Sarah could never look on without bitterness; she had so wanted the Garter for her dear Marl, her husband, who, she believed, was possessed of genius and could rule the country if he only had a chance. Therefore to see the small figure boasting that he was already a Knight of the Garter was a maddening sight; but when she looked at the white periwig, which added a touch of absurdity, and thought of that huge head beneath it, she was thankful that even if Marlborough had been denied the Garter, even if Dutch William was keeping him in the shadows, at least she had a healthy family; and it was only a matter of waiting for the end of William before, with Anne's coming to the throne, they were given what they deserved.

In the royal nursery young Gloucester had displayed the jewel which the King had given him; it was St George on horseback set with diamonds, a magnificent piece; and it was certainly not William's custom to be so generous. But like everyone else at Court he had an affection for the little boy who, with his charming eccentricities, had even been able to break through the King's reserve.

'His Majesty gave me this,' he said, 'when he bestowed the Garter on me. He put on the Garter with his own hands which I assure you is most unusual. It is because he holds me in such regard. Am I not fortunate? But I shall repay His Majesty. Look here, Mamma, this is the note I am sending him.'

Anne had taken the note and Sarah, with the boy's governess, Lady Fitzharding, had looked over her shoulder as she read.

'I, Your Majesty's most dutiful subject, had rather lose my life in Your Majesty's cause than in any man's else, and I hope it will not be long ere you conquer France. We, your Majesty's subjects, will stand by you while we have a drop of blood.

Gloucester.'

Anne had smiled and looked from Barbara Fitzharding to Sarah. Besottedly, thought Sarah. It was true the boy was precocious – but he was a child. And when he offered his soldiers – boys of his own age with toy muskets and swords – to the King it was a joke and nothing more. But even grim William gravely accepted these offers and came to Kensington to review the small troops. Perhaps, thought Sarah sardonically, this was not so foolish as it seemed; for it was only on such occasions, with the crowd looking on, that he managed to raise a cheer for himself.

'I am sure the King will be delighted,' Anne had said.

'Doubtless he will think I am a little too fine,' mused Gloucester thoughtfully. 'But my loyalty may help to divert his impatience with my finery.'

The Princess Anne had rolled her eyes in ecstasy. Was there ever such a boy! What wit! What observation! What a King he would make when his turn came!

When he had left them they had had to listen to accounts – heard many times before – of his wit and wisdom. Sarah was impatient, but Barbara Fitzharding was almost as besotted as the Princess; and there they had sat, like two old goodies, talking about this wonderful boy.

It was later when Sarah and Barbara were together, that Sarah gave way to her impatience.

'I do not think the King cared for all that display,' she commented, a smile which was almost a sneer turning up a corner of her mouth.

'He is, I believe, truly fond of his nephew,' Barbara replied. 'And he is not fond of many people.'

'There are his good friends, Bentinck and Keppel – Bentinck the faithful and Keppel the handsome – and of course his mistress.'

Sarah looked slyly at Barbara, for it was her sister, Elizabeth Villiers, who had been William's mistress almost since the beginning of his marriage to the time of the Queen's death. The Queen had left a letter which had been opened after her death reproaching William and asking him to discontinue the liaison, and which had so shaken the King that he had left Elizabeth alone for a long time. Sarah believed, though, that the relationship had been resumed – very secretively; and Barbara, a spy reporting everything to her sister who passed it on to William, would know if this were so.

'He is so very ill these days,' said Barbara. 'I doubt whether he has the time or energy for diversions.'

12

'His *gentlemen* friends remain at his side. I hear they enjoy themselves on Hollands Gin in the Hampton Banqueting House. He still finds time – and energy – to indulge his Dutchmen.'

'But he is looking more frail every week.'

'That is why it was a mistake to dress Gloucester up in all that finery. It was almost proclaiming him Prince of Wales before his mother is Queen.'

'I wonder,' said Barbara with a hint of sarcasm, 'that you did not warn his mother since she would most assuredly listen to *you*.'

'I did warn her.'

'And she disobeyed?' Veiled insolence! Sarah had never liked Barbara Fitzharding since the days when as young Barbara Villiers she had lived with the circle of girls, Sarah among them, who had been brought up by Barbara's mother, with the young Princesses Anne and Mary in Richmond Palace.

'She is so besotted about that boy.'

'He is her son.'

'He is being pampered. I would not let one of mine be indulged as he is.'

Was this a reflection on Barbara's governess-ship? Barbara disliked Sarah Churchill – who at Court did not? – and although she might rule the Princess Anne's household, Barbara was not going to allow her to interfere in that of the Duke of Gloucester.

'He is by no means indulged. He merely happens to be an extremely intelligent boy. In fact, I have never known one more intelligent.'

'Have you not? I must invite you to St Albans one day and you shall meet *my* children.'

Barbara laughed. 'Everything you have must naturally be better than other people's.'

'*Must* always be? What do you mean by that? My children are strong, healthy, intelligent, which is not to be wondered at. Compare their father with that ... oaf ... I can call him nothing else ... who goes around babbling "Est-il possible?" to everything that is said to him! Prince George of Denmark! I call

13

him Old Est-il-possible! And when I do everyone knows to whom I refer.'

'One would think you were the royal Princess – Her Highness, your servant,' said Barbara. 'You ought to take care, Sarah Churchill. You should think back to the days when you first joined us at Richmond. You were fortunate, were you not, to find a place there? It was the greatest good luck . . . for you. You must admit that you were not of the same social order as the rest of us. We were noble and you . . .'

'Your relative, Barbara Villiers – my lady Castlemaine as she became – put honours in your family's way because she was an expert performer in the King's bedchamber. We had no such ladies in our family.'

'Your husband I believe did very well out of his relationship with my Lady Castlemaine. She paid him for his services to her . . . in the bedchamber. Was it five thousand pounds with which he bought an annuity? You must find that very useful now that my lord Marlborough is out of favour and has no office at the Court.'

If there was one person in the world whom Sarah truly loved it was her husband, John Churchill, Earl of Marlborough; and although he had had a reputation as a rake before their marriage, he had, she was certain, remained absolutely faithful to her since. This reference to past indiscretions aroused her fury.

She slapped Barbara Fitzharding's face.

Barbara, taken aback, stared at her, lifted her hand to retaliate and then remembered that there must be no brawling between women in positions such as theirs.

But her anger matched Sarah's.

'I'm not surprised at your mode of behaviour,' she said. 'It is hardly to be wondered at. And besides being arrogant and ill-mannered you are also cruel. I should be ashamed, not to have poor relations, but to turn my back on them while they starve.'

'What nonsense is this?'

'It is no nonsense. I heard only the other day the distressing story of the Hill family. I was interested . . . and so was my informant . . . because of their connection with the high and mighty Lady Marlborough! Your uncle, aunt and cousins . . .

dying of starvation! Two girls working as servants, I hear, two boys running about the streets, ragged and hungry.'

'A pitiable story and one which does credit to your imagination, Lady Fitzharding.'

'A pitiable story, Lady Marlborough, but it owes nothing to my imagination. Go and see for yourself. And let me tell you this, that I shall not feel it my duty to keep silent about this most shameful matter.'

Sarah for once was speechless, and when Lady Fitzharding flounced out of the room she stared after her, murmuring: 'Hill! Hill!' The name was familiar. Her grandfather Sir John Jennings, she had heard her own father say, had had twenty-two children and one of these, Mary, had married a Francis Hill who was a merchant of London.

Sarah had heard nothing of him since. One did not need to keep in touch with one's merchant connections – except of course when they were likely to bring disrepute.

Sarah made one of her prompt decisions.

Something must be done about the Hills.

It was too delicate a matter to delegate. She must deal with it herself.

Sombrely dressed she drove to the address she had discovered – a perilous journey, for the streets of London were unsafe even by day, and robbers had a way of knowing the quality, however quietly dressed.

She dismounted at the house – a poor place – and told the coachman to wait, for she would not be long. Two boys in ragged clothes were lounging at the door and looked at her in surprise.

'Do the Hills live here?' she asked imperiously.

They told her, in voices which suggested a certain amount of education, that they did.

'And you?' she demanded.

'Our name is Hill.'

Inwardly she shivered. These ragged creatures her relations! It was incredible. Something must be done . . . quickly. She was not going to allow that Fitzharding woman to spread scandal about her.

'Take me to your parents,' she commanded.

The house was clean, for which she was thankful, but when she came face to face with Mary and Francis Hill she was horrified. Their state of emaciation was clearly due to starvation.

'I am Sarah Churchill,' she announced. 'Sarah Jennings that was.'

Mary Hill gave a little cry and said: 'So *you're* Sarah . . . I have of course heard much of you.'

'And I have heard of you. This is terrible. But I will remedy it. Those are your sons. Here, boy, go and buy food . . . as quickly as you can.'

She gave him money and both boys went off.

'Now,' said Sarah, 'you had better tell me everything.'

'You, Francis,' began his wife.

'It is not an unusual story,' Francis explained. 'I was a merchant. My business failed. I became bankrupt and over the last months have had to sell our possessions in order to live. We have become poorer and poorer. We came to this place to live. It is the best we can afford. There is very little money left and I do not know where we shall turn for more.'

'Those boys . . .?'

'They can earn a penny here and there . . . but it is not enough to keep us.'

'And you?'

'I have tried, but my strength seems to have deserted me.'

Sarah could understand why. Malnutrition! There was little strength in either of them.

'So there are you and the two boys.'

'The girls were more fortunate. They found places.'

'Places!'

'Yes. Abigail and Alice are in service. Abigail has a good post with Lady Rivers.'

'What as?'

'As a maid in the house.'

A maid! thought Sarah. My cousin . . . a maid to Lady Rivers! A nice state of affairs! Lady Rivers might come to Court and bring her servants with her. And among these the cousin of Lady Marlborough!

'It is fortunate I have discovered this. You must tell me

everything. Hold nothing back. I will find places for all the children – those two boys and the girls. As for you, I shall leave you ten guineas for the time being and we will decide what has to be done.'

Sarah then began firing questions at the couple who, trembling with excitement and hope, answered them. She sat upright on the chair they had given her, while her busy mind was working. Two boys ... perhaps a place in the Custom House for one and the other ... well, she would see. As for the girls, she must consider what could be done for them, and when the children were in good positions they could help support their parents; in the meantime she would see that they did not starve.

The boys returned with food and it was shocking to see the manner in which it was immediately devoured.

Sarah was horrified; but at the same time pleased by their homage. It was quite clear that they thought her an angel in disguise, the omnipotent, beautiful benefactress!

It was pleasant to be so regarded and she knew that without a great deal of effort she would be able to bestow such benefits on the Hill family that would make them her willing slaves for ever.

Help to Mary and Francis Hill had come a little too late. A few days after Sarah's visit Francis died; Mary was stricken with sorrow, and suffering from the same disease caused by starvation, quickly followed him.

Now Sarah had only the four orphans to settle, and she ordered the two girls to return to their parents' house to attend the funerals. She sent off money and cast-off clothes to the family and busied herself with planning what to do with them.

The boys must be settled first. The thought of them running about the streets in rags horrified her. She told the Princess Anne about her discovery of these needy relations – for she was anxious that Barbara Fitzharding should not start circulating her stories before she had had a chance of putting her own case – and Anne was immediately sympathetic.

'My dear Mrs Freeman has the kindest heart!' she sighed.

'I want to place them all as soon as possible,' Sarah told her.

'I am sure Mrs Freeman will know what to do for the best.'

She did. It was infuriating that Marl should be out of favour; but she consoled herself that all the slights and humiliations would be forgotten once Dutch William was no more and Anne was Queen. She was very impatient for that much longed for event; so after hurrying down to St Albans, where Marl was staying with the children, and talking over the matter with him, she went, with his blessing, to see their old friend Sidney Godolphin.

Godolphin was such an adept politician that although he was a Tory and the Ministry was mainly Whig, he retained his position in the Treasury. Godolphin was well aware that Marlborough's decline into the shadows was only temporary and he was anxious not to offend Sarah, so he listened intently to her request and offered at once to find a place for the eldest Hill boy in the Custom House.

Having taken this step she decided once more to pay a visit to the humble house and see the creatures for herself.

When Lady Marlborough declared her intention of visiting the young Hills, there was immediate tension throughout the house.

'It was,' said Alice, 'like a royal command.'

'It is indeed so,' replied Abigail. 'Everyone knows that our important female relative is greatly admired by the Princess Anne who takes her advice in all things.'

'She rules royalty,' agreed Alice. 'I'll wager she will find places for us.'

'Being penniless you have nothing with which to wager,' Abigail reminded her.

'Don't be so prim, Abby! I do declare you don't seem the least excited. Don't you realize how fortunate we are to have such a benefactress?'

'She is only finding places for us because she can't allow her cousins to be servants.'

'What does the reason matter . . . as long as we get the places?'

Abigail shrugged her shoulders and murmured: 'Come, we should be ready to receive her when she arrives.'

They were thinking of their elder brother who, by the good graces of Lord Godolphin and Lady Marlborough, was already installed in the Custom House, as they made their way to the sparsely furnished bedroom to put on the dresses which Lady Marlborough had sent them. These had belonged to Lady Marlborough's daughters, some of whom were very much the same age as thirteen-year-old Abigail and eleven-year-old Alice.

Abigail wore a mulberry-coloured cloth gown and because she felt it might appear to be a little too grand for a poor relation decided to wear her linen apron over it.

'That spoils it,' declared Alice. 'Why do you do it?'

'I don't want her to think I am aping my betters.'

Alice burst out laughing. 'You stand there looking buttoned up,' she said. 'I know you hate this as much as I do.'

'We have to be grateful to Lady Marlborough.'

'That's why we can't abide her. Whoever liked those to whom they had to be grateful?'

'It could depend.'

'On what?'

'On the manner in which benefits were bestowed.'

'Oh, Abby, you don't talk like Lady Rivers's chamber maid.'

'Why should I when I was never meant to be a servant. You know how Papa always insisted on our doing our lessons.'

'Well, we *were* servants – for whatever reason – until Lady Marlborough decided otherwise. She is like God – all powerful, but I wish that like God she would remain invisible. I might be able to offer more fervent hymns of praise then.'

'You're blaspheming, Alice.'

Alice laughed and struggled with the fastening of Elizabeth Churchill's cast-off gown. 'I wish I knew what you were thinking, Abby.'

'Doubtless the same as you on this occasion.'

'Abigail, do you never lose your temper?'

'Often.'

'You never show it.'

19

'What good would that do?'

Alice sighed. 'There are times, sister, when I think you have more sense than you're given credit for.'

The two girls were standing side by side looking into the mirror.

'Then that is useful,' commented Abigail, 'for I have little else.'

Poor Abigail! thought Alice. She was plain. She was small, thin, and in spite of this she looked older than thirteen. A little woman already. Her hair was fine, limp and a sandy colour; her eyes were pale green and small; her only distinguishing feature was her high bridged nose which was inclined to be pink at the tip; and she had an unfortunate habit of hanging her head as though she wanted to spare people the need to look at such an unprepossessing face. She had no beauty, so it was fortunate that she had good sense and knew how to keep her temper under control.

'Well,' went on Alice, 'I wonder what she has decided for us.' Her face puckered and the assumption of age which the hardness of her life had put upon her, fell away; she looked like the eleven-year-old child she was. 'Oh, Abby, I don't want to go away. How I hate being poor. Don't you?'

Abigail shrugged her shoulders. 'Oh, what use would it be? We are – and there's no help for it.'

'Don't you sometimes dream that you're important ... as she is. That you descend like a tornado on your poor relations ...'

'I have never witnessed a tornado so I do not know how it descends.'

'Have you no imagination? Of course you haven't ... only plain good sense. And when her ladyship finds you your post you will take it most gratefully and you will go about your duties with a quiet efficiency which will be a credit to the great lady who recommended you, while I ...'

'While you, Alice, will do exactly the same.'

Alice smiled at her sister. She was right. And the cast-off clothes of a rich Churchill girl could not help her at all; she looked just as plain as she did in her working clothes. But perhaps when she was poor and had to be grateful for small benefits it was as well to be plain and modest, controlled and hardworking.

Lady Marlborough stepped from her coach and as she entered the house, it immediately appeared to be ten times smaller, shabbier and meaner than it had been before. Her loud voice seemed, to Abigail, to shake its foundations.

The little family were waiting to receive her. Abigail, at its head now, quiet, humble, betraying nothing; Alice apprehensive and finding that all the truculence she had promised herself was fast disappearing; and John who was wondering whether he would have to join his brother in the Custom House or whether he could hope for a place in the Army.

As Lady Marlborough's gaze swept over them and came to rest on Abigail, she was pleased with what she saw. The girl looked after the others as well as could be expected and she was aware of her position. She was old beyond her years. Thirteen was young but her responsibilities had aged her. She might be at least sixteen or even seventeen.

She took off the cloak that she had worn to conceal her fine garments which were in the latest fashion. Although she hated the King and had done her best, during Queen Mary's reign, to alienate the Princess Anne from her sister, she had to wear the Dutch styles if she were to be in the fashion. Over her gown, looped up to make panniers at the side, and so droop at the back, she wore a wide skirted coat of dark blue velvet, the sleeves of which came to the elbows where they were turned back in the form of stiff cuffs, beneath which showed the fine lace at the sleeves of her gown. Her magnificent hair, which was her greatest claim to beauty, being thick, wavy and of a bright golden colour, was dressed in the style of a bob wig, and over this she wore a lace head-dress decorated with ribbons which had been completely hidden by the large hood of the dark cloak. A regal Court lady stood before the children, the more magnificent because she made such a contrast to her surroundings.

'Now Abigail,' she said, 'you are the eldest. I trust you have been looking after your sister and brother.'

'Yes, my lady.'

21

Lady Marlborough looked about her for a chair and Abigail seeing this and immediately bringing her one, was rewarded by a smile of approval.

Sarah beckoned the children to stand before her. She had decided that the boy was to be sent to school while she looked for an opening for him. She had only one post for the girls as yet and she thought it would be suitable for Abigail. As for the other girl she could not live alone and there was only one thing to be done and that was take her to her own house at St Albans until something could be found for her.

She was thoughtful, watching them. This Abigail was a good girl; of the other one she was not sure. Was that a spark of frivolity she saw in Mistress Alice's eyes? One thing was clear; the young one was not of the same docile disposition as her sister.

'In my position,' she began, 'I receive a great many calls on my generosity. The Princess places *all* her affairs in my hands and that means I have posts . . .' She smiled pityingly, implying that these were posts which could not be within the range of the Hills' meagre talents . . . 'important posts of which to dispose. Those who desire them are ready to do me any service to obtain them; but I can assure you I must select most carefully.'

Alice, who since she had left home to become a servant had, so it seemed to Abigail, lost the good manners which their parents had insisted on, was impetuous and said: 'Your ladyship's position is one of great importance. In fact, I have heard it said that in a short time . . .' She caught Abigail's warning glance and finished lamely: 'But perhaps I am indiscreet.'

'Pray go on, Alice,' commanded Lady Marlborough.

'Well, it is said that the King is very weak and that he cannot live much longer and when he dies of course the Princess will be Queen and that means . . .'

Lady Marlborough was smiling complacently. Far from annoying her, Alice's remark was putting her in a good mood.

'I can see Court gossip reaches you here,' she said; and Alice threw a triumphant glance at her sister while Lady Marlborough surveyed the room with the few pieces of furniture which had once been good and were now very shabby, showing

22

signs of having seen, and said goodbye to, better days. 'It is true,' she went on, 'that the Princess places great trust in me, and I do my best to deserve it.'

Alice, emboldened by success, tried again. 'I trust my lord the Earl is back at Court.'

A shadow passed across Lady Marlborough's face. So, thought Abigail, the Earl is still waiting for his opportunity. He is not as fortunate as his wife. And was it to be wondered at? The King had suspected Marlborough of treason on more than one occasion; it was said that he was a 'Jack', which was the name Abigail had heard below stairs applied to Jacobites; in fact he had been in the Tower not so long ago; and then there had been the affair of the flower-pot intrigue. Lady Marlborough might have a great influence over the Princess Anne, but her husband was most certainly on uneasy terms with King William; and it would have been wiser for Alice to wait for Lady Marlborough to mention her husband's name.

'The Earl has much with which to occupy himself,' replied Lady Marlborough coolly. She came to a decision in that moment. The younger girl was pert for she might have heard gossip about Marl and be trying a little impudence. The elder one was much more serious, much more aware of what she owed to her important cousin. The post she had decided on for the elder girl should go to the younger; and she herself would make use of Abigail while she decided what should become of her.

'Now,' she said firmly, 'it is clear that you cannot stay here ... three young people alone! Prompt action is necessary. I have plans for you all and you must be prepared to leave here within the next few days. These bits of furniture will not fetch much.' She addressed Abigail. 'But you should sell them and what you get will mayhap put a little into your pockets. John, you are going to school.'

'To school!' cried John aghast. 'I wanted a place in the Army.'

There was a shocked silence; then Lady Marlborough burst out laughing. 'The Army! At your age. Why, you would have to join his Grace of Gloucester with a wooden sword and a toy musket.'

23

'But . . .' began the boy, and the tears were in his eyes.

Lady Marlborough waved a white hand on which jewels flashed. 'I don't doubt that if you show ability I shall, in time, be able to place you in the Army. But as yet you are but a child. I shall send clothes for you and you will go to school in St Albans. There I shall watch your progress.'

John's lips quivered and Abigail said nervously: 'I am sure my brother is delighted.'

Lady Marlborough gave her a smile of approval. She was not mistaken in the girl. Abigail was the only one of these children who knew her place.

'It may well be,' said Lady Marlborough looking sternly at the boy, 'that if you work hard and are humble, loyal and obedient, the Earl of Marlborough may find you a place in his army.'

He would first, thought Abigail, have to come back into favour; but if the King died and Princess Anne became Queen Anne, it was very possible that he would. Oh how stupid were this brother and sister of hers. Did they not realize that this flamboyant arrogant woman held their futures in her hands? What a marvellous opportunity for them. And all this they owed to their cousin, the brilliant clever Lady Marlborough.

'John,' cried Abigail, 'you should go down on your knees and thank Lady Marlborough.'

A very good girl indeed, thought Sarah, with a proper sense of her duty and that of others.

'Thank you, Lady Marlborough,' said John obediently.

'I am sure you will do me credit.' She turned to Alice. 'And I have an excellent opportunity for you. There is a vacancy in the household of the little Duke of Gloucester for a laundress.'

'A laundress!' gasped Alice.

'A laundress in the household of the young Duke is a post greatly coveted, I do assure you,' said Lady Marlborough acidly.

'My sister is overcome by your ladyship's generosity,' said Abigail, impatient to know her own fate. 'She is young and finds it difficult to express her gratitude.'

Lady Marlborough was soothed. 'And grateful she should be, for the young Duke will be the heir to the throne as soon as

Dutch William goes where he should have gone these many years. How he lingers on! He's been dying ever since I saw him, and it was Mary who went first. I could never abide *her*, but for that Dutch Abortion . . .'

Alice gave a slight nervous giggle; John looked interested, and although Abigail's expression did not change she was thinking: How indiscreet she is! How vulgar. And how odd that indiscretion and vulgarity should have brought her such high rewards!

'You may smile,' went on Lady Marlborough, 'but that is one of the names Mrs Morley and I use for him. Mrs Morley is Anne . . . the Princess, you know. She would have us dispense with formality when we are together and she herself gave us the names of Mrs Freeman – which is mine – and Mrs Morley which is hers. Caliban! The Dutch Monster! That is how *we* speak of His Majesty.'

'But are you not afraid . . .' began too-impetuous Alice.

'Afraid, my dear child. I . . . afraid of that . . . creature!'

She likes Alice's questions, thought Abigail; she wants to talk all the time, hold the centre of the stage while we act as a chorus, to repeat what she wants repeated, to form a background for her.

'I should not think you are ever afraid of anything, Lady Marlborough,' said John sincerely.

Oh when, thought Abigail, is she going to tell me what will happen to me?

'It would take more than that Hollander to strike fear into me, I can tell you. He knows it. He works against me and the Earl . . . which is what I find so hard to forgive . . . but his day is almost over.'

'I hope Alice will be a good laundress,' said Abigail, trying to bring the conversation back to important issues.

'I fear I shall not,' put in Alice.

'Ah!' laughed Lady Marlborough. 'You'll do well enough. When you are given a post in a royal household you use it as a stepping stone to better things. Watch out, girl, and you will see where it will lead you.' She turned to Abigail. 'And for you, I have plans.'

What thoughts could flash through the mind in a short space

of time. A place at Court? She would watch illustrious people at close quarters; she would have a glimpse into matters which she believed could be of great interest to her. A place at Court, a stepping stone to better things.

'I am going to send you to St Albans, Abigail. There you will be with my own children. You will, I am sure, make yourself useful.'

St Albans! A poor relation in her cousin's house! A sort of nursery maid to a family which were doubtless as arrogant as their mother.

Lucky John! Lucky Alice! Both were going to Court while Abigail was to be a poor relation, slightly higher than a chambermaid, but not much, in the house at St Albans.

Lady Marlborough was watching her. She smiled and murmured her thanks.

Only Alice, who knew her so well, would know of the despair in her heart, and that she would guess; there was no sign of anything but abject gratitude on the plain features of Abigail Hill.

The furniture was sold and, with the very little money it had realized between them, the three Hills left the house in which their parents had died, and set out to make their fortunes: John to school; Alice to Campden House where the Duke of Gloucester had his household; and Abigail, after saying a sad farewell to her brother and sister, to take the coach to St Albans.

The journey was one of discomfort and alarms. There were stretches of road made notorious by the robbers who lurked there; and even if the coachman had his blunderbuss and horn of gunpowder, such precautions were known to be of little use against really desperate men.

Abigail was too much concerned with her future to worry about the dangers of the road; she was wondering what her duties at St Albans would be, for although Lady Marlborough had hinted that she would be one of the family she did not believe this would be so. She had discovered that there were five Churchill children and that the two elder girls, Henrietta and Anne, were older than she herself; she believed that

Elizabeth the third daughter would be about two years younger, John, the only boy, three years younger, and Mary four. What could a thirteen-year-old girl do for such a family? she asked herself, for she guessed that she was being installed in the household as a poor relation who would be expected to make herself useful.

How differently Lady Marlborough must travel on her journeys from London to St Albans! Abigail imagined her with her outriders and bodyguard of servants, all armed in preparation for encounters with highwaymen and equipped for emergencies such as ditching or breaking down. There would be running footmen too, to go ahead and announce what important people were on the way. Abigail could picture them dressed in the Marlborough livery, with their jockey caps and long staves trotting along the roads, pausing now to fortify themselves by drinking a little of the spirits they carried at the head of their staves. Oh yes, Lady Marlborough would travel in a very different way from her poor relation!

I am haunted by that woman, thought Abigail. It is unwise because I could never be as she is and I should be grateful if now and then she reminds herself of my existence, which she will do – but only when I can be useful to her.

Then she consoled herself that Lady Marlborough would be at Court and it would be children of her own age – or thereabouts – with whom she had to deal.

Leaving the coach at St Albans, she discovered that no one had come to meet her, but it was easy to find her way, for everyone knew the house built by the Earl of Marlborough on the site of Holywell House which had belonged to the Jennings. They still called it Holywell.

Her belongings, not amounting to much, were easily carried, and thus, quietly and discreetly, Abigail Hill found her way to her new home.

Her reception was much as she had expected it would be.

Who was the new arrival? the servants asked. She was a member of the family but that most despised of connexions – a poor relation. Her clothes – those which were not recognized as Lady Elizabeth's cast-offs – were shabby and much patched

27

and darned. A very poor relation! She was to be put to useful service in the nursery. This was the command of Lady Marlborough, and those in authority would see that it would be carried out in the most humiliating way.

She was to share lessons, because Lady Marlborough could not allow a relative of hers to be uneducated. Not that Lady Marlborough had any great respect for education; her family must learn to conduct themselves as the nobility, to be able to move graciously about the Court when the time came for them to be there; but Latin and Greek, history and literature! 'Bah!' Lady Marlborough had said. 'Don't talk to me of books! I know men and women and that serves me well enough.' But languages? Perhaps a little would be useful, for foreigners came to Court. Her children must be taught arithmetic; for money was important and a knowledge of the subject was necessary to deal with that indispensable asset.

The children were, as Abigail would have expected, on such an academic diet, growing up to be as worldly as their mother.

They were all good looking, having inherited the beautiful hair which was their mother's greatest claim to beauty. It seemed too that some of them had not missed her arrogance either. Henrietta, the eldest, certainly possessed it; and in spite of her youth the same quality was apparent in nine-year-old Mary. Anne was different; she had a gentler nature; she was calm, and although a little aloof from Abigail, she made no attempt to browbeat her. Anne, although a year younger than Henrietta, seemed more mature than her sister. There was a gap of three years between Anne and eleven-year-old Elizabeth, and although the younger sister admired the elder and tried to follow her example now and then the temper would refuse to be restrained. Ten-year-old John was more like Anne. Being the only boy, he was adored by the family, and the servants said he took after his father rather than his mother.

Abigail's room in this household was a small attic; it was a concession, she supposed, that she should have one to herself and not have to share the large one with the female servants. When she stood there for the first time, looking out through the tiny window at the countryside, momentarily she felt at peace; but that was of short duration. Young Mary had come up to look for her.

'So you really are our cousin,' she said.

'I am your mother's cousin.'

'Then you're not ours?'

'Oh, we are connected.'

Mary wrinkled her brows and murmured: 'How odd!' Then: 'How are you going to make yourself useful?'

'I shall have to wait and see what is required of me.'

'But you will make yourself useful because Mamma said you would.'

Henrietta was calling: 'Mary, where are you? Are you up there with Abigail Hill?'

Henrietta came into the attic and began turning over Abigail's belongings, which were laid out on the pallet.

'Are these *all* your things?' The lips curled in that half sneer which was an absolute replica of her mother's. 'Oh, and that's Elizabeth's old gown. Does it fit? You are thin, Abigail Hill. And why have they put you in this attic?' She looked round it and her slightly tiptilted nose sniffed disdainfully. For a moment Abigail wondered if Henrietta thought she should have been treated more as a member of the family and was disgusted that she should have been put in an attic usually reserved for a servant.

'I think,' went on Henrietta, 'that you should have a room near ours. There is a small one. It's a powder closet, but it would serve. Then you can help us dress.'

Abigail saw the point. There would be no difficulty in making herself useful; she would be shown the way. She might be a blood relation but she had been brought into the house to earn her bread.

It would be very bitter bread, Abigail thought to herself; but she restrained her thoughts; she gave no indication of how she disliked Henrietta Churchill. She was demure, acquiescing, resigned as a poor relation should be. Even Henrietta could find no fault with that.

She had settled into her place in the family. She took lessons

29

with the girls; the governess looked down on her and even commented in her hearing that she had not bargained for teaching the likes of her. Abigail applied herself more earnestly to lessons than any of the Churchill children, but she was not commended for her industry. She did not ask for praise; outwardly she appeared grateful; and perhaps when she thought of service in Lady Rivers' household this was just preferable. For one thing she was acquiring a little more education, which was always good; and because it was a little harder to accept insults in a house full of her own family than in one where she was frankly a servant, she was learning greater endurance. She did not attempt to assert herself; meekly she accepted the fact that she was insignificant beside these flamboyant cousins; she was quiet and they were vociferous; they were physically attractive, she was not; she had little hope of bettering herself, whereas they were dazzled by the reflection of their parents' ambition. Abigail guessed that Lady Marlborough, who had talked so frankly before the humble Hills, would have been even more open with her own family. She had spoken as though she were certainly as important as the King, if not more so; and her children, of course, would have grand titles and positions at Court bestowed on them.

There was in Holywell an atmosphere of which Abigail soon became aware. It was a marking time, a waiting for great events. Ambition was ever-present, so that it seemed to have a personality of its own. The children were always talking of what they would do when ... When what? When Anne was Queen and was ruled by their mother; when their father had complete charge of the Army. To them it seemed inevitable that this would happen, but Abigail who had been born into a family which, if not affluent, was comfortably off and had seen its decline to poverty, believed that it was never wise to crow over what might be, until it was.

Being herself Abigail soon settled into her place in the family; she was as unobtrusive as a cupboard or a table, said Anne. Nobody noticed her presence until they wanted something.

Sometimes Abigail pictured her life going on and on in this groove into which she had fallen. She had enough to eat; she had the knowledge that she was related to the Countess of Marlborough, but she had less freedom than the cook, the maids or the governess. Would it always be so?

The idea came to her that it could not go on. This was when she sat with the girls one day stitching for the poor, for Lady Marlborough had ordered that they must do this. So they sat making shapeless garments of rough material which each of them had to complete before they turned to fine needlework. As neither occupation was enjoyed by the Churchill girls it was no more distasteful to do the rough work than the fine. Abigail, stitching diligently, had completed her garments before the others.

'Here, Abigail, do fix this miserable seam for me. It bores me.' That was Henrietta – almost a young woman now. A little fretful, feeling shut in by the quiet life of St Albans, always dreaming of what the next weeks might bring.

'If I were not myself, do you know what I should wish to be?' demanded Henrietta.

'What?' asked Anne.

Henrietta stretched her arms about her head. 'An actress,' she said.

That made Anne and Elizabeth laugh aloud, while Abigail bent over her work as though to shut herself out of the discussion.

'An actress like Anne Bracegirdle,' went on Henrietta.

'How do you know of such people?' asked Elizabeth.

'Idiot! I keep my ears open. Do you know that some of our servants have been to London and to the play?'

'How strange that they should have been and we not,' mused Elizabeth.

'Plays are for low people,' added Anne.

'Indeed they are not,' retorted Henrietta fiercely. 'Queen Mary went to a play. King Charles was always there and so was King James. The King does not go but that is because he hates anything that is gay and amusing. It has nothing to do with being a King.'

'The Dutch monster!' said Elizabeth with a laugh.

So Lady Marlborough talked carelessly of the King before her children, thought Abigail, and was once more astonished that one who was so careless and so vulgar could have made such a position for herself at Court.

'Queen Mary went to a play by Dryden,' said Henrietta. 'I have read it. It's called *The Spanish Friar*. There are some passages in it that made her blush.'

'Why?' asked Elizabeth.

'Oh, be quiet. You don't know anything. But I should like to be an actress like Betterton and Bracegirdle. I love particularly Mr Congreve's play the *Old Bachelor* and the *Double Dealer*; and Dryden says he is the greatest living playwright. Oh how I should love to be on the stage.'

'Mamma would never permit it,' said Elizabeth.

'She didn't really mean it, Elizabeth.' That was Anne.

'Of course I meant that I should love to be on the stage. I should love to play wonderful parts. Beautiful women ... wicked women I should like playing best. And the King would come and see me and all the nobility.'

'Perhaps some of them would want you for a mistress.'

'Anne!'

'Well, that is what happens to actresses. And, Henrietta Churchill, if you think Mamma would ever allow it to happen to you, you are mad.'

'No, I know it won't happen, but . . . I wish it would.'

Anne was suddenly aware of Abigail. 'You're sitting there . . . quietly listening as you always do. What do you think? Would you like to be an actress?'

Henrietta burst into a loud laugh. For the thought of Abigail Hill on the stage charming Kings and Queens, and the nobility falling in love with her, was quite comic.

Elizabeth was rolling on her chair with glee; Anne could not suppress a smile; and Henrietta went on laughing. Only Abigail Hill sat quietly, plying her needle, seeming serene.

But beneath that calm there was dislike for this family which became stronger with every week she spent in their house.

Yes, it was certainly humble pie and bitter bread which was eaten at St Albans.

When the Earl came to St Albans there was a change in the household. He was in some sort of disgrace, Abigail gathered, because of a plot in which his name had been mentioned; it was, as usual, a scheme to bring back James II who had fled to France when William and Mary had taken his throne.

Sir John Fenwick was executed on Tower Hill, and Marlborough had thought it wise to keep in the shadows. Hence his stay at the house.

'Now,' said the cook, 'we must be careful what we serve at table for he will want to know the cost of the meat in the pie and why we did not use more pastry and less meat because he will know that the cost of one is greater than the other.'

'The meanest lord I ever worked for,' was the comment of a groom. 'He'll have us catch the last second of daylight before lighting the lanterns. Every penny counts with my lord.'

And so it seemed. His manservant had said that he possessed only three coats and that these had to be watched carefully so that the slightest tear could be mended at once in order to preserve the life of the garment. He would walk miles through the mud when in London rather than spend the coach face; and most extraordinary of all, his secretaries said that he never dotted his i's because he considered it a waste of ink to do so.

Abigail wondered what he would think of her. He would not want to give her food and shelter unless she earned them. If she did not she would surely be more of a liability than a candle or a drop of ink.

She was surprised, therefore, when she met the Earl. He was tall, very well proportioned and outstandingly handsome; his hair was fair, almost the same colour as Sarah's; his eyes, between well defined brows, were startlingly blue and his features were finely chiselled; but what was so unusual in this family was the serenity of his expression. As soon as she saw him, Abigail understood why Sarah, who seemed incapable of loving anyone but herself, loved him almost as much, and why the notorious Lady Castlemaine had jeopardized her position with the King to become his mistress. There were perhaps more handsome men, but none, Abigail was sure, who possessed such overwhelming charm. John Churchill was courteous to the meanest servant and he did so with an air of not being able to act in any other manner. There was no hint of the meanness of which Abigail had heard so much, although she was quickly to discover that it was by no means exaggerated.

He was charming to Abigail, noticing her as soon as he was in her company, inquiring if she was happy in his household as though it was a matter of concern to him. Abigail, possessing a serenity to match his own, was able to look on at herself being charmed by him and yet remain completely aloof. She wondered whether it was not in her nature to idealize any one person. Perhaps she had suffered such hardship that the prevailing need was to protect herself; and until she felt herself securely settled in life – and whoever in a changing world was ever that? – she would continue to keep one motive in mind.

All the same it was pleasant to find the Earl so different from the rest of the family. If he thought she was a drag on the household expenses he gave no indication of this. How different from his wife!

He even had news of her brother and sister.

'Your young brother is to leave his school for a place has been found for him as page in the household of the Prince of Denmark – husband of Princess Anne,' he told her.

'But that is indeed good news!' she said, lowering her eyes. Oh, lucky John! she thought, fiercely envious for a moment, comparing this life of servitude as poor relation with the opportunities given to her brother and sister.

'He has his eyes on the Army,' went on the Earl. 'He's set on it, and if a lad wants to be a soldier, then so should he be – for such make the best soldiers. We shall see; and I promise you that if there is an opportunity later when he is older, he shall have it, if it is in my power to give it.'

'You are good, my lord.'

'The boy is my wife's cousin, and I would do what I can for him. He'll have to be patient though, for as yet he is only old enough for the Duke of Gloucester's army. When your brother goes into action it should be with more than a wooden sword, eh? And that reminds me of your sister. She asked me to send a message to you. She is happy in her work, and trusts you are the same.'

He smiled at her so charmingly that she answered that she was.

She was glad that he was in the house even though it did mean that the candles were doused early and every economy must be practised. It seemed strange to Abigail that a man who, according to his wife, was a genius capable of holding the highest post in the country should be concerned about the consumption of candles; but she accepted this as one of the idiosyncrasies of the great and was thankful for his presence.

The Earl had been in the house less than a week when the Marlborough outriders arrived at the house to say that the Countess of Marlborough was on her way.

Sarah Churchill swept into the house like a tornado – as Alice had once described her advent. Pots and pans were polished, so was furniture; and there was a smell of baking in the kitchen. The Earl was so delighted at the prospect of seeing his wife that he did not calculate the cost of this extra activity. From a window Abigail watched him go out to greet her. She saw him take her hands, stand a little way from her as though to see her more clearly; then he clasped her in a prolonged embrace. And what would my Lady Marlborough think of that? He was crushing her head-dress but she did not seem to mind. Abigail marvelled to see them laughing together; she had never seen Lady Marlborough look at anyone else like that and would not have believed that she could.

They came in and Abigail could hear her voice penetrating the house.

'And where is my family? Why are they not here to greet me?'

But of course they were all there. They would not dream of displeasing her.

She did not ask for Abigail Hill; as Abigail guessed, she had forgotten her existence.

Lady Marlborough was never happier than when in the company of her husband. Although she loved intrigue and to enjoy it she must live close to the Princess Anne, and if Marlborough were ever to achieve the fame which was his due he

35

could not do so, as she would say, 'in his wife's pocket', these brief sojourns at St Albans with her husband and family were the happiest periods of Sarah Churchill's life.

This time a purpose other than pleasure had brought her to St Albans; and it was one which she would only discuss with her husband in the privacy of their bedchamber.

There she sat at her mirror and let her rich hair, which he loved so much, fall about her shoulders.

'Oh my dear Marl,' she said, 'I am sick to death of this waiting. How long can he live, do you think?'

'It's a question we have been asking ourselves for a very long time, my love.'

'H'm? Sometimes I think he goes on living just to spite us.'

Marlborough laughed. 'Well, my dear, you can hardly expect him to die to please us.'

'We are not the only ones who would be pleased. I wish he'd go back to Holland. We could manage very well without him here. I had thought the crown would be on my fat stupid Morley's head by now.'

'Hush!'

'Nonsense, Marl. No one can hear, and if they could they wouldn't dare talk of what I say.'

'One can never be sure where our enemies are.'

'In our own house! My dearest, we are perfectly safe here. Now I want to talk *sense*. When the great day comes we must be ready, must we not? My dearest Marl, you have genius, I know. And I can do as I will with Morley. But we have our enemies and I believe it is time we began to build up our defences.'

'My dearest Sarah is becoming a general, it seems.'

'Now listen to me. Even when my fat friend is on the throne, she will not be all powerful. There will be her ministers. We shall never have an absolute monarchy again. We need friends, Marl, and we need them badly.'

'And, Sarah dear, I do not think we are very popular, you and I. There is only one person in the world whom I can absolutely trust – and that is you.'

'Why, bless you, Marl, you and I are one and nothing on

36

earth can alter that. But we are going to need friends. Do you agree?'

'Friends are always useful.'

'Useful! They are a necessity.'

'Where shall we find them?'

'By binding them to us.'

'With what?'

'Sometimes I think the most brilliant soldier in the world is lacking in strategy.'

'It is a mercy he has a wife who can supply his lack.'

'Seriously, have you forgotten that we have marriageable daughters?'

'Marriageable. Why Henrietta is . . .'

'Sixteen, Marl. Ripe for marriage.'

'Oh, not yet.'

'You are like all fathers. They want to keep their daughters children for ever just to give themselves an illusion of youth.'

He smiled and said, 'Well, who have you in mind for Henrietta?'

'Godolphin's boy, Francis,' she said.

Marlborough stared at her.

'Well?' demanded Sarah. 'What objections could you have, my lord, to such an alliance? Godolphin is one of the cleverest men in the country. He would be a power, as you would, my dear Marl, on your own; but together . . . You see what I mean?'

'You mean an alliance between the Churchills and the Godolphins.'

'I do, and how better to strengthen such alliances than by marriage? Godolphin's grandchildren will be ours. One family instead of two. Would that not be a good thing?'

'There is one thing you have forgotten.'

'And what is that?'

'Do you remember how we made up our minds to marry?'

'Yes, and your family stood against us. I was not good enough for the Churchills. I remember well. They had someone else in mind for you.'

'That is my point. No one would have induced me to marry anyone but you.'

37

'I should think not.'

'So I say there is one point you have omitted. What of Henrietta?'

'Henrietta will do as she is told.'

'She is your daughter and mine.'

'Bah!' said Sarah. 'I'll have no disobedience from my children.'

The Earl laid his hand on her arm. 'Be gentle,' he begged.

'Are you telling me how to treat my own daughter?'

'I am suggesting how you should treat mine.'

She smiled at him. She adored him; he was the one person who could reason with her.

'Well?' she demanded.

'We will invite them here. Francis and his father. And we will not mention marriage to the young people until we know they are fond of each other.'

'Romantic nonsense!' said Sarah.

But she agreed.

Sarah had long been watchful of Sidney Godolphin, for she had marked him out as a man whom it would be better to have for a friend than an enemy. The Godolphins were a noble Cornish family and Sidney had found favour with Charles II, who had summed up his regard for him in one of his apt phrases. 'Here is a man,' he had said, 'who is never in the way and never out of it.' That was good praise from Charles. It was often the case that a man who was honoured in one reign was out of favour in the next. Sidney Godolphin was too clever to allow this to happen to him. He had received his title when Charles had made him Secretary of State and when Charles died he remained one of James's most trusted ministers and was appointed Chamberlain to James's Queen, Mary Beatrice. He was one of those Tories who had remained faithful to James longer than most; and when he had seen that the exile of James was inevitable, he had voted for a Regency. His fidelity to James had never really wavered, and when Marlborough, deciding that he could not satisfy his ambition through William, had turned to the 'King across the Water', this had made a bond between him and Godolphin. Like Marlborough, Godolphin had wished to show his friendship with James while at the same time he feigned a friendship with William; it was a case of waiting to see which side could be the one an ambitious man should be on; and because of William's undoubted qualities it seemed certain that he was the one whom they must serve – but at the same time they were watchful of what was happening at the Court of St Germains where the exile lived with his Queen and the son whose birth had caused such a controversy in England and who was acknowledged by Louis of France as the Prince of Wales.

Godolphin's name, with that of Marlborough, had been mentioned in the case of Sir John Fenwick; and although neither he nor Marlborough had been brought to trial over that affair, Godolphin had been forced to resign. This was the state of affairs when Sarah had the idea that the two families united by marriage could form the nucleus of a ruling party which would of course be dominated by the Marlboroughs.

In his youth Sidney had made a romantic marriage. He had fallen in love with Margaret Blagge, one of the most beautiful and virtuous young women at Court. Margaret, a maid of honour to Anne Hyde, who was Duchess of York and mother to the Princesses Mary and Anne, had taken part in John Crowne's *Calista* which had been written that the Princess Mary might perform and make her debut at Court. Although Margaret had believed dancing and play-acting was sinful and had been forced to play a part in this, she had scored a success as Diana the Goddess of chastity. Sidney watching her had fallen more deeply in love than ever before. Margaret seemed to him unique; for to find a girl who was virtuous at the Court of King Charles was rare.

He often thought of those days of courtship, the secret marriage, the friendship with John Evelyn, the writer, who, recognizing Margaret's rare qualities, loved her as though she were his daughter. A strange interlude for an ambitious man, to discover that there was a life which did not depend on gaining advantages over other men, fighting for power, enviously watching the progress of rivals – days which later he was to look back on as a dream. In due course they announced their marriage; he remembered the house they had lived in, in Scotland Yard near the palace of Whitehall, during the days when they had been awaiting the birth of their first child.

It was not wise to brood on those days; there was too much sadness in nostalgia for a past which was lost for ever; but he could not stop thinking of how they had walked in the gardens, always talking of the child. They had come that September day – September days had ever after seemed tinged with sadness for him – just as the green leaves were touched with brown; their edges dry and shrivelled ready to fall from the trees to be trampled underfoot or swept up and destroyed, as his happiness had been. But how was he to guess then that soon his joy in life would be gone as surely as those bright leaves upon the trees?

Young Francis had been born on the third day of September – a healthy boy, which was what they had secretly longed for, although neither of them had admitted it. They had stoutly declared to each other that the sex of the child was unimportant, lest the other should think either one would be disappointed.

But a boy brought that moment of triumph. For two days they were at the peak of happiness. Then she took fever, and a week after the birth of Francis, Margaret was dead.

Sidney had had only one desire for a long time – that was to follow her. But he went on living, and in place of the love he had had for his wife he had built up ambition. His great relaxation was gambling and no amount of losses on horse racing could deter him. Consequently he was almost always in debt; but he was a brilliant politician.

John Evelyn, who had been almost as desolate as Sidney when Margaret died, had found his solace in Margaret's son; and Sidney was glad of this, for he had a great respect for the writer. It was Evelyn who took charge of the boy's education, who had advised his father to send him to Eton and afterwards to Cambridge. Francis was, at the time when Sarah Churchill had cast calculating eyes on him, eighteen years old.

Although the Churchill girls despised their cousin Abigail, she was far more observant than they were. When the Godolphins visited St Albans it did not take her long to guess for what reason Sarah had invited them.

She watched Henrietta and Anne riding with Francis and one of the grooms: and she guessed that Francis was being offered a choice of the two girls, although Henrietta was the one her parents hoped he would select.

Why? wondered Abigail. The answer was simple. Because they wanted a marriage to take place as soon as possible, and Henrietta was older than Anne.

Abigail believed that their wish would be granted, for Henrietta, bold and dashing, was determined not to be put aside for her sister. She began to understand why Francis had been brought to St Albans, and summed him up as a docile young man who could be trained to become the kind of husband whom she could dominate. To dominate was a need with her, as it was with her mother. She wanted her freedom. Marriage could give her that – and what better than marriage with a malleable man!

Anne, who had no desire for marriage with Francis Godolphin, was well content to remain in the background, leaving the field clear for Henrietta.

There had been no lavish hospitality for the Godolphins. The Earl of Marlborough had no intention of throwing away good money for that. Sidney Godolphin was a friend of his – at least as near a friend as they could have in their ambitious lives. They could go along together, be of use to each other; they shared their dreams of power; so if Godolphin could be persuaded to the marriage it would not be because of rich food being served from gold plate, but because he saw in it a useful alliance between two ambitious families.

But after the visit the Churchills were still uncertain.

The Earl and Countess walked in the gardens discussing it. Lady Marlborough's strident voice floated over to Abigail Hill who had been sent to weed the flower border in the enclosed garden.

'What do you think, Marl?'

The Earl's voice did not reach Abigail.

Sarah's went on, 'Well, if Sidney Godolphin thinks he's too good for the Marlboroughs ...' A low reproving murmur.

'What do we care for him? And I'll tell you this: I think he was considering very seriously. He knows what will happen when Caliban dies. And it must be soon. It must. It *must*. I had it from one of the pages that he's spitting blood . . . badly. How *does* he go on? He must have a pact with the devil. *That* wouldn't surprise me.' A pause. 'Good gracious, Marl! Who would hear me out here? And what I say about him, I mean. What? Henrietta seemed taken with the boy? She had better be, Marl. She had better be.' Then: 'I know. We married for love. But that boy's not you. And Henrietta's not me. We were different. You must see that.' The sounds of laughter. 'I tell you this, John Churchill, I'll have Henrietta married to Francis Godolphin if I have to whip her to the altar.'

Abigail went on weeding. She was thinking of the future of Henrietta, married to Francis Godolphin. A place of honour at Court. Lady Marlborough would make sure of that – and the children they would have would belong to the Churchills and the Godolphins.

Abigail stood up to press her hands to her aching back. How exciting to play a part in moulding affairs of state. What fun to be at the Court, to make decisions!

How she would enjoy that!

She laughed at herself. She was imagining herself a Godolphin or a Churchill. As if such opportunities would ever come her way!

There were more visits from the Godolphins, and Francis and Henrietta seemed as though they would fall in with their parents' wishes for they clearly enjoyed each other's company.

Henrietta's seventeenth birthday came and although the Earl of Marlborough wished his daughter to wait a little, his wife was impatient and Abigail was sure that soon she would have her way.

Then an event occurred which was clearly the first step towards the change in the Marlboroughs' fortunes.

The King had evidently decided that much as he distrusted Marlborough it was better to have him on his side than against him, and while he was skulking in semi-banishment William could not be sure what mischief he would stir up. He knew of the rapprochement between the Marlborough and Godolphin families; he would therefore feel happier with Marlborough at Court in some post which he valued.

The Duke of Gloucester was now nine years old and it was necessary to establish him in a household of his own. Anne would readily agree to Marlborough's being appointed her son's Governor, so this seemed the obvious solution.

William sent for Marlborough and when the Earl had kissed his hand he said: 'The Princess Anne would welcome your appointment to the household of the Duke of Gloucester and I myself believe that none could do the job better.'

William was indeed in a gracious mood for he went on: 'Teach him to be what you are and my nephew will never want accomplishments.'

Perhaps there was an ambiguity in the remark; but John Churchill was not going to question it. He assured the King that he would accept the post with pleasure and would perform it to the best of his abilities.

When John told Sarah of the good news, she was delighted.

'This is the end of our misfortunes,' she declared. 'Even the Dutchman sees that we cannot be ignored for ever.'

And it seemed that she was right, for following on John's appointment to the governorship William sent for him once more and told him that he should be restored to his old rank in the Army; nor was that all; he was to rejoin the Privy Council.

Sarah was delighted. 'Now,' she said, 'with you back at Court and Henrietta soon to marry Francis Godolphin we really can begin to get to work.'

The Princess Anne reclining on her couch, to rest her swollen legs, listened with pleasure to Sarah's account of Marlborough's restored glory.

'Nothing could delight me more, dear Mrs Freeman,' she said. 'Pray pass the dish.'

Sarah held the sweetmeats before her royal mistress.

'I do declare that these are not so sweet as those we had

yesterday. Do taste, Mrs Freeman, and tell me if I am wrong.'

Sarah nibbled impatiently. 'They taste the same to me, Mrs Morley. I was thinking of the Duke of Gloucester.'

Anne's attention was immediately turned from the sweet-meats for her son was the delight of her heart and she would rather talk of him than of anything else on earth, even food.

'What of my boy, dear Mrs Freeman?'

'He is now growing up. Nine years old. But to tell the truth, Mrs Morley, I should think him much older.'

'I do believe there is not a brighter boy in the kingdom. Such intelligence and with it the kindest heart. Do you know, dear Mrs Freeman, yesterday at my toilet he used an oath which I did not much like and I asked him sharply where he had learned it. It was from one of his attendants I am certain. That tutor of his – Pratt . . . or perhaps Lewis Jenkins. He knew that I was angry with whoever had taught him such a word and he thought a while . . . but only a little while, for, Mrs Freeman, he is so quick. Then he said: "I invented it myself." You see, be-cause he thought to save someone from trouble. Was there ever such a boy?'

Sarah said: 'He spends too much time with that tutor and Lewis Jenkins. He should be with boys nearer his own age, nearer his own rank.'

'I have often thought of that, Mrs Freeman; but he loves his soldiers and I am not sure where he has recruited them from. If any boy wants to join his army and is what he calls a good soldier then he accepts him. You cannot tell my boy what he ought to do.' Anne smiled fondly. 'He always has his answer and such a one to confound you.'

To confound *you*, thought Sarah, and your stupid old hus-band, for both of you are a pair of doting fools where that boy is concerned; but if he were my boy I should have something to say!

'He reminds me so much of my young John,' said Sarah.

Anne smiled, ready for a cosy chat about their boys.

'My John would like to be a soldier. He talks constantly of the Army.'

'Then they are a pair!'

'I often think they ought to be together.'

'My dear Mrs Freeman, what could be more delightful?'

'And as His Highness now has a household of his own, I was wondering whether my boy might have a place in it. Master of Horse or some such post.'

'But it is an excellent idea. Of course we must arrange it. There is nothing I should like better.'

'My John is a little older than the Duke. He is twelve now.'

'But my dear Mrs Freeman my boy is old beyond his years. You would believe *he* was twelve to hear him talk.'

Sarah was triumphant. Her dear Marl back at Court not only Governor to Gloucester but back in the Army and in the Privy Council, and her son with his first Court post – Master of Horse in the newly formed household of the Duke of Gloucester.

Henrietta was to marry Francis Godolphin at the beginning of the next year. Sarah was delighted; everything was working out as she had planned. Now she needed a husband for Anne and she must select with the greatest care; for she had determined on a grand triumvirate which could stand astride the country – a powerful triangle with Marlborough at the apex. Godolphin was an excellent beginning; now she must consider the next move very carefully.

The Earl was as pleased as she was, and his joy was increased because Henrietta was happy. There was one part of the affair which caused him a little disquiet and that was the fact that weddings were expensive, and although he agreed with Sarah that it was an excellent thing to marry into the Godolphin family, Sidney Godolphin, being an habitual gambler would not be able to take his full share in the expenses of the wedding. Spending money had always been painful to John Churchill; as a child his parents had been constantly struggling against poverty and they had been dependent on their wealthy relations; afterwards as a page at Court he had been obliged to live among rich people and this had made him acutely aware of his own poverty; he had determined then that once he had a chance to lay his hands on a little money he would take care not easily to be parted from it. When Barbara Castlemaine had been so enchanted with his powers as a lover that she had bestowed on him a gift of five thousand pounds he had been able to overcome the humiliation of accepting this in the contemplation that it was the beginning of the fortune he intended to make. One of the reasons why he and Sarah were so devoted was because it was natural for a young man in his position and of his nature to seek a wealthy marriage; when he had met Sarah he had fallen so deeply in love that he had been ready to waive the fact that she was penniless; this, in his case, showed so clearly the strength of his devotion that all were astonished. It was something Sarah would always remember; and so would he. She herself had desired a brilliant marriage and John had at that time to prove his genius. Having made their sacrifices they were determined that theirs should be a successful marriage; and as they were both people who were determined to have what they wanted from life, they had, as they both agreed, the perfect union. Much as he loved money John would not have exchanged Sarah for the richest heiress in the kingdom; as for Sarah she preferred a genius for whom she could help to create a career than one who had already proved himself.

Now he discussed with Sarah the need to provide Henrietta with a dowry.

'That is the trouble with daughters. One has to provide a dowry.'

'She ought to have ten thousand pounds,' declared Sarah.

John grew pale at the thought of parting with so much money. 'I might manage five,' he said painfully. 'We have to remember, my love, that it will soon be Anne's turn and then there are Elizabeth and Mary.'

'It's a pity Sidney gambles so. He's continually embarrassed with debts, I hear. If Meg Blagge had lived she would never have allowed him to waste his money on gambling. She would have considered it a sin. But . . . five thousand, you say, Marl. If we can manage that, it will do. You will see.'

He did see, for very shortly afterwards Sarah told him jubilantly: 'Henrietta will have her ten thousand dowry.'

John looked at her in astonishment.

'Dear Mrs Morley *insisted*. She thinks Henrietta charming and implored me to allow her to give her a worthy gift. Do you know, Marl, she offered ten thousand. I wouldn't accept it. You

46

know what a sharp eye Caliban keeps on her income. I've already heard some unpleasant suggestions about favourites taking all she has. I modestly accepted five. Anne can have the other five when her turn comes. And no one can call five thousand *excessive* for one who professes she is so fond of me!'

The Earl smiled at his wife.

'There is no need to tell you, my love, that I think you the most wonderful woman in the world. You must be aware of it.'

There had been talk of nothing in the St Albans house but the marriage of Henrietta. Abigail spent most of her time in the sewing room working on dresses for the girls of the family. Weddings were continually discussed throughout the household and whenever on such occasion any of them became aware of Abigail, they usually gave her a pitying look which she interpreted without difficulty.

Poor plain Abigail! She will never have a handsome husband – nor any husband for that matter. For where would such a humble creature find a dowry; and who would marry her without?

One could not blame them, thought Abigail. It was perfectly true.

So she stitched the dresses and quietly listened to Henrietta's abuse because she had not made a dazzling Court gown out of the materials provided; and she envied Henrietta, not her husband, but for the fact that she would escape from St Albans.

Abigail attended the wedding, keeping well in the background. She briefly made the acquaintance of the Godolphins. 'A connection of ours ... who is so useful in the house!' It spoke for itself; the Godolphins briefly acknowledged the poor relation and promptly forgot she existed.

But there were some members of the household who did not forget her.

'The household has shrunk a little,' commented the Earl. 'When you and I go back to Court and young John takes up his position in Gloucester's household, there will only be the three girls here ... and of course Abigail Hill. Do they need Abigail now, do you think?'

'Need her?' said Sarah. 'They managed well enough before she came, but I understand she is meek and uncomplaining.'

'I do not doubt that, but it is an extra one to feed and those small creatures often have astonishing appetites.'

'My dear Marl, I don't want the creature here, but what can I do?'

'Find her a place somewhere so that she is off our hands.'

'I will keep my eyes open. I do see what you mean. Why should she live at our expense when she might do so at some-one else's. She is useful, of course.'

'But we did not dismiss any of the servants when she came to us.'

'That's true enough. I will see what can be done. If there is a place that it would not disgrace us for her to accept then she shall go. For as you say, why should we feed someone who brings no benefit to us.'

On matters of expense the Marlboroughs saw eye to eye. Abigail was a luxury they could do without; therefore they would give her to someone else.

With Henrietta and John gone, Abigail's life became less secure. She was aware that the Marlboroughs would consider she was scarcely worth her keep. John had now left to take up his position in the household of the Duke of Gloucester; and as there was no longer the wedding to discuss and prepare for, the house seemed much quieter. Anne was apprehensive – knowing her turn would come. She was more sensitive than her sister, but young Mary seemed to grow more and more like her mother and sister Henrietta, and her arrogance was discon-certing. She referred to Abigail as 'that Hill Creature' and turned up her nose when she mentioned her. Abigail disliked the child very much and longed more than ever to get away from St Albans; but she never gave the slightest indication of her feelings; all Mary could provoke her to do was lower her eyes as though she feared that they alone could betray her dislike.

'It's a miracle what she puts up with,' commented the ser-vants. 'Never gives a back answer – not even a look.'

'And what would happen to her if she did? I wouldn't be in

her position – connected with gentry though she may be.'

'These poor relations! I'd rather be a servant . . . good and proper. At least then you know your place.'

'She seems to know hers all right.'

'Her! Oh, she's got no feelings.'

'I wouldn't change places with that Abigail Hill . . . not for all the money in the King's purse!' was the summing up.

While Abigail was wondering how she endured such a life and was contemplating what might happen to her when all the Churchill girls were married, Lady Marlborough arrived at St Albans.

There was the usual fuss of arrival, the fond embraces from her children, the loud voice, raised in affection or delivering a scolding – whatever the occasion demanded. But the entire household sprang to life with the arrival of Lady Marlborough.

She had not been long in the house when she was demanding: 'Where is Abigail Hill?'

Abigail was summoned to the Countess's room and there Sarah, magnificently dressed, fresh from Court, greeted her, if not with affection without displeasure.

'There you are, Abigail Hill. And you are looking better than when I brought you here. Good food has improved you, Abigail. I hope you appreciate what I've done for you.'

'Yes, Lady Marlborough.'

'When I think of the state you were in when I found you all. Those ragged boys! I could not leave you like that, could I? I'll dare say you often think of those days and compare them with what you enjoy at St Albans.'

One had to compare lack of food with lack of freedom, independence with patronage. It was difficult to say, Abigail decided, which was preferable. When one had enough to eat independence and dignity seemed the most precious acquisitions; but then when there was enough to eat one quickly forgot what it was like to be hungry.

She said meekly: 'Yes, Lady Marlborough.'

'I have many duties in the household of the Princess Anne, as you know; and there is a great drain on my time, but I have been thinking of you, which surprises you. Confess it.'

What answer was expected? With any other, one would have been surprised; but one knew that Lady Marlborough was so good, so kind, so thoughtful, so devoted to duty that she would not forget even the most humble and insignificant of poor relations.

Would she detect the sarcasm behind such a remark? Of course not. Her great pride and belief in herself would not permit her to see such irony.

'I did know, Lady Marlborough, that you are so very kind and . . .'

'Ha! And you hoped I had not forgotten you? That was rather impertinent of you, Abigail Hill. Had I forgotten you? Did I not see that you were well provided for in this house?'

'Yes, Lady Marlborough.'

'Well, of what have you to complain?'

'I was not complaining, Lady Marlborough.' The face tinged with pink, the manner alarmed, scared humility in the eyes, the gesture of usually quiet hands.

'But all the same you hoped for a place at Court, did you not?'

'A place at Court? But Lady Marlborough, I . . .'

'Oh, there are places and places. You did not expect that I was going to appoint you Secretary of State to his most Gracious Majesty. Eh, girl?'

'But no, Lady Marlborough.'

Sarah began to shake with laughter at the thought of Caliban's receiving Abigail Hill as his Secretary of State.

'It is not the King's household in which I would place you.'

Nor could you! thought Abigail. You are the last person to whom he would grant favours.

'But that of the Princess.'

'The Princess Anne?'

'Who else? You will see little of the Princess, of course. We need a quiet reliable woman to look after the maids. I thought of you. It will be a good opportunity for you. I did not intend to keep you at St Albans all your life. The Princess leaves the choice of posts to me and when I knew we wanted a Mother of the Maids I thought of you.'

Abigail's face was faintly pink, and even she found it difficult to suppress her excitement. She would be near John and Alice; they could see each other, exchange experiences. At last Abigail was to have what the others were enjoying: a place at Court.

'Well, Abigail?'

'I do not know how to thank you, Lady Marlborough.'

Sarah's eyes narrowed. 'I doubt not that you will find a way of doing so. You will have to keep those women in order. Do you think you can, Abigail Hill?'

'I will do my best, Lady Marlborough.'

'You will find them a feckless band . . . given to gossip and often disrespectful to their betters. If you should hear anything interesting you should let me know at once. I like to be aware of what is being said.'

'Anything interesting . . .?'

'I am sure you are intelligent enough to know what would interest me. Any scrap of knowledge about the Princess or the King; or if anyone should gossip about the Earl or myself in your presence. . . . You understand?'

'Yes, Lady Marlborough.'

'Well then, you should prepare for your journey at once. I see no reason why there should be any delay.'

Abigail went to her powder closet, dazed and bewildered. Escape from this house which she hated; and a place at Court!

But as a spy for Lady Marlborough. At least that was what Lady Marlborough expected; yet perhaps when she had her place it would not be necessary to do all that Lady Marlborough ordered. Who could say?

A few days after that interview, Lady Marlborough left St Albans and Abigail went with her. It was pleasant to travel in such state, but more pleasant still when they reached London.

Lady Marlborough went straight to St James's Palace, taking Abigail with her, and very soon Abigail was being presented to the Princess.

She saw a large woman, with light brown hair and highly coloured complexion, whose expression was mild perhaps on

51

account of her eyes, the lids of which appeared to be contracted. This gave her a helpless look. Her hands were perfectly shaped, her fingers tapering; they were very white and they attracted immediate attention, perhaps because with her sweet and gentle voice they were her only beauty.

'Your Highness,' Lady Marlborough was saying, and Abigail remembered afterwards that her tone was just as imperious in St James's Palace as it was in the house at St Albans, 'this is my relation. The new Mother of the Maids.'

The shortsighted eyes were turned on Abigail. The lips smiled in a very kindly fashion.

'I am pleased to see any relation of Lady Marlborough.'

'I have found places for the whole of the family,' went on Sarah, and added as though Abigail were not present: 'This is the last of them. She has been making herself useful at St Albans while she has been waiting.'

Anne nodded almost sleepily and Lady Marlborough signed to Abigail which meant she must kneel and kiss the Princess's hands.

The beautiful hand was given her; Abigail kissed it; Lady Marlborough nodded. That was the sign for Abigail to retire. Waiting for her outside the door was a woman who would take her to the apartment she would occupy and explain her duties to her.

As she left she heard the Princess say: 'Now my dear Mrs Freeman, you must tell me all your news . . .'

Abigail knew that the Princess Anne had already forgotten she existed.

In the Princess's Apartments

Having married Henrietta satisfactorily, Sarah was looking round for a suitable bridegroom for Anne. There was one family whom she considered worthy to join the triumvirate she had decided on; and that was the Spencers.

Robert Spencer, the second Earl of Sunderland, was a wily politician, a slippery statesman; Marlborough himself did not like him; Sarah had at one time hated him, had maligned him and his wife and persuaded the Princess Anne to do the same in her letters to her sister Mary when the latter was in Holland. But there could be no doubt in Sarah's mind that Sunderland was a man they could not afford to have against them.

The Earl had a son Charles who had married Lady Arabella Cavendish some years before; shortly after Henrietta's marriage Lady Arabella died and Charles, Sarah decided, would need a wife. Why not Anne?

The Spencers were wealthy; Charles was a Whig, it was true, and Marlborough was a Tory; but Sarah was a little more inclined to Whiggery than her husband and she did not regard this as an obstacle. Charles Spencer had already made a name for himself with his democratic notions when he had declared that he would, when the time came refuse the title of Lord and be known as Charles Spencer; he was, according to Sarah, a prig of a Whig, disapproving of his father whose conduct had at times been quite scandalous. But Sarah believed herself capable of directing her son-in-law in the way he would have to go.

Perhaps she was more interested in his colourful father. Robert Spencer, the second earl of Sunderland, had had an exciting career. Feigning fidelity to James II, he had even gone so far as to pose as a Catholic in order to find a way into his favours, while at the same time corresponding through his wife – as wild a character as himself – with the Orange Court supporting the plan to bring William and Mary to England.

Sunderland had been the object of scandal more than once in his life. A young man, with a gay past behind him, deciding to settle down and marry, he chose Anne Digby daughter of the Earl of Bristol, a match which seemed doubly advantageous, for the young lady was not only beautiful but rich. But before the marriage could take place Sunderland had disappeared, having, he afterwards explained, no stomach for matrimony; but he was brought back and the ceremony took place. His wife was an intriguer who, far from being put out by her bridegroom's conduct, welcomed it, for it gave her an opportunity of pursuing her own colourful life. Very soon she formed an attachment to Henry Sidney, her husband's uncle and one of the most attractive men at Court, who had earned for himself the title of The Terror of Husbands. He was even suspected by the Duke of York of making love to the first Duchess, Anne Hyde, and dismissed from Court for a period because of this.

Sunderland however bore no grudges on account of his wife's infidelity. She and he had agreed that one of the ways to favours in those days was the courting of the King's mistresses and this they did by providing lavish entertainments which, since they were given in honour of the King's mistresses, obviously brought the King to their table. When Charles was enamoured of Louise de Keroualle and she wanted a guarantee of security before she succumbed, it was Lady Sunderland who arranged what she called a 'wedding' for King Charles and the

French woman and this was celebrated at the Sunderlands' house.

But with the passing of Charles and the coming to the throne of James it was necessary to decide where it was necessary to bestow one's allegiance. Sunderland was an opportunist – so while he pretended to support James he was in league with William of Orange that he might be ready to leap whichever way would bring him most advantage.

William was shrewd; he did not trust Sunderland; in fact no one trusted Sunderland. Yet he was a man whom no one could ignore. When Queen Mary had died and William was disturbed as to whether his subjects would continue to accept him as King, it was Sunderland who had shrewdly arranged a reconciliation between the King and the Princess Anne, which William had realized afterwards was the best method of placating those who were against him.

Sunderland was a man of brilliance, and William could not afford to do without him – nor, decided Sarah, could the Marlboroughs.

Sarah considered the possibilities of alliance. His son, Charles Spencer, in himself would be an excellent *parti*. Robert Spencer, Sunderland's eldest son, had led a profligate life and died some ten years before: thus Charles was the heir. There had been a third son who had died as a child, and four daughters, two of whom were dead. The vast Spencer wealth would be at Charles's disposal; Charles was a brilliant politician, and Sunderland was one of the most influential men in the country. So union with the Spencers was necessary.

When Sarah told her husband this he was disturbed.

'Charles Spencer for our young Anne?' he demanded.

'*Young* Anne! Really, Marl, what are you thinking? You still see her as a child. She is not I assure you. She will soon be as old as Henrietta was when she married; and look what a success *that* marriage was.'

'I don't like Charles Spencer.'

'Why should you? You don't have to marry him.'

'But our little girl . . .'

'She has been brought up to look after herself. Have no fear she will do that.'

'No,' said Marlborough, 'I don't like it.'

Sarah sighed. Not only had she to arrange this difficult match, but she must make her husband see that it was necessary.

She set to work in her usual indefatigable manner.

Since Marlborough was not eager for the match Sarah herself sounded Sunderland, who at once grasped the importance of what she was trying to do.

By God, thought Sunderland, they already have Godolphin. With Marlborough and myself, the three of us would be invincible.

To Sarah's delight he was wholeheartedly enthusiastic.

'My daughter is a very beautiful and charming girl,' said Sarah.

'I am sure, having such a mother, she could be nothing else,' was Sunderland's reply.

Sarah waved such flattery aside impatiently. 'My Lord Marlborough, however, is not in great favour of the match.'

'And why not, I pray you tell me?'

'Oh, Lord Spencer is a Whig and my lord is a staunch Tory.'

'My son would be guided by me in all matters of importance.'

Would he? wondered Sarah. She remembered how the Whiggish prig had denounced his father's conduct. But that was of no great concern. If Sunderland could not manage his son, she would manage her son-in-law. The important point was to have the three most powerful families together.

'I will tell Lord Marlborough what you say,' she replied; 'it might influence him.'

She was elated. Sunderland seemed so eager for the alliance with the Churchills that she believed he would do her work for her. How much better if *he* would persuade dear sentimental Marl of the advantages. Far better to come from him than from her.

'Perhaps you should see my lord Marlborough,' she told Sunderland. 'He would be interested to hear what you have to say on this matter. As for myself, I must hurry to the Princess. I see I am overdue.'

Sunderland took his leave of her and she thought how much she would have liked to have been present when he talked to her husband. But she had her duties. Always her duties. Those trivial little tasks for which she was always having to hurry back to the Princess's bedchamber.

How much more time she would have to do *useful* things if she could delegate these simple homely tasks to someone whom she could trust. What she wanted was some colourless person whom the Princess would not notice about the apartment; someone who would do what had to be done quietly and efficiently and call no attention to herself.

Abigail Hill!

Why had she not thought of that before? Abigail was just the one she needed. And what advancement for Abigail! From Mother of the Maids to chamber woman in the Princess's own bedchamber. The girl would be grateful to her kind benefactress to the end of her days. She would want to repay her kindness in the only way she could; and that would be to work for the benefit of Lady Marlborough for the rest of her life.

'Abigail Hill!' said Lady Marlborough aloud. 'Why of course. Abigail Hill!'

As Mother of the Maids Abigail had opportunities of seeing her brother and sister. Alice was delighted with her position which brought her two hundred pounds a year – a vast sum – and plenty of entertainment besides.

Abigail soon gathered that, like everyone else in the Duke of Gloucester's household, she adored him. He was an extraordinary boy with his frail body and active mind, his great interest in military matters, his army of ninety boys whom he drilled and inspected daily, his droll sayings, his ability to foretell events, for, declared Alice, he had assuredly foretold the death of his old nurse Mrs Pack, and that was years ago, before the death of Queen Mary.

'Often,' said Alice, 'the Princess comes to visit him and cousin Sarah is sometimes with her. It is true, you know Abigail, the Princess does adore our cousin; and they say she is ruled by her in all things.'

'How strange that she should be,' mused Abigail. 'She . . . a Princess!'

'Well, our cousin is handsome, bold and clever.'

'Brazen, I should say,' mused Abigail. 'I never knew anyone with such effrontery.'

'We at least have to be grateful for it. Remember that.'

'Have no fear, Alice. We shall never be allowed to forget.'

'Do you know, Abby, I feel proud to be connected with her.'

Abigail nodded and said nothing.

When she saw her brother John he talked excitedly about the household of the Prince of Denmark.

'He's kind,' was John's verdict, 'and always on the point of falling asleep. Someone said of him that it is only the fact that he breathes which makes you know he's alive – in all else he is dead. It's true he says little; but you should see him eat – and drink. And his answer to everything is "Est-il possible?" In the household they call him Old Est-il Possible? But he is rarely annoyed and everyone likes working for him as they do for the Princess.'

'Is he often with the Princess?'

'Yes. But when he visits her he falls asleep. Then she talks to our cousin who is always in attendance.'

It was remarkable how the conversation always came back to Sarah.

'How does he feel about cousin Sarah? He must be put out by her influence over his wife.'

'He is never put out. He has the sweetest temper in the world. Besides, the Princess dotes on our cousin and for that reason he too is fond of Cousin Sarah.'

Abigail considered this and believed she would never understand how one who was as overbearing and took no pains to be pleasant should be so admired.

But when she was face to face with her cousin she was conscious of Sarah's power. This happened one day when a message was brought to her that Lady Marlborough wished to speak to her without delay.

Abigail went at once to Sarah's apartment which was connected with the Princess's by a staircase; and there Sarah was impatiently waiting her.

'Ah, Abigail Hill.'

Yes, she was magnificent; her handsome looks, her vitality, her strident voice; her laughter sudden and coarse; her presence commanding.

'You sent for me, Lady Marlborough?'

Sarah nodded. 'I have good news for you. You have done well at your post and I am going to see that you are rewarded.'

'Your Ladyship is good to me.' Abigail gave no indication of her apprehension. What would be her reward? Not to return to St Albans!

'I know that I can trust you. I am going to put you closer to the Princess.'

'I . . . I see.' Abigail's face had become faintly pink; it would show, she was aware, in her nose and she would look even more unattractive than usual.

'Yes,' went on Sarah, 'I know that you are well aware how to be *discreet*. You will be a chambermaid and you will do small tasks for the Princess . . . fetching and carrying when necessary. It is a pleasant post; in fact it is close to my own. You will not only be near the Princess but near *me*.'

'I don't know how to thank you, Lady Marlborough.'

'You will please me if you do your work *well*. The Princess needs you to bring what she wants without her asking. You must anticipate her needs. See that her dish of sweetmeats is replenished, that her cards are always at hand and that none is lost and that they are replaced when necessary; you will see that her clothes are in order, that when she needs gloves you have them. At the same time you must behave as though you are not there. Her Highness would not wish you to *intrude*. Do you understand?'

'Yes, Lady Marlborough.'

'I am glad. You will take over tasks which I once performed and for which I now have not the time. Your duty in fact is to let it seem that *I* am there when I am not. Speak only to the Princess when spoken to. I doubt she will speak to you. You will discover what is needed of you as time goes on. I am going to take you to Her Highness now and explain that you will be there to perform the more menial tasks of the bedchamber. Don't forget. Don't speak unless you are spoken to. You will have to remember that you are in the presence of Royalty. Do you think you can?'

'Yes, I think so.'

'Very good. Then come with me.'

Sarah swept imperiously into the Princess's apartments where Anne was at her table writing a letter.

'My dear, dear Mrs Freeman,' she said, looking up and smiling. She peered past Abigail as though she were not there. 'How pleasant it is to see you. You can seal this letter for me.'

'Abigail Hill will do it, Mrs Morley. I have brought her along that she may be of use to you.'

'Abigail Hill,' murmured the Princess.

'The poor relation I told you about. She is the one who is going to have the bedchamber post. You'll find her a good modest creature.'

'I am so glad, dear Mrs Freeman.'

'I have schooled her thoroughly so you will not have any trouble *there*. She will seal your letters. She will make herself useful without disturbing you in the least. That is what I have trained her to do.'

'How good of you, my dear.'

'As Mrs Morley knows, she can always rely on Mrs Freeman to look to her comfort.'

'I know, I know.'

Sarah signed to Abigail to seal the letter. Abigail's fingers felt wooden; then she realized that neither Sarah nor the Princess were aware of her. How strange, thought Abigail, the letter was addressed to the King. She, homely Abigail Hill, was sealing a letter from the Princess to the King; and what was said in that letter could possibly have a bearing on history. She had never felt quite so important in the whole of her life as she did at that moment.

Sarah was telling the Princess about her newly married daughter Henrietta and that Anne would soon be of an age to marry. The Princess nodded and cooed and now and then spoke of 'my boy' in such an affectionate way that Abigail thought how human she was, and how much less terrifying than Lady Marlborough. One would have thought that Sarah was the Queen and Anne the subject.

When she had sealed the letter she laid it on the table.

'Just make yourself useful,' said Sarah. 'Mrs Danvers will tell you anything you want to know. She has been with the Princess for years. But if there is anything you think she should need, you should ask *me* if she should have it. The great point is to remember not to disturb the Princess. She does not want to see you nor hear you.'

'Dear Mrs Freeman,' murmured Anne, 'what should I do without you?'

Sarah congratulated herself on a shrewd move when she put Abigail into the Princess's bedchamber. Abigail would be recognized as one of Sarah's women and it would be known that she would look out for her benefactress's interests. Moreover, Abigail was efficient; that had been made obvious at St Albans. And what was more important she was no pusher. She would keep her place and not attempt to curry favour with the Princess as some of the others did. She was so colourless (apart, thought Sarah with a snort of amusement, from her nose) and so quiet that one scarcely noticed she was there.

Sarah had tested this by asking the Princess what she thought of the new chamber woman.

'Oh,' Anne had replied, 'is there one?'

'My dear Mrs Morley, don't you remember I presented her to you?'

'You have done me so many favours, Mrs Freeman. Can you expect me to remember them all?'

'All that I hope is that she is not making herself offensive as some of these bold and brazen pieces do.'

'I am sure she has not, for I did not know that she was there.'

'And you have found nothing amiss? All that you have needed has been done?'

'My dear, dear Mrs Freeman, I am so well tended . . . thanks

61

to you. Oh yes, I know it is you I have to thank for the smooth running of my household.'

Nothing could have pleased Sarah better.

Abigail was pleased too. She took her orders from Mrs Danvers, went about the apartment silent-footed and efficient, and she knew that although she was often in the presence of the Princess, perhaps because the latter was shortsighted, perhaps because Abigail was just another woman to her, she was not aware of her as an individual, although any personal service was always rewarded with a kindly smile.

But it was a pleasant life. The fact of being near the Court greatly appealed to Abigail. She listened to all that was said; she enjoyed hearing stories of the Court of King Charles II and the drama which had followed close on his death. There were many who remembered well how Monmouth had collected an army and calling himself King Monmouth – or perhaps others had called him that? – had attempted to take the crown from James. She heard how William had sailed to England from Holland because he had been invited to take the crown; and how Mary his wife had followed him and the two sisters Mary and Anne had, it was said, broken their father's heart.

And this Princess whom she served was that same woman who had defied her father and helped to send him into exile, who had circulated stories about her own half brother not being her father's child at all, but a spurious baby who had been introduced into her step-mother's bed by means of a warming pan.

Abigail felt that she was living close to history; it could be said that people like the plump, lazy-looking woman whom she served made history. Perhaps her own cousin, Sarah Churchill did, for she would tell Anne what to do if ever Anne became Queen and it seemed likely that she would. Why not Abigail Hill?

Life had become suddenly more exciting than she had ever dreamed possible. She even had a notion that she was not quite as unattractive as she had always been led to believe.

Alice sent a message to her telling her that the young Duke of Gloucester was parading his army in the gardens of Kensington

Palace, and as the King was to inspect them this was a special occasion and there would be quite a little party going to see this. Why should not Abigail join in? John would be there and so would a friend of Alice's. She would have an opportunity of seeing the King at closer quarters than she was ever likely to again.

So Abigail asked Mrs Danvers for leave of absence which was readily given. It was rare, Mrs Danvers had commented, that one found a chamber-maid of Abigail Hill's stamp, who moved about so quietly that you did not notice she was there, yet managed that everything that should be done was done. A little gaiety would not come amiss either, thought Mrs Danvers; for although the girl was small and plain, she was also young.

Abigail neatly and very inconspicuously dressed in her discreet grey dress and short black cape found Alice in a red silk gown cut away to show a black satin petticoat with a white calico border; she also wore a black silk scarf and a black and red spotted hood.

Abigail scarcely recognized her and guessed that she was spending a great deal of her salary on her clothes instead of saving as she should. John too showed his love of finery in his brown frieze coat, breeches of the same colour and light drugged waistcoat; he wore a freshly curled wig and looked quite magnificent. Abigail would have seemed incongruous beside such fashionable people but for the fact that John had brought a friend with him, who was as soberly dressed as Abigail herself.

'This is Samuel Masham,' said John. 'I wonder you and my sister haven't met, Sam, for she is now in the Princess's household.'

Samuel Masham bowed over Abigail's hand. He already knew Alice, it seemed.

'I am in the household of the Prince of Denmark,' he said.

Abigail asked if he were satisfied with his post, and he replied that he was very well satisfied.

'One is fortunate to get into the royal household,' he said. 'Particularly in my case. I'm the youngest of eight sons.'

'And I believe,' said Abigail, 'that His Highness is an indulgent master.'

'The best in the world.'

'The Princess is kindly too.'

'Oh yes, we are fortunate indeed.'

'I should not care to be in the service of the King,' put in John.

'I should say not!' cried Alice. 'I'm told he awakes in none too good a temper and lays about him with his cane on those who are unlucky enough to wait on him.'

The four of them laughed and John added: 'The clever ones keep out of his way until the day wears on and he becomes more mellow.'

'It's due to all the Hollands Gin he drinks in the Hampton Banqueting House,' Alice explained. 'What a strange man he is! They say that he is filled with remorse because he was unfaithful to Queen Mary and she left a letter reproaching him. Who would have believed that *he* would ever have been anyone's lover.'

'You've seen the Countess of Orkney, I'll swear,' asked John.

'Yes,' said Alice. 'She's so odd looking. Her eyes are so peculiar. Squinting Betty they call her. Yet she was the only mistress he ever had, so they say; and there's some that are sure he still meets her – but only when he goes to Holland.'

Abigail and Samuel Masham said nothing, but stood quietly listening to the conversation of the other two. There seemed to be an accord between them; and Abigail sensed that he was taking everything in, even as she was, but that he was not eager to let them know what he was thinking.

'We should get into our places,' said Samuel. 'The display is about to begin.'

He did not touch Abigail but was close beside her. She sensed his interest and it seemed strange to her that a young man should be more interested in her than in Alice. It was something which had never happened before.

The King had arrived and was seated in a grandstand which had been erected for the purpose. No trouble, of course, was too much for the young Duke of Gloucester.

Abigail could not take her eyes from the King, William of

Orange, that man of destiny about whose head, so it was said, on the day of his birth had been seen the three crowns of light, meant to be the crowns of England, Scotland and Ireland which he was destined to inherit. He did not look like a hero. He stooped, and a curvature of the spine was obvious; he was small and thin, his legs like a bird's, his nose large and hooked, his eyes small, his mouth unsmiling, his face pallid; and his great wig seemed top-heavy on such a little figure. It was small wonder that the people greeted him in a silence that was almost sullen. He was not the man to inspire cheers, for all his cleverness.

'I heard,' whispered Alice, 'that he spits blood frequently. He looks like a corpse. He can't be long for this world.'

'He dismissed Dr Radcliffe for saying he wouldn't have his two legs for his three kingdoms,' added John.

'It would seem to me,' Alice went on, 'that we shall not long have a King William to rule us.'

Not long a King William, thought Abigail. Well, then there would be a Queen Anne. How strange to think of that mild fat woman ruling a great country. She would not rule in fact; it would be Sarah Churchill who ruled her – Abigail's own cousin. She felt almost lightheaded to be so close to such important people.

'Here comes the young Duke with his army,' said Samuel quietly.

And there they were – the most unusual army which had ever marched into the park. Ninety boys of varying sizes, shouldering wooden muskets, swords at their sides, all in brilliant uniform.

There were cheers and laughter from the lookers-on as the Duke of Gloucester shouted orders to his company.

'Halt! Present arms!'

There he stood – as odd a figure as the King – in his sparkling uniform, his small frail body and enormous head, made more obvious by his white curled periwig. Beneath the wig his face was animated, his eyes alert, for although he suffered from water on the brain he was clever; and his sayings were quoted not only in the Princess's Court but in the King's.

His preoccupation with soldiers had begun in the days when

he was driven through the park in the little carriage especially made for him; and it had never left him; and because he was indulged not only by his parents but by the King himself, he had been allowed to recruit his little army and to supply it with uniform and imitation weapons of war.

A small cannon was now being set off in honour of the King; and there was William, lending himself to the occasion with a tolerance he rarely displayed, walking down the ranks with little Gloucester beside him, inspecting the troops.

'I wouldn't have missed this for the King's crown,' said Alice.

Abigail did not answer; she was thinking of that frail King and the frail boy and marvelling at the strangeness of events.

How strange it would be if she became the servant of the Queen of England!

The display was over; the Duke of Gloucester had dispersed his army and was being conducted by the King into Kensington Palace. They were talking gravely as they went and the watchers even raised a small cheer for the King among the louder ones for young Gloucester.

Gloucester gravely acknowledged their acclaim, which was more than the King did; and all eyes were on the little figure in the dazzling uniform with the blue garter ribbon across his tunic. It was obvious that they would be very willing to accept him as Prince of Wales when the time came; and that would be on the death of William.

The crowd was breaking up and Abigail found that Samuel Masham was at her side. Alice and John had joined some of their friends from the royal household and were chatting and laughing together.

'You look grave,' said Samuel.

'I was thinking how ill the King looks.'

'He has been dying for many years,' Samuel told her.

'I can't believe he will for many more.'

'There is a mighty spirit behind those sick looks.'

'Yes, but surely even that cannot keep him alive much longer.'

'You are satisfied with your post?' he asked.

'I am very fortunate to have it. Did you know that my cousin is Lady Marlborough?'

He nodded and smiled.

'Well, she decided to place us all . . . and she did.'

'She would always do everything she set out to.'

'It was very necessary to place us. I discovered this a few days ago. Someone had heard that her relations were in want, and she did not care that people should know that, hence we all have been provided for. One brother in the Custom House – another in the Prince's household, Alice in that of the Duke of Gloucester and myself now with the Princess.'

'You have the most interesting post of them all.'

'I believe you are right.'

'We shall surely meet now and then; for the Prince and his wife live very amicably together, and I am often taking messages to and from their apartments.'

'I hope we shall,' said Abigail; and she was surprised that she meant it.

Samuel Masham was not handsome, not gallant; but he was rather like she was herself . . . Quiet, unassuming, eager to please, grateful for his place, determined to hold it through his own modesty rather than effrontery, and a little bewildered that such an important post could have fallen into his humble hands.

He was interested in her and asked her questions about herself; she told him frankly of her father's bankruptcy and the desperate state of the family until Cousin Sarah came to rescue them.

'It was too late for my parents,' she said; her voice was quiet and he looked for a trace of bitterness and found none. He decided then that Abigail Hill was an extraordinary woman. One would never be entirely sure what she was thinking and she would be completely discreet.

She told him of those months at St Albans, and although she did not say how humiliating they had been, he understood. Her lips were firmly set and he believed she would make a stand against going back to them.

She did not ask him questions but he told her something of his childhood.

'When you are the youngest of eight sons you cannot hope for very bright prospects,' he told her. 'I think I was very lucky to get a post at Court at all.'

'How was it arranged?'

'My father is distantly related to the Princess Anne, because Margaret the Countess of Salisbury is our kinswoman. That is why I was given the opportunity. It was pleasant to get away from home.'

'You were unhappy there?'

'Scarcely that. My mother died when I was very young and my father married again. Lady Damaris Masham is very clever. She writes on theology. We are all very proud of her, but it was difficult to live up to her. Then when she had a child of her own, naturally she devoted most of her attention to him.'

'I see,' said Abigail. 'So here we are . . . both arrived at the same place but through very different routes.'

They had been walking sedately through the Park towards the Palace where Abigail must join the Princess's household and Samuel that of Prince George.

But before they took leave of each other they had promised they would meet again.

Abigail found herself alone with the Princess Anne and it was rarely that this happened. She was setting the dish of sweetmeats by her couch when she noticed that the silk coverlet had slipped a little and she adjusted it.

For a few seconds the mild shortsighted eyes were concentrated on her as the beautiful white hands – plump and smooth with tapering fingers – grasped the edge of the coverlet.

'Thank you,' said the Princess.

'Your Highness is a little tired today,' ventured Abigail.

'I have been to the display. My boy looked splendid.'

'Your Highness, I . . . I had the honour to see him. I was there.'

The dull eyes brightened. 'So you saw my boy? Did you not think he was magnificent?'

'Your Highness, I have never seen anyone quite like him. So

young and in such command! I would not have missed if for a great deal.'

'I don't think there ever was another boy like him.'

'I am sure Your Highness is right.'

'He is so clever. Sometimes I believe he simply must be older than I have always thought him.' The Princess smiled. 'I think I must have made a mistake in his birth.'

Abigail smiled with the Princess.

'He is so clever . . . I must tell you what he said the other day . . .'

Abigail had heard it before. It had been told to both cousin Sarah and Mrs Danvers, besides several of the waiting women; but Abigail was delighted to have the whole of the Princess's attention to herself and she listened as though she was hearing the story for the first time.

'Can it be really true, Your Highness!'

'Oh yes. I can tell you I would astonish you with my boy's antics. I wish you could have seen him in his new camlet suit with the jewels glittering in it. I had let him wear my jewels for the occasion. Such a sight! And the Garter ribbon! He blessed us both . . . the Prince, his father, and myself . . . and the sweet child told us afterwards that he sincerely meant all that he had said and that it was not the formal greeting a Prince would be expected to give in public to his parents.'

'How proud Your Highness must be!'

'Proud, I can't tell you . . . er . . .'

'Hill,' said Abigail. 'Abigail Hill.'

'No, I cannot tell you. But he is a constant anxiety to us both . . . his father and me. We watch him. You see I have been unfortunate so often and he is so precious. He has been ill often and I can tell you, er . . .'

'Hill, Your Highness.'

'I can tell you, Hill, I nearly died of grief. And so did the Prince. If anything should happen to that boy . . .'

'It must not,' said Abigail quietly.

There were tears in the Princess's eyes and Abigail handed her a kerchief.

'Thank you. So thoughtful,' murmured Anne; but Abigail

knew that she was scarcely aware of her; her mind was at the bedside of her boy during one of his illnesses when she and her husband had experienced all the desolation which would be theirs if they lost this precious boy.

'He is surrounded by care,' said Abigail; 'and he is so bright and interested in life.'

'Yes, you are right.'

The Princess was silent, a smile playing about her lips and Abigail had no excuse for remaining.

She said quietly: 'Is there anything you need, Your Highness?'

Anne shook her head; she wanted to be alone to dream of her wonderful boy.

Abigail went away so quietly that Anne was unaware of her departure. It was some little time later when she awoke from her reverie and looked about for the woman.

She had discreetly retired, but everything she needed was at hand.

A nice creature, thought Anne. Now what did she say her name was?

Abigail was finding life full of interest. After that conversation with the Princess, Anne was aware of her. She could not always remember her name, but there was no doubt that she was not displeased by Abigail's personality.

Her women were a vociferous crowd. They were ostentatiously sycophantish, but they could be careless. Often they forgot to perform some little duty which seemed important to the Princess and she had to ask for what she wanted; she had begun to notice that when Hill was on duty everything she needed was always at her side without her asking.

Once when Sarah had been amusing her and making her laugh with her imitations of some of the ministers, Sarah had made some references to Anne's husband, the Prince of Denmark, which Anne although she smiled, did not quite like. But that was how it was with Sarah. No one was spared.

But it rankled a little, and after Sarah had left it was pleasant to talk to that quiet Hill about the virtues of the Prince.

Hill said that she had a friend who was a page in the Prince's household and she had already heard from him of the wonderful kindness and extraordinary good qualities of the Prince.

Anne was pleased. Who was he? She would tell the Prince what a good and loyal servant he had.

'His name is Samuel Masham, Your Highness.'

'Is it then? You must remind me of that, Hill. For I shall never remember.'

Anne felt sleepy as she always did when talking to Abigail Hill. Abigail was so quiet and so restful. Just the kind of woman she liked to have about her after one of Sarah's stormy visits. Of course she loved dear Mrs Freeman as she would never love another woman; more than she loved dear George who was the kindest of husbands; Sarah came second only to her beloved boy; but it was pleasant to let the placid Hill soothe her now and then.

She dropped off to sleep when Abigail was talking.

Abigail stood looking at her and then tiptoed from the room.

She told Samuel Masham about this relationship with the Princess. He was very interested; in fact he was interested in anything that concerned Abigail, and Samuel interested Abigail; he was so like herself. He knew a great deal about what was going on and no one would have guessed it.

They often walked together in the Park or along the river. Abigail was glad that they were so inconspicuous in their dress and insignificant in their persons because this gave them an opportunity to do what other more notorious people never could. They could even walk through the streets of the city without attracting much attention, as few people attached to the Court could hope to do. They were once among a crowd and saw a pickpocket caught in the act and dragged to a nearby sewer to be ducked there. Ducking was a common enough event. Prostitutes were ducked if they lived in a respectable street and annoyed their neighbours; nagging wives were ducked; complacent husbands were treated to a serenade on iron pots and pans and old tin kettles; bailiffs, the enemies of all, if caught unaware, were taken to a trough and made to drink against their will until they were reduced to a state of great discomfort. Mob law ruled in the streets; and it was astonishing how self-righteous the people were in judging the sins of others. This way of life, which Abigail and Samuel were able to witness, was unknown to people such as Sarah Churchill whose lives were bounded by the Court and their own country houses.

Samuel and Abigail had been watching the fate of a quack doctor whose pills had failed to achieve what he had claimed for them; he was divested of his garments and tipped into a ditch and his clothes thrown in after him; and as they wandered away Samuel remarked on the great love in human nature to rule.

'Did you see their faces?' he asked. 'Each one of those people enjoyed playing judge to that poor quack. There is very little difference in these people and those in high places.'

Abigail nodded. She and Samuel were in such accord that words between them were not always necessary.

'I heard,' went on Samuel, 'that the Marlboroughs' daughter Anne has been secretly married to the Earl of Sunderland's son, Charles Spencer.'

'Is that so?' said Abigail. 'I knew that Lady Marlborough was in favour of the match, but I did not think the Earl would agree to it.'

'It is Lady Marlborough who decides what shall be done in that household . . . and not only in that household.'

'I wonder if Anne married willingly. She is more gentle than her sisters but she has spirit, and I do not believe she would easily be forced to do anything that was very much against her inclination.'

'The marriage is a secret as yet but I heard it said that the Earl of Sunderland was very eager for an alliance between his family and the Churchills and that he promised them that he would guide his son in all things.'

'But Charles Spencer once denounced his father's way of life. So it does not seem that the Earl would be very successful in guiding him.'

'I dare swear Lady Marlborough will succeed where the Earl of Sunderland fails. But Spencer is a Whig and Marlborough a Tory. I wonder how that will work. But you see the point,

Abigail. They are waiting for William to die and Anne to take the crown. Then the rulers of this country will be the Marlboroughs, the Spencers and the Godolphins.'

'It's very exciting to watch . . . like sitting in the stalls at the playhouse.'

'And in a way, Abigail we play our part. Because we are on the stage after all.'

'In very small parts . . . the parts that don't influence the play,' said Abigail with a smile. 'Why I'm not even sure what all this fuss about Whigs and Tories means.'

'You should know, Abigail, for they are the people who rule us.'

'I believe Lady Marlborough to lean towards the Whigs although Lord Marlborough is a staunch Tory.'

'And Charles Spencer is a Whig and he has joined the Marlborough family. There will be fireworks, you see.'

'I don't understand why there should be this conflict between the two parties.'

'But naturally there is for they stand for two opposing opinions. The Whigs are for William because they look upon him as a constitutional monarch; the Tories stand for the old rule – the rule of those Stuart Kings who believed in the Divine Right of Kings. We see where that led Charles I. Charles II had the same beliefs but he was far more clever. He did exactly what he wanted behind the backs of his ministers; but the belief in the Divine Right was there. Then there was James; he was determined to foist Catholicism on a nation which did not want it and you know what happened to him.'

'How clever you are, Samuel.'

'But these facts are common knowledge.'

'And William and Mary were the Whig Sovereigns. I have often heard them called that.'

'Yes, and William never forgets it. That is why he feels so insecure.'

'And when the Princess Anne is Queen, do you think she will be as her uncle and father?'

'I do not know. That is why it is necessary to watch these Whigs and Tories. I think it would depend a great deal on which party was elected.'

'How strange that the Earl of Marlborough should support the Tories.'

'Yes, but his wife is leaning towards the Whigs. *She* does not want an absolute monarch. What she is after is a Sovereign who is ruled, not by her Parliament, but by the Churchills. We shall have to watch very closely to see what her game is.'

We shall have to watch closely! It made an excitingly intriguing situation. A little plot between herself and Samuel. They were watchers in the wings while the players performed. Somewhere in the back of Abigail's mind was the thought that one day she and Samuel might actually perform on that stage. But it would be a part that was not noticed by the audience; they would work in the shadows; but perhaps they would be none the less powerful for that.

What extraordinary thoughts for a chambermaid to have! But Abigail was beginning to believe that she was no ordinary chambermaid.

She wanted to know more of these Whigs and Tories, that she might understand all that Samuel had to tell her.

'The Tories?' he said. 'It certainly is a strange name. It comes from Ireland. It was first used in Cromwell's day and described those Irish who remained as outlaws on their own lands instead of emigrating to Connaught as they were commanded to do. Of course our present Tories have nothing to do with that. It is merely the name of the party which opposes the Whig attitude to the Church and State. They stood for the older order of things and many of them are Jacobites of course.'

'And the Whigs?' asked Abigail.

'That was the name first given to the Covenantors of south west Scotland who fought against the Restoration. Then the name was given to those who championed the Exclusion Bill which was to keep James II from the throne and prevent the risk of Popery. They are the country party, the commercial party, those with more liberal views, while the Tories stand for the old way of life.'

'Why, Samuel, you are very knowledgeable.'

They smiled at each other. Samuel found Abigail's quiet concentration, her modesty, her willingness to learn extremely attractive. Her quiet personality suited his. They enjoyed their meetings and their friendship grew.

Tragedy came to St James's Palace.

The young Duke of Gloucester had celebrated his eleventh birthday and there had been festivities to mark this occasion.

The Princess Anne had been in good spirits and almost animated. Sarah had been a little impatient with her as she could so easily be at the Princess's excessive devotion to her son and Anne, sensing this, had sent for Abigail Hill. Abigail had a soothing manner; she agreed with the Princess; she listened to the monologues on the perfections of the boy and only spoke to express incredulity and wonder at his actions. This was just what the Princess needed at the time, even though her greatest joy was listening to Sarah Churchill's brilliant and often cruel conversations. With Sarah one listened; with Abigail one talked. Usually Anne preferred to listen; but there were occasions when she wanted to talk; and then she found herself enjoying the society of the meek little chambermaid.

'My boy reviewed his troops this morning. Did you see him? My poor Hill, I must see that you get out more. Remind me. He was so excited by his cannon. A new one, Hill, which the King gave to him. I am delighted that the King and my boy are such good friends. Of course even William cannot *help* being charmed by him. I know it astonishes everybody. Did you know, Hill, that my boy offered the King his troops and himself to fight for him in Flanders?'

'Really, Madam. What a boy he is!'

'You may well say so, Hill. "I would be proud to die in Your Majesty's service." That is what he wrote to the King. Oh dear . . .'

'Your Highness is cold?' Abigail had put a shawl about Anne's shoulders.

'Thank you, Hill. I always shiver when I hear the word death in connexion with my boy. If I lost him, Hill, I do not think I could bear it.'

'I thought he looked very healthy when I last saw him, Your Highness.'

75

'You did, Hill, did you? And you are an observant creature. Yes, I fancy he grows stronger as he grows older. But I have lost so many. Sometimes I despair of ever having another child. That is why . . .'

'Your Highness is such a devoted mother.'

'And who would not be, Hill, to such a boy?'

'Who would not indeed, Madam.'

Such pleasant conversations. So comforting!

But the next day the little Duke of Gloucester was taken ill, and the Princess was in despair. He was bled but this did nothing to relieve him. Anne threw off her lethargy; she was at his bedside night and morning; her grief was terrible, but it gave her a dignity she had not shown before.

Abigail remembered the day the little Duke died, for she believed it was a turning point in her life.

The Princess Anne came to her apartments, Prince George of Denmark was with her, and they held hands like two lost children from whom all the joy of living had been removed.

Afterwards Prince George went to his apartments and the Princess was alone.

She did not want to see anyone – not even Lady Marlborough. She sat rocking to and fro, her hands over her face to shut out the world which was so full of memories of her beloved boy.

'I cannot believe it,' she kept murmuring to herself. 'It cannot be true.'

All day she sat alone, refusing food which she had never been known to do before; and when it was time to retire she shook her head and told her women to go away.

Then she caught sight of Abigail and said: 'Let Hill remain. She can give me all the help I need.'

So Abigail helped her to bed and she talked of her boy while the tears slowly ran down her cheeks.

'It is what I dreaded, Hill. I dreaded it more than anything that could happen . . . and now it has come. What can I say, Hill? What can I do now?'

'Talk of him, Madam. Perhaps it will help you.'

So she talked and to her surprise was soothed; and she looked at the young face of her chambermaid, itself stained with tears and she said: 'You're a good creature, Hill.'

When the Princess was in her bed, Abigail turned to go but the Princess said: 'Stay, Hill.'

Abigail stayed and knelt by the bed while the Princess lay and wept silently.

The Princess seemed to have forgotten the chambermaid was kneeling there; but when her eyes did fall on the small figure she said: 'Thank you, Hill. You are a good creature.'

And Abigail remained until the Princess slept.

She knew that the Princess would not quickly forget that at the peak of her suffering she had found comfort in Abigail Hill.

The Princess Anne was listless. Each day she sat dreaming of her lost boy. She confided to Abigail Hill that life would never again be the same for her.

Sarah came bustling into the apartment. 'Come, dear Mrs Morley, you must rouse yourself,' she commanded. 'You must remember that although you are a bereaved mother you are also the heiress to the throne.'

'I do not think you can understand how I feel, Mrs Freeman.'

'I! Not understand. Have I not lost a child . . . a boy? Have you forgotten my dear Charles?'

'No, I have not forgotten and I suffered my dearest Mrs Freeman's loss as my own, but this is my boy . . . my beloved boy.'

'There will be other little Morleys ere long.'

'I wish I could be sure of that.'

'You are certainly not sterile. You have given us good proof of that.'

Sometimes there was almost a sneer in Sarah's voice; Anne, her feelings made raw by her recent loss, was hurt by it; and oddly enough she was reminded of the gentle sympathy of the chambermaid.

She said that she was tired and would sleep a little. Sarah, who nowadays always seemed to be seeking opportunities to leave her company, said at once that that was an excellent idea.

'Send for the chambermaid, Hill,' said Anne. 'She will help me to my bed.'

'And I will see you when you are refreshed,' replied Sarah. 'Then I am sure, Mrs Morley, you will see that I am right when I implore you to stop *showing* your sorrow. I know you grieve. I still do for my darling Charles, but we have to be brave, Mrs Morley. We have to hide our feelings from the world.'

When Sarah had left and Anne was alone with Abigail Hill, the Princess said: 'Of course we cannot all hope to be as strong as dear Lady Marlborough.'

'No, Madam.'

'Although sometimes I think my dearest friend, being so *admirable* herself, has little patience with those who are weaker.'

'Your Highness is not weak.' Abigail spoke more fiercely than usual. 'If I may offer my humble opinion Your Highness has shown the greatest fortitude . . .'

'I have tried, Hill. But sometimes I think the loss of my darling . . .'

Anne began to weep and Abigail tenderly proffered the handkerchief. Anne did not seem to see it, so greatly daring Abigail wiped the tears from her cheeks.

'Thank you, Hill,' said Anne. 'You are very different from . . . your cousin.'

'I fear so, Madam.'

'Do not fear, Hill. I find your quietness to my taste.'

'My cousin is a brilliant woman and I am just Your Highness's chambermaid.'

'Do not fret with labels, Hill. There are times when I find your presence very comforting . . . very comforting indeed.' Anne's face hardened suddenly. 'And there are others when I find Lady Marlborough's most . . . most . . . unkind.'

There was a silence which horrified Anne. At last she had spoken aloud a thought which had been at the back of her mind for some time; and spoken in the hearing of Abigail Hill, Sarah's cousin, who had been given everything she had by Sarah and must therefore be her creature.

Now there will be trouble, thought Anne.

She felt so weary that she closed her eyes and rejected Abigail's suggestion to soothe her forehead with unguents. She felt stricken with misery. Her boy was dead and she had spoken disloyally of a woman who for years she had regarded as her dearest friend. And in the hearing of Abigail Hill who certainly would be obliged to repeat everything she heard to her cousin.

'Leave me,' said Anne weakly.

And when she was alone she began to weep silently, partly for the loss of her son and partly for the loss of an illusion.

The next time Anne saw Sarah she waited for a reference to her disloyalty. It did not come. In fact Sarah behaved as though nothing had happened.

Was Sarah waiting for a telling moment to let fly her reproaches. No! There was one thing one could be sure of with Sarah; she was as she herself had said of a frank and free nature. She was unable to curb her feelings, particularly her anger.

If Sarah did not scold her for the words she had said in Abigail's hearing there could be only one reason: Abigail had not told her.

How strange! She could not understand this; and her interest in the softly spoken chambermaid increased.

'Hill,' she said, some days later, 'you must be very grateful to Lady Marlborough.'

'Oh yes, Madam.'

'I hear that she found your family in great distress and that she has placed your sister and brothers in good places.'

'It is true, Madam.'

'Then I suppose you feel that you must pay her back in some way.'

'I have nothing with which to pay her, Madam. I can only give her my gratitude.'

'Perhaps you feel that she is in a sense your mistress?'

Abigail's eyes were filled with frank awe and respect. 'Oh, Madam,' she said, 'I have only one mistress. I do not think it would be possible for me to serve two at the same time.'

Anne nodded. Her lips framed words which she had used to Abigail several times before: 'You are a good creature.'

But this time she said them with a new sincerity; and afterwards she began to look for Abigail among her women and was very contented that she should be in close attendance.

Now that her two elder daughters were so advantageously married, Sarah was becoming very interested in politics. She and her husband were often in the company of the Godolphins and she was wooing her rather difficult son-in-law, Charles Spencer. The time was fast approaching, she was sure, when Anne would be Queen of England. William simply could not live much longer; his body was a mass of disease; everyone said it was a miracle that he could have lived so long. But he seemed to have found a new reason for living since Louis XIV, his greatest enemy, had begun his plan to rule the whole of Europe. This had been made a possibility by the appointment of his grandson Philip of Anjou to the throne of Spain. If Philip could rule independently this would not be a major issue, but was le Roi Soleil the man to stand back and let that happen? No, he wanted to rule Spain, through his grandson, as well as France and that meant that the balance of European power would be in favour of the French. It was something William could not tolerate; and he was already preparing, with the aid of Austria to stand with Holland against this.

William was more at home with his armies than in the council chambers; and so was Marlborough. This war should prove a source of inspiration and profit to John Churchill; and Sarah wanted to see him exploit his talents.

If William were to die – and any normal man in his physical condition would have been dead years before – then Anne would be ruled by the Marlboroughs, for Sarah would see to that; and with his two influential sons-in-law they would be able to stand firm against any of their political enemies.

With such a dazzling prospect before her it was difficult for Sarah to listen with patience to the tittle-tattle of Anne's conversation.

'I do declare,' she told her husband, 'that I am beginning to loathe that woman.'

'For God's sake, Sarah, have a care of what you say.'

'My dear Marl, there is no need for you to tell me how to

80

behave. Is it not largely my doing that we are where we are today?'

Marlborough had to admit the truth of this. 'But, Sarah,' he added, 'when I think of your frankness I do not know why our enemies have not overthrown us long ago.'

'Old Morley knows me as I am and accepts me as such. I have always been free with her and she has raised no objection. I am not going to change now. But as I was saying she sometimes sickens me so that I feel I shall scream if she touches me. It was clever of me to give her Abigail Hill. That creature now has to do all the *loathsome* tasks. I hear she does them well too and Anne has no complaints. She says she is a good creature. "Good but dull," I said; and she replied "Dullness is sometimes a comfort." But I do declare that she is a trial, particularly since Gloucester's death.'

'Well, I suppose I need not tell you to be careful. You know what you are doing.'

'And when have I ever failed you?'

'Never!' Marlborough assured her.

Sarah not only showed her growing impatience with Anne to her husband, but to Abigail. The girl was so much her creature, Sarah believed, that she had no need to speak anything but freely in her presence.

On several occasions she spoke slightingly of the Princess and Abigail made no comment. She merely listened in that quiet way of hers as though she were not in the least surprised.

Sarah was behaving as though she were already the Sovereign.

Abigail continued surprised and startled at the effrontery of her relation; and she often wondered how Anne would feel if she knew how far Sarah went in her condemnation of her. Sarah was inclined to be what she would call frank, to Anne's face, but of course she reserved the real abuse to be uttered behind her back.

Abigail did not speak of Sarah's abuse of the Princess, even to Samuel Masham. She was by nature discreet and she was not sure what her position would be if Sarah fell out of favour. And she could not believe that Sarah would *not* fall out of favour if Anne heard some of the really wounding things which were said of her.

At the same time she dearly wanted to know what Anne would do if she knew how very disloyal Sarah could be.

One day she was helping the Princess to dress and Anne and she were alone together. Since her quarrel with her sister who had now been dead more than six years Anne had not stood on any great ceremony. For a time she had lived very humbly indeed at The Cockpit and Berkeley House and had even spent a month or so in the country at Twickenham, living the simple life of a noble lady. Now William realized that if he were to keep his throne he must treat Anne as the heiress and she had moved to St James's Palace and spent her summers at Windsor Castle, but she had not gone back to living in the state which would have been natural to her rank. Therefore there were many occasions when she allowed only one of her maids to assist at her toilet.

Abigail was looking for the Princess's gloves when Anne said: 'I remember, Hill, I left them in the adjoining room. Pray go and get them for me.'

Abigail at once obeyed, and as she opened the connecting door between the two rooms saw Lady Marlborough sitting at a table reading a letter while she absentmindedly drew on a pair of gloves which Abigail recognized as those of the Princess Anne.

For a second Abigail hesitated. She could shut the door so that whatever Sarah said would be unheard by the Princess; or she could leave it open and the words would be heard.

A fleeting temptation. Sarah would not know that Anne was within earshot, and Anne did not know that Sarah was in the next room.

Abigail held the door open for a second; then she made up her mind. Without shutting it she went to the table at which Lady Marlborough sat.

She did not speak for a second or two; then gave a discreet cough.

Sarah looked up. 'Oh, it's you, Abigail. How you creep about. You startled me.'

'I am sorry, Lady Marlborough.'

'What is it you want?'

'The Princess's gloves. I believe you have mistaken them for your own.'

'What!' shrieked Sarah, staring down at the gloves on her hands.

'Those are the Princess's, I believe.'

Sarah wrinkled her nose; she was aware of Abigail looking at her with astonishment, and could not resist the temptation to show this meek creature that she cared nothing for royalty, considering herself at least equal, if not above it. Certainly she felt above the foolish Princess Anne.

'That woman's gloves!' she cried.

Abigail stepped back; and had Sarah been more observant she would have noticed that Abigail was betraying an emotion which was unusual with her, but Sarah believed the girl was admiring one who could speak so of a Princess. Well, Sarah would show her.

'You have put them on by mistake, Lady Marlborough,' said Abigail timidly.

'So I am wearing gloves which have touched the odious hands of that disagreeable woman!' shrieked Sarah.

Abigail stood still, trying to stop herself from looking over her shoulder at that open door. Anyone in the next room could not fail to hear that shrill, strident voice.

'Take them away. Take them quickly. Ugh! How unpleasant.'

Abigail picked up the gloves which Sarah had thrown on to the floor and hastily left the room closing the door quietly behind her.

Anne was seated where Abigail had left her, and one look at her face was enough to show that she had overheard every word Sarah had said.

As Abigail laid the gloves on the table beside her, Anne said nothing, but her eyes met those of Abigail and in that moment there was a flash of understanding between them. Sarah Churchill was a disloyal friend to the Princess and they both knew it; the subject was too painful to be mentioned, but neither of them would forget what had happened; and because

83

of it their own relationship had advanced a step further.

The King was a very sick man. He was beset by anxieties which were aggravated by his weak physical condition and his conscience. He would never forget the letter his wife had received on the morning of their coronation which her father James, from his exile in St Germains under the protection of Louis XIV, had sent to her. James had said that Mary could not expect anything but the curses of a father whose crown she had allowed to be snatched from him.

Now he was getting near to death and he was constantly concerned with the problem of who should succeed him.

There was one person to whom he could talk with absolute ease. This was Elizabeth Villiers, whom he had made the Countess of Orkney. Elizabeth was the cleverest woman he had ever known; although she was not a beauty, she was to him the most fascinating woman in the world. It had always been so, from the moment he had first seen her. Her quick clever brain and her extraordinary eyes with the slight cast in them which had earned her the name of Squint-eyed Betty, attracted him now as they ever had. She had shown him, in the early days of his marriage, that he was human, after all, when he had overcome his Calvinistic principles and made her his mistress. He had never had another. Mary his wife had seemed a foolish child in comparison; and often he had wished that Elizabeth had been the eligible Princess, Mary her maid of honour.

Mary had been an admirable wife; now that she was dead he realized that more than ever; but on the last night of her life she had sat up writing a letter to him in which she had implored him, for the sake of his soul, to give up his mistress. That had been disconcerting enough; but this document she had left in the care of the Archbishop of Canterbury with a covering letter to the Archbishop explaining its contents. Thus it was known that his wife's last wish was that he should discontinue the liaison; and such a wish could not be ignored. During the months following Mary's death he had refrained from seeing Elizabeth; he had married her to George Hamilton whom he had created Earl of Orkney and many had believed that this marked the end of a relationship with a suitable prize in appreciation of past services. But he had not been able to cast off Elizabeth as easily as that; and although in England she had ceased to be his mistress, when he was in Holland she joined him there and the old relationship was resumed. But there had been no expressed wish in Mary's last letter that he should not continue to discuss his problems with Elizabeth; and since it was a custom of many years to do this he continued in it. Her wit and wisdom were invaluable to him.

He retired to his cabinet, and using a secret staircase which he had had put in and which led to the apartments of the Countess of Orkney, he went to her.

Elizabeth greeted her lover with great pleasure. At least, she could scarcely call him lover now; but she was not displeased with the change in her fortunes. She had as much influence as she had ever had and a great deal more prestige; she was delighted with her marriage and intended to do all in her power to enhance her husband's career, and this she was effecting very satisfactorily.

She bade him to be seated and tell her his troubles.

'I am growing old, Elizabeth,' he said with his twisted smile. 'And I believe my days are numbered.'

'You have said that often before, yet here you are.'

'I am disturbed about the succession. I would I had a son to follow me.'

Elizabeth nodded sadly.

'To think,' he said, 'that that foolish fat sister-in-law of mine will be Queen of England on my death fills me with horror. When the boy was alive there was hope. He was a bright little fellow. It is a terrible tragedy that we have lost him.'

'The Princess is the complete dupe of the Marlborough woman,' said Elizabeth. 'If she is Queen it will be Sarah Churchill who rules.'

'I should like to prevent that.' He looked at her cautiously and she knew that now he was coming to the object of his visit. 'I am thinking of writing to James at St Germains,' he said.

She waited for him to go on but he remained silent for some seconds; and it was clear to her that he had not yet made up his mind.

'I am thinking of suggesting that I adopt James's son.'

'James would never allow it.'

'Not when he considers what is at stake? If he came over here as my son and was brought up to be a good Protestant he would be the natural heir to the throne.'

'It's a brilliant idea,' said Elizabeth; 'but I do not think you will be allowed to put it into practice. In the first place James would never entrust his son to you; and in the second Anne's friends would be ready to start another revolution to ensure her succession.'

'I believe I could deal with that revolution.'

'Marlborough and Godolphin would stand together. There is Sunderland and his son Spencer, who would be with them. Don't forget the diabolical Sarah has united them and they'll stand together, particularly when the Marlboroughs' grand-children are Sunderland's and Godolphin's.'

'I have dealt with Marlborough before. I should do so again. I intend to broach James.'

'Well, that would be a good move,' agreed Elizabeth. 'Even if James refuses, which he assuredly will, the Jacobites will be pleased.'

'If the boy is sent over, that will be good; and if he is not, at least I have done my best. Though the Jacobites may not be pleased when they know it is my intention to bring the boy up as a Protestant.'

'But even they will realize that only as such will he be acceptable to the English.'

'I feel it is my duty to make him acceptable, Elizabeth.'

She understood; and she was disturbed. William's conscience was greatly troubled and he had the air of a man who wants to set his house in order before he leave this life.

Sarah's fury was uncontrollable. 'Do you know what the Dutch Abortion plans now?' she demanded of Anne. 'He is going to cheat you out of your inheritance! He is going to bring that warming-pan brat to England and foist him on the people! I shall not allow that to happen, Mrs Morley. If you lie there on your couch and accept such abominations, I shall not.'

Anne shook her head. She could scarcely bring herself to look into the face of Sarah since the glove incident. Whenever

Sarah came near her she felt cold with horror. She could not shut out the sound of the strident voice referring to her as that disagreeable woman. And Sarah had said her hands were odious. Her beautiful hands which she knew were lovely! They, with her voice which had been so carefully trained by Mrs Betterton when she and Mary were in the nursery, were the only beauties she possessed. Her beautiful *odious* hands. How could she ever forget! How could she ever feel the same towards Mrs Freeman again! Yet she could not bring herself to reproach her friend with what she had overheard. She was thankful that no one but herself and Abigail Hill knew of it; the secret was safe with that nice quiet creature.

Sarah went on, 'Of course we shall never allow it to happen. I was talking to Mr Freeman about it. He agrees with me that it is preposterous. Bring that little bastard to England! Why, if he is in truth the heir to the throne, what is William doing on it! No. It shall never be. Never, never, *never*!'

'My dear Mrs Freeman is so vehement.'

'*Always* – on behalf of Mrs Morley!'

'It is comforting to know you think so highly of me ... *always*.'

Sarah was more than angry, she was alarmed. She might sneer at William, call him the Dutch Abortion, Caliban, and the Monster, but she had to admit that he was a brilliant leader. When he believed in something he went out to get it with such enthusiasm that he invariably succeeded; such vitality was not natural in one so frail, and Sarah was definitely disturbed.

In an attempt to make the people accept what he was doing William had engaged the brilliant and witty writer Thomas d'Urfey to produce a few ballads about the coming of the boy whom many called the Prince of Wales. William had never forgotten what a part the old Irish song of *Lillibullero* had played in the Irish battles. Many believed it was as responsible for victory as William's tactics. This was an age which was becoming very susceptible to the written word. The pen was actually proving to be mightier than the sword. Those who could produce telling words must be cosseted and wooed; they must be on one's side.

In the streets they were singing,

> *'Strange news, strange news! the Jacks of the city*
> *Have got,' cried Joan. 'But we mind not tales —*
> *That our good King, through wonderful pity,*
> *Will leave the crown to the Prince of Wales.*
> *That peace may be the stronger still.*
> *Here's a health to our master Will.'*

It was small wonder that Sarah was grinding her teeth in anguish. If this boy came over, Anne's position would remain the same as it always had been. And if the boy was brought up as a Protestant who was going to quarrel with that?

But Sarah's fears miraculously disappeared.

James declared that he absolutely refused to put his beloved son in the care of William.

William looked greyer every day; Sarah was more jubilant.

'Warming-pan babies! Who ever heard of such a thing!' cried Sarah gleefully. 'The man is in his dotage, and if ever I saw a fellow with one foot in the grave that man is Dutch William.'

It was a marvel to everyone that Sarah Churchill was not sent to the Tower. She must have uttered twenty treasonable statements a day. The King loathed her, but was afraid of offending the people if he attempted to interfere with Anne's freedom, so she remained.

It was noticed that her manner towards Anne was becoming more overbearing; but since Anne voiced no objection it was presumed that the Princess accepted her friend as she was. But Anne herself was thoughtful. She liked to talk to Abigail Hill when they were alone together; she had discovered the pleasure of talking instead of listening, which was what one was obliged to do with Sarah. Abigail rarely offered an opinion unless it was pressed out of her; and then it was not to be despised. But what was so comforting was to be able to talk as though thinking aloud, and to have her murmuring assent, never contradicting.

Anne was becoming more and more addicted to these mono-logues and looked forward to the time when they should be alone and she might indulge in them.

When news of her father's death reached her she was glad to talk of it to Abigail. Sarah was so impatient if she mentioned it to her; and the matter was so much on the Princess's conscience that she had to talk of it to someone. She went into mourning; and wept a little. She knew that he had wanted her to stand aside for her half-brother. This distressed her; and although she had no intention of confiding her true feelings to a chambermaid, she liked to talk to Abigail who never probed into her innermost thoughts or tried to trap her into some admission she would regret later.

'Of course, Hill,' she mused, 'the King invited that boy over here and his father would not allow him to come. I don't blame him . . . after what William did to him.'

'No, Madam, no one could blame him.'

'So now that he will not come there can be no doubt of my accession. And perhaps soon, for I declare William looks most grievously ill . . . His asthma is quite terrifying, Hill . . or it would be if one were fond of him, which it is quite . . . quite impossible to be. You understand that?'

'Oh yes, Madam.'

'And then he has haemorrhoids . . . a most distressing complaint, Hill, which makes riding so painful for him, although it would be good for his asthma. He spits blood and I have never heard anyone lived long with that, have you, Hill?'

'Never, Madam.'

'Yet he has been doing it for years and still he goes on. Then he has this swelling in the legs. Dropsy, I should think. And Dr Radcliffe was dismissed for being a little too frank about that. Yet he goes on. But one thing I know, Hill: he will not go on for ever and when he does die, Hill, and that boy is not here . . . but a Catholic in France . . . it will be my turn. Your mistress will be Queen of England. I often think about it and I am sometimes afraid that I shall not be a good Queen because I am not very clever, I fear, Hill. I wish that I were. I wanted children very much. I believe I was meant to be a mother. I cannot tell you, Hill, even though I know you understand me as few do . . . but even you cannot know what the loss of my boy meant to me. I should have been happy if all my children had lived. What a large family I should have, Hill, and the Prince says there is

no reason why we should not have many more. A big family . . .
yet. You see, he would be such a good father to them. The
Prince is a kind, indulgent man, Hill. Never allow anyone to tell
you otherwise. But sometimes I think that if God is to continue
denying me children of my body He has a reason and it came to
me last night, Hill, that I shall be the Mother of my people.
When I see the crowds and they cheer me, I think they love me
. . . more than they love William – but then of course they do
not love him at all. I think they love me more than they loved
my father. They see me as the Mother. Hill, if I am ever Queen
of England I want to be a *good* Queen.'

'Your Highness will be a great Queen.'

'But I am a little ignorant, I fear. I never did my lessons as well
as my sister Mary did. I would always make excuses. My eyes,
you know, always troubled me and I would use that as an excuse
not to study. I fear we were over-indulged as children. Perhaps
we should have been forced to learn. Perhaps it is not too late.'

'It is never too late, they say, Madam.'

'You are right, Hill. I shall start preparing myself now. I shall
study history because that is a subject above all others that a
ruler should be conversant with. Tomorrow, Hill, you will bring
me history books and I shall commence my studies.'

Abigail did as she was told and when Sarah came in and saw
what was happening, she snorted her disgust. There was no
need for Mrs Morley to disturb herself. Marlborough would
provide her with all the knowledge and advice she needed.

But Anne plodded on; she studied for a week or so, but confessed to Abigail that she found it all very dull and it really did
give her headaches.

Abigail's soothing fingers, massaging the brow, charmed
away the headaches; and it was so much pleasanter to talk
than to read.

'Sometimes I think,' said Anne, 'that it is unwise to live in
the past. Modern problems need modern solutions. Do you
think that is right, Hill?'

'I am sure you are right, Madam.'

'Then take away these books, and bring out the cards. Call
some of the others. I have a mind for a game.'

*   *   *

William was thoughtful as he rode in Bushey Park on his favourite mount, Sorrel. He was scarcely ever in London at this time, although occasionally he left Hampton for Kensington Palace to attend a meeting of the Council; but he was always glad to return. Sometimes he felt that it was only the need to prosecute the war in Europe which kept him going. He felt death very near at times. But there was comfort in the saddle, as there had been all his life; it was only when he was in the country that he could breathe with ease; but even riding was becoming exhausting.

Riding Sorrel, he wondered whether the horse was aware of the change of masters. Did he ever remember the man who had once ridden him? Sorrel had belonged to Sir John Fenwick, whose goods William had confiscated when Fenwick had been executed for treason. The most precious item had been this Sorrel, who had become William's favourite companion. Horses grew to know their masters; what did Sorrel think of the change? Whimsical thoughts rarely came to William; he was a man of sound common sense; yet on this day he was thoughtful.

Fenwick had been a Jacobite and a plotter, a man who was determined to make trouble; and he had made it. Marlborough's name had been mentioned in connection with Fenwick, and William wondered how deeply the Earl had been involved. One could never be sure with Marlborough; there was a man whom he would never trust, but whom he dared not banish.

What an uneasy reign his had been! Far better, he sometimes thought, if he had remained in Holland. He remembered happier days there, when he had subdued Mary and taken his troubles to Elizabeth Villiers, and planned the building of his beautiful Dutch Palaces. The people of Holland had loved their Stadtholder; they had cheered him when he rode through their towns and compared him with his great ancestor William the Silent who had delivered them from the cruelty of the Spaniard.

'Why, Sorrel, was I not content with my own country?' he murmured. He often talked to Sorrel, imagining the horse sympathized with him. He would never have done so within the hearing of any living person; but he fancied there was a sympathy between Sorrel and himself. 'Why did I have to come to this land and rule it? It was a desire in me, Sorrel, which I could not suppress. It was because the midwife saw those three crowns at my birth. Suppose she had not seen them, would I have schemed and plotted, would I have taken the crown from James? Mary had no wish to do so. How reluctantly she came! How she used to attempt to defend her father in those early days; and how angry she made me! If I had not believed that I was destined to possess three crowns should I be in Holland now; should I be happier than I have been?'

He was not sure. What was happiness? He had never believed it to be the right of human beings to possess it. Such a belief would be in opposition to his puritanical outlook.

'No, Sorrel,' he said. 'It was predestined. It had to be. But is that the more comforting doctrine? What has to be, is. Then no blame attaches to the individual.'

Happiness, he thought. When have I ever been happy? With Elizabeth? But then there was always the guilt. With those dear friends Bentinck and Keppel? With Mary?

'No, I was never meant to be happy, Sorrel. I think that perhaps I am more contented on my lonely rides with you than at any other time.'

He turned towards the Palace. He could see it now – the magnificent walls to which he had given a flavour of Holland. Hampton grew more and more Dutch each day.

'Come, Sorrel,' he said.

Sorrel broke into a gallop; and William remembered nothing more until some time after. Then he learned that Sorrel had trodden on a molehill.

He was in great pain, and when his physician was brought to him it was discovered that his right collar bone was broken.

The King was dying. The King was recovering. He was at Hampton. He was at Kensington.

The Jacobites were rejoicing and drinking to the mole who had made the hill which had thrown William's horse – a toast to the Gentleman in Black Velvet.

'He was riding Sorrel,' it was whispered. 'Sir John Fenwick's horse.' And they remembered the day when Sir John had been beheaded on Tower Hill.

William had sentenced Sir John to death and Sir John's favourite horse had not forgotten. It seemed significant.

Many people were calling on the Princess Anne. Some, who had recently neglected her, now came to pay their respects. Sarah Churchill was with her; she could not bear to tear herself from her dear friend's side. This meant that Abigail Hill was almost completely banished, for naturally Sarah did not seek to share her mistress with a chambermaid.

But William was recovering. He declared it was nothing more than a broken collar bone and he would not remain at Hampton, but set out for Kensington, it being imperative, he said, that he should attend the meeting of his council.

The Bill for the attainder of James Stuart, the so-called Prince of Wales, which had been decided on when James had refused to allow him to come to England as William's adopted son, had not been signed; and this was something which he declared he must put into effect, for if he did not, on his death, that boy would be proclaimed King; in fact the King of France, who had already acknowledged him as Prince of Wales, would most certanly bestow on him the title of James III.

But when William arrived at Kensington he was very ill, for the bones which had been set at Hampton needed resetting. Nor was that all. The shock of the fall, in addition to his habitual ailments, was too much for his frail constitution.

Yet he was determined to sign the attainder and had it brought to him. It was unfortunate that at the very moment when the document was laid before him he was attacked by a spasm which made it quite impossible for him to put his pen to the paper. The Jacobites declared this was a sign that God refused to let him sign the document against the true Prince of Wales.

But there were many who had no wish to call the boy their King; they had decided that Anne should be their Queen. There was no doubt that she was the daughter of James II and she was a staunch Protestant.

William was dying. This time there could be no doubt. Few would mourn him; everyone was looking towards St James's

Palace where the Princess Anne, with her friend Sarah Churchill beside her, was waiting for the news that she was Queen of England.

Queen Anne

The sun shone brilliantly on the March morning. All through the day ministers of the realm were making their way to the presence chamber in the Palace of St James, jostling each other to be first to kiss the hand and swear allegiance to the new Queen.

Anne had assumed a new dignity; she had, after all, been born near the throne and had known for many years that there was a possibility that this day would come. Sarah never left her side; her excitement, though suppressed, showed itself in her shining eyes and her very gestures. She wanted those who entered the presence chamber to be aware of in what relationship Sarah Churchill stood to the Queen.

What power she had! Anne seemed bewitched by her. Abigail, dismissed by Sarah to her proper place in the shadows, looked on wondering how Anne could have forgotten those cruel words she had overheard. Had she forgotten? It seemed so, for her manner was as affectionate as it had ever been towards her dear Mrs Freeman.

But was it? Abigail had come to know her mistress very well; and the affair of the gloves had been very revealing. Not by a look had she shown how hurt she was, how shocked; those who did not know the new Queen very well thought of her as fat, lazy, kind and a little stupid, in fact a woman who could be easily duped. They were mistaken. Anne avoided quarrels simply because she did not want to waste her limited energy in such a way; and Sarah Churchill who was so much aware of her own powerful personality underestimated everyone else. She believed that she could be rude to the Queen one day and have her in leading strings the next. But could she? Abigail was not sure. Yet seeing them together now made her wonder.

It made her excited too. She believed that she understood the Queen far more than Sarah Churchill ever could – far more than anyone else. That was why she, who had comforted Anne at the time of Gloucester's death, who had witnessed the unkindness of Sarah Churchill, now meekly stood aside and made no attempt to call attention to herself. She had a suspicion that Anne was aware of her, demurely in the shadows, aware of her and glad she was there, that there was even a kind of conspiracy between them; as though she and the Queen, together, would fight the overpowering influence of Sarah Churchill from which Anne found it difficult to escape.

Sarah's loud voice filled the apartment.

'Ah! So Clarendon is asking for audience. He is waiting his turn in the ante-room. And will Your Majesty see him?'

'He is my uncle . . .'

'Who had taken the oath of allegiance to your father and that means to your so-called brother. Tell him that when he qualifies himself to enter your presence you will be pleased to see him.' Sarah looked about her. 'Oh, there is Abigail Hill. Summon one of the pages.'

As Anne's shortsighted eyes momentarily fixed themselves on Abigail she smiled faintly, but Sarah did not notice; so Abigail hurried away to do her bidding.

When the page arrived Sarah said: 'My lord Clarendon is without. It is Her Majesty's wish that you tell him that if he chooses to take the oath of allegiance to his legitimate Sovereign, he will be admitted to her presence – and not before.'

As the page went out the Earl of Mulgrave was ushered into

the apartment, a handsome man and a poet of some standing who when he was young had courted Anne. She had wanted to marry him, but Sarah had broken up that romance – although neither of the lovers had known who had been responsible – by telling Anne's uncle, Charles II, what was going on; as a result Anne had lost her lover who had been sent on a mission to Tangiers. When he returned Anne had already been married to Prince George of Denmark; and she was not the woman to indulge in extra-marital affairs. She was too lazy, too fond of George, too busy being pregnant with remarkable regularity; and in any case she preferred the society of women to that of men.

All the same she cherished an affection for this man who had been her first lover; particularly as he had been more faithful to her father than most; he had never been a friend of William's; and becoming leader of the Tory Party had stood in opposition to the Court for some years.

Anne remembered this as he stood before her and her eyes clouded with momentary sentiment. She would always remember him as her lover, although she was happily married and he had already been married twice.

How strange that now he stood before her, she could think of nothing to say to him. And he was waiting for her to speak, for it was the prerogative of the Sovereign to speak first.

The sun was streaming through the windows; it seemed a good omen that the cold March winds should have dropped and the first signs of spring show themselves on her first day as Queen.

'It is a very fine day,' said Anne.

'Your Majesty must allow me to declare that it is the finest day I ever saw in my life,' was the earnest answer.

'I see,' smiled Anne, 'that you have not forgotten how to pay a compliment.'

'Your Majesty will never lose the gift of inspiring them.'

Sarah hastily ushered in the next visitor. She would have to watch Mulgrave if Anne were going to be foolishly sentimental over the fellow.

Abigail was aware of the slightly stubborn set of the Queen's lips, and she was certain that Sarah should take more care what she did. But Sarah was blind, blinded by her own egotism. Should she be warned? Inwardly Abigail laughed at the idea. She pictured Sarah's reaction if Abigail told her to take care, for the proud Lady Marlborough would not relish being told what she should do by a chambermaid. But did the chambermaid want to warn her?

The page had returned and was talking to Sarah.

'My lord Clarendon replies that he has come to talk to his niece and that he will take no other oaths than he has taken.'

'Then pray tell my lord Clarendon that the Queen does not wish to see him until he recognizes her as his Sovereign.'

When the page had left Sarah turned triumphantly to Anne. 'The stupid old man! Does he think he is going to rule this country! We will show him that he will have to take care in future how he treats Your Majesty. I remember how he behaved at the time William and Mary came over. He talked to you as though you were an erring infant in his control. I tell you, Master Clarendon will have to alter his ideas!'

There was no doubt that Sarah believed herself already to be in command of the Queen and the country.

The procession of ministers and courtiers came and went until it was time for the new Queen to attend service. This she did in St James's chapel and then retired to the apartments which had belonged to her dead son, while her own were hung with mourning.

'It is sad,' said Anne, 'that on this day I should have to be reminded of my sorrow.'

'Tush!' retorted Sarah impatiently. 'Mrs Morley will have many children. She should think rather of those than the lost ones.'

Anne's eyes filled with tears. 'I fear there could never be another like my boy.'

It was Abigail who was ready with a handkerchief to wipe away the tears and a quick almost furtive smile passed between them, which Sarah did not see.

'I think Your Majesty should wear purple for mourning,' announced Sarah. 'It will be different from that which you have been wearing for your father.'

'So many deaths . . . all at one time!' mused Anne.

'But such as we need not bother our heads with!' said Sarah harshly.

Abigail thought: She is too confident.

And a great excitement seized her.

Lady Marlborough was in constant attendance. Even those menial tasks which she had left to Abigail were now performed by her. Some of the wits jokingly called her Queen Sarah.

Anne seemed content to have her favourite with her; they addressed each other in the old affectionate terms, but with Anne's new rank Sarah too seemed to have assumed new dignity; it was quite clear that she saw herself as the power behind the throne.

Abigail had become merely the chambermaid and there were occasions when she believed that her original notion that the Queen had not really forgotten Sarah's outburst were quite wrong. Judging by their conversation there appeared to be no doubt that Anne was as devoted as she had ever been.

'My dear Mrs Freeman, I want you to have the Rangership of Windsor Park for life.'

'If Your Majesty insists,' said Sarah, modest for once.

'Of course I insist.'

'I had hoped to be Groom of the Stole and Mistress of the Robes so that I might be in constant attendance.'

'My dearest Mrs Freeman, the posts are yours.'

'And the Privy Purse . . . Frankly, Mrs Morley, I should hesitate to *trust* any with that . . . I would take it on if Your Majesty insisted . . .'

'You must take it on, Mrs Freeman.'

Abigail's heart sank. Anne must be completed besotted. What was this strange power of Sarah's?

'Your Majesty has been so good to *me*,' said Sarah, and that gives me great pleasure; but Your Majesty who so loves dear Mr Morley will understand that I would give up everything that has come my way for one small honour for Mr Freeman.'

'I remember how you once badly wanted the Garter for him.' said Anne.

'I am sure there is no one – just no one – at Court who deserves it more,' was the fierce rejoinder.

'You are right and it is only just that it should be his.'

'My dear Mrs Morley!'

'My dearest Mrs Freeman, so Morley has made you happy?'

It was incredible! thought Abigail. She had miscalculated; she would be an insignificant bedchamber woman for the rest of her days.

Sarah's new posts brought in seven thousand five hundred a year, but Anne said that she needed more.

'You must allow me to give you a further two thousand, Mrs Freeman.'

Sarah's eyes sparkled, but of course she dared not accept. There would be trouble as there had been previously. She did not want it to be said that the Marlboroughs took too large a share of the Queen's income. Their enemies would find some means of cutting down Anne's allowance if that were spread about.

With great self restraint Sarah declined her dear friend's generous offer. But it was very satisfactory, as she explained to dear Marl. A Garter for him; fresh posts for herself; an added income; and most of all – power!

It was Sarah's prerogative to bestow posts and that was one of the most profitable businesses in the country.

'Her Majesty will allow no places to be bestowed without *my* approval,' was her very proud boast.

She was indeed Queen Sarah.

When Anne made her first visit to Parliament as Queen it was Lady Marlborough who rode beside her; and when she entered the House, Prince George was on one side, Sarah on the other, and Marlborough himself carried the Sword of State before her.

A further honour had been bestowed on the family, for John Churchill had been made Captain General of the British Armies abroad.

Anne looking regal and wearing the star on her breast and her robes of velvet and ermine, was very different from the indolent careless Princess, and she seemed very conscious of her dignity. One of her greatest assets was her beautiful voice, and she spoke earnestly and eagerly of her intention to rule well; she wanted no strife through the three kingdoms.

'And as I know my heart to be entirely English, I can very well assure you that there is not anything you can expect or desire from me which I shall not be ready to do for the happiness and prosperity of England, and you shall always find me a strict and religious observer of my word.'

'God Save the Queen!' was the loyal answer.

The new reign had begun, but there were many who, watching the Queen and her courtiers, asked themselves: 'Whose reign? That of Queen Anne or Queen Sarah?'

The day selected for Queen Anne's coronation was April 23rd.

She confided to Abigail: 'Hill, I dread the ceremony, for I do not see how I am going to walk to the Abbey.'

'Your Majesty will have to be carried.'

'A Queen carried to her coronation! Have you ever heard the like? Oh dear, I fear it is going to be a most tiring occasion. I wish that I could dispense with it.'

'Your Majesty will come through it, charming all who behold you.'

'But a Queen carried to her coronation, Hill!'

'The people will love you the more for your misfortune.'

'I believe you are a wise young woman. 'Tis true enough they love when they pity. And they will remember the loss of my boy.'

Anne had formed a habit of talking of her boy to Abigail; she would go over the anecdotes again and again, but Abigail always listened as though she was hearing them for the first time.

'You're a comfort to me, Hill,' Anne said on more than one occasion, for another habit of hers was to make a phrase and repeat it again and again. This irritated Sarah, who would sometimes make an impatient gesture when these repetitious phrases were used; Abigail never gave a sign that she had heard them before. And there were occasions when Abigail suspected that Anne enjoyed those sessions with her more than she did the brisk encounters with Sarah.

So on the morning of the coronation Abigail listened once more to the stories of the dead Duke's perfections until Sarah bustled in to stop the reminiscences.

'I was telling Hill how I wish my boy were here to see this day.'

'I doubt not it would have pleased him mightily,' said Sarah. 'Now I have come to see that everything is in order. Nothing must go wrong today!'

'I am sure it could not with you, dear Mrs Freeman, to attend to all that should be done.'

Abigail faded into the background, forgotten.

'Ah, yes,' mused Anne, 'if only my boy were here . . .'

'I can tell you, Mrs Morley, I am not so pleased with *my* boy.'

'My dear Mrs Freeman, what do you mean?'

'He has a desire, mark you, to join the Army, and serve under his father.'

'A very natural desire when you consider he is Mr Freeman's son. And my dear Mrs Freeman is a fighter too. I am sure if she had been born a man she would have been commanding an army.'

'Lord Blandford is sixteen years old. That is no age to become a soldier. I said that he should go from Eton to Cambridge and that is where he has gone. But he is displeased with me because of it and I can tell you *I* am displeased with him.'

'It is a pity when families quarrel.'

'Quarrel, Mrs Morley! Do you think that I shall allow my own son to go against my wishes?'

Anne sighed. 'And what does Mr Freeman think?'

'Oh, he thinks that there is only one worthwhile profession in the world and would willingly take young John with him into service. I can tell you I put a stop to that nonsense.'

'I believe even Mr Freeman is afraid of you.'

'Then I am the only one in the world he *is* afraid of. Of course later on it may well be that young John will join his father, but not yet.'

'How fortunate you are, Mrs Freeman, to have children. I often think that if my boy had lived and I had been able to give him brothers and sisters I should have been a very happy woman. I would willingly give my crown in exchange for a family of boys and girls. Sometimes when I see my poorest subjects . . .'

'Well, well, we have to accept our lot. And now, Madam, if you are to be in time for your coronation . . .'

Abigail listening, marvelled at the temerity of a woman who could cut short the Queen. Yet here was Sarah taking the important posts while she, Abigail, who let the Queen talk, who always agreed with her and soothed, had to dissolve into the background as soon as Sarah appeared, and emerge again only when she could make herself useful.

It was eleven o'clock when Anne was carried in her sedan chair from St James's Palace to Westminster Hall.

She was deeply conscious of her state, for since she had become Queen she had thought more and more seriously of her position. She wanted to be a good Queen; she wanted her people to love her; as she had told dear George: If she looked upon the people as her children she could find some compensation for the loss of her dear boy.

In the Hall she remained seated while the company was assembled for the procession to the Abbey. As her husband followed the Archbishop of Canterbury into the Hall he looked for her and when he saw her his expression was one of such tenderness that she thanked God for giving her such a good man.

I am happily married, she thought, and the only sorrow in our union is the loss of all our babies and the greatest sorrow of all, that of our boy.

George was a dear man, although he was rather dull; he did eat too much and drink too much, but he was never bad tempered. He became more and more affable as he grew more and more sleepy; and when he murmured 'Est-il possible?' which was his favourite phrase he meant to encourage those who were talking to him. It was true that she found the company of Sarah more amusing and that of Abigail Hill more soothing – but George was a good man, and the best possible husband for her.

He was concerned now for her feet which were so tortured

by gout and dropsy, but she flashed him a smile to assure him that she was managing well enough.

She was helped into the open chair in which she would be carried and the procession set out through New Palace Yard towards the west door of the Abbey. The sight of the Queen in her chair, the circle of gold set with diamonds on her abundant curled hair, the kindliest of smiles on her placid face, set the people cheering and shouting 'God Save the Queen'. Tears were in her eyes; she wanted to tell them that she loved them all, that she regarded them as her children; that she wanted to care for them and bring good to them.

It was a moving ceremony. She thought of all those who had passed through it before her and naturally she must remember her father. She reminded herself that he had forgiven her before he died; and at least he was not alive now, so she was not taking the throne from him. How different it had been with poor Mary who had been crowned while he lived, and had received a letter from him on the very morning of the coronation in which he had cursed her.

It was a thrilling moment when the Archbishop presented her to the people.

'I here present unto you Queen Anne, undoubted Queen of this realm. Whereas all you that are come here this day to do your homages and service, are you willing to do the same?'

The cry echoed through the Abbey. 'God save Queen Anne.'

The trumpets burst forth and the choir rose to sing: 'The Queen shall rejoice in Thy strength, O Lord; exceeding glad shall she be of Thy salvation! Thou shalt present her with the blessings of goodness, and shall set a crown of pure gold on her head.'

Anne deeply moved vowed to herself: I will be all that I desire to be. Before my days are done they shall call me Good Queen Anne.

Her progress to the altar was painful, but she scarcely felt the ache in her feet; she believed that God gave her special strength on that day. When she heard the words 'Thou shalt not appear before the Lord thy God empty! she put the gold which she had brought with her into the proffered basin and thought once more of her sister and William who at this moment of their coronation – owing to the consternation they had felt earlier on receiving the letter from the deposed James – had forgotten to provide themselves with the necessary gold.

Her beautiful clear voice with its perfect enunciation could be heard repeating the declaration after the Archbishop; this was an important part of the coronation, for it assured the people that she did not believe in the theory of transubstantiation, that she considered the worship of the Virgin Mary and any saints idolatrous; in fact that she was a member of the Protestant Church.

And when she answered the questions put to her and came to that one: 'Will you, to the utmost of your power, maintain the laws of God, the true profession of the gospel, and the Protestant reformed religion established by law?' she answered with great fervour: 'All this I promise to do.'

Supported by the Chamberlain she regained the altar and there, laying her right hand on the Bible made a solemn oath to carry out all her promises.

The coronation ring was on her finger; the crown was placed upon her head and the repeated shouts rang out once more.

'God save the Queen. God save the Queen.'

The guns from the Abbey turrets fired a salute which was answered by the guns of the Tower of London. The trumpets sounded.

Seated on her chair of state Anne received the homage of the peers. George was the first to come forward and kiss her cheek, and there was more than homage in his eyes: there was pride and pleasure. Dear, dear George! she thought. He could not be happier if they were crowning him. But was that not like her dear boy's father? How different he was from her sister's husband, William. Poor Mary! I am fortunate when I think of her.

One by one they came to her . . . these important men who would play their part in shaping her reign for good or for evil. The thought sobered her, but the feeling of exultation remained, and for the first time since the death of her beloved son did her grief recede almost to insignificance. It would return, of course; but at this moment she felt her duty so strongly that there was a new purpose in her life, and during this solemn ceremony she believed that if she could win the love and respect of her subjects she could be happy again.

They were singing the anthem now. The triumphant ceremony was over.

But this was not the end; there was the banquet to follow. How willingly she would have dispensed with that; there was nothing she wanted so much now as to lie on her bed and rest her poor aching feet. She would like quiet Abigail Hill to unbind her hair and massage her forehead while she talked to her of the coronation and how she intended to be a good Queen. Abigail Hill would understand; and she would believe that this could be. What pleasure then to be alone in her bedchamber with Abigail Hill!

That could not be. Knowing how wearying she would find this coronation since, although she was carried to the Abbey in her chair, it would be necessary to walk up to the altar and stand for a while, she had vaguely hinted that the banquet might be dispensed with. How horrified Sarah had been at the thought!

'What!' she had cried. 'They would say you were afraid. Have you forgotten what happened at William and Mary's banquet? Then, when Dymoke made his challenge a glove was thrown . . . and what a scandal that made! The Jacobites would say you were afraid the same thing would happen at your coronation. No, banquet there must be, and attend you must.'

She had to agree that Sarah was right; but Sarah's voice seemed to have become louder since the accession and more authoritative.

A banquet always had a certain charm for her; however tired she was she could always show appreciation for good food. At her left hand at the table sat George, benign and uxorious; his little eyes, embedded in fat, glistening at the sight of all the good things on the table.

It would have been a pleasant ending to the ceremonies if she were not so tired.

Dymoke made his appearance and no one accepted his challenge, and the faint embarrassment which memories of the previous coronation had provoked was ended.

It had been an inspiring and invigorating day but she was

glad it was over. Anne was divested of her coronation robes at the Court of Wards and helped into the chair in which she would be carried back to St James's Palace. Back she thought to Abigail's soothing ministrations. Oh, to be lying on her bed with that good woman within call!

There were bonfires in the streets; the sounds of music drifted along the river; and as she entered the Palace Anne heard sounds of revelry in the state apartments. Her attendants were preparing to give her a royal welcome.

She heard the shouts: 'God save Queen Anne.'

There were toasts to be drunk and George's eyes gleamed at the prospect, for much as he loved food he loved wine better.

Anne's heart sank, for she had believed it would be possible to go straight to her bed. Lord Lindsay, the Chamberlain, noticed how tired she was and leaning towards Prince George said 'Perhaps Your Highness would propose going to bed.'

George looked like a child who was in danger of losing a toy he has hoped for. Then he said: 'I cannot propose. I am Her Majesty's subject. I can do nought but what she proposes.'

Anne overhearing this laughed and: 'Well then, George, as I am so very tired I command you to come to bed.'

She held out her hand. George took it; and they retired to the royal bedchamber.

A Death in the Family

While the Queen was sleeping Sarah left the bedchamber in charge of Abigail Hill and went to seek her husband. She found him in their apartment waiting for her and she flew triumphantly into his arms.

'So, at last it has come!' she cried.

' 'Tis so. But this, my love, is the beginning.'

'Never fear. I shall tell her what she must do.'

'That you will, but we must not forget that she has a Parliament. We have to go carefully. Rochester is after the office of Lord Treasurer. He must not get it, Sarah. If he does that is the end of our hopes.'

'Rochester! He shall not have office! I shall forbid Morley to consider it for a moment.'

'Two things you have forgotten, dearest. He is her uncle and she is the Queen.'

'I forget nothing. Uncle or no, he shall not have the post. And Queen or not, she shall obey me.'

'For God's sake, my love, do not let our success go to your head.'

'Marl, I could find it in my heart to be angry with you.'

He took her hand and kissed it. 'Nay,' he said, 'never. You and I are as one, Sarah, and you know it. I am too cautious and you are too quick. Listen, love, let us stand together and with your speed and my caution we cannot fail.'

'Well,' she said with a grudging smile, 'let us hear what you plan.'

'To keep Rochester out. He will vote against war and that will be the ruin of our country. We have to stop the French from commanding Europe. And I am going to do it.'

'Well, you are the commander of the Army.'

'Of what use if the chief minister were against me? Even if I succeeded in prosecuting the war I should be denied the necessary supplies. No. I want a Lord Treasurer who is completely with me and there is one man for the job: Godolphin.'

'Godolphin it shall be. Was it not for this purpose that we allowed Henrietta to marry his boy?'

'I have spoken to him, Sarah, and he tells me he has no love for the job.'

'No love for the job. Then Master Godolphin will have to change his views.'

'I have tried to persuade him.'

'You leave Godolphin to me. I will make him see his duty.'

John smiled. She was fierce; she was forthright; and he fancied Godolphin was a little afraid of her.

'There would be no harm, my dear,' he said, 'in adding your voice to mine. You could remind Anne that Godolphin has always supported her – which is more than Rochester has. Remind her how he tried to stop William and Mary when they wanted to reduce her income and how he remained her friend when she was at the height of disfavour. She is not one to forget past friends.'

'She shall be reminded, I promise you. Have no fear, Marl; the Treasury shall go to Godolphin. And there is one other matter I wish to take up with you. It's our own young John. I believe you have been encouraging him.'

'Oh, come, Sarah, it's natural enough the boy should want to follow his father's profession.'

'In due course. At the moment he stays at Cambridge.'

'Well, that is agreed. But there is surely no need for you to continue to show the boy your displeasure. He has obeyed you. Is that not enough?'

'I do not expect my children to *attempt* to disobey me.'

'He is but a boy.'

'But he was ready to defy *me!*'

John laughed affectionately. She was overbearing and arrogant, but the magic of her presence never failed to enchant him. With her flashing blue eyes and the indignant colour in her cheeks, he thought her the most beautiful woman he had ever seen. Even his daughters – beauties all – could not compete with their mother.

She should have her way, of course – even though he must lay a gentle restraining hand on her.

'Sarah, my love, do not let our son feel the force of your displeasure too long.'

'He will have to learn that I know what is best for him. But . . . there are important matters which need attention. *I* shall see Godolphin without delay and point out where his duty lies.'

Sarah came into the Queen's bedchamber where Abigail was kneeling at Anne's feet, bathing her swollen ankles.

'Hill has such gentle hands,' murmured Anne.

'Yes, yes,' said Sarah, signing to Abigail to get up, take her basin and be gone.

Abigail raised her eyes to the Queen who nodded her head slightly, at which Abigail dried and powdered the royal feet, while Sarah looked on impatiently. With lowered eyes, Abigail was asking herself: How can the Queen allow this? But she seems to enjoy her servitude to this woman.

Sarah waved a hand and Abigail, clasping the bowl in her hand, left the apartment.

As she went on, Abigail heard Anne murmur: 'Such a good creature.'

'I have matters which must be discussed between us two. Hill can come back later and do what you wish.'

'Pray be seated, dear Mrs Freeman.'

'Well,' said Sarah, 'you will have noticed how those who have hitherto treated you with contempt have now miraculously become your friends. We must be very watchful of such; but you can trust me to be on the alert for them.'

'You are thinking of . . .'

'Your uncle, Rochester. Oh, he is now preening himself, I can tell you. Uncle to Her Majesty the Queen of England! Never mind if before he treated her with contempt. Never mind if he sided with that arch scoundrel, that Dutch Abortion! Never mind if he voted to reduce your income! Never mind if he never came near you when your sister and her miserable spouse picked quarrels with you! Oh, never mind! Now he comes creeping back and would be My Lord Treasurer . . . *if* you please.'

'It is true that he was not always my friend, but I have heard that he is an able man, and as my uncle . . .'

'*I* know that Mrs Morley would never forget her true friends. When I think of what a *good* friend Sidney Godolphin has been to you, when I think of the brilliance of that man! I said to Mr Freeman: I know Her Majesty, my dearest Mrs Morley. I know that she is not one to be led astray by the whining of curs who a short time ago were yapping at her heels.'

'It's true of course, Mrs Freeman.'

'Mrs Morley agrees with me that Mr Freeman is a genius . . . an absolute genius. She can safely leave the conduct of her armies to him. In the past he has had to suffer the envy of others less gifted. But that is over now. There is only one man with whom he could work and it is an essential fact that the Queen's commander of the Armies and her Chief Minister must work together.'

'I do agree.'

'Then it can only be the Treasury for Godolphin and Master Rochester must understand that his Queen is not a fool to be duped by his pretty speeches. Godolphin at home; Marlborough abroad. Why, Mrs Morley, you will indeed make England great . . . with their help.'

'I have always liked Sidney Godolphin . . .'

'Then that little matter is settled. He shall be informed. Now

I am going to tell you about the trouble I am having with my son. The boy has dared challenge my plans for his future. What do you think of that?'

'That is a little wicked of the young man, Mrs Freeman.'

'He would join the Army without delay, if you please. He would leave Cambridge forthwith when I have decided he shall stay there.'

'He is eager to be a soldier . . . just like my boy. I can see him now, dear Mrs Freeman, drilling his soldiers in the park. What a boy he was . . .'

Let her rant on a little, thought Sarah. It would be a reward for giving the Treasury to Godolphin.

With Godolphin Lord Treasurer, and himself Commander of the Armed Forces, Marlborough saw that the future looked bright. He meant to wage war on the Continent; he was going to make his country the major power; but he needed absolute support at home. A great deal depended on the Queen – but Sarah could be relied upon to guide her. Even so there would be powerful enemies, for there were many ministers who were opposed to war. Both Whigs and Tories were oddly assorted within their own ranks. The Tory party was the Church party and the landowning classes; the Whigs were the moneyed section of the community, the commercial interest. Both parties had their encumbrances. The Tories the bigoted High Church dignitaries and the Jacobites; the Whigs, the Nonconformists and the Calvinists. But it was the Whigs who would support the war because war meant an expansion of commerce; while the Tories had no such means of enriching themselves and were impoverished by taxes. Yet in spite of his desire for war Marlborough was a Tory and there was dissension even in his close family circle, for Sarah herself was inclining more and more to Whiggery.

But when Marlborough persuaded his Allies to make the Pretender's claim to the throne one of their reasons for continuing the conflict, the war assumed a greater popularity; and as the whole country was firmly behind the new Queen and determined that the Catholic Pretender should not come back, it was ready to go wholeheartedly into battle, and on a May morning Garter King of Arms appeared in the London streets and to the sound of trumpets declared to the people that England was at war.

This was triumph for Marlborough, and he immediately began making his preparations to leave for the Continent.

But he was not easy in his mind as to the situation at home. They had too many enemies, he had said to Sarah.

It was for this reason that he had sought to win Robert Harley to his side.

He had discussed this matter with Godolphin and they had both agreed that Harley was the third pillar needed to support the edifice they intended to set up.

'Your Francis is over-young,' said Marlborough, kindly, for he had quickly realized that Sarah's complete lack of tact meant that he must use his own liberal supply to the full. 'And he is therefore not in a position to be of much use... at the moment.' Francis, husband of Henrietta, was a good enough pawn. Member for Helston, he was a budding politician; but the situation demanded strong men. Marlborough's mind rested fleetingly on his second son-in-law who had become the Earl of Sunderland on his father's recent death. He was clever but rash and of an uncertain temper.

Godolphin was already thinking of Harley.

The three men met in Marlborough's club and as soon as he had been invited Harley knew why. The situation interested him.

Marlborough came straight to the point. He believed, he said, that at all costs the French must be prevented from dominating Europe. It was his duty to see to this; but there was a strong pacifist element in the country.

'It would be only a temporary peace,' said Marlborough, 'and could before long bring our country to her knees.'

Harley nodded. 'I am entirely of your opinion.'

'I shall be out of the country fighting her battles. My Lord Treasurer is of my mind, but we have our enemies and we need the support of strong men.'

'A triumvirate of strong men,' put in Godolphin.

Harley smiled. He understood. He was being invited to share in their success. Being shrewd, he knew how important it was to win the Queen's approval; in fact it was not possible to advance far without it, and the Queen was ruled by one woman: Sarah Churchill. So one might say that the Marlboroughs were the real rulers of the country. Marlborough was a wise man; he knew very well that he was surrounded by enemies; but Sarah could persuade the Queen to anything, and as the Queen's ministers knew this it did not endear them to Marlborough who would have to watch every step he took; but what men among them would be able to stand up to a strong triumvirate such as would be made by himself, Godolphin and Harley?

'And you consider me worthy to be included?' asked Harley.

'You are a good Tory,' said Godolphin.

'That is a recommendation?' asked Harley. 'A Tory today is a Whig tomorrow. One grows dizzy contemplating the turnabout. Why in your own family, my lord Marlborough, you have yourself – staunch Tory. And I have heard that your good lady is inclined to the Whigs; your brother Admiral Churchill is eager to have us all know what a good Tory he is and your son-in-law Sunderland equally anxious to show us he's a regular Whig of a man. While Lady Marlborough's own sister, so I've heard, is all for the Jacks, and Lady Marlborough herself surely the most intimate friend Her Majesty ever had.'

Marlborough smiled coolly at Harley. He was known as Robin the Trickster, and one could never be sure what he was at; but he knew well enough that they needed him.

'Good men now and then find it necessary to turn their coats,' said Marlborough.

'I am in absolute agreement with my lord as usual,' replied Harley with a bow.

'Then,' replied Marlborough, 'it would give me pleasure if you would visit us at St Albans. My wife is anxious to make your closer acquaintance.'

Returning to London from St Albans Robert Harley was congratulating himself. A triumvirate, he was thinking: Marlborough, Godolphin, Harley. It was well to be allied with the Marlboroughs, and when one met Sarah Churchill one understood why. The Queen was completely hers to command, he had heard; and although he had thought previously that statement a little exaggerated now that he had met the lady he no longer did. What fire and fury! Marlborough was, if not afraid of her, in bondage to her. A handsome woman, and an absolute virago.

Robin the Trickster was amused and intrigued. He was looking forward to travelling along with the Marlboroughs . . . for a while.

She was arrogant and quite vain. He was a man who knew how to pay a compliment and he had made her believe that he admired her every bit as much as he had intended that she should.

The Marlboroughs were delighted. They had angled for him and they believed they had him in the net. They needed him; they recognized him as a power in the House. And so he was. He had been elected Speaker because he had a greater knowledge of parliamentary procedure than any one living person, and it was understandable that they should want his support. With Marlborough conducting the war and Godolphin and Harley in charge at home, no one could stand against them.

At St Albans he had been promised a grand appointment. Secretary of State in place of Nottingham whom they had decided must go. Nottingham should certainly go; Harley should decidedly take his place. But in this alliance Harley would be expected to remain contentedly in third place. They did not know Harley, who was already asking himself: What is Marlborough? A soldier with a forceful wife who in some unnatural way has managed to subdue the Queen! What is Godolphin? A timid man, easily disheartened, and obviously in awe of Marlborough's wife. It seemed as though Madam Sarah ruled the roost. But she should not rule Robert Harley.

He left his house and strolled out into the London streets, passing unnoticed, for his appearance was insignificant, and he was by no means a handsome man; perhaps that was why he yearned to be noticed. His powers of oratory were marred by a stammer which he had overcome to some extent but which made him appear hesitant; his voice was harsh and cold, his manners formal. Yet he could produce the telling phrase and could confound his opponents in debate. He had developed these qualities because of his disabilities; in the same way his vanity had grown as though to give the lie to his lack of good looks. There was one characteristic which dominated him: That was envy. He could not endure to see others succeed. At the moment he was prepared to use the friendship of Marlborough and Godolphin; but he could not quietly stand aside and see the power and the glory pass him by to fall into their hands.

That, he realized, would come later. In the meantime it would be a wise policy to ingratiate himself with the Marlboroughs, and he did not anticipate much difficulty in arranging this. He had summed up Sarah and she, of course, was the important one. He would flatter her; he would appear to bow to her will. As her greatest desire was to rule everyone, that should please her. He did not think he would have any difficulty in walking in step with Madame Sarah ... for a while.

She interested him. How he would enjoy going into battle against her! What an interesting situation! But of course one would work skilfully in the dark ... right until the moment when it was appropriate to deliver the fatal blow.

Harley was delighted. Life was becoming interesting.

He turned into a coffee house and as he sat down was almost immediately joined by a young man.

'Ha, Harry,' said Harley. 'Pray be seated.'

'Master,' replied the young man with a somewhat affected bow, 'you have had good news.'

'Do I then betray myself?' asked Harley with a smile.

Henry St John was an exceptionally handsome man of about twenty-four. Harley had selected him as the most brilliant of the younger politicians and St John was a willing disciple, immediately recognizing what the patronage of a man in Harley's position could mean to an ambitious young man; and determined to make the most of it, he never missed an opportunity of sitting at the feet of the master.

'Only to those who know you well, Master.'

'Well, Harry, you are right. I can see the way ahead more clearly than I ever did before. I have recently returned from Holywell near St Albans.'

116

'I heard that you were visiting the Marlboroughs.'

'So that is all over the town?'

'Our most brilliant politician – and the Marlboroughs. Who could fail to prick up ears?'

'So there are speculations, eh? Well, we shall see.'

'You are thoughful. And, I see, in no mood to impart your thoughts.'

'There are thoughts which should be guarded as closely as state secrets.'

'Those sort of thoughts? Then we should indeed expect great events. But you are here in a coffee house where one does not expect to find the greatest statesmen of the day.'

'You are wondering why I am not caressing the bottle, Henry? I am a faithful man, but I was never more faithful to any than I am to Bacchus. Is that what you're thinking? Oh, my boy, don't imagine I have swerved. But tonight I have a fancy to look at a certain section of our London scene which I believe merits more attention than it usually receives.'

St John leaned his elbows on the table and looked intently into his friend's face.

'Develop the powers of observation, Henry, my boy. Have you ever considered the power of words? Ah, I see you have. A man of your er . . . intelligence . . . I almost said genius, Harry; but perhaps that is a word which should not be rashly employed. No word should be rashly employed perhaps. Remember, my dear boy, that this is a discussion on the importance of words. Words! Words! They are more powerful than cannon. Have you ever heard it said that *Lillibullero* won the victory for Dutch William more certainly than his army? In the last few years words have formed a part of our lives. Lampoons . . . sly verses . . . street songs . . . These Harry are the weapons which have made thrones tremble. Just think if Catholic James could have found a scribbler to give the right words to him the Queen might not be on the throne today. Ah, Harry, you smile. I see you think this is one of my discourses. I talk as so many do, for the sake of talking. I am not sure whether I do or not. But tonight when I am in my cups . . . I shall be sure, for drinking – in my case – clears the head, Harry. You see I am not as other

117

men for which I might say Thank God had not the Pharisee said it before me and been held up as an example of hypocrisy. I am a hypocrite perhaps. Who shall say? And who is wise to say anything of a man until his time has run out? You only judge a man's life at his death, Harry. Now look at that fellow over there. I am going to invited him to our table.'

St John was alert. He knew that it was for the purpose of inviting this fellow to the table that Harley had come to the coffee house.

A man of medium height with a sallow complexion and dark hair – he wore no wig – came over to the table.

'Sir,' he said with a bow, 'your servant.'

'Be seated,' said Harley. 'But first meet a friend, Henry St John, who is eager to make your acquaintance.'

St John looked startled, but Harley smiled.

'Harry, this is Daniel Defoe – a literary man. I hope you are acquainted with his work?'

The man turned his eager eyes on St John who, taking his cue from Harley, said modestly: 'It is an omission which I intend to rectify without delay.'

The grey eyes were idealist, the hooked nose and sharp chin betrayed a strength.

What is Harley up to? wondered St John. But he began to guess.

He was going to use Defoe as he used everyone. Harley was a brilliant schemer; he was not called Robin the Trickster for nothing.

He was going to stand with Marlborough and Godolphin as one of the almighty three, but Harley was not the man to be one of three. He would want to stand alone, supreme.

This band of men, of whom Defoe was one, would be the secret army. They held a more deadly weapon than the generals, but the generals were too foolish to realize this. It was men such as Mr Harley who were a step ahead of their contemporaries who became the leaders.

Harley had decided to use the hidden weapon against his foes. The Marlboroughs thought they were going to rule the country because of Sarah's ascendancy over the Queen, but Harley had decided otherwise; *he* was going to stand supreme.

And the fact that he had allowed Henry St John to share this little confidence showed clearly that if St John cared to attach himself to Harley he could go along with him; St John cared. He cared very deeply.

So he was excited as he sat in the coffee house listening to talk between one of the country's leading statesmen and the poor scribbler.

Parting was almost unendurable for John and Sarah. It was at such times that briefly they forgot ambition. Sarah was unable to control her tears — tears of sorrow were unusual with her, though she occasionally shed tears of rage. To let him go, her beloved John, into danger! So many hazards he would face; and he had so many enemies! What if she were never to see him again? Nothing then would be worthwhile. As for John, he had wanted to go to war for only at war could he prove his genius. He was a soldier first and foremost; he believed that this war was necessary to England. And yet what would he not have given at that moment of parting to leave everything and go back with Sarah to St Albans.

He was worried about young John who was at cross purposes with his mother. Henrietta, now that she had escaped from the family circle by marriage, was as her mother said 'saucy'. The only member of the family with whom Sarah really lived on amicable terms was Anne — and this was solely because Anne had a sweet disposition and it was impossible to quarrel with her.

He wanted to be in the circle of his family; he wished momentarily that he and Sarah could have abandoned ambition, the quest for wealth and fame ... everything ... to go and spend their days quietly at St Albans ... together ... all through the days and nights.

Oddly enough he knew as they faced each other that Sarah felt the same — his wild tempestuous Sarah who could be tender only to him, and then rarely so. Yet, he told himself, for him her frequent anger made her occasional sweetness all the more precious.

She clung to him now. 'Oh, John,' she whispered, 'there'll be dangers over there.'

119

'And here there'll be dangers too. You will have to be careful of your behaviour, my love, for although I go to war with a ruthless enemy you stay behind in a country of tigers and wolves.'

Sarah's eyes glinted momentarily. 'I'd like to see them attack me. Just let them try.'

'They'll try, Sarah. They'll never cease to try.'

'I shall be ready for them. Now that I have got young Abigail Hill to take over some of the more unpleasant duties I have more time for important affairs. I'm thankful for that girl, John. She does her task well. And she is respectful and grateful.'

'As she should be.'

'As she should be. She dare not be otherwise. But it is rarely that I have to remind her what I have done for her. She *should* serve me well. But I'll reward her.'

He touched her cheek lightly with his finger. 'It is always well to reward a good servant.'

She took his hand and kissed it. 'You will think of me when you are away?'

'Constantly.'

'Let not thoughts of me turn you from those of war. I want this finished quickly. I want you back in England.'

'You can be sure that I shall lose no time in hurrying to you.'

'Oh, my love, these are great days.'

'Yes,' he replied, 'this will be warfare with a difference. I want to beat the French in the field and then march on to Paris to take their capital. That is the only way to beat the French.'

'And you'll have opposition to those plans, I'll warrant.'

'There is always opposition. To turn to Spain would be suicidal ... and if we succeeded there no decision would have been reached.'

'Well, John Churchill, I do not think you are the man to let others fight your wars for you.'

'As usual my love is right.'

When the hour for parting had come and he must set sail, leaving her behind, Sarah declared her intention of seeing him go aboard, for she was determined to be with him until the very last moment.

'How I wish that I were coming with you!' she cried vehemently.

'Ah, my love, then I should indeed be happy. But there are affairs at home which need your attention.'

She nodded. 'Have no fear. Sidney Godolphin will do as I wish and Harley seems amenable. I believe he is delighted that you selected him to join you. He as much as told me so.'

'He's a clever fellow whom we can't afford to have as an enemy.'

'I shall be watching them. I wish I didn't have to listen to Morley's gossip. Sometimes I could scream at the old fool to be silent.'

'You must never do that, Sarah.'

'I believe that woman would take anything . . . just anything from me.'

'I beg you do not put it to the test.'

'Oh, come, Marl, you can trust me.'

'With all my heart, but you can be a little impetuous, my love.'

'She dotes on me. Her stupid old face looks almost human when she sees me.'

'She is not a fool, Sarah. She is a woman who successfully hides her true feelings as well as any. I've heard that said and I know it to be true.'

'I know what her true feelings are for her beloved Mrs Freeman, I do assure you.'

'God bless you, Sarah. Take care of yourself and the family.'

One last embrace. Then she must let him go. He stood on deck watching her; and she stood waving to him, praying earnestly, and what was so unusual, humbly. 'Let him come safely back to me.'

Marlborough held up his glass that he might see her for as long as possible; and when he could no longer see her he could only endure the parting by writing to her without delay.

'I watched with my perspective glass for a long time in hopes that I might have another sight of you. At this moment I would give my life to come back to you.'

'Hill,' said the Queen, 'pray bathe my feet. They are most painful today.'

Abigail inclined her head and in a few minutes was kneeling at the Queen's feet with the silver bowl half full of water that was neither too hot nor too cold.

Anne smiled placidly and lay back, her eyes closed.

'That feels good,' she said. 'Danvers is either too rough or afraid to touch me. You have magic in your hands, Hill.'

'Your Majesty is so gracious to me.'

'You're a good creature.'

'And the happiest in the world to give pleasure to Your Majesty.'

'You're quiet and there are times when I feel the need for quietness.'

Abigail patted the feet dry, anointed them, powdered them and put them into the large and comfortable slippers.

'Your Majesty feels better now?'

'Greatly refreshed Hill. Did I hear Danvers scolding you this afternoon, my dear?'

'She said I was in too constant attendance on Your Majesty.'

'What nonsense!'

Abigail folded her arms and struck a pose that was so like one of Mrs Danvers' that the Queen opened her eyes wide and laughed. 'I do declare, Hill, you look exactly like her.'

' "Hill," ' mimicked Abigail, ' "you push yourself too much. Lady Marlborough has put you here to do those tasks which are not to her liking, but I have not asked you to take my place." '

'It's Danvers to the life!' cried Anne.

Abigail looked up meekly at an imaginary Danvers and murmured her excuses. Then greatly daring she pretended that Sarah had arrived and mimicked a scene between her and Danvers.

She was almost afraid to look at the Queen. Had she gone too far? What would Anne's reactions be to a little poking of fun at Sarah?

122

'Clever little Hill!' murmured the Queen, smiling. It was a further step forward in their relationship.

'Your Majesty,' said Abigail, 'Mr Masham left a message that the Prince was hoping to visit you this day.'

'Then I am pleased, Hill. I trust this means that his breathing is a little better.'

'Mr Masham tells me that his breathing was much easier this morning and that he enjoyed his dinner.'

'He is a good man, young Masham. I believe he is fond of the Prince.'

'I am sure of it, Madam.'

'He confides in you, does he?'

'A little, Madam.'

'Clever little thing. Now help make me ready to receive the Prince and then Hill you shall play some of your pieces on the harpsichord. Why, Hill, I am always discovering fresh talents in you. I am very fond of the harpsichord and I was telling the Prince what a pleasant touch you have.'

Abigail was delighted with her progress in the bedchamber. If only Sarah would stay away for months. Then she would make a real advance.

George, Prince of Denmark, came to his wife's apartments accompanied by his page, Samuel Masham. There were signs in the Prince's face of past good looks, but he had become so fat through an excessive fondness for good food and wine that he was now almost a ridiculous figure as he trundled painfully along, leaning on a jewelled-topped stick. He wheezed painfully, for he suffered greatly from asthma, but his expression was one of kindliness and a placidity which matched that of his wife.

'My angel,' he said, his Danish accent obvious, for he had never tried to eradicate it. He was far too lazy. 'I trust I find you better today.'

'Yes, my dearest. My good Hill has just made me comfortable. And you are wheezing less, I fancy. Come sit down here beside me so that I may see you clearly.'

George sat down heavily in the chair which Abigail had set close to the Queen's couch. He took the Queen's hand, kissed it and retained it, stroking the beautifully white plump fingers admiringly. Even as he did so he nodded drowsily. He had drunk heavily and always found it hard to keep his eyes open in the afternoon – or at any time for that matter.

'Dear George!' murmured Anne.

He nodded happily. Then they were silent.

He was such a good husband, Anne was thinking, but there was never anything to say to him, except: 'My angel!' Or: 'My dearest George.' Of course when their boy was alive they had had him to talk of and that had been the most engrossing subject in the world; but if they talked of their darling now it could only end in sadness. In actual fact it was so much more enlivening and amusing to talk to – or rather listen to – dearest Mrs Freeman; it was much more pleasant to talk to that quiet little Hill who was turning out to be so clever.

Anne yawned.

In the ante room Abigail was smiling at Samuel Masham.

'If you will forgive me the liberty,' he was saying, 'I should like to say how well you are looking.'

'I *am* well. And you?'

He nodded and his eyes were brighter than usual. 'It is pleasant without Madam Virago at Court.'

Abigail opened her pale green eyes very wide and looked astonished.

'I am sure you suffer at her hands more than most,' went on Samuel. 'The Court seems quiet and peaceful. She will soon be back though. As soon as the Earl sails she will return.'

Abigail lowered her eyes. She agreed with Samuel, but she was not certain whether it was wise to speak of Lady Marlborough disparagingly here in the royal apartments. And she was determined to be discreet. It was true that Sarah Churchill was the most indiscreet woman in the country and she had not appeared to suffer for it, but Abigail was well aware that she could never follow in Sarah's footsteps; she would have to go an entirely different way.

'I am sure,' she said discreetly, 'that Lady Marlborough will lose no time in returning to her duties.'

Samuel too was discreet; and he would take his cue from Abigail, so he changed the subject. 'I heard Her Majesty speak of you to the Prince the other day. She said that she was beginning to wonder what she would do without you.'

Abigail was excited. If Anne spoke of her when she was not present then she must have made a deep impression on the royal mind.

Samuel brought his head close to hers. 'Of course,' he said, 'more and more will depend on the good graces of The Lady. They are saying that the Triumvirate with the Queen behind it, will be all powerful. The Queen behind it! It is The Lady who is behind it. Marlborough, her husband! Godolphin, her daughter's father-in-law! Harley their man! And the Queen completely in the hands of The Lady. Those of us who fail to please Madam will not long retain our posts.'

'We shall have to be watchful to please,' murmured Abigail.

'Hill!' called the Queen.

Abigail came into the apartment where George had slumped forward in his chair and was breathing heavily. He had clearly fallen into a doze.

'Hill, I wish for some music on the harpsichord.'

'Certainly, Madam.'

Abigail sat down and played. Anne beat time with her fingers.

'Hill, one of the dogs wants to come up. Which one, I cannot see.'

Abigail lifted the dog and set it on the Queen's lap. Anne stroked it lovingly. 'There, there! Listen to Hill's playing. Is it not pleasant? Such a clever little thing! Go back to the harpsichord and play something lively.'

Abigail obeyed and the Queen sat smiling at the straight little figure with the limp ginger hair dressed high in the fashion, at the straight back in the neat grey gown.

Such a pleasant creature, she thought. Also so eager to *please* . . . as though it gives her pleasure to serve. Never strident. Always quiet. Oh dear, how I do miss my dearest Mrs Freeman!

George began to snore and she leaned forward and tapped him with the fan which lay on her lap.

'Eh? Vat?' cried George.

'You had fallen asleep, dearest. Listen to Hill's playing. Such a good, clever creature.'

'Very nice . . . Very nice,' murmured George sleepily.

'A little music is very pleasant now and then. I cannot be grateful enough to my dear Mrs Freeman for bringing me this good kind creature.'

George scowled. He was not very pleased with the Freemans. He had had dreams of commanding the Navy or the Army and the Earl of Marlborough had been one of those who had put a stop to that ambition.

'It is gut she's away,' he grumbled. 'She make too much noise.'

Anne laughed. 'Oh, that is Mrs Freeman's way.'

'Don't much like,' murmured George. 'Nice, peaceful . . .' He waved a fat hand.

'Well, George, there is something to be said for peace in one's apartment, I do agree.'

Abigail's fingers faltered because her mind was so alert. But neither the Queen nor the Prince noticed it. She was thinking: The Prince resents the Marlboroughs. It's a mild resentment because he is too lazy to feel deeply but it is there and he'll not forget it easily. The Marlboroughs were getting stronger and stronger and yet there was a place in the royal bedchamber for a quiet and soothing personality.

'George, you are going to sleep again,' Anne was saying. 'A little game of cards will keep you awake. Hill. Get the cards. Call in Masham. He plays a good hand. Then join us.'

Abigail rose from the harpsichord, eager to obey.

Anne smiled at her. The dear good creature!

It was an uneasy summer. Marlborough was out of England fighting the French and Sarah watched constantly for news of him; without him to lay the restraining hand on her – he was the only one who dared do this – she was more blatantly out-spoken than ever. She thought nothing of interrupting the Queen, hectoring her and even showing her irritation. She was nicknamed Queen or Viceroy Sarah. Anne meekly accepted her behaviour, and to Abigail's secret chagrin it seemed to have no undermining effect on their relationship. How could she, wondered Abigail, after overhearing that most unkind and un-warranted attack over the gloves, ever feel the same towards Mrs Freeman again. But apparently she did. What was the magnetic attraction of the woman that could have made a Queen all but grovel to her, and an ambitious libertine, as Marlborough had certainly been before he met her, become her devoted slave? Slave was a word one thought of when one considered people's relationship with Sarah. She would wish to see us all her slaves! thought Abigail. She is invincible.

But often an insistent voice within her said: Not quite. And when she listened to that voice, life became wonderfully exciting to Abigail.

She took every opportunity of talking to Samuel Masham. They discussed affairs; it was surprising what that young man discovered; and he was always eager to impart what he knew to Abigail. There was no doubt, he told Abigail, that John Churchill was a brilliant soldier. He was a born leader; so calm, so serene, so courteous to all, yet he was always firmly in control and his men were ready to follow him to the death. Even those who envied his command grudgingly admitted that when he was engaged in war he showed a quality which might well be genius. Small wonder that Marlborough wanted to conduct a war against England's enemies. Thus he would show the world his own greatness, and at the same time add to England's stature.

'Marlborough abroad, his lady at home . . .' mused Samuel. 'They are invincible.'

During the summer Marlborough drove the French from the Maas and the Lower Rhine. It was an achievement which put new hope into the hearts of the Allies and apprehension in those of the enemy.

Sarah, as news of her husband's triumphs was brought to her, grew more and more aggressive. Sometimes, though, when she received his letters, she would take them to her private apartments and shed a few tears over them. His love for her was always the theme of those letters. He did not consider he had had any real success in the battlefield as yet, he told her, but he knew it would come. He was aware of the power within him, but everything he would give up – all hope of advancement and honour – for the sake of being with his dearest Sarah.

Sarah allowed herself moments of tenderness when she kissed his letters and put them away to be re-read later. Then she set about making everyone aware that as the wife of the greatest genius living she received the respect due to her, and ranting through the apartments, quarrelling with everyone, she was a great trial to all.

Even Anne would sigh sometimes and, when Sarah had left, send for Hill to soothe her with gentle massage and that wonderful gift of being able to *listen*. Hill would ask questions that had been asked before; would ask to hear what the Queen's dear boy had done on such and such occasion although she had heard it many times before. Dear, kind Hill! Anne found herself thinking often. What a contrast to dear Mrs Freeman. So odd that they should be related!

'Your Majesty is very tired,' Hill would murmur.

'So tired, Hill. So very tired.'

'Lady Marlborough is so amusing. But I think her brilliant conversation has tired your Majesty.'

'She is indeed brilliant, Hill. And how handsome she is! I declare it is a joy to look at her. I have so much to be thankful to her for, Hill.'

'And she to Your Majesty.'

'We have been friends since we were children, Hill. I was taken with her from the beginning and so happy when she wanted to become my friend. And one of the nicest things she ever did, was to bring you to me, Hill. There! Just soothe my brow. I have a headache and there is quite a magic in those fingers of yours.'

Triumph . . . in a strange way, thought Abigail.

Sarah had brought her daughter Elizabeth with her to Court. Elizabeth was just passed fifteen and a charming girl. Sarah was fond of her because not only was she very beautiful and accomplished but she did not argue as Henrietta did, nor was she petulant like Mary. Elizabeth was a perfect daughter because she bore such a striking resemblance to her father. Anne was serene also, but her marriage to Sunderland had naturally made her withdrawn from her mother and Sarah was not completely satisfied with her daughter Anne; therefore, at this time Elizabeth was her favourite. Young John, the Marquis of Bland-ford, now at Cambridge, was definitely in her bad books. It was not so much the fact that he wanted to go against her wishes but that he had dared consult his father and tried to form an alliance against her. That was something she would not tol-erate.

Elizabeth however had always been amenable and she was surprised therefore when the girl came to her and told her that she had fallen in love.

'What!' screamed Sarah.

'Mamma, I know I am young but I am certain of my feelings and I shall never have another moment's happiness unless you give your consent.'

'Have you gone out of your mind?'

Elizabeth's lips trembled and Sarah noticed with satisfaction how very much in awe of her she was. But in love! With a man of her own choosing! Could anyone be so ignorant of her duty as a Churchill!

'You had better tell me all about this folly, girl,' said Sarah grimly.

'Scroop says that he does not wish to wait.'

'Scroop?' cried Sarah.

'Scroop Egerton.'

Sarah was silent. Scroop Egerton, fourth Earl of Bridgewater, Master of Horse to Prince George! This was different. She would have no objection to accepting him as her son-in-law. He would be another supporter for dearest Marl.

Her voice softened. 'So, my dearest Elizabeth, you have seen fit to affiance yourself to this young man without my con-sent?'

'Mamma, Scroop wishes to speak to you. He says that he is sure he can persuade you . . .'

'And you little more than fifteen!'

'My sisters were not much older.'

'I cannot think what your dearest father will say.'

'He will be pleased if you are, Mamma.'

She smiled complacently. It was true – although she had had to persuade him to accept Sunderland. It was not that

Sunderland was not an excellent match, but dear Marl had wondered whether his beloved daughter would be *happy* with the man. Dear Marl! Just a little sentimental. And what was he going to say about Elizabeth's marrying at fifteen!

But Scroop Egerton, Earl of Bridgewater! That did warrant some consideration.

'I must have time to think about this, my dear child. You have somewhat thrust it upon me.'

Elizabeth threw herself into her mother's arms. 'Oh, dearest Mamma, please give your consent. I could not *bear* to be separated from Scroop – and equally I could not bear to displease you!'

Sarah patted the girl's head. Sweet creature. Next to Marl, she thought, I believe I love her best in the world.

Sarah shooed everyone out of the apartment and sat down by the Queen's couch.

'Who would have children, Mrs Morley! I do declare it is just one thing after another.'

Anne looked tearful. Who would have children? She would if she could. She would have given her crown to have her boy back again. Did not Mrs Freeman understand that?

'As you know, my dear Mrs Morley, I have been most put out with young Blandford. He will go for a soldier. He will talk to his father. He will try to have these matters arranged without *my* knowledge. Did you ever hear the like?'

'My boy would have understood his desires to . . .'

'Without consulting me, Mrs Freeman! Behind my back! Oh, he knows very well *he* is in disgrace. And if that is not enough what do you think? My Elizabeth has come to me with a tale of being in love.'

'She is but a child.'

'Children nowadays Mrs Morley, seem to think they may flout their parents. In our day it was different. We had to do as we were told . . .'

Anne looked faintly surprised. She was trying to remember when Sarah had waited to be told what to do.

'Now it is, "I am going to do this . . ." "I am going to do that." But I should never be one to allow my children to flout

130

me. It is not good for them. They must learn discipline. But I am telling you. My Elizabeth wishes to marry.'

'Oh but not yet surely . . .'

'She is in love, if you please, with Bridgewater. The Earl you know. The Prince's Master of Horse.'

'I know him well, of course. And I like him. He is a charming young man.'

'I have no objection to Bridgewater. But the girl is only fifteen.'

'Fifteen and in love . . .' murmured Anne, peering back into a past when the Earl of Mulgrave – still a most delightful man – had written his poems to her and hoped he might be allowed to marry her. 'It is very touching.'

'So it is,' agreed Sarah. 'And since they are so much in love, I cannot find it in my heart to deny them what they ask.'

'I understand you well, dear Mrs Freeman. I often used to think about the time when my dear boy would fall in love . . .'

'Of course poor Marl will have to find the dowry. Who would have daughters, Mrs Morley?'

'You must allow me to make a little gift to the couple. Please, Mrs Freeman, do not deny me this happiness.'

'Your Majesty is always generous. *I* do not forget your goodness to my Henrietta and Anne.'

'It gives me pleasure to see the young people happy. Whenever I see young people happy I think of my boy. He had a great capacity for happiness, Mrs Freeman; and the time would have come when he would have married . . . had he lived.'

'But he didn't,' said Sarah impatiently.

Anne's lips quivered.

'My dear Mrs Morley, you do yourself no good by dwelling on your loss. I think it very likely that ere long you will be giving us a Prince.'

'Ah if that could only be so I believe I should suffer less from my terrible loss. I shall give this dear child of yours ten thousand pounds. Please allow me to, Mrs Freeman.'

Ten thousand pounds! Sarah's eyes glittered. Marl would be so pleased. And he was going to be anxious on account of his daughter's youth and he'd be equally so when he thought of the dowry he would have to give her. Ten thousand pounds would be a good dowry for any girl. But there would be the outcry. She knew. It would be the old story of those about the Queen bleeding her and then there might be all sorts of difficulties – even laws made in Parliament. Marl had said that she must be careful not to take gifts which were too large. It was better to take little frequently.

'Your Majesty is too generous. I could not take it.'

'It would give me great pleasure, dear Mrs Freeman.'

Sarah smiled complacently. The fat old creature really doted on her; she could do what she wanted with her. She could be rude and arrogant and still she came pleading for friendship.

'I remember your generosity to the others. You gave them five thousand a piece. Give the same to Elizabeth. That will please me mightily, Mrs Morley.'

'I will speak to my Lord Treasurer about it as soon as I see him.' My Lord Treasurer! Lord Godolphin, her daughter's father-in-law! He would put no obstacle in the way. What an excellent state of affairs when the rulers were all in the family!

Sarah was excited because John was coming home for the winter. He would return as a hero, for although he himself believed that the campaign was only in its very earliest stages, everyone else seemed to think that he had scored great victories.

Anne was delighted for Sarah's sake in his success and it seemed to Abigail that she wished to atone for the momentary feelings of antagonism she must have felt at times towards her great friend. There were times when Anne's main preoccupation seemed to be how best to please Sarah.

Now she had hit on a great plan. A Dukedom for Marlborough. It was not difficult to get official sanction for this because it was agreed in the Commons that Marlborough had retrieved the honour of the English nation.

Anne called for Abigail to bring her writing materials that she might be the first to acquaint her dear friend with the good news.

'Your Majesty is happy today,' murmured Abigail.

'Very happy, Hill. I am going to give pleasure to one I love very dearly. But I shall not tell even you in what way because she must be the one to hear it first.'

She sat down at her table and wrote.

'Dear Mr Freeman deserves all that a rich crown would give, but since there is nothing else at this time, I hope you will give me leave as soon as he comes to make him a Duke. I know my dear Mrs Freeman does not care for things of that kind but . . .'

Anne paused to think of her dear friend. Duchess Sarah! She was worthy of such a title.

She went on writing, for she always enjoyed writing to Sarah; and when she had finished sent for Abigail to seal the letter; and then gave her instructions.

'See that it is delivered into none but her hands,' she said.

'Lady Marlborough's, Your Majesty?'

Anne nodded. Lady Marlborough soon to be the Duchess.

Sarah read the letter with elation. Duchess of Marlborough – Marl a Duke. It was wonderful. But . . . there was no talk of the estates and money they would need to uphold their elevated position. Did not old Morley understand that? There should have been an offer of at least five thousand a year to go with the Dukedom.

She went thoughtfully to the Queen. When she entered Anne looked up hopefully, expecting floods of gratitude. Instead she faced a very subdued Sarah.

'Mrs Freeman cannot have received my letter.'

'Oh yes. I have received it.'

'You seem . . . displeased.'

'When I read Mrs Morley's letter,' said Sarah slowly, 'I let it drop from my hand and for a time I felt as though I had received the news of a death of a dear friend.'

'Mrs Freeman, I do not understand.'

'My dearest Morley I know wishes to please me. And believe me when honour is paid to Mr Freeman nothing could please me more. But we have not the wealth to sustain a Dukedom. There, I am a simple woman and I give a simple answer. I do not couch my thoughts in flowery sentiments. So I give you the

133

plain truth. A Dukedom is not for us, Mrs Morley, because we simply have not wealth for such a title. And I will say this – it is but a matter of precedence – and that bothers me little. I do not care so much that I pass through one door and others of lesser rank through another, I know my good Mrs Morley thought to please me. But it is difficult for one such as Your Majesty to understand the financial difficulties of others.'

Anne looked as though she would burst into tears.

But Sarah having made her point, asked leave to retire.

Sarah was furious. Anne had of course immediately sought some means of providing an income for the Churchills which would enable them to accept the Dukedom and proposed an annual grant of five thousand pounds which would be taken from Post Office revenues. This she declared was necessary in view of Marlborough's new title, and as his son would inherit that title in due course the income must be granted to the new Duke's heirs.

The Government revolted. Marlborough's services to the nation were appreciated but bestowing hereditary grants on individuals was frowned on; and to avoid an adverse vote Marlborough, now home once more, could only decline the offer of revenue from that source.

Sarah raged and ranted, but John tried in vain to soothe her.

'They are so ungrateful!' she cried. 'When I think of all you have done for them. And now for a miserable five thousand . . .'

She went to the Queen.

'You see, Mrs Morley, how wise I was to refuse the Dukedom in the first place. I know Mr Freeman has no wish to accept so called honours when they are so grudgingly given. If he had taken *my* advice he would *never* have accepted the title. But now it is done . . . and here he is – the man who brought honour to his country, a Duke without the means to keep up his rank. A pretty state of affairs! A pretty example of a country's ingratitude! I said to Mr Freeman: It is folly to take this from a country who so clearly does not wish to honour you . . . rather to humiliate you.'

'My dear, *dear* Mrs Freeman, this is most distressing. You shall have two thousand from my privy purse. No one shall know of it. It shall be a secret between us . . .'

'Mrs Morley should know that Mrs Freeman could not easily be persuaded to enter into secret bargains . . .'

She could not be comforted, and when she left the Queen was trembling and in tears.

Abigail came to her and bathed her forehead.

'There, Madam.' Anne accepted the brandy. 'Would Your Majesty wish me to play a little on the harpsichord?'

'No, Hill. Just sit beside me. Your presence comforts me.'

Abigail took the trembling hand in hers and the Queen smiled at her.

'It seems peaceful now, Hill. Let us talk for a while and later perhaps when I am sleepy you will play me to sleep.'

Sarah stormed back to Marlborough.

'She is ready to pay us two thousand from the privy purse,' she said. 'What's the use of that?'

John shook his head. 'We couldn't take it, Sarah. It could be embarrassing if it leaked out that we were being supplied in this way. But there is something else. I've a letter here from Sidney Godolphin. He writes from Newmarket.'

'Newmarket. I should have thought he might have been in London. Here is the Government treating you in this churlish way and he is at Newmarket if you please.'

'Our John is with him.'

'*Our* John! But why is he not at Cambridge?'

'There's smallpox in Cambridge.'

Sarah turned pale. 'John?'

'He's all right. Sidney thought it better for him to leave Cambridge and go to stay at Newmarket. The air there is fresh and good. But I was a little uneasy.'

Smallpox! The dreaded scourge. Sarah could not bear to think of it having come near her only son.

'Perhaps he should come home,' she said.

'Sidney says he's very well. I thought you might write to him and tell him that you are no longer displeased with him.'

'But I *am* still displeased with him.'

'He wrote to me asking me to plead with you on his behalf.'

'Then he should have written to me himself.'

'Sarah!' Marlborough laid his hand on her arm and gave her that sweet smile which never failed to charm. 'I know you love him dearly – as you do the whole family, but could you not show it a little now and then?'

'Are you telling me how to treat my son, John Churchill!'

'Our son,' he reminded her.

She laughed. 'We'll have him home. I do not care that he should be near a pox-laden atmosphere.'

'Write to him and tell him he is forgiven.'

'No. He must write to me first. And what of this matter of our income . . .'

He laid his hands on her shoulders and drew her towards him.

'That is a matter which will, I doubt not, in time work out to our advantage . . . my Duchess.'

Anne was determined that her dear Mrs Freeman should happily accept the new honour and Sarah had no intention of standing in her way. It was certainly gratifying to be Her Grace, and she derived great pleasure from referring to Marl as The Duke.

With the coming of spring he would set out once more on his campaigns and the separations would begin again. 'How I wish that you had chosen to become a statesman instead of a soldier!' she would exclaim angrily.

Christmas was just over and young John had written to his father to tell him that he was leaving the Godolphins to return to Cambridge.

'I trust,' said Sarah grimly, 'that there he will learn some sense.'

It was in January when she had news from Cambridge.

When she read the letter which was from her son's tutor she was silent, and those watching her saw the colour drain from her face.

Then she cried: 'I am going to Cambridge. At once.'

She stared at her maid who, accustomed to her mistress's

sudden outbursts, was aware that there was something of great importance behind this one.

'My son,' she said slowly, 'has the smallpox. My only son,' she repeated.

Abigail was with Anne when she heard the news.

'My poor, poor Mrs Freeman. So she has gone with all speed to Cambridge. We must pray for her, Hill. If she should lose this beloved child, how she will suffer! I know, Hill. I know full well. I could not bear to think of what poor Mrs Freeman will have to suffer if the blow which struck her unfortunate Morley should strike her.'

'Your Majesty is so good to concern herself.'

'You have never borne a child, Hill. This makes such understanding between us. But we must not *think* of his dying. While there is hope ... But the smallpox. My poor sister died of it. And we were not good friends ... I often think of it, Hill. Oh, the tragedy! But I am forgetting my poor Mrs Freeman. I want you to do this, Hill. Call my doctors ... all of them. I want to send them to Cambridge so that they can give their services to poor little Blandford. We must do everything ... simply everything, for I could not bear that what happened to me should happen to my poor Mrs Freeman.'

Sarah sat by her son's bedside and wept. He opened his eyes and saw her.

'Papa,' he said. 'Papa.'

'He will come to you, my love. He is on his way.'

She thought he understood because he smiled so sweetly and he reminded her poignantly of his father. He would have been another such, she thought; and then angrily: He *will* be another such.

She would not let him die. But even Sarah could not hold back death.

'He is my son,' she cried. 'My only son.'

'Your Grace,' said the doctors. 'You should send for the Duke.'

When Marlborough came to Cambridge with all speed, Sarah flung herself at him and burst into loud weeping. 'It cannot be. It cannot be. They are saying there is little hope. But only such a short while ago he was strong and well . . .'

'Sarah, my beloved, I suffer with you. We must pray for courage. If this terrible tragedy should come to pass we must meet it with resignation.'

'Resignation. This is my son . . . my only son!'

He did not remind her that the boy was his son too. He was wonderfully gentle and she clung to him in her despair which, even at such a time, was tempered by rage. What right had death to threaten her son – her only son who would one day have been the Duke of Marlborough?

She was suddenly overcome by fear. 'John, *you* must take care. You must not go near him. There could be an even greater blow than this.'

She looked into his face and he saw the fear there and he marvelled that she of whom it had been said she cared for neither God nor man could care so much for him.

He turned away; his emotions were betraying him.

John Churchill, sixteen-years-old Lord Blandford, died at Cambridge and was buried in King's College Chapel.

Sarah was bewildered by her grief and astonished all by her quietness. She and the Duke went to their home in St Albans and remained quietly there. John was the only one who could make any attempt to comfort Sarah and he must soon make preparations to join his army which had been delayed by the death of his son.

Sarah wandered from room to room. She could not believe that young John was dead. It was so short a time since he was pleading to become a soldier.

She who had never attempted to control her rage and arrogance now could not control her grief. She would throw herself on to her bed and sob so wildly that it was feared she would injure her health. If only there had been someone on whom she could have vented her wrath she would have felt better. But how could she shake her fist and insult Providence; how could she warn Death that she would have her revenge on him for flouting Sarah Churchill's wishes.

'My dearest,' soothed the Duke, 'we will have another son.'

'He is dead . . . he is dead . . . he is dead . . . And soon *you* will go from me.'

'I shall be back with you soon.'

She clung to him, weeping bitterly.

Her beautiful complexion was blotched with tears; her blue eyes once so bold and flashing were red and swollen with so much crying.

The servants said: 'She will lose her reason if she goes on giving way to grief in this way.'

The Queen who had heard the news immediately wrote to express the sympathy of Mrs Freeman's poor unfortunate faithful Morley. 'Christ Jesus comfort and support you under this terribly affliction, and it is His Mercy alone that can do it.'

When Sarah read the letter she threw it from her.

'Poor unfortunate Morley!' she cried. 'Now I suppose we must sit together mingling our maudlin memories. Does she compare that bigheaded boy of hers with my Blandford?'

The Duke suppressed the impulse to restrain her. Let her rant against the Queen. At least it had turned her thoughts from her son's death.

She hated her relationship with the Queen; she hated the cloying affection, the protestations of fidelity and devotion. Yet, it was due to the Queen's love for Sarah that they had come so far.

When Sarah was calmer he must warn her of her attitude towards the Queen. He could understand how she found Anne a bore, how she disliked making a show of affection she could not feel, but the Queen's approval was necessary to any ambitious man or woman.

But at the moment let her rage against the Queen. It was an outlet for her grief.

And from that moment it seemed that Sarah grew a little more resigned.

King's Evil

The Court was peaceful without Sarah; and peace was what
Anne really enjoyed. She had never greatly cared for balls and
banquets. She was too infirm to dance; so was George; and as
for banquets – one enjoyed food, but more so when it was
eaten comfortably in one's own apartments. Of course it was
not always possible to eat in comfort. There must be state
occasions; one must eat in public. But when she remembered
the Court of her uncle Charles II she realized how different was
her own. William had set the mode in Courts which could
hardly be called by the name. He had spent as much time as
was possible in more or less retirement at Hampton or
Kensington, making gardens and superintending building; and
had only come up to London for council meetings when absolutely necessary. But the people had not liked William; and
whenever he had appeared he had never added to the gaiety of
the occasion. They had never cheered him and even now drank
toasts to The Little Gentleman in Black Velvet. It was different
with herself. They knew that she was a martyr to the gout and
the dropsy; they knew that she had had to be carried to her
coronation; but they had never heard scandal about her private

life. They saw her with the Prince and to see them together was to know how devoted they were to each other. The Prince took no mistresses; the Queen took no lovers. Even William had had one mistress and there had been a mild scandal about Mary and Shrewsbury. But Queen Anne and her consort remained the perfect example of conjugal bliss.

Sovereigns set manners. There had never been a more profligate period than that of Charles II. Why? Because he made no secret of the mistresses, of whom he kept many at a time; he would saunter through St James's Park with them and his dogs and acknowledge the greetings of the passers-by as he did so. The whole of London speculated as to which was most important to his comfort; and the names of Cleveland, Portsmouth, Mancini, Moll Davies and Nell Gwyn were on every tongue.

The people had so loved the scandal their King provided that they forgave him everything else, but it had been so because they had lived through the dreary years of puritanism and needed a violent change. Now that was over; and they wanted to settle down with a good and virtuous woman as their figurehead.

Anne often thought of this as she sat fondling her little dogs.

I want to be a good ruler, she assured herself. I want to be remembered as Good Queen Anne.

She must rouse herself. She was not going to be persuaded to what she did not want to do by anyone . . . *anyone*. That was a fact she would make clear in her own way, which was not to quarrel with a person's opinion. She loathed quarrelling. It demanded too much energy and it was pointless. She was the Queen and she would have her way — only she wanted people to realize it without a great deal of discussion.

To set a good example to her people; to do good; to make England great. What a pleasant subject to contemplate while her dear little dogs nuzzled against her and she nibbled sweetmeats from the dish at her elbow, or sipped a cup of chocolate, or simply lay back contentedly while the efficient and most skilful hands of Abigail Hill massaged her swollen limbs.

George came into the Queen's apartments, more animated than usual and with him he brought an odd pair – a country man and woman, in all possibility his wife – who looked so incongruous in the Windsor apartments that Anne was startled.

Abigail who had been playing the harpsichord stopped and turned to watch; Anne's attention was all for her husband and the odd little pair.

'My dearest,' cried George, 'I must present to you these good people. This is John Duddlestone of Bristol and this his good wife. You remember, my dear, vot I haf told you of the gootness of John Duddlestone.'

Anne smiled at the pair of them, who seemed struck dumb, and said, 'John Duddlestone, my dearest? Of Bristol?'

'You remember, my love.' He turned to them. 'The Queen is so goot. She remember everything I tell her ... and she likes much those who haf shown me the kindness.'

Anne mildly wished that George would express himself more clearly and come to the point, but she sat smiling graciously, never betraying by a fleeting expression that she had no notion who these people were.

Abigail, watching, thought then that it would be a great mistake to dismiss the Queen as a foolish woman. She was by no means so. Physical debility might make her seem lazy, amenable; but it was not so. Anne was so like many calm good-natured people; she could give way frequently until she decided to make a stand; then none could be more stubborn. Moreover, a great determination to be worthy of her office had come to her. To watch her now with these two country people was a lesson in good manners and diplomacy. She had not wished to be disturbed; she could not be greatly interested in the Duddlestones; she could not remember what she had heard of them; yet she betrayed nothing of this.

George went on: 'It is ven I am in Bristol. Ven I vas at the Exchange and none asked me to dine. The Master John Duddlestone came to me and he says: "Vos you the husband of our Queen Anne?" And I say, my love, that I haf that great joy and honour and he say "I am a humble bodice-maker of Bristol and no one asks you to dine because they think you too great

142

and important gentleman because you are husband to our Queen. But the shame of Bristol would be great if the husband of our Queen must dine at an inn because no Bristol door was opened to him." So, my love, he takes me to his home.'

George was beaming with pleasure and Anne was always delighted to see him pleased.

She looked at John Duddlestone and said: 'Anyone who has shown kindness to the Prince, my husband, is a friend of mine.'

The Prince whispered: 'You must kneel to Her Majesty.'

John Duddlestone did so with some awkwardness and Anne gave him her hand to kiss.

Then his wife came forward and made her clumsy obeisance.

George chuckled. 'He call to his wife and say: "Wife, the Queen's husband haf come to dine with us, so put on a clean apron and come down to greet the guest." So down she came in a clean apron . . .'

'It were blue, Your Majesty,' said Mistress Duddlestone.

Anne smiled as though the colour of the apron was a matter of great interest.

'And a very good dinner it was,' said George reminiscently.

'His Highness is very particular about his food,' put in Anne; and again Abigail was surprised by her ability to take part in such a scene.

'So pleased,' went on George, 'that I say, when next he comes to Windsor he must call and I give him dinner.'

'We came to buy whalebone, Your Majesty,' John Duddlestone told Anne.

'And you make . . .?'

'Stays, now, Your Majesty. For the fashion has changed. Once we made bodices but now we make stays.'

'So, they haf come to dine with me,' said the beaming Prince.

'Then,' said Anne, 'they must dine with me also. Hill! Oh there you are, Hill. You will take Master and Mistress Duddlestone and tell them what they will need, and see that it is supplied for them.'

'Yes, Your Majesty,' said Abigail, and led the couple away.

The Queen's servants were discussing the affair.

The pages, Saxton, Smith and Kirk paused in their game of cards to offer their comment.

William Lovegrove, the coffer-bearer, said to Mrs Abrahal, the Queen's starcher: 'Such a thing would never have happened if the Duchess were at Court.'

'Who ever heard of a stays-maker dining with the Queen?' demanded Mrs Ravensford, the Queen's seamstress.

'I repeat,' said Lovegrove, 'the Duchess would never have allowed it.'

'Fitted out with Court dresses, if you please . . . provided from her own wardrobe and made to fit!'

'Purple velvet. Because when the Prince dined with them that was what he wore.'

'And the Queen knighting the fellow so that the bodice- and stays-maker will return to Bristol Sir John Duddlestone . . . and all because he gave a dinner to the Queen's husband! Did you ever hear the like?'

'And what do you think? Not content with giving the man and his wife their titles the Queen took a gold watch from her side and gave it to *Lady* Duddlestone.'

Amid the shrill laughter that followed Mrs Abrahal said that she reckoned *Lady* Duddlestone would go to market in her apron wearing the Queen's gold watch.

The picture increased the hilarity to such an extent that Mrs Danvers looked in to see what all the merriment was about. When she was told she tut-tutted with disapproval.

'I never heard the like!' she declared. 'I wish I had been told earlier that the wardrobe was going to be raided to provide purple velvet for bodice-makers.'

'Mrs Hill received the orders, Mrs Danvers,' said Mrs Abrahal. 'I wonder I was not asked to starch a head for the new lady when I was doing the Queen's.'

'Mrs Hill receives most of the Queen's orders now,' added Lovegrove.

'It's true,' agreed Mrs Danvers thoughtfully. 'That girl is with Her Majesty most of the day.'

'On the Duchess's orders, Mrs Danvers.'

'Yes,' said Mrs Danvers slowly, 'on the Duchess's orders. If it were not so I would have a word to say to Her Grace about Mrs Hill.'

'You can't say the creature gives herself airs, Mrs Danvers.'

'Indeed no. She creeps about so that you can never be sure when she has entered a room.'

'It struck me, Mrs Danvers, that Her Majesty does not fret for the Duchess so much as she did at one time . . . now that she has her good Hill to look to her comfort.'

'I have noticed it,' said Mrs Danvers. 'But she *was* put there by Her Grace so there is nothing we can do . . . as yet.'

Prince George was dozing. It was those two hours in the afternoon when Anne and her husband were together and more and more of the time George spent asleep.

He is growing fatter, mused Anne. Poor dear George. When he is not eating and drinking, he is sleeping; and he wheezes more than ever. Perhaps it is good for him to rest.

She wanted to talk to him this afternoon. Coming from Windsor to St James's the people had cheered her. They had called: 'Long Live the Queen. Long Live *Good* Queen Anne.' *Good*. She wanted to be good. People in rags had called to her and she fancied she had seen hope in their looks. They hoped because she was their Queen, and she did not want to fail them. Dear Mr Freeman was helping to make England great abroad. They were saying he was the finest general in the world. That was good. Perhaps he would make a quick conquest and there would be peace so that she and her ministers would have an opportunity of bringing prosperity home. She did not care to see her subjects in need. And they had called to her: 'Good Queen Anne!'

'George,' she said. 'I want to be good. I want to deserve the name Good Queen Anne.'

'Eh?' said George.

She leaned towards the sleeping figure in the chair and touched him lightly with her fan. 'I saw the poor today. George, on our drive. I want to be good to them so that they call me Good Queen Anne from their hearts.'

'Goot,' he murmured. 'You are very goot, my love. Nobody in the vorld so goot as my angel.'

Dear George. But a little dull. The park had looked so beautiful and the Mall ... the dear Mall. Half a mile of beautiful trees, planted in even rows on either side of the broad gravel path. The talented French gardener Le Notre had made it for Uncle Charles and after that the aviary of Birdcage Walk. And then the Palace with its battlements and towers which Henry VIII had ordered Holbein to design; it was built, Anne's father used to tell her, on the site where once had stood a hospital for maiden lepers.

Maiden lepers! Anne shivered; and some of those poor people who had cheered her on her way had been diseased, she had noticed.

That was why she was thinking as she lay back in her chair, her eyes closed, that she would like to bring prosperity and better living conditions to her subjects. What a pleasure it had been to entertain that bodice-maker and his wife! How grateful they had been! The woman – who talked more than the man – had said that the happiest moment of her life had been when the Queen had taken the watch from her side and presented it to her. The watch! Not the title she had gained! Not the fine clothes she had worn! 'Every time I touch it I say to myself: My hands are where the Queen's have been. And I feel some goodness comes to me and I'm proud and happy to wear something which Your Majesty has touched.'

Well, the heirs of St Edward the Confessor were said to have a healing touch. And was she not in the direct line of Kings? Some sovereigns had practised the healing touch. Henry III was one. Edward I and II were others; and it was Edward III whose alchymist Raymond Lully actually made gold for him. On the coins he made were impressed the figures of angels and these coins were supposed to have a healing power and if they were bound on the arms of those who suffered from scrofula by royal hands the patients were said to be healed. Scrofula had become known as the King's Evil, and this practice which ensured the popularity of sovereigns, was known as touching for the King's Evil.

To have sufferers brought to her that she might cure them was a blessing Anne could bestow on her subjects.

'George,' she said, 'I have decided that I will bring back the custom of touching for the King's Evil.'

'Eh?' mumbled George.

She looked at him in tender exasperation.

'Oh George, George, you sleep your life away. Hill! Come here, Hill.'

Hill came at once. She always did. Vaguely Anne wondered where she secreted herself so that she was always within earshot.

'Ah, Hill, there you are. I have made a decision. I was so moved by the sight of some of my subjects this morning . . . so many of them poor and ill . . . that I have decided to bring back the custom of touching for the King's Evil. Why, Hill, if I can bring some of those poor people back to health I should be most happy. And it is a duty.'

'Your Majesty is so good.'

'I intend to do all I can for my people, Hill.'

Hill merely nodded and turned away as though she was afraid of betraying how moved she was.

'Now, Hill, I want you to write a letter for me. My hands are troubling me today. I want you to write to Lord Godolphin. I will sign it. Tell him of my decision. Now what shall we say. "This is our will and pleasure . . ." '

'Our will and pleasure . . .' wrote Abigail.

Anne smiled at the head bent over the paper. Small, and meek. Dear Hill, she never argued; she never attempted to advise.

What a comfort she was! And how peaceful it was living with such a creature in close attendance.

Anne was seated in the Banqueting Hall in St James's Palace. About her chair were the officials and her chaplains. The sick and the infirm were crowding into the hall and they gazed at her with adoration. She felt happier than she had since the death of her son.

On the arm of her chaplain were white ribbons to which had been fixed the pieces of 'angel' gold; these the Queen would place with her own hands about the necks of the sufferers.

The service was beginning and Anne, who was deeply religious, felt exalted. She believed then that the most important duty of all was to maintain the Church and this she would do no matter what opposition she had to face. There were some who had not been in favour of this Touching ceremony; but she had made them understand that it was her will.

One of the Chaplains was reading the Collect: 'Prevent us, O Lord, with Thy most gracious favour, and further us with Thy continued help, that in all our works begun, continued and ending in Thee, we may glorify Thy holy name, and finally, by Thy mercy, attain everlasting life, through Jesus Christ our Lord.'

And then the reading:

'They shall lay their hands on the sick, and they shall recover . . .'

Anne looked down at her beautiful hands – so smooth and white. How happy it made her to bestow this gift, and what greater gift was there than that of healing?

Now they were bringing forward the sick to be presented to her.

One by one they knelt before her and she stroked their arms and their faces; then she attached the ribbons with the angel gold to their arms while the chaplain murmured the words:

'God give a blessing to this work, and grant that those sick persons on whom the Queen lays her hands, may recover, through Jesus Christ our Lord.'

When the ceremony was over, and she retired to her private apartments, she sent for Abigail.

'I feel happier than I have since I lost my boy,' she told her.

'Your Majesty is so good,' replied Abigail with tears in her eyes.

'The service was beautiful, Hill.'

'Yes, Your Majesty.'

'I believe there are some in this realm who would seek to undermine the Church. They will never have my support.'

'Nor mine, Madam,' said Abigail quietly.

It was so pleasant afterwards to talk of the ceremony with Hill. The dear creature had such a way of *listening* which was very comforting and pleasant.

Queen's Bounty

Robert Harley, with his friend and disciple Henry St John,
stood on the edge of the crowd which was assembled near the
pillory in Cornhill.

St John knew that Harley was deeply disturbed, more so
than he would admit; and the reason was this affair of
Defoe.

Harley had said: 'There is one of the greatest writers of our
age. I want him to work for me.'

And before he could put that project into action here was
Defoe – a prisoner during the Queen's pleasure and sentenced
to stand three times in the Pillory – at Cornhill, at Cheapside
and at Temple Bar.

'I could have warned him,' muttered Harley. 'I wish I had
seen that pamphlet of his before it had been published.'

'It's a brilliant pamphlet,' said St John.

'Too brilliant. That's the trouble, I've told you that the pen is
a mighty weapon, St John. It is because others are beginning to
realize this that Defoe stands where he is today.'

'He's coming now . . .' warned St John.

And there he was, the unrepentant scribe, the martyr to his

cause, riding in the cart on his way to the pillory. This was usually the moment for which the crowd waited – when they would see the poor condemned wretch set in the wooden frame, his hands hanging before him, his neck and head in the holes provided for them, and himself helpless to face the scorn and fury of the mob. It was the custom to pelt the victim with rotten fruit and vegetables, stinking fish and any filth that could be found; many died of exposure to a cruel mob. And that this should be the fate of a man of great talent, perhaps genius – particularly a man who could be useful to him – filled Harley with indignation.

'He was a fool,' said St John.

'He wrote nothing that was not true.'

'But this pamphlet of his *The Shortest way with the Dissenters* – why it gave pleasure to no one.'

'It gave pleasure to me, St John, as all good writing must.'

'But the sentiments, Master, the sentiments.'

'All this conformity controversy in Parliament nowadays needs to be ridiculed, and that is precisely what Defoe did.'

'Yes, but in such a way that the High-Flyers took him seriously.'

'These High Churchmen take themselves so seriously that they think everyone else does the same. They have no humour – and that's what Defoe has. If they hadn't at first supported the Pamphlet before they realized Defoe was writing with his tongue in his cheek, they would not have made this trouble for him. So he is prosecuted for libelling the Church.'

'And what now?'

'God knows if he'll withstand the pillory. If he survives Cornhill, it'll be Cheapside tomorrow and the day after that Temple Bar. Come away, St John. I don't care to see the man subjected to insults.'

'Is there nothing we can do?'

Harley shook his head. 'I shall do my best to have him released, but that would take time. If only I could talk to the Queen.'

'Well, why not?'

'I need to bring her to my way of thinking and I could not do that by a formal visit. I need to be on terms with her ... as Marlborough is.'

'Ah, he has the Duchess to help him.'

'Yes and Anne dotes on the woman. Would that I could find someone to plead for me as Marlborough's wife does for him.'

'There's only one Viceroy Sarah.'

'God be praised for that. It is a marvel to me that she keeps her place in the Queen's favour. Look. The crowd has divided. How silent they are! Usually the mob shouts so that you cannot hear yourself speak. How strange! What's happening?'

The two men were silent while Daniel Defoe was set in the pillory. His expression was serene and untroubled; he looked as though he had no fear of the crowd and was completely unrepentant.

This was most unusual. A band of men with cudgels had placed themselves about the pillory.

'Listen now,' said one. 'This is our Daniel. Anyone who tries to harm Daniel will get a crack on the head. Is it understood?'

'Aye,' roared the crowd. ' 'Tis understood.'

Someone in the crowd lifted a pot of beer and cried: 'Good health and long life to you, Daniel.'

The crowd took up the cry.

Harley and St John exchanged looks and Harley began to laugh.

'By God,' he cried. 'He's got the crowd with him. He's got them, St John.'

The hot July sun poured down on the prisoner's head; he was clearly in great discomfort; yet his eyes lit up with appreciation for he had realized that the crowd was friendly.

A handful of roses was tossed at the pillory. Two girls ran forward and twined their ready-made garlands about it. Someone brought up a pot of beer and held it up to Daniel to drink.

'God bless you, Daniel,' cried someone in the crowd.

'Aye,' went up the shout. 'We're with you, Daniel.'

A ballad seller accosted the two men.

'Buy a ballad, sir. Daniel's own. Buy a ballad. He's a good man with seven children to support.'

Harley bought the verses and signed to St John to do the same.

When the man had moved off, Harley said: 'This is a sight such as I have never seen before. They'll take him to Newgate after this. But I'll have him out, I tell you.'

The crowd was becoming more noisy as Daniel's supporters were growing. The guard about the pillory had doubled and if any man had dared throw anything but flowers at Daniel Defoe he would probably have paid for it with his life.

Harley said: 'There's no need to see more. Daniel will be well cared for.'

As they moved away he glanced at the verses and read aloud:

> *Tell them the men that placed him here*
> *Are scandals of the times,*
> *Are at a loss to find his guilt*
> *And can't commit his crimes . . .'*

'You see what I mean, St John. Words like that can't be ignored. Why do you think the crowd is pelting Defoe with roses? Why are they drinking his health? Because of words, St John. Words . . . words . . . words! We are going to do battle and our first weapon will be words.'

Sarah had made her grief an excuse for staying away from Court, but when news reached her in St Albans that the Lords had thrown out the Occasional Conformity Bill, and that the Tories finding themselves beaten had created four new Tory peers, she was incensed.

Marl was a Tory by instinct, but much as she loved and admired him she had a greater respect for her own views and these were growing more and more Whig. Marl ought to see that the Tories were against the prosecution of the war which he himself so firmly supported. The fact was that he was so occupied in Flanders that he could not see clearly what was happening at home and it was her duty to take command on the home front.

153

Four new Tory peers in order to get a Bill passed through the Lords! Sarah was not going to stand aside and see that happen. She was going to demand that there be at least one new Whig peer.

This was the best tonic for grief. Sarah left St Albans at once for St James's.

Storming into the Queen's apartments she found Abigail Hill seated at the harpsichord, and Anne dozing pleasantly in her chair.

Abigail stopped playing as she entered and turning saw the look of delight on the Queen's face.

'My dearest, dearest Mrs Freeman!'

'Yes, Mrs Morley I am here!'

'So welcome! So welcome!'

Abigail watched the fond embrace. Anne was almost in tears.

'Do not think that my thoughts have not been with you all through this long and trying time. Do not think that I would not have been at St Albans had you allowed me to come.'

'I was so filled with grief that I thought I should lose my reason – and so did those about me. Mr Freeman even thought of giving up everything . . . everything to be with me.'

'Dear, *dear* Mr Freeman! What a comfort. I understand your loss and your great solace. How alike our lives are, dear Mrs Freeman.'

Sarah grunted with something of the old freedom of expression. If there was one thing she found hard to tolerate it was comparing her handsome brilliant genius of a Marl with that lazy witless Danish Prince.

'Well, now I am here,' she said, 'and I wonder how Mrs Morley has been faring in my absence.'

'Each day longing for our reunion.'

'When I heard the disturbing news I thought I could no longer stay away.'

'The disturbing news, my dear Mrs Freeman?'

'This matter of new Tory peers being created to get the Conformity Bill through.'

'Oh, I am sure my ministers know what is right, Mrs Freeman.'

'But I, Mrs Morley, am far from sure.'

Anne gave a little gasp. Being absent from Sarah for so long she had not heard anyone contradict her so forcibly during that time, and when it happened it was a shock.

Sarah was aware of Abigail Hill still seated at the harpsichord.

'You may go,' she said.

Abigail's eyes were on the Queen and Anne knew that she was thinking: Is it your wish that I should obey the Duchess?

Anne nodded dismissal and Abigail went away. What was the use of thinking she had a firm place in the Queen's affections when Sarah only had to appear to make her understand how insecure that place was. Sarah could say this very day: Dismiss Hill. And Anne would meekly obey. Would she? She might put up a small resistance but it would soon be overridden.

Now this matter of the Occasional Conformity Bill. What would be the outcome? As far as Abigail could see, the greatest controversies in the country were concerned with religion; and the trouble over the Conformity Bill was an example of this. The Test Act had demanded that all public servants partake in communion in accordance with the rites of the Church of England when appointed to their posts; after that they might attend at intervals or not at all, but go to the services they preferred. This Act passed in the time of Charles II was typical of that monarch's desire to placate two schools of thought at the same time. Occasional Conformity was all that was needed. The Tories had wanted to abolish this act and in its place set up another which was far less tolerant. This was the Occasional Conformity Act and would impose large fines on any person who took office and performed an act of conformity and afterwards attended a disssenting service. A second visit would make the offender liable to even heavier fines and banned from his office for three years.

Anne was a High Tory, a fervent churchwoman; and she had been convinced by her Tory Government that the Act of Conformity was necessary to the welfare of the state. Strangely enough the Lords had thrown out the Bill because William III had been a Whig and during his reign he had created a large number of Low Church Bishops.

And it was this act of creating four new Tory peers in order to pass the Bill through the Lords which had brought Sarah's Whiggish principles into the fore and sent her hurrying to Court.

As Abigail left the Queen and the Duchess together she was not thinking so much of the rights and wrongs of the Bill as to the power which Sarah held over Anne. What happened now would be significant. Sarah was not only pitting herself against the Queen but against the Tory House of Commons.

As soon as the door shut on Abigail Sarah turned to the Queen.

'These matters are of too great an importance to be discussed before servants,' she said.

'Hill is most discreet.'

'I know it. It was for that reason I brought her to you. And I can see that she is giving satisfaction.'

'Such a good creature!' The Queen settled happily into her chair. How much more pleasant to talk of the virtues of dear Hill, for whom she had to be so grateful to her dearest Mrs Freeman, than politics.

But Sarah of course had not come to discuss serving women.

'I confess, Mrs Morley, that I was *most* disturbed. If men are going to be created to pass laws what are we coming to.'

'It has been done before . . .'

'It may have been done before! You think that a good reason for repeating an iniquity? Mayhem and murder have been done before, Mrs Morley, but that does not mean it is good and reasonable and *right* to do them again.'

'Mrs Freeman misunderstands me.'

'I misunderstand nothing! This Conformity Bill has been thrown out of the Lords . . . so your ministers have advised you to create four new Tory peers in order to get it through. It must not be.'

'It is already being done.'

'I'll not have it!'

Anne was astonished. She had longed to see Mrs Freeman at

Court, and now she had come there was this trouble. She had no intention of arguing. She hated argument. But even dearest Mrs Freeman could not decide matters of state policy merely by demanding to do so.

'Well, Mrs Freeman, come and sit beside me,' said Anne. 'I want to hear all your news.'

'My news is too sombre, Mrs Morley. For these last months I have thought of nothing but my loss.'

'My poor, poor Mrs Freeman. There is no one who can understand that like your unfortunate Morley.'

'But,' said Sarah fiercely, 'we have to grow away from our grief. It is selfish to mourn for ever.'

Anne flinched a little. It was most exciting to have the dazzling and beautiful Sarah with her, but just a little uncomfortable.

'I came to you because I have to talk to you about this disgraceful matter. Four Tory peers! It is a scandal. If you are going to create four Tory peers you must at any rate create one Whig peer. I shall insist on that.'

'My dear Mrs Freeman, this is a matter for our ministers.'

'This is a matter for *us*,' corrected Sarah.

She began to pace the apartment while she expounded the follies of the Bill. It was iniquitous. It was intolerant. Anne repeated placidly: 'It is a matter for our ministers.'

'Ministers!' stormed Sarah. 'What concern have they for anything but their own advancement? We need to keep a firm grip on ministers. You will remember how difficult it was to get the Prince's grant through. That was ministers for you.'

'I do remember and I shall be eternally grateful to you and Mr Freeman for working so hard on the Prince's behalf.'

'You will also remember that that grant was passed with a majority of one vote and that had not Mr Freeman and I worked day and night it could never have come to pass and Mr Morley would be some hundred thousand pounds a year the poorer.'

'We shall never, never forget the pains you and Mr Freeman took, and I do assure you that both Mr Morley and I can never express our gratitude. I remember my dear George was so ill at the time. Dear Mrs Freeman, his asthma gives me the greatest cause for anxiety. I was nursing him at the time. Do you remember? I really believed I was going to lose him. I thought that fate was going to strike yet another blow at your poor unfortunate Morley.'

'That was when your ministers needed a little prodding and they got it. Now here is another occasion.'

'But, dear Mrs Freeman, I declare you have become a Whig. I do not share your affection for those gentlemen – and I can tell you that it is a great sorrow not to be able to share everything with my dear Mrs Freeman.'

'Let us get back to this matter of the peers.'

'Dear Mrs Freeman, it really is a matter for our ministers.'

Sarah thought: I shall scream at her if she says that again. There she sits, the old parrot, not listening, not paying attention once she has found her parrot phrase, 'It is a matter for our ministers.' We shall see, Mrs Morley, we shall see.

'I suppose Godolphin is partly responsible for this,' said Sarah.

Anne did not answer and Sarah thought: And I have allowed his son to marry my daughter! I have brought him into our circle and this is how he repays me!

'He is our minister,' Anne reminded her.

Anything, thought Sarah, rather than send the fat creature off on to that minister refrain.

'I will speak to him,' said Sarah.

'One cannot be held responsible for one's relatives,' Anne reminded her. 'I know how grieved you were when Sunderland voted against the Prince's Bill. I believe he was one of its greatest opponents. And my poor George suffering so with his asthma . . . fighting for his breath, and Sunderland working up feelings about him in the Lords. I remember thinking at the time: And this Sunderland is my dear Mrs Freeman's son-in-law. I shall never like that man again . . . but it does not make me any less fond of my dearest Mrs Freeman. Nothing could change my affection for her.'

'I shall speak to Godolphin; I shall write to Mr Freeman. If these Tory peers are going to take their places in the Lords then there must be at least one new Whig peer.'

'It is really a matter for the ministers.'

Infuriating old fool! thought Sarah. It is time I was back.

She had bullied Godolphin who could never stand up to her; she had written to Marlborough. They both advised caution. But when had Sarah ever been cautious? She was beginning to realize that she had been foolish to shut herself away from affairs. Marl was a genius, but he was not so perceptive as she was, and Godolphin was too timid. Neither of them – Tories that they were – had grasped the fact that they needed the support of the Whigs if they were going to carry on the war because the Whigs represented the commerce and finance of the country.

Sarah was fiercely on the side of those who wanted to throw out the Occasional Conformity Bill and although Anne supported it she was determined to bring the Queen to her way of thinking.

In this she would have Prince George on her side for he, when he had been appointed Lord High Admiral of England, had been obliged to take the Sacrament according to the rites of the Church of England and afterwards continued to worship at the Lutheran Chapel which he had attended all his life. It was therefore absurd for George to have voted for the Bill; nor would he have done so had not Anne insisted that he did.

The old fool, thought Sarah. Too good-natured to say no, too anxious to please his dear angel, and too fat and lazy to discuss the matter with her.

Anne had to see Sarah's point of view and Sarah was going to bring all her powers of persuasion to making her.

But first she intended to have her Whig peer and she had selected a certain John Hervey for the honour.

The Queen bleated that it was a matter for the ministers until Sarah's fury could no longer be controlled.

'Unless Mr Hervey is elevated to the peerage I shall leave Court and never set foot in it again!'

The Queen was distressed; Godolphin was shocked; Marlborough, deeply engaged in military operations, was horrified.

There was only one outcome. John Hervey became Lord

Hervey and Sarah bowed her head in acknowledgement of victory.

Sarah was delighted when the Bill went through the Lords and emerged with an amendment which the House of Commons must surely reject.

She felt elated by her victory – for small though it was, it proved her to be a power.

It is time I came back, she told herself.

Sarah sent for Abigail Hill.

'You have done well while I have been away,' she said. 'That flibbertigibbit sister of yours will have to mend her ways though.'

'I trust Alice has done nothing to displease your Grace.'

'Displease me,' cried Sarah. 'I should quickly box her ears if she did. I should remind her that I took her from a broom – as I told you – and made her laundress in the household of his Grace of Gloucester. And now she has her pension and her place here – all due to me. I find her idle and scarcely worth her salt. She gossips too much.'

'I will tell her of Your Grace's displeasure.'

'And that brother of yours.'

'Jack!'

'Jack indeed. *He* has been importuning the Duke for a place in the Army, if you please.'

'Oh, it is too much,' said Abigail, lowering her eyes and folding her hands together.

Sarah watched her with gratification. Abigail Hill had not disappointed her, although she had carried no tales. Perhaps Danvers and the rest took care what they said in front of the girl, knowing her relationship to the Marlboroughs and realizing of course that she would lose no time in reporting all she heard. There was no doubt about it – she was a good influence in the Queen's apartment.

'Never mind, never mind. Although it would have been better if the boy had come to *me*. The Duke has much with which to occupy himself.'

'As has your Grace.'

'That's true enough. I only have to turn my back and we have bodice-makers given grand titles. We'll be hearing that grooms are being turned into noble Dukes next. And then, if you please, we have to show our piety by touching for the King's Evil. *Medieval*, I call it. You should have told me what was going on.'

Aibgail looked contrite. 'Your Grace, I knew that you were in mourning . . .'

'It's of no account. Well, now I am here and I shall see that all goes smoothly and as it should. I believe the Queen has been pleased with you. You have looked to her comfort without intruding. That's being a good servant. I am going to reward you.'

'Your Grace is so good.'

'My youngest daughter is with me. I did not care to leave her at St Albans now that her sister is married and her brother . . . gone. So I have brought her with me. I want you to keep an eye on her. It means that you will accompany us perhaps to the opera or to the play. You will watch my daughter and make sure no harm befalls her.'

'And the Queen . . .' Abigail was terrified for the moment. Did this mean that she was going to be taken from Anne's service? She could not have endured that. She pictured herself going to the Queen, throwing herself on her knees and demanding to be kept.

But Sarah went on impatiently: 'Certainly not. The Queen would not wish to lose you. You have proved yourself a good chambermaid. This will be in the nature of a little treat for your good services.'

A treat! A duenna for the hot-tempered Mary who was too like her mother for comfort. She hoped that Anne would soon ask for her to resume her duties.

Anne said fretfully: 'And where is Hill?'

'Your Majesty,' said Mrs Danvers, 'the Duchess said she was taking her to the opera.'

'The opera! Hill! But how very strange.'

'Yes, Your Majesty. It is strange that the Duchess should take the chambermaid to the opera.'

'Danvers, I should like you to bathe my feet. They are very

swollen today. Oh dear, how I should love to go to the opera, but frankly, Danvers, I do not care to be *carried* there . . . and that is how it would have to be. I do believe my gout has been worse these last days. Hill had such soothing hands.'

Mrs Danvers brought the bowl and bathed the royal feet.

There was not the magic in her hands that was in Hill's. She closed her eyes. How tiring it had been this afternoon. Dinner at three of the clock had made George as sleepy as usual; and he had slept away that pleasant hour or two which she usually so enjoyed in her beloved green closet. It was Hill's duty to sit at the tea table and pour the tea – she had rather pretty white hands. Her only beauty, poor Hill! Anne looked at her own. We have that in common, she thought. Poor Hill! So *thin* and plain. But such pretty hands and such a touch on the harpsichord, and her imitations were really amusing. They made George laugh. How she enjoyed seeing him amused – although not too much, for it could bring on the asthma. Hill had never done that. She was so discreet. If she saw it coming on – and she would be watchful – she would stop.

Such pleasant afternoons! And that nice page, Samuel Masham, usually accompanied the Prince. He looked a little glum this afternoon. In fact they were all glum – except the Prince, who was quickly asleep.

'We missed Abigail Hill,' said Anne to herself, with a little jolt of surprise. 'All of us. Even George. I am sure he didn't sleep quite so comfortably.'

And now Sarah had swooped on Abigail Hill and carried her off to the opera. Suppose Sarah should discover the charm of Abigail Hill. Suppose she carried her off to St Albans. Then she would never want to lose her. Anne's face grew long. She pictured them together – handsome flamboyant Sarah and quite *indispensable* Abigail Hill.

Her feet felt limp and only half dry.

'Danvers . . .' she began. But what was the use? It was only Abigail who could bring comfort to her poor aching feet.

Abigail . . . and Sarah! Together. And she confined to her couch or her chair with her dropsy and her gout. How she would enjoy being at the opera, listening to Sarah's wit and with Hill close by to see to her wants.

Danvers was awaiting her command.

'Bring me writing materials. I want to write to the Duchess of Marlborough.'

While Danvers was obeying her she thought of Sarah who had been absent from her for several days and had not written. Sarah was always remiss in her correspondence; Anne had constantly to be reminding her to write. And now of course she would have less time than usual, since she had discovered the virtues of Abigail Hill.

'Dear Mrs Freeman hates writing so much I fear, though she should stay away two or three days, she would hardly let me hear from her, and therefore for my own sake I must write her a line or two. I fancy now you are in Town you will be tempted to see the Opera, which I should not wonder at, for I should be so too if I were able to stir, but when that will be God knows, for I am still so lame I cannot go without limping. I hope Mrs Freeman has no thoughts of going to the Opera with Mrs Hill and will have a care of engaging herself too much in her company, for if you give way to that it is a thing which will insensibly grow upon you. Therefore give me leave once more to beg for your sake, as well as poor Mrs Morley's, that you would have as little to do with that enchantress as 'tis possible, and pray pardon me for saying it. Your poor unfortunate Morley.'

She sent for Danvers to seal the letter and see that it was delivered. And afterwards when she sat dozing in her chair she thought: That was a strange letter I wrote to Mrs Freeman. I wonder why I wrote it. Yet there is truth in it, little Abigail Hill is an enchantress of sorts. One does not notice her when she is there, but when she is away, how one misses her!

'Danvers.'

'Your Majesty.'

'When Hill returns please tell her that she is taking too much leave of absence.'

'Yes, Your Majesty.'

'And send her to me . . . as soon as she comes.'

*　　*　　*

163

The Duchess of Marlborough was with her daughter Mary when the Queen's letter was delivered to her. Mary sat sullenly watching her mother while she opened the letter.

The young girl's blue eyes were fretful, her mouth – so like Sarah's – was petulant. She was longing to return to St Albans. He would be waiting for her. She would slip out in the evening and they would plan the future. Perhaps they would have to elope for it was certain that Mamma would never allow one of her daughters to marry a simple country gentleman. And that was all he was, even though he was the most handsome, most perfect man in the world. Wasn't it enough that Henrietta's husband was Lord Rialton and would be the Earl of Godolphin when his father died? Anne was Lady Sunderland and Elizabeth, Lady Bridgewater. Grand marriages for all three. They had married where their mother wished them to; so why shouldn't Mary the youngest choose for herself?

She was so young yet, and dared say nothing, for she knew well enough how fierce Mamma could be when she did not want something – and she would certainly not want this marriage.

'But it is going to be,' said Mary to herself; and in her face was all her mother's determination.

Watching Sarah reading the letter Mary thought: I shall hate her for ever and ever if she stops our marriage.

'H'm!' said the Duchess. 'Sometimes I think that woman grows madder every day.'

Mary knew to whom she referred when she spoke in that slighting way. Mamma loved to speak contemptuously of the Queen, who had done so much for her. Perhaps, thought Mary, she will send me back to St Albans with Abigail Hill in charge. That would be wonderful. One could do exactly what one liked with Abigail Hill. One could bully and browbeat *her* into accepting just anything.

'Is it from the Queen?' asked Mary.

'It is. She is a jealous old fool. She cannot bear that I should be with anyone but herself. What next!'

'Mamma, do you propose to send Abigail Hill to St Albans with me?'

'No I do not. She is too useful at Court. The Queen would not like that at all.'

'She would not wish to lose Abigail then?'

Sarah let out a spurt of laughter. 'Abigail! She cares nothing for her. She's a good chambermaid ... nothing more. The Queen likes her there because she does what is expected of her without obtruding. But she is so jealous of my noticing anyone ... just anyone ... that she thinks of a plain little chambermaid as an enchantress. Think of that! Abigail Hill.'

'I was only thinking, Mamma, that you might have wanted her to be in charge of me. It would take me off your hands if Abigail and I went back to St Albans.'

The Duchess's glittering eyes were fixed on her daughter.

'Both you and Abigail stay precisely where you are,' she said coolly.

Mary quailed. How much does she know? she wondered.

How pleasant it was in the green closet! Abigail poured the tea and brought it to her mistress, so quietly, so efficiently, just the right amount of sugar. Why was it that it was never quite the same when others made it? George sat in his chair, so contented now – except of course when his asthma troubled him, and even then so patient ... so resigned. Dear George! He seemed not to mind that he had never fulfilled his early promise of becoming a great soldier or sailor, just as she had accepted the fate of never having had the children they had longed for. Now she dreamed of being a great Queen. Often she talked to Hill about her hopes, for to talk to Hill was like talking to oneself. *She* never shouted or contradicted or burst into loud laughter that had a hint of derision in it.

'I look upon my people as my children, Hill, the children I never had. Then I see myself as the Mother of them all and I want to do what is best for them just as I should for my babies had they lived.'

'Your Majesty, I believe the people look upon you as the Mother of them all.'

'Do you think Hill that a Queen can – if she has good ministers – be an inspiration to her people that a King can never be?'

'I do, Your Majesty. Think of Queen Elizabeth. An inspiration . . . it is exactly that.'

Anne nodded contentedly. 'When I think of that, Hill, I cease to mourn quite so sadly.'

'It is God's consolation,' answered Abigail.

Dear Hill. So right-thinking! So deeply religious!

'And there is the Church, Hill. To uphold the Church and the state – that is my duty.'

'Oh, Your Majesty is good . . . *good!*'

Dear Hill! Not only were her deeds a perpetual comfort but her words also.

What happy days! And she was beginning to grasp affairs of state. Here in the green closet she received her favoured ministers and how much easier it was to grasp a situation over a dish of tea than at a Council meeting. She felt so at peace, with one of the dogs on her lap and George dozing in his chair and Hill never far distant.

Samuel Masham was a frequent visitor because he always accompanied the Prince, and he was a young man on whom George seemed to depend as she did on Abigail. Not quite as much, of course; that would be impossible.

'There is a cold wind today, Your Majesty.' Abigail laid the shawl about her shoulders.

'I notice it now you mention it.'

She always anticipated a want. What a creature!

'The Duchess is still at St Albans, I suppose.'

'I believe that to be so, Your Majesty.'

Abigail lowered her eyes to hide the faint mischief in them. The Duchess's children did lead her a dance. Now it was Mary wanting to marry someone whom the Duchess considered unsuitable. Abigail hoped that little affair would keep Mamma occupied at St Albans for some time. It was so peaceful at Court without her.

'How peaceful it is!' said the Queen. 'Do you know Hill, I think one of the states most desirable as one gets older is *peace*. I am sure His Highness would agree with me.'

'I am sure he would, Your Majesty.'

How long, wondered Abigail, before she began to understand who was the disturber of the peace, how long would she allow the Duchess to dominate her and set the pattern of her life? Sometimes it seemed as though the answer was: For ever. There were others when Abigail was not so sure.

'Hill, who is invited to the closet this afternoon?'

'Mr Harley, Madam, and Mr St John.'

'Oh yes, yes. Marlborough's protégés. He seems to think highly of them and he is a very clever man. The Duchess is not so sure of them. Well, perhaps we shall discover, eh, Hill?'

Perhaps we shall discover! There were moments when Anne lifted her from her position as a chambermaid and made a confidante of her, and to be a confidante of a Queen was to take part in politics.

'It might be that Mr Harley would like a dish of tea, Hill.'

Abigail stood before him and a shiver of excitement tinged with apprehension ran through her. His eyes, betraying nothing of his feelings, rested on her not lightly but as though they would probe the depth of her mind. As he accepted the tea she caught the smell of wine on his breath; he had been drinking before he came. Why not? she asked herself. So had the Prince, over his dinner; that was why he could not keep awake.

'Thank you, Mistress Hill,' he said. His tone was courteous but his voice harsh.

'And Mr St John?'

What a handsome young man! Considerably younger than Mr Harley. Twenty years? Not quite so much as that. Fifteen perhaps. And clearly his disciple. Mr St John was too bold. Abigail had heard from Samuel Masham that he had the reputation of being a rake. Now his eyes were on Abigail appraisingly, but differently from the manner in which Mr Harley watched her. St John was no doubt noticing her sandy hair, the freckles of which she could never rid herself, the pinkness at the tip of the nose which was too long, the colourlessness of eyes that were too small. He would be dismissing her as unbedworthy. But still he was interested. Yet not so interested as Mr Harley.

The realization came to Abigail that she was no longer

merely the chambermaid to pour the tea, to fetch and carry the Queen's fans, cards or shawls, and that these men, who were clearly going to be important in the country's affairs had discovered this startling fact even before she had.

Mr Harley was talking to the Queen of Daniel Defoe. Abigail seated herself on a stool close to the Queen's chair, where Anne liked her to be, and listened. Mr Harley was now trying to plead for Defoe. What an extraordinary voice he had; it was inharmonious, and he all but stuttered; yet he made his points with a brilliance and tact which was admirable.

'Your Majesty's reign will be one remembered through the ages,' he was telling Anne. How had he known that that was one of the dearest wishes of her heart? 'Conquest, yes, Madam. That makes for greatness, but there is something more valuable, more endurable: Literature.'

'I believe you have a wonderful collection of books, Mr Harley.'

'To collect books is a hobby of mine, Madam. And I believe that at this time our country has a greater contribution to make to literature than ever before.'

The Queen folded her hands. What pleasant conversation! What an accomplished man! Yes, she had heard of the people he mentioned and it was admirable, quite *admirable*, that they found so much in the *times* to inspire them.

'Sometimes, it does not inspire them to admiration, Madam,' suggested St John.

'It is of slight importance,' retorted Mr Harley. 'It matters only that they are inspired.'

Mr Harley led the conversation this way and that. He mentioned Jonathan Swift, Matthew Prior, Joseph Addison, Richard Steele, William Congreve, John Dryden and at last he came to the point of the discussion: Daniel Defoe.

'I believe he is under sentence for some misdemeanour,' said Anne, frowning.

'For writing a pamphlet, Madam.'

Anne shivered. 'I would not compare such a man with Mr Dryden whose work I admire. Such amusing plays! I think we should have one performed for my birthday, Hill. Remind me.'

'Yes, Madam.'

'Had he been a less brilliant writer, Madam, he would now be free.'

Anne nodded. 'Such amusing plays,' she answered.

Mr Harley had a way of bringing the conversation back to what he wanted to say, and he had come to talk of Daniel Defoe for whom he obviously had a great admiration. Abigail realized at once that his idea was to have the man released from Newgate. But he did not know Anne if he thought that because she found his company stimulating she would grant any request. These people underestimated their Queen; she could be as determined as any of them to have what she wanted. She never raged and stormed as some people were apt to do. But she made her point and clung to it as stubbornly as any mule.

She had not invited Mr Harley and Mr St John to the friendly intimacies of the green closet to discuss the affairs of a scribbler who had foolishly been caught up in politics and in consequence found himself in Newgate Jail.

Abigail inwardly laughed. It was so amusing to listen to Mr Harley on the theme of Defoe while the Queen repeated at intervals, 'Such a clever man, Mr Dryden. Hill do remind me. We will have the play at St James's for my birthday.'

And when they left they must have been deeply disappointed, for they had gained nothing, in Abigail's opinion, but perhaps a little understanding that the Queen was not what they had believed her to be.

She would have been surprised if she could have heard their conversation as they sauntered across the path.

'What did you think of her, St John?'

'Scarce a beauty and devilish sly.'

'It may well be that her mental accomplishments make up for her lack of physical attraction.'

'She's quiet as a mouse. They call her the shuffling little wretch at court, so I heard. Danvers and the rest are pleased to put on her all the most unpleasant tasks.'

'Danvers and the rest could well be fools.'

'Come, Master, don't tell me you're taken with the woman.'

'Mightily taken.'

'And you not a man for the wenches.'

'Your mind runs along wearisomely well-worn paths, Harry. Did you know there are other games more amusing, more exciting than those of the bedchamber?'

'An impossibility,' answered St John.

'Rake! Libertine! You're missing much in life.'

'You are proposing to play games with Mistress Hill?'

'Perhaps. She's a deep one that. Worth watching. Who is she, do you think?'

'Brought to court by Viceroy Sarah, being some distant relation in service, which could not be tolerated, of course. Connexion of Her High and Mightiness a serving wench! Never! Better to have her at Court – in a post of spy, you understand.'

'So she is a Marlborough spy! I doubt it, Harry. I doubt it very much.'

Robert Harley was smiling complacently. He was well pleased with his visit to the green closet.

Abigail would have been surprised, for he had failed completely to do anything for Daniel Defoe. She did not guess then that he had achieved his main object. He had seen Abigail Hill and had decided that he had not been mistaken in her.

It was on the night of November 26th that the great storm broke over London.

The Queen slept through the beginning for she could sleep through most things, but the sound of the rising wind which seemed to shake the very battlements of St James's Palace kept Abigail awake.

She rose from her pallet on the floor in the Queen's room and wrapped her robe about her, for she was certain that even Anne could not continue to sleep through such noise. Even as she did so the chamber was lightened by a brilliant flash of lightning followed immediately by the loudest clap of thunder Abigail had ever heard.

'What is it?' called Anne. 'Hill! Hill!'

'I am here, Madam. It's the thunder and lightning. It seems to be a bad storm. Shall I make some tea or would Your Majesty prefer brandy?'

'I think brandy in the circumstances, Hill.'

Abigail had disappeared, but before she was back there was another violent clap and the sound of falling masonry.

'I think, Madam, that it might be wise to leave your bed.'

There was Hill with a warm robe to put about the Queen's shoulders.

'Shall I need this, Hill?'

'I am afraid the draughts might bring on the shoulder pains, Madam.'

'You are right, Hill. Of course you are right. Oh dear ... what is happening?'

'It's a very violent storm, Madam.'

'And right overhead. Oh dear me ... Hill. There again!'

The Queen shut her eyes. Abigail knew that whenever any disaster threatened she thought of the wrong she had done her father and that some curse had come upon her.

'It's only a storm, Madam.'

'I do hope damage has not been done to the *poor*, Hill.'

'We must see what can be done about it, if that should be so, Madam.'

'Yes, yes, Hill.'

'My angel. My dearest.' George was bursting into the apartment, a robe about him, his wig, having been put on in a hurry, awry. He was wheezing painfully. 'Vot is this? You are safe, my angel. Ah, thank Got. Thank Got.'

'I'm safe enough, George. I have Hill here. You must not get so excited, dear love. You know it brings on the wheeze. Is that Masham? Oh, Masham, is His Highness warmly clad? I do not want him to take a chill again.'

'Yes, Your Majesty. He is wearing his warm underwear.'

'I want no more chills.'

'Masham,' said the Prince. 'We need a little something for the cold to keep out.'

'Yes, Your Highness.'

'Hill,' said Anne, 'brandy for his Highness. Oh dear, who is that screaming?'

It was some of the maids of honour who were terrified of the storm.

'Bring them in, Hill. We will all be together.'

171

Abigail obeyed, and all through that horrifying night she remained beside the Queen.

That was the most fearful night Abigail had ever lived through and it was not until the next morning that the furious gale had abated; by that time it had left behind tremendous damage.

The streets were blocked with fallen masonry; trees had been uprooted by the hundred; the Thames was blocked with broken craft of all description and many battleships had been damaged in the North Sea.

All through the days that followed news of the disaster was brought to the Queen. Fifteen of her warships with countless smaller craft had been destroyed, hundreds of merchant ships were missing; the sea had swept inland; the rivers had overflowed; houses had been demolished.

There had never before been such a storm in living memory; all prayed that there never would be again.

The south of England lay shattered beneath its impact, although in the north it had been scarcely felt, and it was said that nowhere in London had it struck so fiercely as at St James's Palace where part of the battlements and many of the chimneys had been wrenched off. In the parks, trees had been pulled up and flung aside as though by some giant hand – trees which had stood there for many, many years.

'Nothing,' said the Queen, 'will ever be the same again.'

They were sad days which followed the great storm as news of disaster after disaster kept coming in.

Anne was horrified to learn that a stack of old chimneys in the episcopal palace of Bath and Wells had fallen and that the Bishop and his wife, Dr and Mrs Kidder, had been killed in their beds.

'What terrible disaster, Hill! It is like a judgement.'

Then the news reached the Court that the recently built Eddystone Lighthouse had been swept into the sea and that its architect Mr Winstanley had gone with it.

'It is like a judgement,' repeated the Queen.

Abigail, who knew how the Queen's thoughts were running, refrained from mentioning the cause of the Queen's remorse –

her disloyalty to her father. 'Instead she said: 'Madam, you will doubtless decide to help those who have suffered from the storm.'

'I shall indeed, Hill.'

'And perhaps a service to thank God for bringing us safely through the storm and asking him not to send such a one again.'

'Oh, Hill, of course. Of course. That is what we must do.'

So the Queen's thoughts were turned from the possible curse which might have fallen upon her and gave her mind to good deeds.

'Madam,' said Abigail, 'in the streets they begin to call you Good Queen Anne.'

Good could come out of evil then. The storm had been quite terrible, but it did help her people to understand how much she cared for their welfare.

She sent for Godolphin and they arranged that there should be a fast throughout the country – a public fast with special services in the church.

There should be a general proclamation.

'Hill,' she said, when Hill was massaging her painful limbs, 'I sometimes think that good can come out of evil.'

'I am sure you are right, Madam.'

Soon after the great storm the Archduke Charles of Austria was expected to spend a few days in England on his way to Spain to claim the throne.

He had been proclaimed King of Spain in Vienna and had met the Duke of Marlborough in Düsseldorf that October. There he had presented the Duke with a diamond encrusted sword and earnestly thanked him for all he had done.

It was important therefore that the Duke be in England to receive the visitor when he arrived. Sarah was delighted to see her Marl. No matter what success or failure they had to suffer, for both of them these reunions were the most enjoyable periods of their lives. Some might maliciously say it was fortunate for John Churchill that he did not have to live day after day with Sarah without hope of escape; they might hint that the great felicity of the marriage – which none could deny – was based on the long absences, the fact remained that both could be completely happy in those short weeks when they were together.

Sarah raged about the follies of the Queen, the intractability of their daughter Mary who – at her ridiculous age – was trying to make a most unsuitable match: she might talk of the absurd knighting of bodice-makers, the difficulties of bringing son-in-law Sunderland to heel, her suspicions of Robert Harley and Henry St John – of whom Marl and Godolphin seemed to have such a high opinion – but all the same there was no joy like having her husband home with her – safe within her sight.

And the same applied to Marlborough. He might be one of the most ambitious men alive; his heart was deep in military affairs; he longed to continue the war, but he yearned all the time to be at Sarah's side. None but himself saw her soft, tender and gentle, for she had no softness, tenderness nor gentleness for any but him.

Marlborough, with the Duke of Somerset, went to Portsmouth to greet Charles of Austria; and it had been arranged that Prince George should go to Petworth, the Duke of Somerset's mansion, there to greet the guest in the name of the Queen and bring him on to Windsor.

'I do declare,' said Anne, 'that I am a little worried for Mr Morley to make the journey at this time of the year.'

'It'll do him good,' countered Sarah, who was now at Court superintending all the preparations for the visit.

'But you know, Mrs Freeman, how bad his asthma has been this winter. He was bled three times in forty-eight hours and it was only the blisters that relieved him.'

'A little more action would be good for him.'

'Dear Mrs Freeman, you enjoy such rude health yourself that you do not always understand the weakness of others.'

Sarah allowed the faintest look of exasperation to cross her face.

Hill would have understood my anxiety, thought the Queen; and dismissed the thought at once. It was disloyalty to dear Mrs Freeman, and it was such a pleasure to have her back at Court. There was not the same peace, but how *vital* Mrs Freeman was, and what a pleasure to look at those flashing scornful eyes and to listen to the invective which came tripping from that fluent tongue. One felt so *alive* with Mrs Freeman about. And how handsome she was! One forgot how handsome until one saw her – with her beautiful golden hair hanging about her shoulders or dressed high for a state occasion.

All the same she was worried about George and she did wish Mrs Freeman would have been a *little* sympathetic. The roads would be even worse than usual at this time of the year after the bad storm.

So George had gone off to Petworth, and when he returned he would be accompanied by their august visitor with Somerset and dear Mr Freeman.

It was clear that Sarah believed this was as much her occasion as anyone else. Who, for instance, had made it possible for Charles of Austria to go to Spain and lay claim to the throne? Marlborough! Whose military genius was deciding the fate of Europe – and England? The answer was the same. And on whom did Marlborough depend for counsel and comfort and to fight his battles at home? His Duchess.

She behaved as though the Queen were her puppet. She all but ordered her; but not quite. Anne never argued; she would nod and smile and then go her own way; or sometimes make up her mind, find the phrase she needed to express it, and go on repeating it at intervals.

Nothing could have maddened Sarah more, but at the same time even she could not be blind to the warning it implied. John had cautioned her a hundred times. He was, of course *over*-cautious; but in her calmer moments Sarah did admit to herself that the Queen was a stubborn woman who could at times, as she put it, brandish the orb and sceptre.

It was evening when the party arrived at Windsor. Anne had ordered that every alternate man in the guard of honour should hold high a lighted flambeau, and the sight was impressive. The Queen, with Sarah – who should have been behind her – almost at her side, stood at the top of the staircase to greet her guests.

The Archduke was a delicate looking young man, handsome yet with a melancholy expression, and graceful manners; his blue coat with its gold and silver galoon was very becoming.

Poor young man, thought Anne. He looks tired.

He stooped and kissed the hem of her gown, then he kissed her cheek.

Sarah exchanged glances with John. But for you, she was reminding him, that young man would not be on his way to Spain. I hope they realize this.

John returned the smile. Never did a man have a more faithful champion.

Before meeting for supper the company would retire to their apartments and the guest taking the Queen's hand led her to hers and, when that was over, Prince George conducted the Archduke to his.

Anne was pleased to see Hill in the apartment quietly waiting to be of use, and for a moment she thought how pleasant it would be if instead of going down to the banquet she could visit the green closet where she could lie back in her chair and leave everything to Hill.

Almost immediately it was time to assemble before supper and the ceremonies began. All the ladies of the Court must be presented to the Archduke. He seemed to like them, for he kissed them all with a little more heartiness than seemed necessary and, during dinner when he was seated at the right hand of the Queen, he kept rising to attend to the wants of some lady.

Anne glanced about the table at Sarah who was completely absorbed in Mr Freeman and he in her, at George who was completely absorbed in, to him, the most serious business of life – eating and drinking.

What a handsome young man! thought Anne. My boy would be a young man now. Would she never have a child? Fruitless pregnancies came and went and she had almost accepted them as part of her life. They were no more inconvenient than the gout and the dropsy. But never a child.

How morbid she was – and at a banquet! And this was such an important occasion. When that young man was King of Spain how friendly England would be with his country for he would be grateful for ever – and it was all due to the Freemans.

Dearly beloved Sarah! But how much more *comfortable* to

176

lie back in the green closet. She thought of Hill's white hands among the tea things. So pleasant.

She was relieved when she could retire to her apartments.

George sat wheezing in his chair. She noticed that he was very breathless after a banquet – even though George's appetite made a banquet of every meal.

'I fear this has been a little trial to you, my dearest,' she said.

'Bed vill be goot.' George's pronunciation grew more broad when he was tired.

'The journey was too much for you, my love. I was saying to Mrs Freeman I was uneasy about your making it.'

'Oh . . . that journey. Never shall I forget. How glad I am, I said to Masham, how glad the Queen does not come. The roads . . . my dear love . . . the roads . . .'

'The storm of course has devastated everything. It was really not necessary for you to go. I would rather have gone myself.'

'That, my angel, I vould never allow.'

Dear George – only stern when he felt the need to protect her!

'It iss forty miles from Vindsor to Petvorth, they tell me. Fourteen hours it took, my angel, and no stop ve made safe vhen the coach was turned over and ve vas stuck in the mud.'

'My poor, *poor* George. And how was your wheeze then?'

'My veeze vas terrible, my love, vas very terrible.'

'My poor, poor George.'

'And ve should be there now, but for the men who lift up the coach vith bare hands, my angel, vith their bare hands . . . and they carry the coach and set it on the road.'

'That was wonderful, George. What good and faithful servants! You must present them to me and I will tell them how grateful I am. I was so anxious. I said continuously to Mrs Freeman how I wished you had not gone.'

'But I vould not haf allowed my angel to go.'

'Nor should I have allowed mine.'

'Vell, ve are safe now . . . and tired . . . and let us to bed. But a little brandy vould be varming.'

'A little brandy. I will call Hill. Hill! Hill!'

She came at once. She could not have been far away. How

pleasant she looked – how simple after all the brilliant costumes of the evening!

'His Highness fancies a little brandy, Hill. I will take some, too. Such a tiring day ... and another before us tomorrow. It will help us sleep.'

'Yes, Your Majesty.'

And almost at once – how was she so quiet and so quick? – there she was.

So pleasant ... sipping brandy with George dozing in the chair and Hill hovering in case she should be wanted.

'Hill, tell Masham His Highness is ready for bed.'

'Yes, Your Majesty.'

'I too, Hill. Oh, what a tiring day!'

Samuel Masham went with the Prince into George's dressing-room and Abigail remained with the Queen.

'Such a day, Hill! What ceremonies! And this young Archduke – King as he is now. I hope he is allowed to remain so, poor boy. But I daresay Mr Freeman will see to that. I thought Mrs Freeman looked magnificent. And so delighted to have Mr Freeman back. But I am worried about the Prince, Hill. He does not look well to me and that journey to Petworth must have been an ordeal. His coach stuck in the mud ... overturned, if you please. And the boors had to lift it out. I really cannot think it has done His Highness any good at all. I wish you would speak to Masham, Hill. I want the greatest care taken of His Highness. Make sure that his underwear is of the warmest and he should not be in draughts.'

'Your Majesty can trust me to speak to Masham.'

'I know, Hill. I know. And now to bed ... I am so tired. And tomorrow of course there will be more and more ceremonies ...'

More and more ceremonies, thought Abigail, with the Duchess of Marlborough at the Queen's right hand, forcing herself forward, already recognized as the power behind the throne, as no King's mistress had ever been more so. And Abigail Hill – confined to the bedchamber, but only for the term of Her Grace's pleasure.

The Archduke Charles was considerably refreshed next day

178

when he joined the Queen in preparation for the ceremonies. Dinner must be taken in public, to be followed by a concert – instrumental and vocal – and after that there would be more music and, of course, cards.

Charles looked even more handsome than he had the previous night, as dressed in his crimson coat he greeted the Queen and her attendants.

Anne found it difficult to suppress her yawns as the day went on. Dinner at three and then the long afternoon of entertainment before supper. Oh for an hour or so in the green closet! She saw that George felt as she did and was thinking longingly of that comfort.

Sarah of course felt no such desire. What energy! What vitality! Dear Mrs Freeman makes me feel tired merely to look at her. But how handsome! How admired! And no wonder.

Charles was paying attention to her. Like everyone else he knew her importance. And how she enjoyed it! Such occasions were perfection to her. We are really quite different! thought Anne.

How glad she was that the supper was now over and there was dear Mrs Freeman ready to perform her duty, standing before her with the bowl in which she would wash her hands and the towel across her arm.

But Charles had risen and was attempting to take the towel from Sarah's arm.

Sarah said: 'It was my duty and my honour to do this service for Her Majesty.'

Charles replied: 'But at this time you will let me have that honour?'

He took the towel from Sarah and dipping it in the water, lifted one of Anne's hands and washed it and when he had done this he washed his own, while Sarah stood holding the bowl, with all eyes upon her; and then Charles took off a diamond ring and taking Sarah's hand slipped it on her finger.

Sarah's eyes gleamed with satisfaction. This was an acknowledgement of her importance.

In their apartments Sarah held out her hand with the flashing diamond in it.

'Worth a fortune,' she said.

John took the hand and kissed it.

'You know why he did it?' he said.

'Because he knows that if he wishes for England's support he has to have mine.'

'Spoken like my Sarah.'

'And how else should I speak, pray?'

'In no other way, for I would not have my Sarah different in any small detail.'

'So I am appreciated.'

He caught her in his arms.

'It pleases me,' she said, 'to be embraced by the greatest genius of our day.'

'No,' he said, 'it is the great genius who is being embraced.'

'Together we are supreme, John.'

'You understand the meaning of that gesture of the Archduke?' he asked her.

'Of course. I have just told you.'

'It's more than that. His ancestor Charles V gave a diamond ring to the mistress of François Premier when she held the bowl for him in similar circumstances. But he left his in the bowl. Charles put his on your finger. He could not treat the Duchess of Marlborough as a King's mistress.'

'I should hope not. I am a respectable woman and I am thankful that at least my fat friend sets a good moral example to her subjects.'

'Ah, Sarah, what of the Queen? Should you not be in attendance?'

'There is only one on whom I intend to attend this night, my lord. Why do you think I got Abigail Hill her place?'

'You think it wise to neglect her . . .' began John.

But she laughed in his face and such times as these were the most precious occasions for them both.

All over Christmas John remained in England, but he was making plans for his spring campaign. Sarah spent her time between the Queen and her husband and whenever possible they escaped to St Albans. A sullen Mary had been given a place in the Queen's household as lady in waiting on the death of Lady Charlotte Beverwaret. 'Where I can keep an eye on her,' said Sarah grimly. But relations between mother and daughter were decidedly strained, for Mary was not one meekly to accept meddling in her life. John, distressed by the relationship between wife and daughter, did all he could to put it right, but while Mary continued affectionate towards him she made it clear that she had no love for her mother.

'Who would have children!' cried Sarah. 'Ungrateful creatures!' But Mary continued resentful and brooding, and avoided her mother as much as she could. 'It'll pass,' said Sarah. 'I remember her sullen moods of the past.'

During Anne's birthday celebrations John Dryden's play *All for Love* was performed in St James's Palace.

It was a pleasant occasion, particularly as Anne had announced on that day that she intended to celebrate her birthday by making an endowment to poor clergy. It had disturbed her for some time, she had explained to her ministers, because those who were working in the Church were so ill paid.

She had talked about this with Hill during those winter days when George had dozed, awaking now and then to emit a grunt when she addressed him, and Hill had understood perfectly how anxious she was, for she had heard that some of the clergy and their families were actually in want. 'Doing the Church's work, Hill, and in want! I remember Bishop Burnet's advising my sister Mary and her husband William to do this. But it was useless. William thought only of war ... and Mary thought exactly what he wanted her to think. I am thankful that the dear Prince is quite different. There could not be a better husband ...'

Abigail only interrupted with: 'Nor a better wife than Your Majesty.'

Anne smiled. 'Thank you, Hill. I could wish all my subjects could enjoy the happiness of marriage as I have done. There is only one sorrow, Hill. My babies ... and particularly my boy. But I was telling you of my plan. I intend to establish a fund for the clergy. I shall make over my entire revenue from the First Fruits and the Tenths ... which is from the Church ... back to the Church for the benefit of the Clergy. I have been discussing this with my ministers and I have asked them to make it legal. My uncle Charles took this money to give to his mistresses, Hill. But I want to give it to those who are dedicating their lives to my church.'

'Your Majesty is so good.'

'I want to do good to my people, Hill. You, I know, understand that.'

Hill lowered her eyes and nodded.

Shortly afterwards the fund was created and made known throughout the country. It was called Queen Anne's Bounty; and when the Queen rode out the people cheered her. She was becoming generally known as Good Queen Anne.

The Jealous Duchess

All through the spring John was making preparations for his campaign.

'I have done with sieges and petty battles,' he told Sarah. 'Now the time has come to settle the fate of Europe.'

'I long for the time,' Sarah told him, 'when your battles are over and you come home to enjoy your deserts.'

'Sometimes,' he answered passionately, 'I think I would give up ambition ... everything ... for the sake of a life we could share together.'

Gratifying, thought Sarah, but impossible. It was because of his ambition that she loved him.

She spent a great deal of time with him at St Albans, for, as she said, I can safely leave Hill to look after the Queen. But there were frequent interruptions to their idyll when Marlborough must be in London; and often on this occasion she remained waiting for his return.

She saw a great deal of her daughters, particularly Henrietta and Anne, for she looked upon their husbands as her creatures who must, since they were politicians, take their orders from her. Francis Godolphin, Member for Helston, was a mild man, and under the thumb of his wife, and although Henrietta was inclined to be truculent with her mother, there had been no open quarrel. Sunderland who, since his father's death, had inherited the title as well as vast wealth, was a different matter. He it was who had voted against Prince George's annuity which, in Sarah's mind, was a foolish thing to do for it brought no gain to the family and at the same time antagonized both the Prince and the Queen. He was a rash man and notoriously quick-tempered. Anne, his wife, was one of the gentlest of the Churchill girls, and unlike her mother avoided rather than made quarrels. But there was constant friction between Sunderland and Sarah.

It was while Sarah was visiting the Sunderlands that the Earl made some reference to Marlborough's visits to London. He smiled as he did so and this Sarah passed, but when she heard Sunderland in conversation with one of his guests beneath her window she listened in horror.

'You can scarcely blame my father-in-law. He must have some respite from that tongue.'

'I thought it was impossible for a man of his nature to remain a virtuous husband. Why, before Sarah got her talons into him he was one of the biggest rakes in Town.'

Sunderland's burst of laughter maddened Sarah, but she had to go on listening.

'He braved the King of England when he slept with Barbara Castlemaine, so why shouldn't he brave Sarah for this woman. I hear she is very attractive . . . kind and gentle. A change. A man must have variety. But after Hurricane Sarah the most blatant fishwife would seem like a soft breeze.'

Sarah could bear no more; she leaned out of the window.

'What wicked scandal is this?'

They were silent for a few seconds.

'I am sorry Your Grace overheard us,' said Sunderland, then, sardonically, caring for nothing, 'We were discussing the news from London.'

'The news from London! I'd like to hear more of such news. And where you heard it.'

She came down to the gardens to find Sunderland alone – his

friend having fled. Not many would care to face Sarah in such a mood.

'Now, young man, what is all this.'

Sunderland tried to remind her by his haughty demeanour that as the son of a great family he was in no mood to be so addressed by her, for Duchess though she might be, her background was not to be compared with his.

'Don't prevaricate,' cried Sarah, her rage blinding her to everything else. 'I want the truth from you or you'll be sorry.'

'The truth, Madam? Who knows the truth of these affairs but those who participate in them? You have come to the wrong man. I am sure the Duke can tell you far more of this matter than I. Why not ask him?'

Why not? Sarah was going to lose no time. She was going straight to John Churchill to tell him that the tricks he got up to before his marriage could not be played now. Or if they were, that was the end of his life with her.

She raged up and down the room. In vain did he try to comfort her.

'Sarah, there is no other woman.'

'And what of this story of Sunderland's?'

'It is a lie.'

'I am not certain of that.'

'Then you don't know me. How could it possibly be?'

'It could possibly be in the past, John Churchill. A fine fool you must have looked leaping out of Castlemaine's window – *naked*! A fine sight indeed. And the King laughing at you from the window, insulting you, calling out that you were only earning your living.'

He was stricken. The story was one he had hoped was forgotten. Now she was recalling it and giving it more lurid details than it had possessed in reality.

'And,' she shrieked, 'getting paid for your attentions. Five thousand pounds for serving in the bed of the King's mistress. You must have been most worthy, for you have to admit your price was high.'

He took her by the shoulders and shook her, but it was no use. She was deeply wounded; she was filled with rage; and

Sarah loved her rage; she loved to flagellate it into wilder and wilder fury, and at this moment she loved that fury more than she loved John Churchill.

'Listen to me, Sarah,' he said.

'I want no lies.'

'There is no need to tell lies.'

'So now you are going to say that you were never Barbara Castlemaine's lover.'

'I was going to say no such thing. What happened before we married is past and done with. It is what happens now that is important. I tell you I have always been faithful to you. These are lies you have heard. Sunderland told you, you say. I wish we had never allowed that marriage. I shall never forgive him for this.'

'He only repeated what he heard and it is right that I should know.'

'There is no truth in this. You must believe me. You must.'

But Sarah was not going to be placated. She had been jolted out of her complacent belief. She paced the apartment like a mad woman and when John tried to embrace her, she cried out: 'Don't dare touch me, John Churchill. I'll never share your bed again. So you had better find yourself more women. One will not be enough for such as you.'

There was nothing to be done with Sarah in such a mood.

Soon John would leave for the battlefield and Sarah still refused to speak to him. No matter how he pleaded, how much he begged to be allowed to explain, she would not listen.

John's only way of communicating with her was by means of letters. At first she refused to read them, but she thrust them into a drawer, knowing that she would do so later.

John could not understand this change in her. She had always been forceful and naturally was angry when Sunderland had told his lies, but he was bewildered by her refusal to listen to him. He was innocent. He wanted no one but Sarah; he was as completely fascinated by her now as he had been in the days of their courtship and early marriage. And she would not listen to him!

Sarah was a little astonished at herself. Deep in her heart she did not believe in this scandal. There was always scandal concerning people in high places. To be successful was to create envy; and no one in England could have more enemies than Sarah Churchill. She made little attempt to keep her friends and none to lose her enemies. She was married to the war hero who adored her. Her successful marriage was the envy of all those who had failed to achieve such an ideal partnership. Therefore it was natural enough that those who had failed should seek to besmirch that which they could not emulate. In vain did John try to make her see this.

The truth was that Sarah had recently lost her son and almost immediately afterwards became pregnant. Unfortunately this had ended in miscarriage, and the realization had come to Sarah that she was forty-five years old. She had no son. Would she ever have one now? She felt herself ageing; the change of life was upon her. The faint depression which had been with her since her miscarriage was affected by the gossip she had heard from Sunderland and John's infidelity had not seemed the impossibility it would have, a little earlier.

She stayed at St Albans nursing her misery. Henrietta showing quite clearly that she no longer cared for her mother's opinion; Mary hating her because she had prevented that ridiculous romance; young Blandford dead. Anne and Elizabeth were pleasant creatures but Anne was married to the hateful Sunderland and who knew what *he* would do. And soon her beloved John would have left England and, since the death of Blandford, she had begun to wonder what greater blow could strike her. There was only one: the death of John himself. And now ... there was this horrible gossip about him and the unknown woman.

She read one of the letters he had written:

'As for your suspicion of me as to this woman, that will vanish, but it can never go out of my mind the opinion you must have of me, after my solemn protesting and swearing, that it did not gain any belief with you. This thought has made me take no rest this night and will forever make me unhappy.'

* * *

The relationship was no longer perfect. This would always be between them. And worse still, she could not let herself believe that her dearest Marl still loved her.

'He must hate me,' she told herself, 'because I stand between him and . . . that woman!'

Again he wrote to her :

'When I swear to you as I do that I love you, it is not dissembling. As I know your temper, I am very sensible that what I say signified nothing. However, I cannot forbear repeating what I said yesterday, which is that I have never sent to her in my life, and may my happiness in the other world as well as this depend upon the truth of this.'

It is true, she told herself. There could not be anyone else. Yet the scandals of him in his youth were true enough. He had been a philanderer then.

He was begging her to come back to him. He was reminding her that the time was short and that he could not long delay his departure. She must come back to him, live with him as his wife, believe in him.

'If the thought of the children that we have had, or aught else that has ever been dear to us, can oblige you to be so goodnatured as not to leave my bed for the remaining time, I shall take it kindly to my dying day, and do most faithfully promise you that I will take the first opportunity of leaving England, and assure you that you may rest quiet that from that time you shall never more be troubled with my hated sight. My heart is so full that if I do not vent this truth it will break, which is that I do from my soul curse that hour in which I gave my poor dear child to a man that has made me of all mankind the most unhappiest.'

When Sarah read that letter she was shaken. What was happening to them, they who had been so close, so happy all these years? She was wrong, of course she was wrong; but it was not easy for Sarah to admit that she was wrong.

Bed! she grumbled. Bed! That's all he thinks of!

But she went to him and said: 'You are my husband and I shall accompany you to Harwich to bid you farewell.'

He was pathetically eager to accept her on any grounds, but she refused to rid herself of her suspicions. She wrote an angry letter which she gave him on parting, but as she stood watching the ship disappear she was overcome by a longing for him; and with a return of that feeling which she had experienced she knew that the charge against him was false, that he loved her as wholeheartedly as she loved him; and that a madness had come to her, perhaps because she loved him so deeply, so possessively, that the very thought that he could prefer someone else drove her to fury.

There was only one thing to do and that was sit down and write the truth to him.

She had been foolish. She loved him. What madness was it that made them believe they could ever be parted or their interests be divided? She would come out to him, that she might be beside him, for the children were settled now – with the exception of Mary who was well looked after in her Court post – and she need not consider their welfare but her own inclination.

When John read the letter he was overcome with joy.

The nightmare was past. They were together in spirit again. Life was good again, intensely worth living.

He thanked her for her dear letter; he would read it again and again. She had preserved his quiet and made him believe in his life once more. There must never again be trouble between them, for there was no happiness for him without her and he dared hope that there was none for her without him.

Sarah now settled down to await his return.

Blenheim

Those were trying months. Tension was rising and even the people in the streets knew that what was happening on the Continent at this time could be decisive. Louis XIV was anxious to settle the European conflict and was planning a march on Vienna; his armies had already passed through the Black Forest and were with the Elector of Bavaria on the Danube. The Dutch were apprehensive at the thought of a conflict so far from home; so were the English. Sarah knew that John was not going to make the attack on the Moselle which he had allowed the Dutch and Parliament to believe. He was going to take the battle right into Germany; and when the news came that Marlborough had taken his Dutch and English armies up the Rhine to Mainz there was consternation at home and in Holland.

The Tories – who had never wanted the war – were furious, and Marlborough was attacked both in the Commons and the Lords. He was exceeding orders; he was making decisions which should be left to the Government; he was conducting a war of his own.

'Impeach him!' was the cry.

Sarah was furious with those who dared suggest this – none did in her presence.

'Let him fail,' was the comment, 'and we'll have his head.'

'I'll see them all in hell first!' was Sarah's retort.

Anne was faithful to her. She was aware of the sly looks which came Mrs Freeman's way. Sarah stormed about the royal apartments as bombastic as ever – no, even more so. She was going to make them eat their words.

There was bad news from Scotland. Godolphin came in trembling to the Queen. He was always a timid creature, was Sarah's comment. But Godolphin advised Anne to placate Scotland, for if she did not, a civil war might be the result and that would not be a very healthy position for England considering the flower of the Army was with Marlborough.

Anne then agreed to a passage in the Act of Security which allowed Scotland to choose its own King irrespective of what England did.

A backward step, was the comment; and one which could bring back the old days of war between the North and South.

It was a hot summer and George could not breathe in London so Anne and he went to Windsor.

George shook his head over the state of affairs. He was clearly thinking how different it would have been had he been allowed to be Commander-in-Chief.

'I believe in Mr Freeman,' said Anne; and no matter what criticism was levelled at Marlborough she repeated the phrase.

Abigail had returned to her old place, for Sarah was often at St Albans. She had found the court unendurable during those hot days and believed that if she had to endure more of Anne's exasperating ways she would scream the truth at her which was that she was a foolish old woman and Sarah hated to be near her.

Sarah wanted none of these passionate relationships with her own sex. Sarah wanted John with her – a John returned successful from his campaigns.

She had to face the fact that the position looked grim, and that made her all the more eager for his return. But he must come triumphant or they would put him in the Tower. She remembered the agonies of those days when he had been a prisoner there.

She raged against his enemies: Rochester, Nottingham in the House of Lords; Sir Edward Seymour in the Commons. How dared they – just because he was bold and adventurous. Did they not know that that was the only way to success?

Let them beware. Marlborough would succeed and then he would be the most powerful man in England.

Anne lay back in her chair. She was so tired.

'Hill,' she called. 'Hill! Oh, there you are. Never far away.'

'Your Majesty would like me to make you tea.'

'I think that would be very pleasant.'

Anne stroked the dog in her lap. Life had become very difficult lately, after having been so pleasant. Her people had loved her for bringing back the old custom of touching for the King's Evil and then of course there was her Bounty. But wars made Kings and Queens unpopular and Mr Freeman's boldness was not appreciated at home. She had had news from France which she found very worrying.

There was Hill with the tea. It was soothing.

'Your Majesty is disturbed, I fear,' said Hill.

'I am, Hill. I don't know what is going to happen to our Armies.'

'They are safe with the Duke, Madam, do you not think?' Abigail tried to keep the note of excitement out of her voice. She had talked quite often lately with Samuel Masham about the growing unpopularity of the Marlboroughs.

'I hope so, Hill. I hope and pray so.'

'But Your Majesty has the utmost confidence in the Duke?'

'Oh yes, Hill. But the Government seems quite angry with him. They are talking of impeachment.'

'It would never come to that, Madam, surely.'

'No, because the Duke will succeed. Of course he will succeed. But the French seem very confident. I have a despatch here, Hill.'

Abigail was trembling slightly. A despatch. So it had come to this. The Queen was going to show her a despatch!

'The King of France gave a great fête and banquet, Hill, at Marly on the Seine, and the banquet was for my step-brother and his mother. He is calling them the King and Queen of England.'

'It cannot be so, Madam.'

'Yes, I fear so. Read this. Read it aloud to me.'

'It was a sumptuous repast,' read Abigail, 'with new services of porcelain and glass on tables of white marble. At nightfall, drums, trumpets, cymbals and hautbois announced that the fireworks were about to begin and after supper the King and Queen of England returned to St Germains.'

'The King and Queen of England!' repeated the Queen. 'You see that is an insult, Hill . . . to me.'

'But it is only the King of France, Madam.'

'And Marlborough has the Army in Germany. Oh dear, I do hope he succeeds in what he is trying to do, for the Government is very angry with him. Really, Hill, I don't know what should be done.'

'We can pray, Madam.'

Pray! Dear, good, pious creature. It was comforting to be with her.

Anne was at Windsor and Sarah in London during that hot August. The tension was too great, Sarah told herself, for her to be able to endure Anne's inanities at this time. It was better therefore that they should be apart and she could trust Abigail Hill to do what was necessary.

She longed for news of John. She was even a little remorseful that, the last time they had been together, she had been so cruel to him. Now that his enemies were preparing to tear him apart she wanted the whole world to know – but most of all John – that she was beside him and would defend him with her life.

What was happening on the Continent? The rumours grew daily. Godolphin was no comfort. Spineless fool! thought Sarah. It was being said that John had disobeyed instructions. Whose? Those who did not know what warfare meant? Those who stayed behind in London and told the greatest general in the world how the war should be run? And they were waiting for disaster. Almost hoping for disaster, not caring if they saw the downfall of England as long as it brought with it the downfall of John Churchill, Duke of Marlborough.

Occasionally letters reached her, but she knew that for every one she received there were two or perhaps more that went astray. John was marching through Germany; he had told her that the weather was alternately uncomfortably hot or, almost worse still, very wet. She knew from the scrappiness of his letters that he was often apprehensive and she wished that she could be with him to encourage him.

It was the twenty-first of August and there had been no news for some time; tension was growing; she was afraid every time a servant knocked at her door that ill news was being brought to her. She, who never found it easy to remain calm, was now overwrought. She bullied her servants and any members of her family who came near her; it was her only way of releasing her feelings.

And on that day the news came. It began with a scratching on her door.

'Yes, what is it?' cried Sarah, her voice almost shrill.

'A gentleman to see Your Grace. He says he is Colonel Parke.'

Colonel Parke! John's aide-de-camp. Sarah cried: 'Bring him to me. No . . . I'll go to him.'

She was running down the stairs and there he was – travel-stained and weary, holding out a letter to her.

'From the Duke,' she cried and snatched it.

> August 13th, 1704.
>
> 'I have not time to say more, but to beg you will give my duty to the Queen and let her know her Army has had a glorious victory. Monsieur Talland and two other Generals are in my coach and I am following the rest: the bearer, my aide-de-camp Colonel Parke, will give her an account of what has passed. I shall do it in a day or two by another more at large.
>
> Marlborough.'

Sarah read the note through and read it through again. No loving message. No word of tenderness. Then she realized that the battle had just been over when he had written that note – it was scrawled on a bill of tavern expenses – and that he had bidden Colonel Parke ride with all speed to *her*. It had taken a week for the Colonel to reach her.

'The Duke has been victorious,' she cried.

'Yes, Madam, and he wrote first to you. He spread the only paper he could lay hands on on his saddle and wrote. Then he said: "Carry that to the Duchess with all speed." '

'To me first . . .' she said. 'Tell me the name of this battle.'

'It was the battle of Blenheim, Your Grace, and it is one of the greatest victories of all time.'

'Blenheim,' she repeated. 'Now,' she went on briskly. 'This note must be carried to the Queen with all speed. You must take it, Colonel Parke. But stay a short while for refreshment. You need it. Then be off.'

'Thank you, Your Grace.'

Sarah herself ordered the refreshment and was with the Colonel while he ate and drank, plying him with questions.

And all the time she was thinking, 'A great victory. And *I* am the first to receive the news. This will be a slap in the face for all our enemies. This will show Mrs Morley and the rest that they had better take care next time before they revile the Duke of Marlborough and his Duchess.'

The Queen was in her boudoir at Windsor – the polygonal room in the turret over the Norman gateway – with Abigail in attendance.

Anne was in a silent mood, thinking of the disagreement of her ministers and Marlborough. It was most disturbing. Abigail had brought her her favourite Bohea tea and ratafia biscuits, but she could not drive from her mind the memory of discord. Mr Freeman was determined to have his way and the ministers were determined to have theirs . . . and that meant strife and great trouble on the Continent.

A scratching at the door. Silent-footed Hill was there.

'Her Majesty is resting . . .'

'This is a messenger from the Duchess of Marlborough. She

says he is to be taken to Her Majesty without delay.'

'Who is it, Hill?'

'A messenger from the Duchess.'

'Bring him in then.'

So he came and bowed to her and put into her hands the tavern bill on which was the first news of the victory at Blenheim.

'A great victory, Madam. The Duke himself says that it is a decisive battle and that it is the greatest victory of his career.'

'My dear Colonel, you have ridden far. Hill, bring some bohea for the Colonel. But perhaps you would prefer something a little stronger. Now tell me everything.'

The Colonel told, and as he did so Anne glowed with pride and pleasure.

'He was justified in his action,' she murmured. 'I am so pleased. He is the greatest general in the whole world and he works for me. My dear Colonel, how can I tell you how happy this has made us?'

'This will make all England happy, Your Majesty.'

'And rightly so. We will have the Duke's note copied and circulated in thousands throughout the City. I do not want this wonderful news withheld a moment longer than it need be. And you, my dear Colonel, shall have your reward of five hundred pounds for being the bearer of such news. I shall never be more glad to see a messenger so rewarded.'

'If you please, Your Majesty, I should prefer a portrait of yourself.'

'My dear Colonel,' laughed Anne, 'your request shall be granted.'

The next day Colonel Parke received a miniature of the Queen set with diamonds; and as Anne realized that this victory was indeed the greatest of her reign she added a thousand pounds to the miniature, that the bearer of such news might be doubly rewarded.

Sarah, flushed with triumph, treasuring the fact that she had been the first person in the country to hear of the victory at Blenheim – even before the Queen – came hurrying down to Windsor. There she took triumphant charge of affairs; truculent, laughing in the faces of those who had dared criticize the Duke, she was ready to show them who was mistress of them all – the Queen included.

'We must,' announced Sarah, 'return at once to London. The people must be made to realize that this is indeed a great victory. There must be celebrations . . .'

'And thanksgiving,' put in Anne. 'We must give thanks to God to whom we owe this victory.'

'Well, Mrs Morley,' cried Sarah with a loud laugh. '*I* think we owe this victory to Mr Freeman.'

Anne was shocked by such irreverence, but she had always known that dear Mrs Freeman had never been really devout.

'We shall be eternally grateful to Mr Freeman,' said Anne with dignity, 'but we must not forget that victory or defeat – both are in the hands of Almighty God.'

'There should, of course, be a thanksgiving service at St Paul's,' cut in Sarah, her mind forging ahead, making plans. A carriage with herself and the Queen. It was fitting that *she* should share the Queen's carriage. This was the Duke of Marlborough's victory and no one was going to forget it.

The Queen was delighted at the prospect of a thanksgiving service and willing enough to discuss it.

'You should be most splendidly attired,' said Sarah, 'and wear your most dazzling jewels. I will choose them. Both should be quite splendid.'

'Oh dear, I am a little worried about Mr Morley. I do hope his asthma will not worry him unduly. These ceremonies tire him so and there is nothing like fatigue for bringing on an attack.'

'I was referring to us, Mrs Morley, for *I* think it only right and fitting that I should accompany you to St Paul's. I am sure Mr Freeman would wish it. You will remember it was to me that he sent the first news of the victory.'

'But of course, dear Mrs Freeman should ride with her unfortunate Morley.'

'I do not think the King of France is calling you unfortunate at this moment!' laughed Sarah. 'Well, I shall choose our jewels and I think we should have the service as soon as possible.'

'I am in entire agreement,' said Anne.

So Sarah and Anne returned to London with Abigail — now relegated to be the chambermaid once more — and in her post as Mistress of the Robes, Sarah chose what the Queen should wear.

Such splendour she could never match, and as she was not one to take second place she decided to attract attention by the very simplicity of her own attire.

They rode from St James's Palace to St Paul's — Anne resplendent, Sarah simply clad: but Anne's jewels could not compete with Sarah's beauty; and in any case she was the wife of the hero of the day.

Anne was elated as she was always by her visits to church, and a thanksgiving service for a great victory must be doubly inspiring.

When they returned and Sarah had dismissed the Queen's attendants, Anne said to her, 'I and the nation will never cease to be grateful to Mr Freeman.'

Sarah bowed her head graciously.

'And I have been thinking,' went on the Queen, 'that it is only fitting that we should show our gratitude, and how better than by bestowing on Mr Freeman and yourself some fine estate.'

Sarah's eyes had begun to shine.

'It would be a magnificent gesture,' she agreed, 'if we could persuade Mr Freeman to accept it.'

'I am sure,' said Anne, with the glint of a smile, 'that if it is *Mrs* Freeman's wish it will be Mr Freeman's.'

'I may endeavour to persuade him,' agreed Sarah. 'What has Mrs Morley in mind?'

'I was thinking of the Manor of Woodstock, a delightful place in a charming setting. It is my plan that that site might be used to build a house . . . a palace . . . for nothing else would be worthy to celebrate this great event . . . for the use of Mr and Mrs Freeman and their heirs.'

'Woodstock,' murmured Sarah, subdued for once. 'It is an excellent spot.'

'Yes, a palace,' went on the Queen, 'which you and Mr Freeman should plan together.'

Sarah's eyes were shining now. A palace! A pile of stones, gracious and imposing, which in the centuries to come should be the home of the Marlboroughs.

'No expense should be spared in the building of this palace,' went on the Queen, seeing how excited her beloved Mrs Freeman was becoming. 'It should be the gift of a grateful nation to its greatest general. I should only ask one concession.'

'Concession?' said Sarah.

'Yes, Mrs Freeman, I would ask that it be called Blenheim Palace so that none should ever forget this famous victory and the man who was responsible for it.'

'Blenheim Palace,' repeated Sarah. 'I like it. I like it very much.'

Intrigue in the Green Closet

Robert Harley sat in his favourite spot at the Apollo Club, indulging his favourite pastime – drinking. Harley enjoyed the night-life of London. He liked the atmosphere of the clubs which were springing up all over the City. He even visited the coffee houses and taverns in order to exchange conversation with literary acquaintances who frequented them. Next to drinking he enjoyed talking, and when Harley talked others enjoyed listening; for he was witty, brilliant and persuasive, in spite of his discordant voice and hesitant delivery.

Since his new appointment – he had recently replaced Nottingham and become Secretary of State for the Northern Department – he still found time to mingle with his literary friends and if he was not at the Apollo he would be at the Rota, invariably accompanied by his friend and disciple, Henry St John, who, naturally enough, had received an appointment at the same time as Harley and was the new Secretary at War.

They had made their way through streets in which the celebrations for the victory of Blenheim were at their height. The coffee houses were full of people sipping hot coffee, chocolate or Nants brandy. The taverns were even more crowded. There were already signs of drunkenness and as the evening progressed these would naturally increase. Harley, with St John beside him, had had to push his way through the crowds.

The comparative peace of the Apollo was very pleasant, so was the taste of good brandy.

Harley looked sardonically at St John and said: 'This could well be called Duke's Day. That screaming hysterical herd will crown the ducal head with laurels when he returns – the victorious conqueror. But remember they would as readily have screamed for that head to be cut from the ducal shoulders and placed at Temple Bar to be spat at and scorned, had the battle gone the other way. There's the mob for you, Harry.'

'Well, 'twas always so.'

'True enough. Nor was I intending to make an original observation in stating the obvious. No, I am merely asking you to observe an action natural to the hysterical screaming uneducated mob and to realize that since it is possible successfully to gauge its reaction, how easily it could be to control it.'

St John looked intently at his mentor.

'Marlborough!' went on Harley. 'That name is on every tongue. The Great Duke! The Victorious Duke! The Victor of Blenheim! He disobeyed instructions from home and by great fortune – for him – he won his battle. Ah, if it had gone the other way. That screaming mass of ignorance would have torn him to pieces. And now, it would appear that we shall be ruled by the Marlboroughs.'

'And so have we been since Anne came to the throne, for does not Anne rule us, and is not Anne ruled by Sarah?'

'Ruled by women. Is it a healthy state of affairs, Harry? For I would take the sad story further and say that Marlborough is ruled by his wife – so we might all call ourselves Sarah's subjects.'

'Has the Queen no will of her own?'

'She has a stubbornness. She comes to a point when she makes up her mind and will not be turned from her opinion – even, I believe, by Sarah. One realizes this by the summing up of opinion which is repeated and repeated in face of all arguments. I often wonder whether even Sarah can break that down. And therein lies my hope.'

201

'Your hope, Master?'

'Well, do you wish to remain one of Sarah's subjects?'

'I loathe the woman, but while the Queen is besotted by her how can we help it?'

'There are always ways, my dear fellow. The Marlboroughs are supreme now . . . at their peak, shall we say. Never can they climb higher than they are at this moment. Now is the time to assess their power, to find their weaknesses.'

'But . . .'

'I know. I know. We are Marlborough's men. We are his protégés. To him we owe our advancement. He trusts us. Now we come to his weakness. It is never wise – in politics to trust anyone.'

'I have trusted you.'

'My dear fellow, we are travelling companions – we go together. Your support is useful to me; my influence is useful to you. We are not rivals. We move in unison. It is the Marlboroughs who are our rivals. If we are not careful we shall find that we must agree with Marlborough in all things – and that, like as not, means obeying Sarah – and if we do not, we shall be *out*.'

St John shrugged his shoulders.

'You would accept this state of affairs? A great mistake, Harry. Never accept anything unless it is agreeable. Pray accept some more brandy for that at least you know to be agreeable without doubt.'

'So . . . you intend to work against Marlborough?'

'You express yourself crudely. Let us say this, Harry, if we would advance we do not stand still. We go forward. We explore the territory and assess its advantages. Well, that is what I intend to do.'

'But how?'

Harley laughed. 'Can you not guess? I shall tell you then, because we are in this together, St John. You know that as I march forward I take you with me. That's agreed, is it not?'

'We have worked together; you have helped me, encouraged me.'

'And when I receive my Government appointments you have yours. We're in harness, Harry. Don't forget. Now in what territory would you reconnoitre if you were surveying the coming battle? You are at a loss, Harry. That's rare with you. In the Queen's bedchamber, my dear fellow! That is the place. And the time is now. You will see I am ready to go into action.'

Glorious days! thought Sarah. Letters from Marl telling of his plans and his love for her. 'I would give up ambition, my hopes for future glory, for the sake of my dearest soul.' They were bound together again and there must be no more follies. She was certain that if by any chance there had been a little truth in the rumour Sunderland had reported to her, Marl had learned his lesson. He would never risk looking at another woman.

She had been down to look at the site for the new Palace. Woodstock was both delightful and romantic. There Henry II had dallied with the Fair Rosamond Clifford, and to avoid the jealousy of Queen Eleanor had had a bower built for her within a maze to which few had the clue. Eleanor determined to destroy her rival, arranged that a skein of silk be put in Rosamond's pocket that it should be unravelled as she walked through the maze, and thus Eleanor, following the silken clue, was led to the bower where she offered Rosamond a choice between a dagger or a bowl of poison.

Rumour! thought Sarah mockingly, knowing how rumour could arise. But the fact remained that Rosamond died soon after her liaison with the King was made known and there seemed little doubt that Eleanor had had a hand in it.

Sarah could well sympathize with the Queen. I'd be ready with the dagger and the poisoned bowl for any woman Marl preferred to me! she thought. But how foolish! He preferred only her. Did she not carry a letter in her pocket in which he told her so with the utmost emphasis?'

The romantic past of Woodstock made even her imaginative. Here the Black Prince had been born; here Elizabeth had been imprisoned; Charles I had sheltered here after the battle of Edgehill; but now in place of Woodstock there would be Blenheim, and when people passed this way they would not think of Elizabeth or Charles or the Fair Rosamond – they would say: There is Blenheim which commemorates one of the greatest victories in English history made possible by England's greatest soldier.

It was a beautiful spot; two thousand acres of parkland watered by the River Glyme. Sarah was impatient, and when she had viewed the site engaged Sir Christopher Wren to draw up plans.

Wren of course was getting old and perhaps it was wise to engage another architect to submit his ideas. She had heard that the Controller of Works was doing a very fine job for the Earl of Carlisle, rebuilding his mansion – Castle Howard. He was the rising architect; Wren was the waning one.

'Your Grace should certainly give John Vanbrugh a trial. He's an amusing fellow besides being an excellent architect. He's the man who writes those witty plays.'

'He can show me what he can do,' Sarah had said; and as a result the plans submitted by John Vanbrugh had been chosen in preference to those of Wren.

So far so good. But there were troubles in the family circle and again it was Mary. She was only sixteen and very beautiful – perhaps the most beautiful of an extremely handsome family.

She was young, but Sarah had seen since that unfortunate affair at St Albans that Mary was the sort who needed to be married young.

She had not talked to Marl about their daughter. He was far too indulgent where his daughters were concerned. In fact had he had not been so devoted to her they might have joined forces against her. But Marl would never do that. Throughout her stormy relationships with her family John had always done everything in his power to bring her children back to her. 'You must listen to your mother. Really she knows best.' And those bold girls of hers – Henrietta and Mary particularly – would fling their arms about his neck and say: 'But Papa, *you* understand. We know you do!' There could have been conflict in the family but for Marl's complete loyalty to her.

And now there was Mary. She remained sullen and on bad terms with her mother. Really the girl should be whipped. And, Sarah told herself and Mary, if I had more time I might be tempted to do so.

Mary's lips curled in contemptuous disregard and it was all

Sarah could do to prevent herself striking the girl.

In any case she knew that she must get her married quickly.

There were suitors in plenty. In the first place who would not want to mate with the Marlboroughs? And in the second, in spite of her present sullenness, Mary was a very attractive girl.

Lord Tullibardine had tentatively approached Sarah and she was by no means adverse to such a match. The Earl of Peterborough's heir was clearly attracted by the girl; and Lord Huntingdon had hinted that he was interested. Besides these there were others whom Sarah could not consider, but it was obvious that it would be the simplest matter to get Mary married.

But every time Sarah approached the girl she was sullen.

'I have no wish to marry any man you may choose for me.'

'So you intend to die unmarried?' demanded Sarah.

'I did not say that.'

'You will marry whom I choose for you or not at all.'

'Then there is no alternative but to die unmarried,' retorted the insolent creature.

'Lord Huntingdon is the son of the Earl of Cromartie,' Sarah reminded her daughter.

'I am aware of it.'

'So you consider he is not good enough?'

'I consider I am too young to marry – as you told me recently.'

'Too young for an unsuitable marriage.'

'I cannot see how suitability affects age.'

'I can see how *your* insolence is affecting *me*.'

That was how it was. Perpetual strife; and now Lord Monthermer, son of the Earl of Montague, was expressing interest.

'Lord Monthermer is a very worthy young man,' said Sarah.

'Being the future Earl of Montague?' asked Mary.

'Those who turn away the best prizes often have to accept something less valuable later on.'

'I am still too young, Mamma, to be interested in these glittering prizes.'

Who would have daughters!

And thus it was. Taking Mary to St Albans in the hope that a sojourn from Court would enable her energetic mother to instill a little sense into her foolish young head; going down to Woodstock, having meetings with John Vanbrugh. It took so much time so she could not be with Anne as much as the latter would have liked.

Mrs Morley must realize how busy I am with my affairs, Sarah told herself. In any case there is Abigail Hill to make sure that everything runs smoothly in my absence. That is exactly why she was put where she is.

So during those weeks when Harley was planning his strategy, Sarah, immersed in her own affairs, left the fort wide open to her enemies.

The Queen was preparing to go into the green closet. George had come to her apartment to accompany her there and was at the moment standing at the window commenting on the passers-by. His remarks were malicious; he enjoyed poking fun at the oddities of others, although, thought Abigail, his own obesity was scarcely attractive; but perhaps this was the reason for his delight in the physical disability of others.

'We are ready now, my dearest,' said Anne.

George turned reluctantly from the window and yawned.

'You'll have your nap, my dear, in the green closet. Hill will make some bohea after a little while and *that* will revive you.'

'The sucking pig was goot,' said George. 'But I think I haf ate too much of it.'

'Dearest, you always eat too much sucking pig – and then there was the wild fowls and fricasse. You'll sleep it off, never fear. Hill, who will be in the closet today?'

'Mr Harley, Madam, and Mr St John . . . among others.'

'Pleasant creatures, both,' said Anne; and they went to the green closet.

Abigail, while waiting on the Queen, was conscious of Mr Harley's interest. Every time she lifted her eyes it seemed that she met his. His smile was warm and friendly; and she wondered what had happened to arouse his interest in her. She did not imagine that he was attracted by her, for she was not an attractive woman, except to perhaps Samuel Masham who was clearly affected by her; but Samuel was not a great politician – merely a humble servant to royalty like herself, meek and never forgetful of his place. Robert Harley was different. He was one of the most important men in the Government; and surely there was only one reason why he could show his interest in a humble person such as herself.

Yet he had not attracted scandal by his affairs with women. He was respectably married and by all accounts was faithful to his wife, although he was a notoriously heavy drinker and a lover of the night-life of London. But what did it mean?

She watched him talking to the Queen. He knew how to pay a compliment and Anne was obviously pleased with his company. And Mr St John could supply his own particular brand of wit.

It was a successful afternoon – Prince George comfortably sleeping without snoring too loudly, Anne sipping tea and listening contentedly while Mr Harley talked of the advantages which had come to the country since the Queen's reign. He did not mention Blenheim, though.

It was when he was taking his leave that he found an opportunity of coming close enough to Abigail to whisper: 'Could I have a word with you alone?'

She looked startled and he went on, 'I have a matter to discuss with you which I think will be of great interest . . . to us both.'

'Why . . . yes,' she murmured.

'I will wait in the ante-room. Come when you can.'

Shortly afterwards she made her way there to find him patiently waiting for her.

'I knew you would come,' he said, his voice warm and friendly.

'You said you had a matter to discuss.'

'Yes, I have made a very pleasing discovery.'

'About . . . me?'

'You and myself. We are cousins.'

'Cousins! Is it indeed so?'

'You are in the same relationship to me as you are to the

Duchess of Marlborough. Your father was my cousin.'

'Mr Harley, is it really so?'

He laughed. 'You seem more surprised than pleased. But I can prove it to you.'

'But of course I am honoured to be so ... so well connected.'

'It was your name that caught my attention. Abigail is my mother's name. It is a popular name in our family.'

'It is scarcely unusual.'

'But that was what interested me and then ... I discovered the connection. I was ... delighted, and I could not refrain from telling you so.'

'It is a pleasure for me,' said Abigail, 'but for you ...'

'You are indeed as modest as I have always heard you are. There is one thing I wished to say to you and it is this: Cousins should meet now and then, should they not? A relationship is a bond. Do you agree? I hope therefore that we shall meet often in Her Majesty's green closet.'

'I am sure Her Majesty will be pleased to see you at any time.'

'And you too?'

'I, of a certainty,' said Abigail with a blush.

She went back to the Queen a little bewildered but pleased. What exalted relatives she possessed! And how much more charming was Mr Harley than the Duchess of Marlborough. He talked to her as though she were a friend – not as the Duchess did, like a poor relation only fitted to be a glorified servant.

Abigail was excited. Why, she asked herself, had Mr Harley seemed so pleased by the relationship? He was not a young man to be easily excited. He was a very ambitious middle-aged one.

A thought came to her. Could it possibly be that Robert Harley, one of the leading politicians, believed the acquaintance of a chambermaid was worth cultivating?

What did Harley want? Abigail was no fool. He wanted a closer relationship with the Queen and he believed he could reach it through his cousin. People were noticing the Queen's fondness for her. This must be the case. It had come to Robert

Harley's ears, and because of it he was proud to recognize his cousin.

For, pondered Abigail, I have been his cousin for a very long time, but it is only now that he has taken the trouble to find out.

She could think of nothing else but Harley's pleasure in his discovery, the courteous manner in which he had spoken to her.

I am important, thought Abigail. Not only to fetch and carry for the Queen, but for the influence I can have with her. I am becoming a little like my cousin Sarah.

What if one day I should be in Sarah's position?

Samuel Masham noticed the change in Abigail.

'Something has happened,' he said when she joined him in the ante-room after the Queen and her husband had retired for the night. 'You are different.'

Did she then betray her feelings, Abigail wondered, she who had always prided herself on so successfully hiding them. She studied Samuel shrewdly. They were very close friends; he sought her company whenever possible and she trusted him as she did few people.

'Nothing has happened,' she told him. 'I have, though, discovered a new cousin.'

'Who is that?' asked Samuel sharply.

'Mr Harley.'

'The Secretary of State?'

'Yes, he asked to speak to me and then told me he had discovered the relationship. He seemed very pleased about it. I have been wondering why.'

'People are beginning to appreciate you, Abigail. I was afraid . . .'

'Yes, of what were you afraid?'

'That perhaps . . . someone was paying court to you . . . and you were rather pleased about it.'

'No, no one is paying court to me, Samuel.'

'You are wrong, Abigail,' he told her vehemently. 'It is what I have been doing for a long time.'

She lifted her green eyes to his. 'But, Samuel . . .'

'I think we could be very happy together, Abigail.'

'You mean . . .'

'I mean in marriage.'

Marriage! She considered it. The Prince's page and the Queen's chambermaid. Their children growing up at Court. She remembered the marriages of the Churchill girls and how Anne had presented them all with handsome dowries. They would make good marriages . . . if their parents were important at Court. No, not their parents. It would be their mother, for Samuel would never be important. Perhaps he knew it. Perhaps that was why he admired her. If she married Samuel – and if she were to have a husband it would have to be Samuel, for who else would want to marry her? – she would guide his destiny as well as her own, as well as their children.

And the Queen was fond of her. Not as fond as she was of Sarah Churchill, of course; but the Queen was capable of great fondness for her female friends. People were noticing . . . That was what she kept coming back to. Robert Harley was anxious to claim her as cousin because people were noticing her, Abigail Hill.

'Well, Abigail,' he said. 'You don't hate me, do you?'

'No, Samuel. You know I'm very fond of you.'

'Fond enough for marriage?'

'I'd like to think about it.'

He was contented. Samuel would be easily contented.

What an exciting life was opening out for Abigail Hill! She was asked in marriage – which was something she had once thought would never happen to her. More than that, ambitious men sought her friendship – because of the influence they believed her to hold with the Queen.

'Good day to you, cousin.'

She was in the garden and she could have sworn he had waylaid her.

'Good day to you . . . cousin.'

'You hesitate.'

'It is a somewhat distant relationship. You were my father's cousin.'

'Well, that makes me yours of a sort, and as I told you once

210

before I am as nearly related to you as the Duchess of Marl-borough. Though I promise you I shall not attempt to treat you with the scorn I have seen her give you.'

Abigail said: 'I was a poor relation.'

'My lady was not always so rich; but she knew how to feather the nest, eh?'

'She is, I am sure, very clever.'

'At feathering nests? But there are times when I think the lady is but one half as clever as she believes herself to be, and do you know, little cousin, it is a very dangerous thing to do to overestimate one's brilliance.'

'I am convinced of it.'

'There may come the day when the Queen of Bedchamber loses her crown.'

'That is scarcely likely to be permitted.'

'The improbability often becomes the possible. You would be surprised how often!'

'And you would be pleased to see it.'

'I did not say so, cousin. But I should always be pleased to see merit rewarded. Pray tell me, will the Queen be receiving in the green closet today?'

'I believe she will.'

'And who is to be there?'

'The Queen will be alone with the Prince. She did not sleep well, so I shall play to her on the harpsichord and perhaps sing a little.'

'I should like to hear you play on the harpsichord. I have always admired your singing.'

She lifted her eyes to his and regarded him steadily for some seconds.

'You wish an audience with the Queen this afternoon?'

'An audience? That has a formal ring. I should like to be there . . . to talk to the Queen . . . soothingly . . . but without others present.'

Abigail's heart began to beat faster.

'Would that be possible?' he asked.

'It might be.'

'If you suggested it to Her Majesty? That I had no tiresome business with which to weary her. Just a dish of bohea . . .'

'It might be possible . . .'

'I should esteem it a cousinly favour.'

'I will speak to Her Majesty. Present yourself and if . . . it is possible, you shall be invited.'

He took her hand and kissed it gallantly.

'How pleasant it is,' he said, 'to have relations in high places.'

A hint of mockery? Perhaps. But his eyes were gleaming; and he was asking a favour.

She was beginning to understand something about him. He hated the Churchills – and so did she. How could one love someone who had done one so much good and never allowed one to forget it?

No wonder she was excited. She had entered into a liaison – strange and mysterious as yet – with one of the Queen's leading ministers. She, Abigail Hill, might yet take a part in shaping her country's destiny.

A delightful man, this Robert Harley, thought Anne. Such pleasant conversation. Hill played the harpsichord softly – a piece of Purcell's which was among Anne's favourites. George dozed contentedly and Mr Harley told her what she most wanted to hear, how fortunate her dear people were to have such a monarch. In the coffee houses and taverns they talked continually of her as the Good Queen. The revival of touching for the King's Evil had touched *them* deeply. Such a clever way Mr Harley had of expressing himself. He hinted that the people of England rejoiced in their Queen and that they felt it was an act of Providence which had brought her to the throne. That was very comforting, for always at the back of her mind was the memory of her father, who had been so devoted to her, and whom she had been led to betray.

Led to betray. Mrs Freeman had been so vehement against him, and in those days she had believed that Mrs Freeman was always right.

Mrs Freeman was still her very best and dearest friend, but she did spend a lot of time away from the Court. She was continually going to St Albans and always managed to be at Windsor Lodge when the Court was *not* in residence. If one did not know what heavy family commitments were Mrs Freeman's, one would almost think she deliberately set out to *avoid* her poor unfortunate Morley.

How her thoughts ran on, and there was amusing Mr Harley being so pleasant.

He had discovered he was Hill's cousin and seemed pleased about it. She was pleased too. It was good for Hill to be connected with a family like the Harleys.

'We have something more in common, Madam, than our cousinship, and that is our desire to serve you – a desire which is unrivalled throughout your kingdom.'

What charming things he said! And when he had gone she told Hill how pleased she was to discover that she had such an exalted relative. Of course she was some distant connection of Mrs Freeman, but Mrs Freeman had never treated her as anything but the humblest of poor relations. Mr Harley on the other hand had nothing but respect for her.

Anne felt a flicker of uneasiness. If Hill became too exalted, might that not alter her? Suppose she became too proud to perform the menial tasks which she now did so cheerfully? Suppose she became arrogant and demanding ... like some people.

Nonsense, said the Queen to herself, that would not be *my* Hill!

That was the first of many meetings, and it became the accepted procedure that on those occasions when the Queen said: 'No visitors,' Abigail would let in Mr Harley and he and the Queen would chat together – not necessarily of state affairs, but now and then they crept in and Mr Harley never made them dull or boring. He explained everything so perfectly and was never arrogant or obscure. Secretly Anne much preferred him to Sidney Godolphin, who was so cold and formal in spite of his timidity and desire to please. Mr Harley amused one and laughed at people in the nicest possible way so that one could not help joining in the fun.

George's asthma was troubling him more than ever, which meant that his night's sleep was often broken; he dozed more frequently during the day and perhaps this was as well, for he had become such a staunch admirer of the Freemans since Blenheim that he might not have appreciated some of Mr Harley's wit.

It was not that it was exactly aimed at Marlborough and his Duchess, but somehow they were included in it; and Anne, in spite of her desire to be loyal to her dearest friend, had to recognize the truth of some of Mr Harley's comments.

Mr Harley was so devoted to the Church, and anyone who cared so much for the spiritual wellbeing of the nation was Anne's friend. Dear Mrs Freeman had never been reverent; in fact sometimes Anne had feared that she was almost irreligious; so how pleasant it was to listen to a clever politician talk with such reverence for the Church!

'The Church,' said Mr Harley, 'could be in danger from certain elements in this country. I am sure Your Majesty would want above all else to keep it strong and aloof from conflict.'

'It would be my first consideration, Mr. Harley.'

'I knew it.'

'And you really think that the Church is being put in jeopardy in . . . certain quarters?'

'I think this may be so, and when I have some proof of this I shall crave permission to set it before Your Majesty.'

'I pray you will without delay.'

He talked to her about the glorious age which was opening out for England. There were certain times in a country's history, he said, which were known as glorious ages. The Elizabethan age had been one; and now there was another glorious Queen on the throne and the glory of the age was becoming apparent through the literature of the times.

There were some in the country who sought to suppress this. One of the greatest writers of the age was at this moment languishing in prison.

Who was this? Anne wanted to know.

It was Daniel Defoe. A charge had been trumped up against him. An age which imprisoned its great writers was defeating itself.

Anne wanted to hear more about Daniel Defoe, and Harley talked of him – his brilliance, his wit, his works. He told how the people had been angered when he was set in the pillory, how they had garlanded him with flowers, had drunk his health and set a guard about him.

Anne listened, indignant.

It was well she had Mr Harley to visit her informally and let her know everything that was going on, for there was much of importance that was kept from a ruler.

Harley was delighted with his discovery of the new relationship. He hoped Abigail Hill understood how important it was. He was certain she did, for there was subtlety behind that demure smile. She had her part to play in this. She was very necessary to him; he never lost a chance of telling her so. His gaze was caressing and Abigail was a little bewildered. He fascinated her, as more than a cousin or a conspirator – for she was well aware that this was a conspiracy. She had never met such a man before. She knew that he was overwhelmingly ambitious, that he was determined to be at the head of the Government, to rule the country; and it was the most flattering thing that had ever happened to her to be selected as his partner. She could not understand her emotions; she was less calm than before and although she hid her excitement she believed that she did not completely succeed as far as he was concerned. He was deferential towards her. Who before had ever been deferential to Abigail Hill, except Samuel Masham? She had shelved that matter for she was too excited by Robert Harley to think very much about Samuel Masham at this time. He paid her delicate compliments – even about her appearance. She was different from the pretty dolls with their paint and their powder and their ridiculously dressed hair. She had character. She was changing. Her sister Alice noticed it. 'Lor, Abby,' she said, 'what's happened to you? Are you in love?' With a subtlety which matched Harley's, she confided in Alice that Samuel Masham had asked her to marry him. Alice was excited. 'Abby! Married! Who ever would have thought it!'

'I have not accepted his offer yet,' said Abigail; a remark which sent Alice into fits of laughter.

'The airs!' she cried. For she did not believe Abigail would refuse such an offer, since when would she be likely to get another?

How could she explain to Alice, even if it had been desirable for her to do so, which of course it was not, that she had matters of far more interest than marriage with Samuel Masham with which to occupy herself.

Sometimes Abigail allowed herself to dream. Suppose Robert Harley were unmarried; suppose he married *her*. She would remain with the Queen; she must never leave the Queen; others less wise than herself might imagine that their influence was so great that they could bully and neglect and keep it. Abigail would never make such a mistake.

To keep Anne's need of one, one must be constantly there, always ready to console, listen, and comfort with those menial attentions (washing feet, massaging limbs swollen with the gout and dropsy, to play, to sing, to do what was required of one at any moment, to make sure that one's absence would immediately be noticed with regret). That was the secret some had forgotten. Not that Sarah Churchill had ever retained her hold on Anne through the comfort she offered. Sarah was brilliant, vivacious, domineering, arrogant; she was the exact opposite of Anne and when they were children the Princess must have admired the forceful girl who had nothing but her good looks and her flamboyant personality. But the Princess had become a Queen and the brilliant Sarah was showing herself to be a fool.

And so would Abigail Hill be if she allowed herself to dream too much. Robert Harley and she were partners, but the love of power was at the root of their relationship. Power for him. And for me, thought Abigail.

I must keep my feet on the ground. I must not let Robert Harley dominate me, for if I do I shall be as foolish as Sarah Churchill has become.

Daniel Defoe was released from prison as a result of Robert Harley's conversations with the Queen; he was conveying to her that while certain people were in power she would be only a cypher, for that was what they intended. There was no doubt to whom the epithet 'Certain People' referred, though as yet Harley had not mentioned the names of Churchill and Godolphin.

To turn her thoughts from Robert Harley, Abigail began to

216

think increasingly of Samuel Masham. He was as yet a page in the household of the Queen's husband. But then she was only a chambermaid in that of the Queen. That was what they appeared to be to the undiscerning. But that could be easily changed.

Lord Masham ... Lady Masham? Why not? Had Harley been free, had his interest in her been due to love instead of her peculiar influence with the Queen, she might have been a Duchess. For it was not difficult to imagine Harley a Duke – never Samuel Masham, though.

But Samuel would do exactly as she wished; there could be many advantages in a marriage with Samuel.

When she was with Robert Harley she forgot all about Samuel Masham. He talked to her in his caressing way which was full of hidden meanings.

It was natural at this stage not to state too openly what their intentions were, but there was one major issue and both were very much aware of it.

Together they were going to bring about the downfall of the Churchills. Harley was going to take the place in the country's affairs now occupied by the Marlboroughs and their faction; and the power behind the throne which for so long had rested in Sarah was to be Abigail's.

The Sunderland Controversy

Sarah returned to St James's and installed herself in her apartments there. From these there was a secret staircase which led down to the Queen's apartment and which in the old days had delighted them both.

Anne was pleased to see her; whenever Sarah put in an appearance she always forgot the alarming thoughts which had beset her previously, for such was the power of Sarah's personality that when she was there Anne still believed that she was the one person in the whole world for whose society she longed more than any other.

'So, Mrs Morley,' she was saying, 'I shall get my Mary married at last.'

'She is so young yet, dear Mrs Freeman.'

'She is old enough for marriage, that one. I can tell you she has led me a pretty dance. Who would have daughters?' Sarah did not notice how her companion winced, nor did she give a thought to the many miscarriages which had become a pattern of the royal existence. So many disappointments that Anne was losing all hope; but that did not mean she wanted continual references to those who were more fortunate than herself.

Didn't her sad mode of signing letters as 'your poor *unfortunate* Morley' explain her feelings? But Sarah was heedless of the thoughts of others. She was without tact, a failing which she called honesty; but that which she saw as honesty in herself she would call rudeness in others. Sarah cared for no opinion but her own – not even the Queen's. In Sarah's opinion Sarah was always right and that applied even when people like Godolphin or even Marlborough himself contradicted her.

Sarah swept on: 'The sooner the marriage takes place the better. It's an excellent match. Both her father and I will be pleased to welcome Lord Monthermer as a son-in-law. He'll be the Earl of Montague in due course and the marriage is as good as those of her sisters.'

'She is only a child.'

'You deceive yourself, Mrs Morley. Mary's no child. She has already found a bridegroom for herself . . . a most unsuitable one, I call tell you. Of course I soon put an end to that bit of nonsense.'

'Poor Mary! I suppose she was in love.'

'In love! My dear Mrs Morley! In love with a man who had nothing but a poor estate! A fine thing for Marlborough's daughter.'

Anne continued to look sad. Sentimental fool! thought Sarah. Why do I have to waste my time with her! What does she ever think of but the cards . . . and food! Of course she must give Mary a dowry like the others. Marl will be horrified if he has to provide the lot.

'This is most satisfactory and I shall be glad to see the girl settled. I hope your Majesty approves of the match.'

'If Mr and Mrs Freeman approve so do I. You must allow me to give her a dowry.'

'You are the most generous friend in the world, Mrs Morley.'

'My dearest Mrs Freeman, you are the best friend in the world to allow your poor unfortunate Morley to take a share in your children's marriages, since she can have no hope of such *personal* happiness.'

'You are so good to Mrs Freeman.'

How much? wondered Sarah. Five thousand like the rest?

Sarah also had another reason for being at Court. Her first grandchild was to be christened and she hoped the Queen would be his godmother.

Anne wept with joy at the prospect.

'The next best thing my dear Mrs Freeman to being a grandmother is to be a godmother.'

'I had hoped you would think so. Godolphin and Sunderland will be the child's godfathers.'

The Queen nodded. She had never liked Sunderland who had voted against dear George's allowance being increased, and that was something for which she would never forgive him; and since she had become so friendly with dear Mr Harley she was beginning to find Lord Godolphin rather tiresome.

'We're going to call him William,' said Sarah. 'His mother has already given him the name of Willigo.'

'Willigo for William. He's named after my boy. It's so charming,' said Anne. 'I long to see the dear little creature.'

So cosy! she thought. It was like the old days when they had talked about their children, when her dear boy had been alive and Sarah's son too. Poor Mrs Freeman, she had lost a beloved son, the same as the Queen had; it made such a bond between them; but Sarah was the more fortunate. She had her daughters and now her darling grandchild. Little Willigo!

The door opened suddenly and Abigail came in; she was smiling and turning, Sarah stared at her in astonishment.

What an unusual way for a chambermaid to enter the Queen's presence! No scratching at the door, no humble approach!

How odd! thought Sarah. How very odd.

Abigail stopped short, seeing who was with the Queen.

'You . . . Your Majesty rang?' she asked.

Anne looked at the bellrope as though with surprise. 'No, Hill,' she said with a pleasant smile, 'I didn't ring.'

'I ask pardon of Your Majesty and Your Grace.'

Anne nodded pleasantly and Sarah haughtily inclined her head, while Abigail closed the door.

Sarah forgot the incident immediately. The manners of the chambermaid were scarcely worthy of her consideration at such a time when she had the marriage of her daughter and the christening of her grandson to occupy her mind.

Abigail stood outside the door and for once she allowed her features to fall into an expression of hatred. That woman had only to appear and she was immediately delegated to the position of humble chambermaid and poor relation.

Would it ever be possible to oust the proud Churchill woman from her place – even with the help of Robert Harley?

During the weeks that followed Abigail began to believe that her fears were justified. Sarah had only to appear and Anne it seemed was ready to forget all past neglect and become her slave.

Never, it seemed, had Sarah been so powerful. In the past they had differed in their views, Anne being at heart a staunch Tory and Sarah inclining strongly towards the Whigs; but now the Whigs had been successful at the polls and even the Queen was favouring them; and because they knew how much they owed to Sarah they were ready to give her the adulation she expected. Tories such as Robert Harley and Henry St John sought her favour – outwardly – and it did not occur to her that they had anything but the utmost respect for her, while like so many others, they hoped for her friendship.

Sarah was more powerful than she had ever been before.

Harley was watching eagerly. The more powerful she became the more careless she grew. Not once during those days when her ascendancy seemed complete did he despair of sending her hurtling down to failure. He hoped that she would continue in her arrogant blindness for he realized that his greatest ally was Sarah herself.

The woman was dazzling, brilliant – and a fool.

Some day, someone was going to carry those slighting remarks about the Queen right back to the Queen. At the moment no one dared ... but the time would come.

In the meantime his friends, the wits and wags of the coffee houses, were playing the part he expected of them, and laughing at the situation; Viceroy Sarah was Queen Sarah now, and sometime their lampoons might reach the Queen.

'And Anne shall wear the crown but Sarah reign,' they wrote.

'Churchill shall rise on easy Stuart's fall
And Blenheim's tower shall triumph o'er Whitehall.'

And then came a chance to discountenance Sarah.

It was only to be expected that Sarah should believe that the Member of Parliament for St Albans should be chosen by her, and she selected as Whig candidate Henry Killigrew whom she was certain, with a little persuasion to the electorate from her, would be elected.

The Tory candidate was a Mr Gape and Sarah set out to attack him, but in spite of her efforts he was elected, and Henry Killigrew, believing that he could not fail if he had the support of the Duchess of Marlborough, was certain that Gape could only have won through bribery, and promptly accused him of it.

Gape took the matter to court where his counsel turned the tables by making a public announcement that the Duchess of Marlborough in her support of Killigrew had been guilty of ill practices. This the Duchess poohpoohed with her usual scorn, but when witnesses were brought forward Sarah's enemies began to chortle with glee.

Robert Harley called on Abigail and they took a little walk in the gardens of the Palace to discuss this interesting affair.

'I've seen Gape's counsel,' Harley told Abigail. 'This is most illuminating. The Duchess of Marlborough has been ordering members of the electorate to Holywell House to give them little homilies as to how they should vote. You can guess what they were like. More warnings than homilies, "If you don't vote as I tell you it will be the worse for you!" I'll swear.'

'But this is certainly an ill practice.'

'No doubt of it. We'll have Madame Sarah taken up for bribery and corruption yet.'

'She must be quite furious.'

Harley laid his hand on Abigail's arm and she lifted her face to his. Sometimes she thought he was fully aware of the effect he had on her. She was fascinated and yet in a way repelled, but the fascination was the strong emotion.

'You allow her to intimidate you, cousin.'

'She is an intimidating person.'

'Don't forget each day you grow farther and farther from her reach.'

'I believe she would still have the power to dismiss me . . . if she should decide to do so.'

'Then we must make sure she is robbed of that power as soon as possible. This affair might well help to divest her of some. She has been telling people of St Albans that Mr Gape and his kind would unhinge the Government; she has paid one man twenty guineas; unfortunately there was no mention in writing that the gift was in exchange for his help in the election.'

'She is the most indiscreet woman in the world, but it seems everyone is afraid of her.'

'It will not always be so, little cousin. This pleases me. Let us hope that she has been even more indiscreet than usual and put something in writing which can be used against her.'

In spite of Sarah's indiscretions on that occasion nothing was proved against her; but her enemies – and in particular the Tories – were loud in their condemnation of her.

And she was as bold as ever. She assured herself that she had done much to procure the Whig support which Marlborough needed to prolong the war. She wrote to the Duke that she wanted more news of what he was doing and assuring him that he could rely on her to look after their interests at home.

She was truly at the peak of her success; she had tried to turn the Queen towards the Whigs and had succeeded, perhaps because the Tories themselves had helped to arouse Anne's animosity. They had not taken into account the fact that the Queen who must now seriously begin to think of her successor was more inclined to favour the House of Stuart than that of Hanover. Anne, a sentimentalist at heart, had never ceased to be troubled by the manner in which she had treated her father; her stepbrother was now at St Germains and what could salve her conscience better than making him her heir; if he would swear to support the Church of England that was all that would be asked of him. She was a Jacobite for reasons of conscience. But the Tories declaring that the Church of England would be in jeopardy if the Stuart was brought back wanted to make advances to Princess Sophia of Hanover and even suggested that she should be invited to pay a visit to England.

The idea of receiving her in England was repulsive to Anne; and when Nottingham suggested in the House of Lords that this must be done for fear the Queen should live till she did not know what she did, and be like a child in the hands of others, Anne was moved to an anger rare with her. To suggest that she might become a victim of senile decay and to do so in one of her Houses of Parliament was too much to be borne.

Had not Mrs Freeman warned her of Nottingham and the Tories? Although she was angry with Nottingham it was such a pleasure to be in agreement with Sarah over politics.

She wrote to her, for she was very happy to be back on the old terms of friendship when letters frequently passed between them:

'I believe, dear Mrs Freeman and I shall not disagree as we have formerly done; for I am sensible of the services these people have done me that you have a good opinion of, and will countenance them, and am thoroughly convinced of the malice and insolence of them that you have always been speaking against.'

So Sarah was back in high favour; and it seemed clear that although she might stay away from Court, and speak contemptuously of the Queen, all she had to do was graciously return and Anne was delighted to have her.

Sarah revelled in her position. She would cut short the Queen when she rambled on. 'Yes, yes, yes, Madam. It must be so!' and would openly yawn.

'How that woman bores me!' she cried to Lord Godolphin, and did not care that servants heard her. 'I'd as lief be shut up in a dungeon as spend my time listening to her bumbling on.'

Godolphin would have liked to warn her but of course he dared not. He was very much in awe of her and carried out her instructions without attempting to disagree with her.

Abigail from the shadows watched in amazement. How could the Queen so forget the dignity due to her rank to accept such conduct! Sarah now performed those tasks which Abigail had been doing for the Queen, although the more menial services of the bedchamber were still left for her to do. To see Sarah hand the Queen her gloves was a revelation. Her dislike for the Queen seemed to be apparent to everyone but Anne. Anne suffered a great deal from gout and dropsy, and Sarah, who was full of health, seemed to find the Queen's illnesses very distasteful. When the Queen talked of her symptoms – which she loved to do – Sarah would turn away disgusted and sometimes when she handed her something for which she had asked she would turn her head away as the Queen's hand touched hers as though, said those who were watching, the Queen had offensive smells.

The relationship between the Queen and the Duchess was discussed at length in the women's quarters. Mrs Abrahal said she was surprised Her Majesty did not send some people packing, that she did. To which Mrs Danvers replied that: Nobody would dare send the Duchess of Marlborough packing ... not even God nor the devil.

Seeing Abigail enter Mrs Abrahal said: 'This puts Hill's nose out of joint, I'd swear.'

Mrs Danvers tittered because, Abigail knew, the nose referred to was too large for the small face it adorned – though adorned was scarcely the right description – and was now, as so often, pink at the tip. Through, she believed they had said of her when they had noticed her rising favour with the Queen and been jealous of it, having it poking where it had no right.

'In what way?' asked Abigail lightly.

'Well, no little tête-à-têtes over the bohea, dear! No little cosy chats with Her Majesty ... not now Her Grace is back! They haven't the time for you now, Mrs Hill.'

'It is natural that when Her Grace of Marlborough is at Court she performs the duties which I took over during her absence. My nose suffers not at all from this perfectly natural procedure.'

Abigail picked up the little dog for which she had been searching and walked calmly out of the room. Mrs Danvers who considered herself the Duchess's woman grimaced at Mrs Abrahal.

'All the same,' she insisted, 'it's a change she doesn't like.'

She was thoughtful. 'There was a time,' she went on, 'when I thought I ought to mention to Her Grace what a friend Her Majesty was making of that woman. Sometimes I used to think that Abigail Hill rather fancied herself as the Queen's special favourite. Well, it shows, doesn't it? Her Grace only has to put her handsome nose in the place and back scuttles Hill to her corner. I needn't have worried.'

They both agreed that she need not have worried.

With Sarah back at Court the pleasant intimacies of the past were lost. Now dressing was a formality. Every time Anne changed her dress she must be surrounded by women who did the tasks which had been allotted to them in order of precedence. Each garment was passed from hand to hand until it reached that of the Duchess who then handed it to the Queen or put on for her. It was on these occasions that Sarah was more and more openly showing her disgust, turning away, nose in the air, as the garment passed from her hands to the Queen's. Every time Anne washed her hands, the page of the backstairs must bring the basin and ewer; then one of the bedchamber women must place it beside the Queen and kneel at the side of the table, and another bedchamber woman must pour the water over the Queen's hands.

When the Duchess was away the ceremony was relaxed, and Abigail Hill was happy to do all the services the Queen desired – no matter how menial; she would put on the Queen's gloves with tenderness, for often Anne's hands were too gouty to do this for herself; she would put on the Queen's shoes in the same gentle manner, and when it was necessary to poultice those poor swollen feet she never allowed a poultice to be too hot on application, and was always ready to suggest it might be getting cold that minute or so before the Queen realized it.

It was Abigail who had brought the Queen's chocolate to her before she lay down to rest; and what comfort it was to sip the warm sweet drink which she so much enjoyed and chat to Abigail of all the irritations or the pleasures of the day.

Of course it was so stimulating to have dear Mrs Freeman at Court. Something was always happening to Mrs Freeman, and it was almost always something to arouse her indignation. With Mrs Freeman there was never a dull moment; and it was pleasant to find that they were not so politically divergent as they once were.

Sarah came into the royal apartments one day, her face purposeful. She received the Queen's embrace coolly and sat down beside her, her lips set in lines of determination.

'I have been thinking,' said Sarah, 'that it is time there was a change of office in the Secretaryship of State.'

Anne gasped. 'But I am very fond of Sir Charles Hedges. He is a very good man.'

Sarah clicked her teeth impatiently, 'Lord, Madam,' she said, 'a man must be a little more than *good* to hold a high office in the Government.'

'But Sir Charles has always given the utmost satisfaction.'

Sarah looked distastefully at the large figure in the chair. She was going to be in one of her stubborn moods and Sarah had counted on getting this matter settled as quickly as possible. What on earth did the fat fool think she was wasting her time here for if it was not to arrange affairs to her liking. Marl had warned her, but she knew her dear cautious old Marl. Godolphin was even more cautious – cowardice she called that. A fine state of affairs with Marlborough abroad and Godolphin afraid and an obstinate old queen on whom so much time had to be wasted.

'Mrs Morley knows that I always make her affairs my constant concern,' said Sarah sternly. 'I do assure her that the time has come for Hedges to go.'

'On what grounds?' asked the Queen.

'He is a bumbling old fool.'

'He has never shown me that he is anything but fitted for his duties.'

'Mrs Morley is apt to form attachments and in her kindness be blinded to truths.'

Here was another suggestion that she was edging towards senility. Anne set her painful feet firmly on their stool and a cool note crept into her voice.

'And whom have you in mind to fill the position?'

'Who could do it but Sunderland.'

Sunderland! Sarah's son-in-law, a man whom Anne had never liked, a man who had opposed the proposal for dear

227

George's annuity! No, said Anne to herself and wished that she dared say it openly to Sarah. No, no, no!

'A brilliant young man,' went on Sarah almost angrily. 'Oh, I know he has had his strange ideas. But what young man worth his salt has not? He is a brilliant fellow. Adventurous!'

'I do not think I should care for him,' said Anne. 'His temper is not one which appeals to me. I do not think we should be friends.'

'Nonsense, Mrs Morley would soon begin to understand him.'

'I understand all I want to now, Mrs Freeman.'

'You don't know the fellow. I'll tell you this: Mr Freeman has not always been fond of him, but now he agrees with me that he has a touch of genius.'

No, thought Sarah, Marl had not always been fond of him. Not very long ago – before Blenheim – he had felt like murdering the fellow. It was Sunderland who had dropped that hint to her of Marl's infidelity and caused them both such anguish. Why should she speak for him now? Because the need for complete power was beyond minor personal irritation. Because Sunderland was a Whig and Hedges a Tory, because he was her son-in-law and it was her desire to make a strong family warhead to fight off all their enemies. Marlborough, Commander in chief. Godolphin, head of the Government. Sunderland, Secretary of State. And Sarah the Queen. Who could stand against that combination? If she could bring that about the whole of the country and of Europe would know who ruled England.

'I do not like his temper,' persisted Anne, 'and should never have a friendly relationship with him.'

'I will send him along to talk to you.'

'Pray do not, Mrs Freeman. I have no wish to talk to him.'

'I do assure you you are making a mistake.'

'I do not like his temper, and should never have a friendly relationship with him.'

Here we go! thought Sarah angrily. The parrot has taken charge of my fat friend.

'If the Duke of Marlborough wrote to you and told you that he believed Sunderland would make an excellent Secretary of State would you believe me then?'

'It grieves me not to be in agreement with my dear Mrs Freeman, but I can say that I know as much as I wish to know of my Lord Sunderland.'

'Personal likes cannot come into such a matter,' cried Sarah.

'I have always found it so useful to be on friendly terms with my ministers.'

'If Mrs Morley would only listen to me.'

'But Mrs Freeman knows nothing gives me greater pleasure than to listen to her.'

'You have set yourself against me on this occasion.'

'It is because I do not like the man's temper and should never have a friendly relationship with him.'

The Queen, who had been playing with her fan, lifted it up to her lips and kept it there. It was a gesture which Sarah knew well and which never failed to exasperate her. It meant that Anne had made up her mind on a certain point and in her obstinate way was not going to be moved from it.

'I can see, Madam,' said Sarah coldly, 'that it is useless to talk to you further . . . on this day.'

Anne did not answer, but kept the fan to her mouth.

'It is time,' said Sarah, 'that I went down to Woodstock to see how the work is progressing. I must say that I am not very pleased at the dilatoriness. Your Majesty knows how long it is since Mr Freeman won the greatest battle in history for you. And they have done scarcely anything yet.'

Anne continued to press her fan to her lips. Sarah thought: She's saying her parrot phrase over and over again in her mind, I'll swear. But she'll come round. I'll see that she does. In the meantime it was a relief to escape from Court and the need to listen to such sentimental or senile bleatings.

Anne was relieved when Sarah went. Sunderland! she thought. That man. Never.

She pulled the bell rope.

'Hill,' she said. 'Send Hill.'

Abigail came, green eyes anxious.

'Your Majesty is unwell?'

'So tired, Hill. So very tired.'

229

'Is it a headache, Madam? Shall I bathe your forehead? There is that new lotion I found the other day.'

'Yes, Hill. Please.'

How quietly Hill moved about the apartment.

'Hill, my feet are so painful.'

'Perhaps a warm poultice, Madam.'

'It might be good. But bathe them first.'

'After I have soothed your head, Madam?'

'Yes, Hill, after.'

Such a comfort to feel those gentle hands; such a comfort to watch the dear creature. She was so different . . . so soothing.

I believe, thought the Queen, that I am *glad* Mrs Freeman has gone.

That was impossible of course. She loved Mrs Freeman beyond anyone . . . even dear George, her own husband. Mrs Freeman was so vital, so beautiful. It was a joy to watch her eyes flash and the sun on that magnificent hair of hers. But that man! After having dared vote against George's allowance! He was a crank in any case. At one time he had talked about giving up his title and remaining plain Charles Spencer. No sign of that when his father had died. He was the Earl of Sunderland now.

'I do not like the man's temper and should never have a friendly relationship with him,' she said aloud.

'You spoke, Madam?'

'I was thinking aloud, Hill.'

'Something has happened to disturb Your Majesty?'

'The Duchess suggests I make Sunderland Secretary of State. Sunderland! I never did like the man.'

'No, Your Majesty, and that is understandable.'

'He has never been a friend to the Prince and as you know, Hill, no one who was not a friend of the Prince could be a friend of mine.'

'Your Majesty and the Prince are an example to all married couples in this realm.'

'I have been fortunate, Hill, in marrying one of the kindest men alive.'

'It is only necessary to see the Prince's care for Your Majesty to realize that.'

'Such a good man, Hill! And Sunderland voted against his allowance and now would like to be my Secretary of State in place of dear Sir Charles Hedges – such a charming man whom I have always liked.'

'How fortunate that it is for Your Majesty to choose her ministers.'

'Of course, Hill.'

Anne felt better already. Dear Hill, always so soothing!

'I hate to disappoint the Duchess, Hill.'

'But, Madam, the Duchess must hate to disappoint you.'

The Queen was silent as a memory of Sarah's flushed and angry face floated before her.

'The Duchess left in a hurry,' said Hill, speaking more boldly than she usually did, for it was rarely that she offered an opinion or an observation. 'She seemed angry. She must be so . . . with herself . . . for having offended Your Majesty.'

Anne pressed the small freckled hand of her attendant. Dear Hill! So tactful! So different.

'I do not like the man's temper, Hill,' she said firmly, 'and I should never have a friendly relationship with him.'

Abigail Hill put on a cloak which concealed her from top to toe and coming out of the Palace sped across the park.

She paused before a mansion in Albemarle Street, knocked, and when she was admitted asked that Mr Harley be told Mrs Abigail Hill wished to speak to him without delay.

She did not have to wait long. She was taken into a drawing room and there was joined after a few minutes by Harley himself.

As ever she was excited by his presence. He was like a different person in his own home – less formal – and she could not help picturing herself as the mistress of such a home.

His eyes were a trifle glassy and as he came into the room even before he approached her she could smell the wine on his breath. But he was by no means intoxicated. She realized that the smell of wine or spirits was always with him; yet never did he appear influenced by it in the slightest way.

'My dear cousin,' he said: coming to her and taking her hands; as he did so the hood fell back from her head and he smiled into her eyes; and in that moment he conveyed nothing but his pleasure to see her, completely hiding the urgent desire to know why she had taken this unusual step.

She did not keep him in suspense.

'The Queen is agitated and even angry I suspect with the Duchess who has suggested that Sunderland replace Hedges.'

He was alert at once.

'Sunderland!' he said. 'What a position! We must not let that happen, cousin.'

'So I thought.'

'And the Queen . . . she is at least angry.'

Abigail nodded. 'She keeps repeating that she doesn't like him and would never be friends with him. Sarah has left in a huff.'

'What fool she is. Thank God! She has left Court?'

'I think so.'

'Make sure of that. She must not have any idea that we enjoy those friendly little sessions in the green closet. If she does that will be an end to them, for she is not such a fool as to allow them to go on.'

'She has no suspicion.'

'We must keep her in ignorance, but I should see the Queen without delay. Dear clever little cousin, find some means of conveying a message to me when you are sure Sarah is well away, and try to get the Queen *alone* in the closet.'

Abigail nodded. 'The Prince . . .'

'Does not count, dear coz, providing he sleeps – and he is almost certain to do that. Hot chocolate is very soothing. Suggest it and get him well asleep. He is inclined to favour the Marlboroughs and might have a favourable word to say for them.'

'He fancies himself as a great soldier and therefore admires the Duke.'

'Now is the time, cousin, to work swiftly and in secret. Sunderland must not have the post. We must prevent it.'

'I will let you know as soon as I am sure Sarah has left Court. Then . . . the green closet meeting.'

'My sweet cousin. It is good, is it not that we can work together thus?'

'It gives me great pleasure to do as you wish,' answered Abigail.

He smiled at her and lifting her hood pulled it up over her head.

'Go now,' he said. 'It would not be good for it to be known you had come here.'

She nodded, excited as always by the conspiracy between them, by the secret allure of this man.

He conducted her down the beautiful curved staircase. She saw an open door and in the room beyond a woman was seated at a table.

She knew who that woman was. His wife!

She hurried down the stairs and out into the air.

How ridiculous it was to dream! And of what did she dream?

She should be content with what was hers, for she had a great deal. She, who had lived in poverty in this City which she now saw straggling out before her, who had been a maid in the house of Lady Rivers, was now a friend of the Queen of England – yes, she was a friend; no one was going to say she was not. Anne was fond of her. Perhaps more fond than she realized. Only, at present she was bemused by Sarah Churchill – perhaps in much the same way in which Abigail Hill was bemused by Robert Harley. Such enchantments gave no satisfaction. There was pleasure in reality. Anne found more ease and comfort with plain quiet Abigail Hill than she ever would with brilliant Sarah Churchill; and Abigail Hill would never find lasting happiness if she looked to Robert Harley for it.

Abigail made a decision as she walked briskly across the Park.

The next time Samuel Masham asked her to marry him she would accept.

The Queen was seated in her chair sipping hot chocolate. So pleasant and Hill made it deliciously. The Prince in spite of his heavy dinner at three o'clock when he had partaken a little too much of the sucking pig, was ready for his chocolate, and as Hill had suggested it, she had had some too.

Hill was at the harpsichord and it was a long time since the Queen had been so contented.

A scratching at the door! How lightly and quickly Hill sped across a room!

Now she was back at the Queen's chair.

'Mr Harley, Your Majesty. He humbly begs to be admitted.'

'Dear Mr Harley. Such a pleasure to see him!'

Harley came in; he bowed; he took the white hand – a little swollen at the moment, but still beautiful – and kissed it.

'Your Majesty is so gracious to receive me thus.'

'My dear Mr Harley I was just thinking what pleasant times we have had here.'

'Your Majesty's goodness overwhelms me.'

'Perhaps Mr Harley would care to take some chocolate, Hill.'

Mr Harley assured the Queen that he had come straight from dinner and would take no chocolate.

Harley complimented the Queen on her looks. He was certain that she looked more healthful than when they had last met.

'My dear good Hill takes care of me,' said the Queen.

'And the Prince seems better too.'

'His asthma troubles him greatly. He had difficulty in breathing last night. It is worse after dinner and supper. I have told him that if his appetite were less good his asthma might be better. But Hill makes a good brew which he inhales and that has brought him some relief. Hill, you must tell Mr Harley about this brew of yours.'

'Yes, Your Majesty.'

'I shall be most interested to hear of it.'

'The Prince's health is a matter of great concern to me,' went on the Queen.

'Your Majesty is such a devoted wife. He is the most fortunate Prince alive.'

'And I am most fortunate to have him.'

The Prince muttered in his sleep.

'It is all right, George,' said the Queen. 'Mr Harley is saying charming things about you.'

The Prince grunted while Harley watched him cautiously. It was when he assured himself that George was fast asleep that he said: 'I've heard a disturbing rumour, Madam.'

'Oh!' The pleasure slipped from Anne's face.

'It need *not* disturb Your Majesty,' said Harley hastily. 'In fact, I am sure it will not because, Madam, you will never allow ambitious people to choose your ministers for you.'

'Is it that man?'

'Sunderland, yes.'

'I do not like the man's temper and I should never have a friendly relationship with him.'

'It is not to be wondered at. Like Your Majesty I do not like his temper and I know I could never have a friendly relationship with him.'

Delight spread across the Queen's face. It was always pleasing when someone took up her phrases and used them as their own.

'Your Majesty will agree with me,' went on Harley, 'that we must not allow this to come to pass.'

'I am so pleased, Mr Harley, that you are in such agreement with me.'

'Your Majesty is so gracious that you forget you are the ruler of this realm.'

'I could not rule it without the help of my ministers and it is necessary that I enjoy a friendly relationship with them.'

'Of the utmost necessity,' agreed Harley.

'And with that man . . .'

'Your Majesty never could.'

'It is so very, very true.'

'I fear, Madam, that there is a conspiracy afoot.'

'A conspiracy!'

'To form a strong alliance of a certain family . . .'

Abigail was holding her breath. This was very dangerous ground. Anyone who had seen the Queen and Sarah together must know how strong were Anne's feelings for her friend. This was coming out into the open most dangerously.

'Madam,' went on Harley hurriedly, for he was well aware of the danger, 'I owe much to the great Duke. I was his protégé. He helped me to my place. But I serve my Queen with all my heart, and if to show my gratitude to those who had been my benefactors in the past means betraying my Sovereign – then, Madam, I must needs be ungrateful.'

'Dear Mr Harley, I understand you. I understand perfectly.'

'Your Majesty's powers of perception have always encouraged me. It is for this reason that I dare speak to you thus now.'

'Pray, Mr Harley, be completely frank with me.'

'Then, Madam, I will say this. It is not good for the welfare of this country that one family should be so strongly represented that it is in fact the ruling family. There is one ruler of this country and one only. I will serve my Queen with all my heart and soul but I will serve no family which by clever contrivance has ousted her from her birthright.'

'Contrivance!' gasped the Queen. 'Ousted!'

'I speak too strongly. I crave Your Majesty's pardon.'

'No, Mr Harley. You speak sincerely and that is what I would wish.'

'Then have I Your Majesty's leave to continue?'

'You have, Mr Harley. Indeed you have.'

'Then, Madam, I say this, that if Marlborough's son-in-law is Secretary of State, while Marlborough is Commander in chief and Godolphin, father-in-law to Marlborough's daughter, is your Lord Treasurer, and the Duchess continues to select your ministers ... then it would seem you are no longer Queen in truth. You will be a cipher to the Churchill family, Madam. And that is something it would grieve me to see; and while I serve my Queen with all my heart and soul I should not serve these ... usurpers.'

There was silence in the green closet. The Queen was shaken. Harley stared down at his hands. Had he gone too far? It was all very well to attack Sunderland and Godolphin; even Marlborough. But Sarah – the Queen's beloved friend!

He was reassured when he heard Anne's voice, a little trembling, but with the obstinacy as strong as ever.

'I could never endure Lord Sunderland's temper and there would never be a good relationship between us.'

Sarah was down at Woodstock harrying John Vanbrugh, who wanted to retain part of the old Manor of Woodstock on account, he said, of its archaeological interest. Sarah, who had no feeling for archaeological interest declared that the house was to be a monument to the Duke of Marlborough's genius and nothing else need be considered. She was unsure of the plans, too. The place was going to be vast, and although she approved of all the very best workmanship and materials going into the building, at the same time she wanted the Palace to be a residence as well as a monument.

This occupied her attention, but she had only shelved the matter of Sunderland and intended to come back to the attack later on. The Queen at the moment was intensely stubborn, but if she was denied the company of her beloved Mrs Freeman for a while, Sarah believed that she would be ready to have it back ... at any price.

Meanwhile the Queen was worried about the Prince's asthma, and consulted Abigail.

'I'm afraid the air here is not as good for him, Hill. His wheeze was terrible last night. I could not sleep for it ... and nor could my poor angel.'

Abigail suggested that a visit to Kensington might be beneficial. It was nearer London than Hampton and she was sure that the air was very good indeed there. Did the Queen remember how well the Prince had been there during their last sojourn?

'Now that you remind me, Hill, I do. We will go to Kensington.'

George was delighted. Kensington had always been one of his favourite palaces. Anne smiled to herself, remembering how as soon as William was dead George had said: 'Now we haf Kensington.' And he had taken possession of the palace without much delay. It was good to see him in a place he so loved. She herself found it delightful and there was the additional interest of seeing how the gardens were progressing. She kept a hundred gardeners at work on it and the result of their labours was beginning to be obvious. The banqueting hall which she had had built was magnificent with its Corinthian pillars and niches in which were branched chandeliers. How pleasant it would be to give concerts and balls there; the public so enjoyed being admitted to the gardens.

'Yes,' she murmured, 'we will go to Kensington.'

237

So they went to Kensington, and when Hill explained that if Her Majesty did not object she would take possession of the apartments which led by a stairway into the Queen's own, Anne agreed that she should. Previously these apartments had been occupied by Sarah and they were consequently more magnificent than Abigail had ever used before. She was delighted therefore with Anne's consent and installed herself there.

Mrs Danvers expressed surprise that she occupied them.

'The Queen wishes me to be close in case I am needed,' said Abigail.

'But those are Her Grace's apartments.'

'I can see no objection to using them while Her Grace is not at Court . . . providing Her Majesty has none.'

Mrs Danvers went away to grumble to Mrs Abrahal that Hill was giving herself airs and she'd like to know what she would be getting up to next.

The Queen was happy to have Abigail in constant attention. The unfortunate affair of Sunderland seemed to have been forgotten and Anne did not seem to be greatly disturbed because the Duchess of Marlborough stayed away from Court.

She gave entertainments and the people were delighted to be admitted to the royal gardens. It was the fashion to attend gloriously clad; and to the sound of music Anne's subjects wandered about, as one of the court writers said, in brocaded robes, hoops, fly-caps and fans.

D'Urfey, the court lyrist, wrote special verses and songs for the occasions and from all over London Anne's subjects flocked to see their Queen.

'Such pleasant days and evenings!' sighed Anne, when she retired to her apartments for the ministrations of Hill.

Sarah meanwhile was consulting with Godolphin as to the next step she should take with regard to Sunderland's appointment; she was also writing at great length to her son-in-law. She wrote to Marlborough, too and told him that he simply must join his voice to hers, for as the victor of Blenheim the Queen could simply not deny him anything.

She visited Kensington to talk to the Queen once more and coming unexpectedly to her apartments there found them in use.

She stood in the centre of the room staring at the bed on which lay a robe. She picked it up and frowned at it, and while she stood there, on her face that expression of one enduring an unpleasant smell, Abigail came into the room, as she told herself later – much later – gaily, brazenly, with a smile on her lips.

'What are you doing here?' she demanded.

'I . . . I . . . thought as these rooms were not being used.'

'You thought *what*?'

'That as the Queen needs me constantly . . .'

'You thought that you might use *my* apartments . . . without my permission you thought *you* might use them?'

'I beg Your Grace's pardon . . .' It was on the edge of Abigail's tongue to say that the Queen had approved her use of these apartments, but no. Sarah would reproach Anne, and Abigail wanted no trouble through her. Far better to take all the blame. So lowering her head she said no more.

'You will move yourself and your possessions without delay,' commanded Sarah.

'Yes, Your Grace.'

Abigail gathered her robe and everything she could lay her hands on; and with downcast eyes scuttled away; as she went she heard Sarah say: 'What can one expect? No breeding. No manners. After all I took her from a broom!'

Sarah had more important things than the insolence of underlings with which to occupy herself; she had spoken to the Queen once more about Sunderland only to evoke what Sarah called the old parrot cry. There was no doubt that Anne was very set against Sunderland's appointment. But Sarah was all the more determined to secure it. She would write to Marl at once and tell him that he simply must add his voice to hers.

In her fury she busied herself with the Queen's wardrobe.

'Mrs Danvers,' she cried angrily. 'It seems to me that some of the Queen's mantuas are missing. I should like to know where they are.'

Mrs Danvers flushed with apprehension, replied that the mantuas were worn and it was the bedchamber woman's prerogative to have her share of the Queen's cast off wardrobe.

'Not without my permission,' stormed the Duchess. 'I am the Mistress of the Robes. Have you forgotten it?'

'Of a certainty I have not, Your Grace, but I believed I had a right to take these mantuas.'

'I wish to see them.'

'But Your Grace . . .'

'Unless I do I shall lay this matter before Her Majesty.'

'Your Grace I have been with Her Majesty since she was a child.'

'It is no reason why you should remain there if you do not give *me* satisfaction.'

'I have always given Her Majesty satisfaction, Your Grace.'

'I am the Queen's Mistress of the Robes and I wish to see those mantuas.'

'I will show them to Your Grace.'

'Pray do – at the earliest possible moment. And I would wish to see the jupes and kirtles and the fans.'

Mrs Danvers, hoping to divert the Duchess's fury said: 'Your Grace, I would like to speak to you about Mrs Hill.'

'What about Mrs Hill?'

'It would seem, Your Grace, that she is too often with Her Majesty.'

The Duchess's eyes narrowed, and Mrs Danvers went on: 'And in the green closet too, Your Grace . . .'

'Do you know, Mrs Danvers, that Mrs Hill has her place through me?'

'Yes, Your Grace.'

'Then, Mrs Danvers, you can safely leave me to decide what Abigail Hill's duties shall or shall not be. Now to those jupes . . .'

Danvers shall go, decided Sarah. She is talking against Abigail Hill whom she suspects is spying for me. We shall see, Madam Danvers, who will go . . . my woman or you.

When she had dismissed Mrs Danvers, after imparting that she had somewhat grave doubts as to the manner in which the Queen's wardrobe was being looked after, she went to the Queen.

Anne was sipping the chocolate Abigail had just brought to her.

'Do try a little, dear Mrs Freeman. Hill makes it most deliciously.'

'No thank you,' said Sarah. 'Mrs Morley is I believe pleased with Hill, whom *I* brought to wait on her.'

'Such a *good* creature, dear Mrs Freeman. Your unfortunate Morley can never thank you enough.'

'I am glad she gives satisfaction, for some in your bedchamber do not.'

'Oh dear . . .' Anne looked alarmed.

'I refer to Danvers.'

'Danvers! Oh, she is getting old, you know. She is like a dear old nurse to me.'

'That is no reason why she should be insolent to *me*.'

'Oh dear me. How terrible! My poor dear Mrs Freeman.'

'The woman is a spy.'

'A spy, Mrs Freeman. For whom she is spying?'

'That we shall endeavour to find out. But she has been helping herself from the wardrobe. She has had four mantuas, she confessed to me. She thought they were her *right* and you had no further use for them.'

'But Danvers has often had these things you know. In her position it is accepted that she should have these things now and then.'

'But my dear Mrs Morley, as Mistress of the Robes *I* should have charge of the wardrobe.'

Oh dear, thought Anne, how my head aches! I shall have to ask Hill to put that soothing lotion of hers on it.

'Danvers must not pilfer from the wardrobe,' went on Sarah.

'I will tell her that she must take nothing without your consent.'

'And she should be dismissed.'

'I will speak to her.'

Sarah was smiling sweetly and bending towards the Queen. 'And there is that other little matter which Mrs Morley has been turning over in her mind.'

'What matter is that, dear Mrs Freeman?'

'Sunderland . . .'

Anne's fan came up to her mouth and rested there.

'I have not changed my mind on that,' she said. 'I could never enjoy a good relationship with him for I could not endure his temper.'

At least, thought Sarah viciously, the refrain has changed a little.

She left the Queen who immediately sent for Abigail.

'Such a headache, Hill.'

No need to ask. Hill was ready with the treatment.

Such soothing fingers! What a comfort to be alone with Hill who did not shout.

And poor Danvers! How could one dismiss a servant who had been with one all one's life?

I shall not dismiss Danvers. I will give a little annuity and special gifts and tell her she must allow the Duchess to have the disposal of the wardrobe.

Anxiety — mainly about this appointment of Sunderland's — seemed to increase the gout. Anne, her feet bound up with poultices, her face red and spotty, her gown unbuttoned, would lie back in her chair and find comfort in little but the presence of Abigail. She was scarcely recognizable as the dazzlingly clad Queen of her public appearances. She was becoming one of the most important sovereigns in Europe and was well aware that she owed this in a large measure to the Duke of Marlborough.

This was enhanced when Colonel Richards, the Duke's aide, brought her news of the great victory of Ramillies.

Marlborough wrote that he wished the Queen to know the truth of his heart and that the greatest pleasure he had in this success was that it might be a great service in her affairs, for he was sincerely sensible of all her goodness to him and his.

Anne read this with tears in her eyes. Dear Mr Freeman! Had she allowed herself to become irritated by all the importunings for that man whose temper she did not like? Such a pity of course that Anne Churchill had married him.

Sarah came to see her, beaming with delight.

'Why, Mrs Morley, do you realize what this means. It is the greatest victory since that of Blenheim which Mr Freeman won for you. This is going to make a difference to the whole course of the war. I have heard that Louis is desolate . . . quite desolate. I can assure you that the enemy trembles . . . yes, trembles at the very mention of Marlborough's name.'

'It is indeed a great victory, Mrs Freeman, and I shall never, never forget the genius of Mr Freeman.'

'It would give him great pleasure to see Sunderland's appointment.'

Even on such an occasion Anne retained her stubbornness.

She turned her head away. 'Dear Mr Freeman will have much to occupy him on the Continent. There must be a thanksgiving service for this victory. I will speak to my Lord Godolphin of my wishes in this matter.'

Sarah did not pursue the subject of Sunderland which was a great relief to the Queen. In fact Sarah was a little subdued which, in the circumstances was surprising, but when she told Anne the reason, Anne was full of sympathy and understanding.

'It might easily have been the end of Mr Freeman,' Sarah burst out. 'I can scarcely bear to think of it, for when I do I must remind myself that every hour he spends over there he is in danger. It was so nearly the end at Ramillies.'

'My poor poor Mrs Freeman!'

'He was leaping across a ditch when his horse was shot from under him; he fell. If his aide, Captain Molesworth, had not been there to give him his horse, the Duke might have fallen to the enemy. I shudder to think of it.'

In a moment of rare introspective Sarah saw life without Marlborough. She could not have endured it. She almost wanted to throw away ambition, to have him safe with her at Holywell House, home and safe.

'That's not all,' she said grimly. 'While his equerry, Colonel Bringfield was helping him to mount, a cannon ball struck the Colonel and took his head right off. It might so easily have been . . .'

'It was Providence, dearest Mrs Freeman,' soothed Anne.

'I have been to see the Colonel's widow,' went on Sarah. 'Poor creature. She is nigh on demented. I comforted her and told her what a great service her husband had done to his country and that you would not wish to let it go unrewarded. I promised her a pension, knowing my dear Mrs Morley's generosity, I was sure it was what she would have wished.'

'Certainly she must have a pension. Oh, this terrible war! I shall give such heartfelt thanks, Mrs Freeman, not only for this glorious victory, but for the preservation of dear Mr Freeman's life.'

Godolphin sat beside the Queen and told her what this would mean.

'The King of France lost one of his finest armies at the Battle of Blenheim, Madam, besides all the country between the Danube and the Rhine. But with his defeat at Ramillies he has lost all Flanders.'

'The Duke is a genius,' replied Anne.

'It will be said of him that he helped to make England great, Madam.'

'News has reached me that the French are desolate . . . quite desolate.'

'In a panic, I should say Madam. Marshall Villeroy was afraid to acquaint his master with the disaster and remained shut in his tent five days.'

'Poor old man,' said the Queen. 'I hear he is turned sixty.'

'Louis himself is almost seventy.'

'It is a pity that old men, so near the end, should be concerned with killing others. But that is war, Mr Montgomery.'

Godolphin was pleased that the Queen should have slipped back to the familiar name with which she had endowed him. Since she knew that he supported Sarah in her demands for Sunderland she had dropped the pet name and referred to him formally as my Lord Godolphin. Ramillies, he realized, had made her see what she owed to the Churchill family; and as a member of it, by marriage, he shared in the glory.

'Well,' went on the Queen, 'let us hope that the end of war is in sight . . . a victorious end. For I would rather see money spent on improving the lot of my people than in killing them.'

'There is no doubt, Madam, that the Duke's victories in France are improving the lot of your subjects.'

'You are right, Mr Montgomery, and we must have a thanksgiving service at St Paul's to remind them of all they owe to God for this great victory.'

'And to the great Duke,' Godolphin reminded her.

'And to the Duke,' echoed Anne.

There was consternation throughout the Court. Sarah was ill.

Her servants had gone to her room and found her lying on the floor in a fit.

As the news spread there was more excitement than there had been over the news of the victory at Ramillies. Sarah dead! What would happen at Court then? Who would take her place?

Never had Abigail found it so difficult to cloak her feelings. The feared and hated rival gone. To what glory might *she* not come? The battle would be over; Abigail had no fears as to who would step into Sarah's place. She wondered what *he* was thinking and could guess. This would make a difference to everything.

But when she saw how distressed the Queen was she felt uneasy.

'Hill, Hill. Have you heard the news? Oh my poor dearest Mrs Freeman. What should I do if I lost her? I have suffered many tragedies in my life Hill, and among them the greatest a mother can endure! The loss of my boy. But if Mrs Freeman should die . . . if she should leave me . . .'

'Madam, you must not distress yourself,' said Abigail, interrupting for once. But Anne did not notice this; she allowed Hill to put an arm round her and hold her against her breast.

'Oh, Hill, Hill she has been so close to me . . . for so many years.'

Abigail looked down at the red, flabby face, wet with tears, and understood the repulsion Sarah did not trouble to disguise.

How could Anne be so besottedly fond of that woman who would never have bothered to speak to her if she had not been Queen. One thing was clear: Anne could not escape from the spell of Sarah Churchill. Abigail thought of these last months when Anne had been perpetually bullied over this matter of

Sunderland and she could not understand the Queen's sincere grief.

'My doctors must be sent to her at once, Hill.'

'Yes, Madam. I will pass on your orders.'

'Thank you, Hill. I don't know what I should do without you. And even you . . . I owe to her.'

Yes, thought Abigail, that was the irony of the situation. The more devoted Anne became to Abigail, the more grateful she must be to Sarah.

Before the thanksgiving service Sarah had recovered. She came to the Court, only a little paler than usual and certainly not in the least subdued.

The Queen embraced her warmly. 'My dearest, *dearest* Mrs Freeman, what anxieties I have suffered on your behalf.'

'I am recovered now. You did not think I would stay away from the thanksgiving to Marlborough, did you?'

Anne did not remind her that it was a thanksgiving to God; Sarah could not see it that way; and in any case she was really quite irreligious.

'I am so happy to see you here,' said Anne sincerely.

'I must of course decide what jewels you will wear.'

'Hill has already put them ready. We thought to save you trouble, Mrs Freeman.'

'A chambermaid putting out your jewels! What do you expect her to choose? No, Mrs Morley, that will not do. Those rubies. Ridiculous! They shall all be taken away and I shall make up my mind what will best become the occasion.'

'I thought Hill made a good choice.'

Sarah blew her lips, dismissing Hill and her choice. She was smiling. 'I have written to Mr Freeman. Poor man, they had told him of my illness. I would not have had him disturbed. He threatens to leave everything and come back to me.'

'Such a devoted husband! How fortunate we are . . . both of us. Not many women have husbands like ours.'

Sarah's lips curled in disdain. This comparing of fat stupid George with Marl was more than she could stomach.

She went on: 'I told him I should soon be well. It was the anxiety of the battle and then of course this affair at Ramillies when I might so easily have lost him. There are so many anxieties at home. I am not sure that Vanbrugh is the man for Blenheim. I don't get on with him at all. Then of course those from whom I would expect friendship will not listen to my advice.'

Anne's lips set sternly. In a moment, Sarah thought, she will be telling me that she can't endure his temper and won't have a good relationship with him. In which case I shall scream to her to stop or she'll send me into another fit.

Sunderland shall most certainly have the post but this is perhaps not the time.

So Sarah busied herself with choosing the Queen's jewels while Anne told her how worried she was about George's asthma which was undoubtedly getting worse.

'He is so bad during the night, Mrs Freeman, it breaks my heart to watch him. He worries about me. He says it is too much for me to help him, but I remind him that he is my very dear husband and that it is my privilege.'

'You should have one of his pages sleep on a pallet in the room while you have a chamber to yourself and get your rest.'

'We have shared the same bed for so many years, and he admits that he would not rest without me beside him. And nor should I without him. But do not concern yourself, dearest Mrs Freeman. Your unfortunate Morley is well served. I have Hill sleep on a pallet in the antechamber so that I can call her at a moment's notice. She is such a good creature. I never have to call her twice. There she is ... so ready ... so willing. Neither the Prince nor I know what we should do without her. And I always remember I have to thank *you* for her.'

'I took her from a broom, as you know, and she is eager to show me her gratitude. I have told her that she can best please me by pleasing you.'

'Dearest Mrs Freeman, how can I ever repay you?'

Sunderland? thought Sarah. No perhaps not yet. After the ceremony. That would be the time.

Anne, dressed in a splendid gown over a petticoat of cloth of gold, adorned by the jewels of Sarah's choice looked very different from the poor creature who a few days before had sat slumped in her chair, her feet in wrappings that concealed the poultices.

She looked at George in his embroidered suit which was trimmed with silver. So splendid he looked and yet the sight of him broke her heart. He had had a trying night and his wheezing had frightened her. She had been obliged to call Hill three times. How comforting Hill was in the middle of the night; and how quickly she came to the call! She almost seemed to *sense* that she was needed.

'George,' she said, 'I'm afraid it is going to be a long day.'

'I vill be viv you, my love,' George told her.

'I shall watch you, and I shall insist on your return to the Palace if you feel ill. I have told Masham to be watchful.'

George nodded and smiled at her. Poor dearest George! He was becoming fatter and more feeble every day.

Sarah looked splendid. She never overdressed on such occasions, relying on personal charms. In any case she was the wife of the hero of the occasion.

'My dear Mrs Freeman must ride in my coach,' said Anne.

'I am sure the people would expect it,' Sarah replied.

'I am worried about George,' Anne told her.

'I agree with you that he is not well enough to accompany us. It is such a strain on him and we should not wish him to have an attack during the service.'

'I should be so anxious.'

'Then he should remain behind. Let Masham and Hill look after him. You can trust them.'

'I can certainly trust Hill and she seems to be able to manage Masham too.'

'She is very eager to please me,' said Sarah.

And she was delighted to ride in the royal coach with the Queen, with the horse and foot guards to escort them – all splendid in new uniforms for the occasion; the streets were lined with people who had come out to cheer the Queen and the wife of the hero; and the sound of music from the bands filled the air.

The Lord Mayor and Sheriffs met the Queen and Duchess at Temple Bar and led them to St Paul's where the Dean of

Canterbury preached the thanksgiving service.

There were fireworks that night and a salute of guns was fired from the Tower.

The coffee houses were crowded; but as the day wore on it was to the taverns that the people made their way to drink to the health of England, the Queen and the Duke.

There was singing and dancing and some grew quarrelsome. In his club Harley sat with St John and some of his literary friends – Defoe, who would always owe him a debt of gratitude, Dean Swift who liked to air his views, Joseph Addison and Richard Steele.

The wit and the wine flowed freely and it was Harley who pointed out what Marlborough's victory cost the country in taxes and the blood of its menfolk. He pointed out too that a country's affairs were not guided so much by the sword as the pen – a theory which, since his listeners were wielders of the pen and not the sword, they were ready to endorse.

It was a theory, Harley pointed out, that he would like to put to the test. He did not see why it should not prove very effective.

The talk went on and it was profitable talk, so Harley told St John afterwards. They would see whether his army of writers could not achieve as resounding a victory as Marlborough's with his soldiers.

And over the Prince's sleeping body Abigail Hill promised to become the wife of Samuel Masham.

'My dearest Soul,' wrote Marlborough to Sarah. 'My heart is full of joy for this good success that should I write more I should say a great many follies.'

Sarah kept his letters and read and re-read them. She had chided him after the affair of Ramillies, telling him what terrible anxiety he caused her by his recklessness.

'As I would deserve and keep the kindness of this Army [he replied], I must let them see that when I expose them I would not exempt myself. But I love you so well and am so desirous of ending my days quietly with you that I shall not venture myself but when it is absolutely necessary. I am so

249

persuaded that this campaign will bring us a good peace that I beg of you do all you can that the house at Woodstock may be carried up as much as possible that I may have a prospect of living in it.'

She would do it. She would go down to Blenheim and harry them; she would give John Vanbrugh a talking to. But most important of all the war must be carried to a successful conclusion. The Whigs had made it clear that unless Sunderland – that Whig of Whigs – were made Secretary of State they would not give their support to the war; and even Godolphin admitted that the appointment was necessary if the means of carrying on the war were to be provided.

Sarah sent for him and he came humbly. He had been against the appointment in the first place and she had had to persuade him to it, but now he agreed with her.

'You see,' she said triumphantly. 'Sunderland must have the appointment. The Whigs insist.'

Godolphin, who could always be browbeaten by Sarah, shook his head mournfully.

'The Queen continues stubborn.'

'She must be brought to heel.'

He could not resist a smile at the simile, Sarah talking as though the Queen of England was a dog! But Sarah saw nothing amusing in her remark. She was weary of the matter which she told herself should have been concluded long ago.

'I would write to Marl,' she said, 'and get his support. The Queen would never be able to refuse him now. But he is so busy with his campaign and I feel it is a matter which we should be able to settle here.'

'If the Queen will relent for anyone it would be for you.'

That was true. 'Leave it to me,' said Sarah. 'I have been trying to persuade her. Now I shall have to force her.'

Godolphin said that he would write to the Queen and tell her that the prosecution of the war depended on the appointment. If that did not suffice, they must find some other means of persuading her.

The result was a letter from Anne in which she set out her objections to accepting Sunderland. When she was dealing with her Lord Treasurer she had a more valid reason to offer than the fact that she did not like Sunderland's temper and did not feel she could have a good relationship with him.

Sunderland was a party man and in making a party man Secretary of State she was throwing herself into the hands of a party.

'That [she wrote], is something which I have been desirous to avoid, and what I have heard both the Duke of Marlborough and you say I should never do. All I desire is my liberty in encouraging and employing all those that concur faithfully in my service whether they are called Whigs or Tories – and not to be tied to one or the other; for if I shall be so unfortunate as to fall into the hands of either, I shall look upon myself, though I have the name of Queen, to be in reality but their slave.'

This was reasonable, Godolphin had to admit; but it was necessary, if there was to be Whig support for the war, to secure Sunderland's appointment.

Sarah was never inclined to listen to anyone else's point of view. Godolphin was too mild, she said, so she would take over. She began by writing long letters to the Queen in which, because they were written by Mrs Freeman to Mrs Morley, she seemed completely to forget the respect she owed her sovereign. Sarah was angry and impatient and she believed that Anne was quite devoted to her and was in such need of her friendship, that she would accept any insult.

'Your security and the nation's is my chief wish [she wrote], and I beg of God Almighty as sincerely as I shall do for his pardon at my last hour, that Mr and Mrs Morley may see their errors as to this notion before it is too late; but considering how little impression anything makes that comes from your faithful Freeman, I have troubled you too much and I beg your pardon for it.'

Anne was with Abigail when this letter arrived and, reading it through, paused when she came to the word notion. Sarah

251

had written in great haste and her scrawl was not always easy to read; and Anne read the word notion as nation.

A dull resentment seized her. Was Mrs Freeman suggesting that she and dear George had wronged the nation? Oh, but this was too much to take – even from Mrs Freeman.

'Hill,' she called. 'Hill, come here.'

Hill came and stood demurely before her, but there was alarm in the good creature's eyes. 'Your Majesty is unwell?'

Anne shook her head. 'I am . . . disturbed. I think my eyes deceive me. Yours are younger. Read this to me. Begin there.'

Abigail read in a clear distinct voice: '. . . Mr and Mrs Morley may see their errors as to this nation . . .'

There! She had read it. It was true. Abigail was staring at the Queen with round horrified eyes.

'But, Madam . . .'

'It is most uncalled for!' cried the Queen, almost in tears, 'the welfare of the nation has been my chief concern since I came to the throne.'

'Madam,' said Abigail. 'I am overcome with shame that a connexion of mine could be capable of such . . . such false-hood.'

'There, Hill. You must not be upset. She has whipped herself to a fury, I suppose. I shall try to forget it.'

'And Your Majesty wishes to answer this . . . insult.'

'No, Hill, I think I shall ignore it.'

It was Lord Godolphin who heard the reason for the Queen's silence. She showed him the letter.

'It would seem,' said Anne coolly, 'that the Duchess of Marlborough forgets that I am the Queen.'

He read the letter and stuttered over it.

'But, Madam,' he said, 'the word is not nation. It is notion.'

'Notion,' repeated Anne. '. . . may see their errors as to this notion . . . That is different, of course. But you will agree with me, my lord Treasurer, that the tone of the letter is scarcely that of a subject to her Sovereign.'

Godolphin smiled apologetically. 'The relationship between Your Majesty and the Duchess has not always been that of

Sovereign and subject. I will tell the Duchess of this unfortunate mistake and I doubt not that she will wish to write you an apology.'

Anne was pleased, for although this matter of Sunderland was very tiresome indeed she could not bear to be on bad terms with Sarah.

In due course Sarah's 'apology' reached the Queen.

'Your Majesty's great indifference and contempt in taking no notice of my last letter, did not so much surprise me as to hear my Lord Treasurer say you had complained much of it, which makes me presume to give you this trouble to repeat what I can be very positive was the aim of the letter and I believe very near the words . . .'

She then set out more or less what she had written in the previous letter in the same high handed manner and gave it into Godolphin's hands to deliver.

Anne however still kept her resentment against Sarah and confided to Abigail that she was heartily sick of this matter of Sunderland and the Secretaryship; and Godolphin was obliged to report to Sarah that she was no nearer her goal than she had been when the unfortunate letter writing had begun.

But Sarah was more determined than ever to have her way and she wrote to the Duke and told him that he must write to her and tell her that if the Queen did not make Sunderland Secretary of State he would resign from the Queen's armies.

When Marlborough realized that the Whigs would withdraw their support unless Sunderland received the appointment he was obliged to give his consent; and this letter Sarah sent to the Queen.

It was the ultimatum. Anne needed Marlborough, and she could not endure the thought of Sarah's leaving Court.

She gave way, because there was nothing else to do. But she was resentful.

She sat silently while Abigail poulticed her feet, and when Sarah's name was mentioned her lips hardened, her fan went to her lips and stayed there.

The Masham Marriage

Harley, watching events closely, was not sure how great a victory this was for the Churchills; indeed he was hoping that it might be turned to a defeat. Anne had been shown that she had not a free hand to choose her ministers. It was a blow for her. With the appointment of Sunderland the Tories were now out of the Privy Council; the Whigs were in power and the only Tories who remained in office were Robert Harley and Henry St John, two men on whom Marlborough and Godolphin had believed they could rely.

Sarah was triumphant. She was more arrogant than ever.

But Abigail was aware of a great confidence which had come to Robert Harley; and she shared in it.

She had told the Queen that Samuel Masham had asked her to marry him and Anne was delighted. She would give the marriage her blessing, which meant a handsome dowry as well; and she did not suggest that Sarah should be told.

That was significant. The relationship between Mrs Morley and Mrs Freeman had not been strengthened by Mrs Freeman's victory.

*　　　*　　　*

There seemed no reason why Abigail's marriage should be delayed any longer. Samuel was eager for it and Abigail was willing.

Dr Arbuthnot, the Queen's Scottish doctor, who had learned to admire and respect Abigail during their encounters in the sick-room, was interested in the couple.

'I would not care,' he had said, 'to see Your Majesty bereft of Mrs Hill. This is a marriage after my own heart, for the bride's home will still be in Your Majesty's bedchamber.'

'I am pleased too,' agreed Anne, 'for I could not do without Hill. And it is a great pleasure to me to see her happy. I have had the best husband in the world and my marriage would have been completely happy if it had been . . . fruitful.'

'Well we'll hope that Mrs Hill enjoys both the felicity and the fruit, Madam.'

'I shall pray that she does.'

'And when is the ceremony to take place, Madam?'

'You must consult Hill about that, Dr Arbuthnot,' said the Queen benignly.

So the doctor did. It was difficult, Abigail explained. She could scarcely expect to be married in the royal apartments, and she was anxious for the marriage to remain something of a secret for a time. She and Samuel wanted no hindrances.

Dr Arbuthnot nodded. Like Abigail he was thinking of the Duchess of Marlborough. She had no right to interfere with Abigail's marriage, but she was not one to look for a right before interfering.

This matter of Sunderland had in Arbuthnot's opinion not helped the Queen's health. He had said to his wife: 'The more we keep that woman from the Court the better for Her Majesty.'

'Mrs Arbuthnot would take it an honour if you were wedded in our apartment,' he said.

Abigail's plain face was alight with pleasure.

'Oh, doctor, that is kind of you and Mrs Arbuthnot!'

'Get away with ye,' said the doctor. 'We'll be glad to do a turn for you.'

When Abigail went back to the Queen, Anne noticed that

she was looking pleased and Abigail told her of Dr Arbuthnot's suggestion.

'He is a good man,' said Anne. 'I am pleased. Sit down, Hill. Oh dear, I shall have to learn to call you Masham. I shall come to the wedding to give you my blessing, my dear.'

Abigail took the swollen hand and kissed it.

'How can I ever thank Your Majesty.'

'Hill, I have much for which to thank you. You are a comfort to me . . . a very great comfort.'

There was silence for a few moments then Abigail said: 'Madam, Masham and I thought that it might be better to keep our marriage a secret for a while. There might be some who, in the first place, might try to prevent it and, in the second, might grow angry because permission had not been asked. Have I your Majesty's permission to avoid this . . . this inconvenience?'

Anne's lips tightened for a moment. Abigail without looking at her was aware of this and knew that she was thinking of the Duchess of Marlborough who had so recently scored the victory of Sunderland – at least she thought it was a victory.

'I think it is good, Hill, always to avoid inconvenience when possible.'

The matter was settled.

Abigail Hill was to be married to Samuel Masham in the apartments of Dr Arbuthnot. The Queen would be present – but the Duchess of Marlborough should be kept in ignorance of the event.

Mrs Danvers had been feeling unwell for a long time, and one morning she awoke and said to herself: 'I believe I am dying.'

She rose from her bed and tottered to her mirror. Her face looked yellow. Of course she was getting old. She had come to the Queen when Anne was a young girl and had been with her all through the reigns of Charles II, James II, William and Mary, and now Anne's own. Not that they were long reigns, but still they represented a number of years.

Life had been interesting, living close to great events; perquisites had been rewarding – at least they had until Her Grace of Marlborough had become so watchful of the wardrobe.

And today Her Grace might be coming to visit her, on the invitation of Mrs Danvers herself. On the other hand she might not come, for the Duchess of Marlborough could ignore what was almost a summons from one in Mrs Danvers' position.

'Lord,' thought Mrs Danvers, 'I'd never dared have asked her but for the child.'

The child was her daughter – not such a child either, for she was old enough to have a place in the Queen's bedchamber. Of course she could have asked the Queen herself and been sure of a sympathetic hearing; but over the last years it had become a habit only to ask favours of the Queen through the Duchess. For if the Queen granted a favour and the Duchess thought it should not have been granted, she would find some means to prevent the benefit being bestowed.

All those about the Queen had long ago realized that it was the Duchess who ruled.

Nothing could change that, Mrs Danvers told herself, nothing at all. That was why, in spite of the Duchess's overbearing manner one continued to placate her, and realized that it was necessary to serve her.

Lately there had been a change in the immediate royal circle. The Queen was clearly growing more and more incapacitated; but she did not seem to fret for the Duchess's company as she once did. It was always: 'Hill! Hill! Where is Hill?'

One would have thought that Hill had been the servant who had been with her since she was a child, by the confidence she put into that young woman!

Danvers did not like Hill. Hill was calm, never lost her temper, never answered back; but Mrs Danvers was convinced that Hill was 'deep'. When the Duchess was angry the whole Court knew it; she was frank and open, as she was fond of saying. With Hill it was another matter.

One had to beware of Hill. Everyone should beware of Hill. Perhaps even the Duchess.

Mrs Danvers had been turning over in her mind for some time how to approach this matter, how to explain why she, the humble Danvers, had dared ask the mighty Duchess to visit her. She could not say: 'I want you to look after my daughter when I am gone.' But she could say: 'I think I should warn Your

Grace that something strange is going on between the Queen and Abigail Hill.'

She dressed slowly and rested, for the Queen had given her leave of absence from her duties and as she lay on her bed she rehearsed what she would say if and when the Duchess arrived.

Sarah came to the Castle from the Lodge. She intended to see the Queen over the matter of a certain Mrs Vain for whom she wanted a place in the bedchamber.

The Queen had been piqued since the affair of Sunderland, but Sarah had made up her mind that she would not allow such nonsense to persist. There was no need for Anne to sulk because Sarah and her ministers had made her see that her duty to the country came before personal prejudice.

It was for this reason doubtless that she had refused the appointment to Mrs Vain. Godolphin had asked for it and Marl was in favour of it. The woman would be a friend to them and Godolphin and Marlborough believed they needed more friends in the bedchamber.

'I have installed Hill there,' she had told them. 'Hill will never forget what I have done for her.'

'Hill is too dull and too servile. She scarcely sees anything,' was Godolphin's answer.

'No, but she is often with the Queen and I fancy no one would dare speak against me in Hill's hearing knowing her to be my woman and that I should certainly be told.'

'All the same it would be good to have Mrs Vain there.'

'I will speak to her this very day,' Sarah promised.

She scarcely waited to greet the Queen before she brought up the matter of Mrs Vain.

'Such an excellent woman, Mrs Morley. I can vouch for her. I know that she would give you good service.'

'I am sure anyone recommended by Mrs Freeman would be excellent.'

'Then I shall send her to you without delay.'

'But,' said Anne, 'I do not want a bedchamber woman.'

'Mrs Vain is a most agreeable creature.'

'I am sure she is all that Mrs Freeman says she is.'

258

'Danvers has not been looking well lately.'

'Poor Danvers, I fear she is getting old.'

'She should be sent away for a holiday. With Mrs Vain in attendance she would not be missed.'

'We could manage very well without Danvers for a while.'

'There would be no need to *manage*. With Mrs Vain . . .'

'But I do not want a bedchamber woman,' said Anne. 'And when I have one, she will not be a married woman.'

'My dear Mrs Morley must take greater care of her health.'

'I am very well served and Mrs Freeman need have no fears on that account.'

'But with Danvers' health failing . . .'

'Hill and the others manage very well.'

'I will send Mrs Vain to you and then Your Majesty will see for yourself.'

Anne's fan came up to her lips and stayed here.

'I do not want a bedchamber woman,' she said. 'And when I do I shall choose an unmarried woman.'

Really, thought Sarah, this was becoming too tiresome when there had to be a battle over the installation of a new bedchamber woman! But it was no use talking to Anne when she was in that mood.

Sarah took her leave and went to keep her appointment with Mrs Danvers.

The woman certainly looked ill.

'It was good of Your Grace to come,' she said, curtseying with great respect.

'What's the matter, Danvers?'

'I am getting old, Your Grace and I fancy I haven't long for this world. I have something on my mind . . . and I felt it was my duty to put this before Your Grace.'

'Well, what is it?'

'It is not easy to say it, but I'm anxious on account of my daughter. If I should die I should like to know that Your Grace would . . . keep an eye on her.'

'Oh,' said the Duchess.

'Yes, Your Grace. She's a good girl and would be most grateful to Your Grace, and you will understand a mother's anxiety.'

'I understand,' said the Duchess, 'and if an opportunity should arise I will see that your daughter is not forgotten.'

'She would serve you well and would not be like some . . . It is on this matter that I asked Your Grace to call.'

The Duchess's brilliant blue eyes opened wider and she cried: 'What's that?'

'Well, Your Grace, I was thinking of Abigail Hill.'

'What of Abigail Hill?'

'Your Grace did everything for her but she has not repaid you well. I meant that my daughter would . . .'

'Not repaid me well! What does that mean?'

'Your Grace knows that it is her most earnest endeavour to take your place with Her Majesty.'

'Take my place! Are you mad, Danvers? That . . . *insect!*'

'She is sly, Madam.'

'Sly! She's . . . insignificant.'

'The Queen does not find her so.'

'The Queen says she makes a good poultice. That is the limit of Madam Abigail's abilities.'

'No, Your Grace . . .'

The Duchess was speechless. That this bedchamber woman should have the effrontery to contradict her! It was incredible!

'Danvers, allow me to know best.'

'Certainly, Your Grace.'

'You're wandering in your mind, Danvers.'

'I think . . . my mind is clear, Your Grace, and my only intention was to tell you what I thought you ought to know.'

'Well, go on. Don't sit spluttering there.'

'She spends hours alone with the Queen . . . in the green closet . . . playing the harpsichord and singing.'

'Well, there's no harm in that.'

'She entertains the Queen with her mimicry. Your Grace would be surprised to see the insolence of that. I have heard her imitation of my Lord Treasurer, the Duke and . . . Your Grace.'

'If I believed that I would box the slut's ears.'

'I assure Your Grace that it is true. Would I, a dying woman, make such a charge if it were not?'

'You bedchamber women are all alike. You're all jealous of each other. It is not so long ago that I found it necessary to reprove you, Danvers, for helping yourself to the Queen's mantuas.'

'Your Grace, I took what was due to me.'

'I trust you have not again been helping yourself to what you considered your dues.'

'Since Your Grace's orders I have touched nothing ... although ...'

The Duchess looked haughty. There was some underhand business here. Danvers wanted to get her girl into the bedchamber, that was certain. So perhaps that was why she wanted to get Abigail Hill out. Abigail playing the harpsichord, making poultices, emptying the slops ... what did it matter. Sarah had no desire to do such things. But mimicry, that was a different matter. But not demure, deprecating Hill! She would never believe that of her. No, Danvers was jealous for some reason.

'I am glad to hear you have filched nothing,' said the Duchess. 'While I am here I will examine the wardrobe to assure myself that everything is in order.'

Mrs Danvers said desperately: 'Your Grace, I overheard Mrs Hill speaking of Mrs Vain to the Queen.'

'What's that?'

'Mrs Hill does not wish Mrs Vain to be brought into the bedchamber.'

'Not wish ... But what concern is that of hers?'

'That is a question I should like to ask her, Your Grace, but I swear I heard her speaking to the Queen and telling Her Majesty why they did not need her.'

This made sense. Hill did not want Vain. Hill had spoken to the Queen on this matter and persuaded Anne to agree with her. And for this reason Anne had set herself against employing Vain in the bedchamber.

Impossible! Anne would never listen to Hill when Sarah expressed a wish. But it was strange. Anne had been so ... stubborn, and about such a minor matter. One could understand the Sunderland affair. But a bedchamber woman was somewhat different from a Secretary of State.

Mrs Danvers saw that she had succeeded in making the Duchess uneasy, so at least the visit had not been wasted. She would do what she could for Mrs Danvers' daughter and at the same time she was uneasy about Hill.

The Duchess rose to go. 'Don't worry about your girl,' she said. 'I'll keep an eye on her.'

'I thank Your Grace with all my heart and I trust you do not take amiss what I have said of Abigail Hill. I know she is a kinswoman of Your Grace.'

'You were right to tell me,' said the Duchess.

Her first impulse was to go to the Queen and demand corroboration of what Danvers had told her. But in a moment of rare hesitation she decided she would ponder this matter for a while; and perhaps in the meantime sound Abigail.

'It is a pleasure, George,' said the Queen as she lay beside her husband in the big connubial bed, 'to know that Hill and Masham are so close to us. I am sure they will be happy.'

'You haf been kind to them, my angel.'

'George, dear, you're lying too flat. It'll bring on the wheeze.'

George hoisted himself up a little. 'The fish was goot,' he said, 'but it repeats.'

'George, you should drink a little less. Dr Arbuthnot says so.'

'It makes no difference, my angel.'

'Dear George, this romance. It takes me back so ... Do you remember the first years? How happy we were!'

'I remember, my love. I am the happiest man ...'

'Yes, we fell in love at sight and that is a rare thing in royal marriages. Now Hill has become Masham. I shall never get used to calling her Masham, but of course just now it is as well, for the marriage remains a secret. I am pleased about that. And it is such a pleasure to see how Masham adores her. I am sure he realizes her good qualities and holds himself the luckiest man alive ... which is how it should be. I have told Hill that I hope she will soon be bringing her first-born to me. I shall take a very particular interest in Hill's first-born, George, and I hope you will too. You know, George, I believe you were the first to notice how taken Masham was with Hill. You pointed it out to me. It is so delightful to see young people in love and when marriages are so suitable ... I think you are rather fond of Masham, George ... just as I am of Hill, and is it not a pleasure to think of them together in their apartment within easy call should we need them. Eh, George?'

But George was fast asleep. In a few moments he would begin to snore.

Anne smiled at him; she did not see his unlovely face, the mouth slightly ajar, the heavy breathing that might at any moment become painful. She thought of him as he had been as a bridegroom. Dear George, so handsome, so ready to fall in love.

It was so pleasant to think of Masham and Hill – dear Hill – in the next apartment ... together.

Abigail was wide awake. Samuel lay beside her, pleasantly weary, satisfied. Marriage! she was thinking. It gave one a certain standing. Even her sister's attitude towards her had changed. Alice had come to the ceremony in Dr Arbuthnot's apartments and had been frankly envious. Alice was getting fat – too much good living, too much purposeless living. She thought herself fortunate to have a pension after such short service in the household of the young Duke of Gloucester and then a place in the Queen's household which was very undemanding. But perhaps Alice was beginning to respect her sister for more reasons than the fact that she was now a married woman.

It was not possible for a woman to be so constantly with the Queen and not arouse some curiosity. And how curious they all were. Why should a Queen select a plain insignificant mouse like Abigail Hill for a favourite!

'Hill makes good poultices.' 'Hill keeps her mouth shut.' 'Hill listens and agrees and soothes.' 'Hill is mealymouthed. Sly. Deep.'

They said all these things of her. It was inevitable.

And now she had Samuel.

Samuel was the devoted husband, and she was lucky since she did not look for romance. But perhaps in foolish moments all women looked for romance. It didn't matter whether they had somewhat scanty sandy hair or an abundance of corn coloured waves, whether they were handsome or plain. They all looked for romance.

The Duchess had found it, surely. The Duke was the man of her choice; he was handsome, courteous and at the moment the national hero. Yet the Duchess was not satisfied. She was not content to be a dearly loved woman; she must rule the country as well.

She is related to me, thought Abigail, and though I am not handsome as she is I am as ambitious.

Suppose Harley had been free ... Suppose she had married him. What a union theirs would have been! It would have been compared with that of the Marlboroughs. They could have gone as far together. Harley would have his Earldom some day; he would have had his Dukedom perhaps. And she would have been a Duchess; the women of the Queen's bedchamber would have trembled when she entered; they would have curtseyed to her as fearfully as they did to Sarah Churchill.

Why not? Why not?

Because Fate had not been so kind to her, because she had not been born handsome; the man whose love she had won was Samuel Masham, whose looks and temperament were similar to her own. Robert Harley had had no feeling for her except amusement, because he understood hers for him, and a desire to cultivate her for the good she could bring him.

But the Queen loved her. Yes, in the secret places of Anne's mind Abigail Masham was more important to her than Sarah Churchill.

That was her strength. The Queen's need of her which was real while her need for Sarah was a myth ... a fantasy ... a dream left over from childhood.

'Sam,' she whispered.

'My dearest ...' was his tired answer.

'The Duchess came to the Queen today. I heard she was looking for me. She wished to speak to me.'

'She'll not be pleased ...'

'She'll have to be displeased then. We are married now ...
no one can alter that.'

His hand closed over hers and he grunted with satisfaction.

She felt impatient with him because he would never be a
leader. He had no real ambition. Perhaps that was good though
because it would leave her a free hand.

But she lay there thinking of Robert Harley – his witty comments, his amusing manners, his worldliness, his ambition.

He would have been the head of the Government and she
would have ruled the Queen.

Now they would still work together but it was only ambition
that bound them. Abigail felt desolate, disappointed and defeated.

She had wanted Harley and she had been given Masham.

She remembered the days when she had been in servitude at
Holywell House – those occasions when the Duke and Duchess
had been in residence. Like lovers they were; it was impossible
to be in the house and not know it. She remembered how the
servants used to titter on those occasions when the Duke returned home after an absence. They used to say that the Duke
would not stop to take off his boots before going to bed with
Sarah – so impatient was he.

Such lovers they were – and it was impossible to be in the
house and not know it. Love like that was enduring and rare.
When one became aware of it, one dreamed of sharing such an
emotion, one longed for it.

Sarah had been singularly blessed. She had extraordinary
beauty and vitality and the devotion of the man she adored.
She might have been the luckiest woman in the world if she had
allowed herself to be, for all the most precious gifts in life had
been bestowed upon her. But she didn't deserve them.

If only I had had her good fortune! mused Abigail; and she
saw herself in a great mansion, and Harley riding into the
courtyard, his face alight with love for Abigail as she had seen
John Churchill's for Sarah.

The bell was ringing.

'Wake up, Sam, they want us. It's the Prince's asthma
again.'

He groaned, but she was already out of bed. 'Don't be foolish, Sam,' she said. 'Rejoice rather. They can't do without us, you know . . . and ask yourself this: What would we be without them?'

'Hill,' said the Queen, 'you are looking a little tired.'

'Your Majesty is so kind . . .'

'With Danvers spending so much time in her bed there is a great deal for you to do.'

She is relenting! thought Abigail. She is going to please the Duchess by taking Mrs Vain after all. Let that happen and Sarah would have scored another victory. It must not be.

'Mrs Danvers has a daughter who is seeking a place,' said Abigail. 'Poor Mrs Danvers, I believe she worries a great deal now that she is ill. She would be very happy if you could take the girl into your household.'

'My poor Danvers! Tell her to come to me when she is a little recovered and I will speak to her.'

'And Your Majesty in the goodness of your heart will ease her mind by offering her girl a bedchamber post?'

'It was you who brought it to my notice yet I fancy Danvers has not always been kind to you.'

'I had so much to learn when I first entered Your Majesty's service.'

Anne's white fingers caressed the sandy locks for Abigail was seated on the stool at her feet where she liked her to be.

'You are such a good creature, Hill . . . Masham I mean. Do you know I fancy I shall never grow accustomed to calling you Masham. I was saying so to the Prince last night in bed.'

It was impossible to keep secret the fact that Masham and Abigail Hill shared those apartments adjoining the royal ones. They slept in the same bed. This could mean only one thing, for the Queen and the Prince must be aware of this which, if the pair were unmarried, Anne would never have countenanced.

Mrs Danvers, feeling better and still clinging to the belief that the Duchess was her true patron asked the Duchess to call upon her once more; and this time Sarah did not hesitate. Since the last interview she had decided to have a word with

Abigail when they met, but to her amazement she found that she never met Abigail. It was not until she received this invitation from Mrs Danvers that it occurred to her that Abigail might have deliberately avoided her.

'Well?' she demanded of Mrs Danvers.

'There are rumours about Mrs Hill, Your Grace ... Mrs Hill and Masham.'

'What rumours?'

'That they are married.'

'Nonsense. Hill would not marry without informing me.'

'It is said that they share an apartment close to the Queen's, Your Grace ... to be handy should they be needed for the Prince in the night.'

'I never heard such nonsense. Hill and Masham would not share an apartment unless they were married, and if they were I should know. If Hill was so deceitful as to keep the matter from me, the Queen would tell me and if they have an apartment next to hers and are together on night duty Her Majesty would be in the secret. I never heard such stuff and nonsense.'

'I merely thought Your Grace would not wish me to keep such a persistent rumour from you.'

'I'm not blaming you for telling me, Danvers, but for believing such rubbish. I hear your girl is now in the bedchamber.'

'Yes, Your Grace, Mrs Hill kindly spoke to the Queen for her.'

'Mrs Hill spoke to the Queen!'

'Yes, Your Grace, and Her Majesty kindly gave her the place.'

As Sarah left Mrs Danvers she remembered Alice Hill. There was another of the indigent ones who had been well treated by her. If there was any truth in this absurd story, which was beginning to give Sarah a qualm or two, Alice would be likely to know.

There was a flutter of excitement among the maids at the approach of the Duchess. Such a visit must mean trouble for someone, for wherever the Duchess went there was a train of complaints.

'I want to speak to Alice Hill,' she said. 'And without delay.'

Alice, flushed, alarmed, and *fat*, came hurrying to the Duchess.

Slut! thought Sarah. I have done too much for these Hills. What is this one doing to earn her very comfortable livelihood, I should like to know.

'You've grown fat,' she said.

'I'm sorry, Your Grace,' replied Alice, bobbing a curtsey.

'Too much rich food.' Sarah made a note that she would take a look at the accounts and see how much was being spent on servants' food. 'I want to talk to you about your sister.'

'Oh yes, Your Grace.' Alice flushed scarlet. Guilty! thought the Duchess. Yes, something is afoot.

'When did you last see her?'

'Oh ... er ... Your Grace, I'm not sure. It might have been yesterday. She is very thin, Your Grace. You would certainly not find her *fat*.'

'I want to ask you a plain question, Alice Hill. Do you know whether your sister is married to Samuel Masham?'

Alice gave a little cry and clapped her hand to her lips.

'Oh ... Your Grace ...'

'Is she?'

Sarah advanced and catching the girl by the shoulders shook her.

'Yes ... Your Grace.'

Sarah released the girl.

'Why was I not told?'

'I ... I believe my sister thought that such a matter would be of small moment to such a great lady, Your Grace.'

'I see,' said Sarah. 'But I should have been told.'

Abigail could not hope to avoid the Duchess for ever; and now being determined to see her, Sarah soon arranged a meeting. When Abigail came from the Queen's apartments she found the Duchess waiting for her in one of the ante-rooms.

'Your Grace!' cried Abigail, flushing and lowering her eyes.

'I've been hearing news of you. So you are married.'

'Yes, Your Grace.'

'And to Samuel Masham.'

'Your Grace knows him?'

'I know him for a young man who is always making bows to everyone and is ever ready to skip and open a door.'

'He is aware of his humble situation, Your Grace, and has a desire to please; his manners are such that he would hasten to open a door for a lady.'

'H'm,' said Sarah. 'An odd affair, was it not? Why should it not be open? Why this secret?'

Abigail opened her eyes very wide. 'There was no need for secrecy, Your Grace. I did not tell you because I felt you were too busy with more important affairs.'

'You forget that I had brought you to Court, that I was your benefactress.'

'It is a fact I shall never forget, Your Grace.'

'Nor should you. You were nothing but a serving girl when I brought you from Lady Rivers. I should have thought it was ordinary politeness to tell me you hoped to marry, and to ask my consent.'

'Your Grace, I must humbly beg your pardon.'

'I'm not against the marriage. In fact, I think it suitable. You continue to serve the Queen and Masham continues to serve the Prince. I should have put nothing in the way of it. Of course you have not been well brought up, otherwise you would not have made the mistake of behaving in this way.'

'So Your Grace forgives me?'

'I will overlook your fault, but do try to behave with more grace in future. So ... you are a married woman now. The Queen will not be pleased. She does not care for all this secrecy, but I don't doubt I can explain to her. I will ask her to give you a better lodging. Now that you are married you should have some standing. If there are children you will have to think of them. But in spite of your folly and your lack of consideration to me I will inform the Queen.'

'Er ...' began Abigail.

'What?' cried the Duchess, appalled that Abigail after having committed one breach of good manners by keeping her marriage secret could be guilty of another and as great – daring to break in on the Duchess's conversation.

'I . . . I believe that Her Majesty has already been informed.'

'Nonsense! You don't imagine that Her Majesty would not have told *me*!'

What could Abigail say to that? She lowered her eyes and looked embarrassed; but inwardly she was laughing. Her Grace was going to receive a shock.

Sarah was looking into the accounts. That girl was far too fat. It was probable that she and her fellow servants were following the Queen's habit of drinking chocolate last thing at night.

The consumption of chocolate had not been excessive . . . She glanced through the Queen's account. What was this three thousand pounds?

The Queen had wanted it for a private matter. As keeper of the Privy Purse she remembered the occasion well.

'A private matter,' said the Queen; and Sarah had been too concerned about the Vain matter to try to discover why.

This would be just about the time of the Masham marriage.

Horror dawned on Sarah. Could it be possible? Had Anne given the girl a *dowry*?

That would be like Anne. She was a generous woman. The dowry was not really important and naturally she would want to give a relative of Sarah's a dowry. But it was rather a large sum for a bedchamber woman! And why had the Queen kept the secret? Why had she not told Sarah?

The more Sarah thought of it, the more certain she became that the three thousand pounds had gone to Abigail – and the greater was her perturbation.

Sarah came briskly into the Queen's apartments and with a wave of the hand dismissed two of the women who were in attendance. Abigail must have heard of her approach for she was nowhere in sight.

Anne, lying back in her chair, picked up her fan and smiled at Sarah.

'My dearest Mrs Freeman.'

'I have just heard of Hill's marriage to Samuel Masham.'

'Oh yes,' said the Queen. 'Hill is Masham now. I find it difficult to remember to call her Masham. I was saying so to Mr Morley last night.'

'I cannot understand why Your Majesty has not been kind enough to tell *me* of the marriage.'

'Oh, I have bid Masham to tell you, but she would not.'

'I brought her to this Court. I took her from a broom. But for me where would she be now? Yet she marries and it appears that the whole Court knows of it and I do not.'

Anne fanned herself unconcernedly. What had become of her? Didn't she care that she had upset Mrs Freeman?

'I find it most extraordinary. In the past Mrs Morley would never have kept secrets from Mrs Freeman.'

'I always liked to share secrets,' said Anne, 'and particularly with you. I remember thinking to myself "I must tell Sarah that". It was in the days before we became Mrs Freeman and Mrs Morley.'

'And yet you did not tell me of this marriage.'

'I have bid Masham tell you . . . but she would not.'

How was it possible to keep one's temper with such a woman?

Sarah took the first opportunity of leaving the Queen, and went at once to Mrs Danvers.

'You had better tell me everything you know about this affair,' she cried.

'Your Grace is now satisfied that there has been a marriage?'

'I have ascertained that – and that *I* have been kept in the dark. Now, Danvers, you must tell me anything else you know.'

'I know that Abigail Hill spends some two hours every day with the Queen in the green closet. The Prince is there, but he sleeps most of the time and often Hill is alone with the Queen.'

'Talking to the Queen?'

'Yes, Your Grace.'

Talking to the Queen! Advising her not to take Mrs Vain but

a woman of her choice instead – the Danvers girl in this instance. Not that Hill was interested in the Danvers girl. Her only object would be to keep out Sarah's choice.

'She plays the harpsichord to Her Majesty, does the poulticing and massaging. Often I have seen her sitting on the stool at Her Majesty's feet. If she is not there Her Majesty sends for her. I have heard them laughing and the . . . mimicry.'

Sarah's eyes narrowed. Ridiculing her. Ridiculing the Duke! Oh, this was an enemy indeed. But she would go in and smite her. Soon no one at Court would dare mention the name of Masham!

'And then, of course, Your Grace, there is her cousin. She is very friendly with him and he makes a great fuss of her.'

'Her cousin?'

'Mr Harley, Your Grace.'

Sarah's heart began to beat faster. In a word or two Danvers had put a very different colour on the entire affair.

'Very affectionate, they are. He calls her his dear coz, and afternoon on afternoon she'll let him in to the green closet and they'll be there together . . . the Queen, Mr Harley, Abigail Hill . . . and the Prince, but he sleeps through most of it.'

'Why did you not tell me of this before?'

'I tried to tell Your Grace . . . but Your Grace didn't seem to want to listen.'

'Harley with the Queen in the green closet and you think I don't want to hear! You're mad, Danvers. You're in your dotage. What else?'

'Mr St John sometimes comes with Mr Harley, Your Grace. They are all very friendly with Hill.'

'How long has this been going on?'

'I don't know, Your Grace . . . for a very long time I think.'

The Duchess rose and left. Rarely in her life had she been so shaken. What she had believed to be the social *gaffe* of an ill-bred chambermaid was turning out to be a major court intrigue.

Sarah was bewildered. For the first time in her life she did not know how to act. John was abroad. Godolphin was useless; Sunderland and she had never been in tune. What she had to discover was how far had Abigail Hill supplanted her in the Queen's affections.

She knew Anne depended on her friendship with women. It had always been so from her childhood; and Mary, her sister had been the same, until she had married William. Anne had selected Sarah as the adored one, but Sarah had disliked the cloying affection bestowed upon her; she had turned from it in disgust – and had, she knew, on occasions betrayed her feelings. But for the fact that Anne was Queen she would never have become involved in such a relationship. It was against her nature; and the older she grew the more repulsive was Anne to her. But she needed Anne's favour; she needed to rule the woman if she were going to bring that fame and fortune to her family which she had decided they must have.

She had been occupied outside the Court; it was true that she had avoided the Queen; and insidiously, while she neglected Anne, that creature, that insect, that little-better-than-a-servant had been creeping in with her lotions and poultices, her Purcell and her mimicry, her flattery and her solicitude.

'It makes me sick!' cried Sarah.

But she knew that she had to do all in her power to end such a situation. How she wished that dear Marl was at home. With his cool reasoning he would know how to act. There were times when she had upbraided him for his caution. But she had need of that caution now.

What should she do next? It was no use seeing that old parrot who was in full cry with her. 'I have bid Masham tell you and she would not'. That was going to be her answer to everything.

So she must see Abigail again, and if necessary shake the truth out of the creature.

Sarah went down to Woodstock. There at least was the evidence of the respect in which the Marlboroughs were held. Blenheim was going to be one of the biggest palaces in the country, and it was built for the Marlboroughs in honour of the Duke's great victory.

That was balm; but she could not get on with Vanbrugh and wished his plans had never been accepted. He was arrogant,

One would have thought the house was being built for him.

It was soothing to some extent to harangue Vanbrugh – but little use in the present situation.

Sarah could never resist the pen. It soothed her always to pour out her anger in words and writing them was almost as comforting as speaking them.

She wrote to the Queen, reproaching her for her duplicity. Why, why, why had she kept her in the dark about the Masham marriage? What could have been the point? Mrs Freeman who had always had such concern for Mrs Morley was astonished that Mrs Morley could have treated her so.

Anne wrote back:

'You are pleased to accuse me in your last letter very un-justly, especially concerning Masham. You say I avoid giving you a direct answer to what I must know is your greatest uneasiness, giving it a turn as if it were the only business of the day that had occasioned your suspicion. What I told you is very true and no turn as you are pleased to call it . . .'

The tone of that letter, so different from those which Sarah was accustomed to receive from her 'unfortunate and faithful Morley' should have warned Sarah, but Sarah had never heeded warnings.

As she said, she wanted plain answers to plain questions and she wanted to know how deep was this friendship between Abigail and Anne, whether Abigail had replaced her in the Queen's affections, and what had happened at those meetings in the green closet between the Queen, Harley, St John and Abigail Hill.

She wrote to Abigail demanding a meeting as soon as she returned to London from Woodstock; but when she did come back Abigail kept out of her way and Sarah's fury rose.

She imagined that the 'chambermaid' as she referred to her, was being deliberately insolent, particularly when Abigail called on her at a time when she would be aware that she would not be at home.

'If that chambermaid should call again,' shouted Sarah, 'I am not at home.'

274

But Sarah knew that if she could speak with Abigail she would be more likely to get the truth of the situation, and when Abigail wrote a meek little note asking for an interview she granted it.

So carefully worded was that note that Sarah was sure Harley had dictated it. The entire situation was becoming horribly clear. Harley and St John were the enemies of the Churchills. They always had been, in spite of mealymouthed Harley's sycophantic admiration for the Duke. Those two had put their heads together to destroy the Churchill faction. She had never liked them. She had told John a hundred times. John had trusted Harley; so had Godolphin. She was the only one with insight into character, and she had known those two were not to be trusted. And all the time they had been in secret conference with the Queen – let in by that snake Abigail Hill, whom she herself had put into the position, to betray them!

They faced each other in Abigail's apartment.

Oh yes, thought Sarah, she has changed. Not so demure now. The sly creature. Harley has groomed her. She is very sure of herself.

She was dignified, serene and outwardly gracious, knowing her place – Masham now instead of Hill. The Queen's favourite but still her chambermaid in the presence of the great Duchess of Marlborough.

'So at last I see you!' said Sarah. 'I will tell you this that I am astonished by your conduct.'

'I am grieved,' replied Abigail demurely, 'and not a little astonished that Your Grace should have found my humble marriage of such concern.'

'Not your marriage – the secrecy that attended it. But let us have the plain truth. The Queen has changed towards me.'

'Your Grace has been much absent. You have so much with which to occupy your time. And added to all else, the building at Woodstock.'

'There is no need to tell me what I do. I know far better than you. I say this – that the Queen has changed towards me because of you, Masham.'

Abigail's green eyes were very faintly insolent. 'Surely that is impossible, Your Grace. A humble chambermaid could not affect the friendship between Her Majesty and the Duchess of Marlborough.'

'Through sly and secret management, yes.'

'Your Grace gives me credit for a diplomacy which is surely beyond my powers.'

'I am just discovering what your powers are. You have been frequently with Her Majesty in private . . .'

'As her chambermaid.'

'Don't evade the truth. You have been with Her Majesty as . . . a friend. Don't deny it. Do you think I don't know *her*. You have slipped in like the serpent in Eden.'

Abigail smiled.

'Take that smirk off your face, woman. You have wormed your way into the Queen's favour; and while you have been doing this you have taken every measure possible to hide it. And to hide it from *me*. I have been a friend to her for years . . . and you have changed this.'

'I have no power to direct the Queen's affection.'

'You . . . snake! Anyone who can behave as you have done is proved to have a very bad purpose at bottom.'

'I do not think Your Grace should be unduly alarmed.'

'*You* do not think!'

'I know that the Queen has loved you in the past and that she will always be kind to you.'

Sarah could scarcely believe she had heard correctly. This insolence was intolerable. This chambermaid, this hanger-on, this ex-servant girl whom she had taken from a broom was now promising her the Queen's kindness! She was without words for a few seconds. It was unbelievable. Moreover, it was quite alarming, for Abigail was not the woman to speak such words unless she had the authority to back them.

Sarah felt sick with rage and fear.

What had happened? Could it really be that she had lost the Queen's favour . . . lost it to a chambermaid!

'You . . . wicked creature!' she cried as her powers of speech returned to her and the words came rushing out. 'You . . . snake and serpent . . . you *insect*. How dare you smile!'

'There is such a disparity between an insect and a reptile, Your Grace.'

'Oh, the insolence! The ingratitude. Would to God I had never taken you from your broom.'

'It was never my duty to sweep floors, Your Grace.'

'Don't answer me, you *slut*! I took you from a broom. I brought you to my house where I fed you and clothed you . . .'

'As an unpaid servant, Your Grace.'

'The wicked ingratitude! I brought you to Court.'

'That I might take over duties which you found distasteful.'

'And you dare . . . attempt to usurp my place!'

Abigail was faintly alarmed. The Queen had by no means escaped from the spell of this woman. It was possible that there would be a reconciliation. She must not allow the brief triumph of the moment to tempt her to act foolishly. Mr Harley would never forgive her if she did.

She became demure again. 'Your Grace, I would not attempt the impossible.'

'You attempted to turn the Queen against the great Duke, against myself and Lord Godolphin. Her attitude has changed towards us and it is due to you.'

'Your Grace, I do not discuss business with Her Majesty. I only bring to her petitions with which Your Grace does not wish to trouble herself.'

Sarah wanted to shout: 'And Harley! And St John! What of them!' But she was remembering John's constant warnings of caution. At the moment it would be unwise to bring in the names of these men. No, she must work in secret, until she found out how deep was the rot.

When she thought of Anne she almost laughed. Of course she would win her way back into the old fool's affections. Had she not always been eager to be friends? There was the Sunderland affair, the Vain affair. Indications which should have been a warning. Harley had told Abigail Hill that they must undermine the Marlboroughs and this was the result.

Thank God she knew the truth now. But she must be cautious. She must remember that the creature who sat facing her with her green eyes cast down and her pale crafty face was not the insignificant dependant she had thought her. She was a sly and scheming woman who had won the regard of the Queen.

Sarah was unusually silent; and at last Abigail rose, saying that she had taken up too much of Her Grace's valuable time and must intrude no longer.

She curtsied with the greatest respect; and with lowered eyes said: 'I trust Your Grace will permit me to call now and then to inquire for your health.'

Sarah nodded her assent; and Abigail was gone.

Sarah remained seated.

Then she began to laugh. 'It is not possible,' she said aloud. 'It is simply not possible.'

But Sarah was to find that it was possible. Anne had changed towards her, and although the Queen wrote that she would always be pleased to hear from Mrs Freeman, she was cool during their meetings, and when she received Sarah would remain standing so that it was impossible for Sarah to sit, which was an indication in itself that the audience would be one of short duration.

Sarah did not know how to meet such a situation. Tact had never been one of her qualities. There were times when she believed that with a little effort she could win back the Queen's affections, but Sarah had never sought to win any affection in her life; she had simply taken as a right that which was given her.

Even when she wrote to the Queen her tactlessness was in every line. She could only write angrily and reproachfully. She attacked Abigail continuously, and Anne defended her.

'Your Majesty says this lady is the very reverse of what I take her to be. To which I can only answer that she is the very reverse of what I once took her to be, and I don't at all doubt but when her master Harley has tutored her a little longer – if I do not die very soon – Your Majesty and I shall come to agree in our opinion of her.'

Sarah could not see that the way to win Anne back was not through attacking Abigail.

Then she accused the Queen of not being frank with her. She

herself had always been of the frankest nature and had not Mrs Morley always admired that quality in Mrs Freeman?

But this was more than a break between the Queen and the Duchess. The Court watched with interest, the Government with alarm; and the man of the moment was Harley who had alienated the Queen from Marlborough and Godolphin.

Harley was a Tory and the Queen had always been a Tory at heart. There was only one thing a Whig Ministry could do and that was get rid of Harley.

Harley had engaged several of the great writers of the day to work for him. Pamphlets were being circulated throughout the city; but his enemies had realized the value of the literary weapon and the age of lampoons had begun.

The story of Abigail Hill's friendship with the Queen could, the Whigs believed, be used to advantage. It was very different, they believed, from her devotion to the Duchess.

In the streets they had begun to sing the Whig song:

> *'And when Queen Anne of great renown*
> *Great Britain's Sceptre swayed.*
> *Besides the Church she dearly loved*
> *A dirty chambermaid.'*

Abigail listened quietly; Harley was mildly annoyed; and when the Duke returned from his activities on the Continent for the winter, he grasped the danger of the situation and went into consultation with Godolphin to decide what should be done.

After Oudenarde

Lord Godolphin went down to Holywell House to make plans with the Marlboroughs.

The Duke, realizing that Sarah had herself been largely responsible for her own unpopularity with the Queen, but not daring to tell her so, was torn between his schemes for further conquests abroad and those for ending this intolerable situation at Court.

Godolphin, old, tired and having little love for his task, needed guidance and the Queen's recent appointment of two new Bishops to Exeter and to Chester had aroused his suspicion.

With Sarah they walked in the gardens, for she said, after the perfidy of that chambermaid she trusted no one – least of all her servants.

It was Sarah who talked. 'Blackhall to Exeter and Dawes to Chester!' she cried. 'That will mean two more Tory votes in the Lords. We can't afford it. And you know why Anne has appointed them, don't you? Because Masham has let Harley into the green closet and he has brought her round to his view that they are the men for the jobs. I tell you this, Marl, and you,

280

Sidney . . . we cannot stand idle any longer.'

'She is as usual right,' said the Duke, slipping his arm through that of his wife. 'We have to be rid of Harley.'

'But how?' asked Godolphin.

Sarah looked at the Lord Treasurer's heavy eyes and pock-marked skin. A poor ally, she thought, lacking adventure. But what pleasure it gave her to turn from him to dearest Marl, who seemed to grow more handsome year by year and whose genius would win this battle for them as it had won Blenheim and Ramillies.

'You are right, Marl,' she said. 'We have to be rid of Harley.'

'How?' repeated Godolphin.

'He must be asked to resign,' said the Duke.

'Ha!' laughed Sarah. 'And you think this creeper into green closets, this friend of our dirty little chambermaid will do that?'

'I think,' the Duke replied, 'that he will have to be forced to do it.'

'How?'

'If Sidney and I refuse to serve with him, he will have to go.'

'And you will do that?'

'We will feel our way first.'

'Trust you for that!' laughed Sarah affectionately.

'In the old days,' said Marlborough sadly, 'it would have been easy for you to have explained to the Queen.'

'And now alas she won't listen to any but that dirty chambermaid.'

'Who,' put in Godolphin, 'will fight for Harley!'

'Marl,' said Sarah, 'you go and see her. She is fond of you, and if she has any gratitude she should not be able to refuse you anything.'

It was agreed that Marlborough should see the Queen.

The Queen sat back in her chair exhausted, and sent for Masham.

'Your Majesty is very tired,' said Abigail anxiously. 'I fear the Duke has wearied you.'

'So tired, Masham. Far more so than when I go hunting the stag, I can assure you.'

Abigail said that she was terrified every time the Queen hunted in the high wheeled chair which was drawn by the fastest horse in her stables. 'I sit and tremble until Your Majesty returns. You are quite intrepid, Madam.'

Anne pushed aside Abigail's fears. 'I have hunted since I was a child, Masham; and my one-horse chaise is excellent for me nowadays.'

'And now Your Majesty is as tired as after the hunt.'

'More so, Masham, more so.'

'Your visitor proved tiresome?'

'I'm afraid so, Hill. The Duke is such a charming man and I have always been so fond of him; and of course I never forget his brilliance in battles. But . . . I cannot give way in everything however brilliant a commander he is, can I?'

'I am sure Your Majesty should never give way. It is others who should give way to you.'

'I have grown so fond of dear Mr Harley. Of course the Duke does not like him. He says that he does not care to serve in a ministry which contains Mr Harley.'

'I see,' said Abigail.

'Yes, that is what he wants. And Godolphin is with him. It would not grieve me greatly to do without Godolphin, but I do not see what our armies would do without the Duke.'

Abigail was silent.

'Oh dear,' went on the Queen. 'There seems to be nothing but quarrels. Make me some tea. I feel I need a little sustenance.'

Abigail made the tea and planned at the same time as to how she could get the news to Harley that Marlborough and Godolphin were attempting to oust him from his post.

When she returned with the tea she sat on the stool at the Queen's feet.

'That's better,' said Anne. 'Just the right amount of sugar. Of course I told the Duke that I could not do without Mr Harley. I have come to depend upon him. I shall summon a meeting of Council; then they will have to attend. Perhaps then they will put their complaints of Mr Harley to his face.'

'But Your Majesty will not ask him to resign?'

'Certainly I shall not,' said the Queen.

Abigail made her way to Albemarle Street; she was let in without question and taken up to Harley's private study.

He took both her hands and kissed her on the forehead; it was the chaste greeting he often bestowed upon her.

'Marlborough has been to see the Queen.'

He nodded. 'I know he is determined to ruin me.'

'He hasn't a chance. The Queen is firmly behind you.'

'A position, my dear coz, in which you have helped to place her.'

'She won't allow you to resign.'

'I am wondering if it mightn't be a necessity.'

'A necessity!' Abigail was aghast.

'My dear cousin, you are so concerned?'

'But everything we have worked for . . .'

'Will not be lost. Depend upon it, in the long run we will drive Marlborough and his virago of a Duchess out of office. But the time is not yet.'

'Something has happened?'

He nodded.

'Something bad . . . for us?'

He nodded again.

She, who was habitually so calm, stamped foot in sudden anger.

'They have been clever, our enemies,' he said. 'Perhaps we underestimated them. We have been congratulating ourselves on the follies of Sarah, but her friends are strong and ingenious.'

'Tell me,' she said impatiently.

'They have arrested a clerk in my office.'

'What has this to do with us?'

'A great deal. A communication he sent to Chamillart was opened in Holland.'

'Who is Chamillart?'

'The French Secretary of State.'

'Good God!' cried Abigail.

'You may well exclaim. He will be tried for High Treason.'

'And you?'

'You can guess what our enemies are saying, can you not?'

'That you are guilty of . . . treason?'

'Well, they couldn't have hoped for better luck, could they?'

'But you . . .'

'I knew nothing of it, but the clerk was in my office. It is information which passes through my hands which has been discovered on its way to the enemy. You can imagine that Sarah is choking with laughter over this. It may not be only my office that I may have to give up, but my head.'

Abigail was pale.

'It won't come to this.'

'Powerful people are doing all they know to make it.'

'We will defeat them.'

'How fierce you are, cousin!'

'But, this must not be. Everything we have worked for . . .'

He came close to her and smiled his enigmatic smile which never failed to excite her.

'You are not disturbed,' she asked. 'You seem as though you do not care.'

'But you do, cousin,' he said smiling. 'Odd, is it not . . . that you should be more concerned than I?'

Marlborough and Godolphin had absented themselves from the Council meeting, and although Harley attempted to open it he was not allowed to do so for the Duke of Somerset pointed out that there could not be such a meeting if both the Lord Treasurer and the Commander in Chief were absent. The Queen was angry, for she had meant to show Marlborough and Godolphin that she could do very well without them.

It was an anxious day for Abigail when it was proved that William Gregg, the clerk in Harley's employ, had attempted to sell information to France and that he had received a hundred guineas for his pains.

The Whig writers were busy inflaming the people against Harley. Harley was the traitor, they said; he was hiding behind Gregg; and the Marlborough Junta waited eagerly for Gregg to betray his master.

In the green closet Abigail brought Harley to the Queen.

'My dear friend,' cried Anne, with tears in her eyes, 'I know full well what your enemies are trying to do to you. I'll not allow it. You know that I trust you.'

'Your Majesty's kindness overwhelms me,' Harley told her. 'If I possess that, I care for naught else.'

'Such trouble!' sighed the Queen. 'And at such a time!'

She glanced towards the Prince who was propped up in his chair and it was clear that his breathing was more painful than usual.

'Masham has been with me all night,' said the Queen. 'We have had to be in constant attention upon my poor angel. He does not hear what we say. I fear he is very bad indeed. And all this trouble . . .'

'Madam,' said Harley, 'I shall offer my resignation. I believe that is the way at this time to save you trouble.'

'Mr Harley, I could not accept it.'

'Madam, you need to give your attention to His Highness. This is not the time to be plagued by the squabbles of your ministers.'

'I don't know what I should do without you, my dear friend.'

'I do not suggest that Your Majesty should do without my advice. It is yours when you wish it. I live but to serve you, Madam. My cousin, your Majesty's most faithful servant, will bring me to you as before. You shall discuss your desires with me and if you think my opinion of value I shall continue to give it. Madam, it will make no difference. I shall sever myself from your Government but I shall continue to serve you with all my power.'

'You mean that you will come as before? You will advise me . . . and at the same time put a stop to this dreadful squabbling.'

'I shall leave you Marlborough and Godolphin, Madam. And you will not lose my services . . . for as long as you need them.'

'I think we had better call Masham. Masham, my dear, I think you should call the Prince's doctors.'

* * *

George was a little better the next day and Anne summoned Marlborough to tell him that Harley had resigned.

The Marlborough faction was delighted, but the Duke was the first to wonder whether victory had been so complete. Harley's friends, St John, Sir Simon Harcourt and Sir Thomas Mansell resigned with him and their places were taken by Whigs.

The topic of the moment was the resignation of Harley and the Gregg affair, and Harley was warned not to be seen in the streets for fear he should be attacked. Sarah congratulated herself that this little rebellion would soon be over; and the presumptuous little chambermaid and her master, as she called Harley, banished; Harley to oblivion – the hell of all ambitious politicians – and Abigail back to her broom.

The Queen was deeply distressed, but all other emotions were swamped by her growing anxieties for her husband. There was no disguising the fact that he was nearing the end.

She and Abigail suffered constantly disturbed nights. Anne was sleeping very lightly and as soon as she heard the Prince begin to fight for his breath she would call to Abigail and together they would hold him up while Samuel ran for one of the doctors. Arbuthnot said that the Prince continued to live only because of the devoted attention of the Queen and Mrs Masham.

Often when the Prince was fighting his grim battles for life the eyes of the two women would meet and Anne's would convey her gratitude and love, Abigail's her undying devotion.

Both knew that only death could sever a friendship like theirs and that these nocturnal duties put a closer bond between them than Sarah with all her bombastic beauty ever could.

Abigail was young and the interrupted nights did not seem to affect her, but the Queen looked very tired and the ophthalmic disease which had troubled her since she was a child grew worse.

And in addition there was this terrible Gregg affair which was so exciting the people.

One night sipping the brandy Abigail had brought while she

sat up in bed with George, at last breathing more easily and sleeping beside her, Anne said: 'It is terrible to witness such suffering, Masham, particularly in a loved one . . . I have been thinking of that poor man Gregg.'

'Mr Harley had nothing to do with it, Your Majesty,' said Abigail speaking more fiercely than usual.

'I know. I know, and poor man, he may be guilty and doubtless he was very poor and did this terrible thing for that reason. But now he is in prison and they say he is ill unto death.'

'If he died, Madam, it would save the executioner his trouble.'

'It is so,' sighed the Queen. 'He is a traitor and I, as the Queen, must sentence him to death. It grieves me, Masham.'

'But the man is evil. He has worked against Your Majesty. He has worked against Mr Harley . . . and delivered him to his enemies.'

'But he is lying in a wretched prison, hungry and ill. And he knows the executioner is waiting for him. He is one of my subjects and I told you once how I felt as a mother to all my subjects . . . even to those who would harm me. I shall send Arbuthnot to him tomorrow – and with some comfort from the kitchens.'

'The goodness of Your Majesty never ceases to amaze me,' said Abigail; and she was thinking that when the Marlboroughs knew that the Queen had sent comforts to Gregg, they would believe that Anne was firmly on the side of Harley against them . . . which would be to the good.

When Arbuthnot visited the prisoner, Gregg, Harley's enemies set up a howl of protest. Godolphin came to the Queen who told him in her most regal manner that it was her custom in every case when a man was under sentence of death to see that his last days on Earth were made as comfortable as possible. It was true that there had been no noise and shouting about other cases, but it was a fact that she never allowed any such prisoner to go without these attentions.

This had to be accepted; and when William Gregg was executed he gave a letter to a fellow clerk in which he exonerated his master, Robert Harley, from all complicity in treason.

The victory seemed less complete. Marlborough was well aware that nothing was achieved without sacrifice. They had rid the Ministry of Harley, but Godolphin, whose official work he had shared, found himself at a loss without him. Godolphin realized more than ever how old he was growing, how feeble he was becoming, and that his health was beginning to fail. Marlborough was the only man whom he could really trust and Marlborough was a soldier rather than a politician.

The people were becoming uneasy for they did not care to see the supreme power of the Whigs. The Whigs were the warmongers, they said. And what benefits, they asked, did Marlborough's war bring to them ... apart from the glory of victory?

Meanwhile Harley was preparing to wait. He was now the hope of the Tories; and his dear cousin Abigail Masham saw that he was conducted very frequently into the Queen's intimate circle.

Now that Harley was out of office Sarah's great desire was to have Abigail banished. The thought of Abigail obsessed her; she could not rid her mind of that whey-faced creature as she called her; she gave up great energy into thinking up new names for her; and all the time she was reviling Abigail she was asking herself how she could have been such a fool as to allow the woman to rise to her present position.

There was one thing Sarah could not bear to be – that was made a fool of – and everywhere people were discussing her fall and the rise of Abigail Masham.

She harangued the Duke, Godolphin, Sunderland and members of the Ministry outside her family. Were they going to allow this chambermaid to hold her position with the Queen? she demanded; and an attempt was even made to bring a case against Abigail, but it failed. The Members of the Government could not but see that they were being rather ridiculous in devoting their time to the activities of a chambermaid.

Moreover, Anne could be regal, and when she had made up

her mind, adamant. She had let them banish Harley, but that was only because he himself had convinced her that it would be better for him to go . . . temporarily. Never would she give up Abigail. How could she do without her when George was as ill as he was. Abigail was not only her personal attendant; she was the Prince's nurse. Dr Arbuthnot had said that there could not have been a better in the kingdom. She was her mistress's companion, confidante and comforter in this terrible time.

But though the attack against Abigail might be called off by Sarah's friends in the Ministry, Sarah herself would continue to fight.

She still held her posts with the Queen, and as she declared that while that chamberwoman was with the Queen *she* could not be, she went to the Queen to tell her so.

Anne received her with a show of affection which deceived Sarah although the Duke had often warned his wife that she underestimated the Queen, who had an extraordinary gift for concealing her feelings, and as she had a great dislike for unpleasant scenes went to great lengths to avoid them. Sarah, however, had never had time to study the idiosyncrasies of others; she saw everyone else in her own image – smaller, pale copies of herself; so even after all these years with Anne, she failed to detect the change in the Queen's manner towards her.

'It would seem,' she said grimly, 'that Mrs Morley is pleased to see me.'

'Mrs Freeman has been told many times that I am always pleased to see her.'

'Mrs Morley might see more of Mrs Freeman if these rooms were not contaminated by the presence of a certain chambermaid.'

'Contaminated?' answered Anne. 'I was not aware of it.'

'Masham is here night and day.'

'Such a good nurse! Dr Arbuthnot says he has never seen a better. I do not know what we should do without Masham. I was saying so only to George this morning. I am very anxious about him.'

'You are looking exhausted. You should allow me to arrange for nurses to be in constant attendance.'

'I am sure if Mrs Freeman were in my position she would

never allow anyone else to nurse Mr Freeman. No. Mr Morley would be most unhappy if I were not present. He has said so. In the midst of one of his fearful attacks he sees me and a smile comes over his dear face, and he says: 'My Anna . . . my angel . . . you are there.' It is most affecting.'

'Don't weep. It'll make your eyes worse.'

'Sometimes I think I am suffering for past sins.'

Oh dear, thought Sarah, now we shall have to go through that unless I'm careful.

'Nonsense, Mrs Morley. You have led a good life. The past is done with.'

'I often think of that brother of mine over the water.'

'The King of France does not flaunt his acceptance of the King of England so much since Mr Freeman gave him something else to think about.'

'Dear Mr Freeman! What should we do without him?'

'Well, you could so easily lose his services, and came near to it . . . not so long ago.'

'Oh, these squabbles!'

'Squabbles, Mrs Morley? You call the concern of your ministers for the country's good, squabbles? In fact, Mrs Morley, the Court has changed so much and Mrs Morley herself has changed so much that I am wondering whether *my* presence is needed here any longer.'

'But of course I shall always need you here.'

'Surely Masham is sufficient for Your Majesty?'

'Masham does very well, but I should be sad to lose my dearest Mrs Freeman.'

'But for the presence of Masham, Mrs Freeman would be in constant attendance on Mrs Morley.'

The Queen said: 'Dr Arbuthnot was saying Masham is the best nurse in the kingdom.'

So that was the answer, thought Sarah. Very well. She chooses Masham.

'I have daughters all married into the most noble families. I would take it as a favour if they might share between them the post Mrs Morley was once so happy to bestow on me.'

The Queen was silent and Sarah went on, 'You would have three to serve you where you once had one and I would see that you had nothing of which to complain.'

The Queen still said nothing and Sarah asked harshly: 'Well, what has Mrs Morley to say? Do not tell Mrs Freeman that you regret parting with her. You have shown so clearly that you prefer Masham.'

'I cannot agree to this suggestion,' said the Queen.

'Mrs Morley does not think that my children would serve her well?'

'I am sure that being Mrs Freeman's children they would perform their duties most excellently. But it is inconceivable that Mrs Freeman and Mrs Morley should be parted while they live.'

Sarah was exultant. Here was a return to the old standing. The Queen was merely temporarily piqued. All right, Sarah would soon be back.

'Mrs Morley is gracious to her poor Freeman. Now as to Mrs Masham...'

'Dr Arbuthnot says she is the best nurse in the kingdom.'

So there was nothing to be done in that quarter while the Prince lived; but Sarah was not going to let Anne think that she merely had to beckon Sarah Churchill and she would come hurrying back.

Sarah settled down to make arrangements about the town house she intended to have. She had had her eyes on it for some time when it had been occupied by Catherine of Braganza. It was on the south side of Pall Mall and King Charles II had planted an acorn in its gardens, and this acorn came from the oak tree which had hidden him at Boscobel.

Sarah planned to build in place of that old house a much grander one which should be her family's town residence; she had decided it should be called Marlborough House.

Now she reminded Anne of an old promise to give her this house; and Anne, happy to turn the conversation away from Mrs Masham and the replacement of Sarah by her daughters, agreed that the site should be Sarah's.

Sarah emerged triumphant from that interview; and throughout the Court it was said that not only had Godolphin and Marlborough scored over Harley, but Sarah would soon be putting Mrs Masham in her place.

Anne was disturbed. There was alarming news. The King of France having been so often defeated by Marlborough in Europe was seeking to attack the Queen of England in a way most calculated to alarm her.

Her ministers had informed her that her half-brother, whom the French King openly called James III, King of England, was being given the aid he would need to land in Scotland where they were ready to rise in his favour and come against her.

Marlborough came in all haste to St James's.

How fortunate that he was in England! There was a strength about the man. A genius which she could not fail to recognize. What should I *do* without dear Mr Freeman! She asked George who, poor dear angel, was too ill to give much thought to the matter.

The best of the Army was in Europe but this would be a matter for the fleet, said Marlborough. Sir George Byng was setting sail immediately to prevent the hostile force landing.

But they must be watchful, for Scotland and the Northern counties were ready to revolt.

When Marlborough left, Anne immediately summoned Abigail to bring her brandy.

'It is so alarming,' she said as she sipped gratefully. 'The Prince so ill . . . and all this trouble!'

Abigail wiped the poor eyes which watered frequently.

'Thank you, my dear. How I wish there need not be this strife. He is my brother for all that he comes against me.'

'Your Majesty is sure of that?'

'Oh, there were rumours. Some thought at the time that he was brought into the bed by means of a warming pan . . . but I have heard that he is very like my dear father. So good my father was to me, Masham. And to my sister Mary. He doted on us. He was a good father . . . but so distressingly fond of women . . . like my Uncle Charles. But the people were fond of him. By the way, I hear that they are not pleased because the Duchess has taken his old house near the Mall. She has had the oak cut down which he planted.'

'The people loved that oak, Madam. To them it was a symbol of royalty. The oak saved King Charles's life and they loved it for that reason.'

'They still wear the oak apple in memory of the occasion, Masham. Yes, my uncle was much loved, but my father . . . alas, he had his enemies. I often think of those days and I wish . . . I wish with all my heart, Masham . . .'

'Your Majesty must not upset yourself.'

'But there is this conflict . . . and now my own brother comes against me. He is but a boy. Is it not sad, Masham? I often think of all the babies I have lost and I wondered whether it was a curse on me. And my dearest husband . . . There will be no hope of more children.'

Abigail did not know how to comfort the Queen; she could not speak of the possibility of a more fruitful marriage while the Prince still clung to life.

'No, I shall have no heirs of my body,' went on Anne. 'And we must think of the succession. I do not like the Germans, Masham. And this boy is my father's own son. I am sure of it.'

'But Madam, you cannot wish that this venture of his will be victorious!'

Anne smiled at her dear friend's horror, and took Abigail's freckled hand in hers.

'No, my dear. He will not be successful. The Duke would never allow that. I can only hope that he will not be harmed. That is what I fear. I should like him to go quietly back to France and wait . . . and when I am gone . . .'

'Your Majesty would make him your heir?'

'I think that would please my father and that then every-thing would be right.'

'He would have to become a member of the Church of England, Madam.'

'Oh, yes. He would have to be that. And if he were . . . then I think it would be the happiest solution. Meanwhile, poor boy, he will try to take by force that which, if he would but wait in patience, I should be very happy to hand over to him.'

Abigail laid her head against the Queen's hand.

'What is it, Masham? Your cheeks are wet.'

'I cannot bear to hear Your Majesty speak of the days when you will not be here.'

'Dear Masham! You make my life so much more bear-able than it would otherwise be. But I have lost my boy. It is over now, *some* say, but to me it is as fresh as though it happened yesterday. Always I hoped that there would be others . . . but now . . . I am losing my dearest husband. Oh, Masham. I hope you enjoy with Samuel what I have with George.'

'It is Your Majesty's goodness which makes everything good about you.'

'You are a dear creature. But all is not good. And now my own brother comes against me.'

'He will not succeed, Your Majesty.'

'I know it. But he comes to try to take that which I hold and which he thinks I usurped from him. It is not so, Masham. The people would never have a papist on the throne.'

'Your Majesty has always faithfully upheld the Church of England.'

'Therein I find my strength, Masham. In the Church, which assures me I did right.'

Abigail kissed the Queen's hand and while she wept with her she told herself that she must let Harley know that the Queen was against the Hanoverian succession and was for the Stuart James.

News filtered through to the Court of what was happening to the invading forces.

As Marlborough had predicted, they had no chance against Sir George Byng, and the remnants of the invading forces were soon fleeing back to France.

There were rumours that Prince James had been captured and was a prisoner on board an English ship.

The Queen told Abigail that she was deeply disturbed because if the young man was brought to her, she would have to remember that he was her own brother and she could never find it in her heart to punish him.

The Chevalier de St George, as James was known in France, was after all a young man in his twentieth year; it was said that he was bold and handsome. The position would be very difficult if he were brought to London for trial.

But she could trust Admiral Byng to do better than that; Anne was very pleased when the report reached her that her brother, of whom she now spoke as The Pretender, had been treated with the respect due to his rank and landed on the French coast.

The attempted invasion had come to nothing; and the Queen need have no fear on that score, but there was a little uneasiness when she heard that Lord Griffin, an ardent Jacobite who had been with her brother in France and had come with him to Scotland, had been captured and was being brought to the Tower where he would be sentenced as a traitor.

Troubled, Anne turned to Abigail. 'You see, Masham, I know Griffin well. I have known him all my life. How can I sign his death warrant? I know he fought with my brother and his plan was to set him up in my place, but he is an old friend. I cannot sentence old friends to death, and be at peace with my conscience.'

Abigail had talked with Harley. He was a Jacobite; so was she. They did not wish to see Anne deposed during her life time naturally, but when she died – for she would almost certainly die without heirs of her body – they would wish to see James Stuart on the throne and not Sophia of Hanover.

'They will bring Lord Griffin to the tower, Your Majesty, but they will not be able to execute him if you do not sign the death warrant.'

'But it will be expected of me.'

'Your Majesty answers to no one. I believe that some people who have mistakenly thought they could put you in leading strings are beginning to discover that.'

Abigail had folded her arms and pursed her lips. Extraordinarily, it seemed to Anne, her face was transformed and it might have been Sarah standing there.

Anne began to laugh.

'I feel so relieved that my poor brother is safe in France. And you're right, Masham, they won't be able to execute him until the death warrant is signed, and if I don't sign it ... then Griffin will live on.'

They laughed together.

Now that Masham behaved less like a servant they were growing closer than ever.

George was clearly worse, and as he loved Kensington perhaps more than any other place, Anne decided to take him there and, with Abigail, nurse him as quietly as she could.

It was Abigail who suggested that the Prince should have apartments on the ground floor of the palace.

The Prince's difficulty in breathing, increased by his corpulence – and now that he was unable to take exercise he was becoming visibly fatter every day – made it difficult for him to mount staircases; and Abigail's idea was hailed as an excellent one.

'He loves his plants,' said the Queen indulgently, 'and it will be so easy for him to slip out into the gardens to be among them, with the least possible strain.'

So to Kensington went the royal party, and as the Queen could not be parted from Abigail and it was essential that her apartments should be immediately adjoining those of the Queen and Prince, Abigail and Samuel found themselves magnificently lodged at Kensington.

Sarah was flitting from St Albans to Blenheim and back to see how Marlborough House was progressing and had little time to spare for the Queen. Moreover, she believed that if she remained aloof Anne would be unable to endure the separation and would humbly ask her to come to her.

She waited in vain for the summons, but her daughter Henrietta, who had been visiting at the palace, came to her to tell her what magnificent apartments Abigail was occupying there, and when Sarah asked her to describe them her eyes narrowed with anger.

'Why,' she cried, 'I know those apartments although I have never occupied them. William had them made for Keppel. You remember Keppel was at one time a very great favourite with William and he could scarce bear the young man out of his sight. When William died and George took over the Palace – which he did with scarcely respectable speed – Anne said that those apartments should be mine. And that gooseberry-eyed slut is occupying them! I shall soon put a stop to that.'

Although she had pleaded lack of time to go to Court before this, Sarah went straight there and demanded that the housekeeper show her the rooms which were being occupied by the Mashams.

As soon as she saw them she gave vent to her rage.

'These rooms were given to me by the Queen when she first came to the throne!' she declared, and went off to see the Queen, thrusting aside those who would restrain her.

'I can assure you that Her Majesty will put nothing in the way of seeing *me*!' she declared.

It may have been that Abigail had seen her approach or it might have been one of those rare occasions when she was not in attendance, but Sarah found one of the other bedchamber women with the Queen.

'It is not often that we have the pleasure of Mrs Freeman's company,' began the Queen.

But Sarah burst out, 'I have heard disturbing news. Mrs Masham has taken my lodgings.'

Anne looked dismayed and Sarah rushed on. 'It is not the first time that she has sought to take that which belongs to me. I'll not have her in my apartments.'

'Masham has none of your rooms,' said the Queen.

'The housekeeper has shown me that she has. Your Majesty gave me those rooms and I will not have Masham using them.'

'But Masham has none of your rooms,' repeated the Queen, 'and to say to the contrary is false and a lie.'

'If Your Majesty will send for the housekeeper, who knows very well which apartments here are being used by whom, he will tell you that Masham is using that apartment which William gave to Keppel and which you gave me. I will summon him.'

'Pray do not,' said the Queen coldly. 'I do not wish to see him because I know Masham has none of your rooms.'

Sarah asked leave to depart and the Queen did not detain her. She was so certain that Abigail was using her rooms and could not let pass an occasion for proving herself in the right. It did not occur to her that the Queen was telling her politely that she could no longer consider the apartment hers, and that it had been given to Abigail.

Sarah must prove herself right.

She went once more to the housekeeper. She looked at the apartments again and stalked back to the Queen.

'Masham *is* in my apartment,' she said.

'Masham has not made use of your apartment,' retorted the Queen coldly.

'I can bring those to Mrs Morley who will assure her that Masham *is* in my apartment.'

'How could she help using an apartment which is near my own?' demanded the Queen. 'She must be at hand, for the Prince and I need her.'

Sarah was exasperated. How could one talk to a woman who one moment was so emphatic, and then calmly admitted what one had been trying to prove.

Anne made no attempt to placate her; so Sarah took her leave and as she did so she heard her say: 'Where is Masham? I have such a headache. Send her to me.'

This was too much to be borne and Sarah was furious. So the Queen no longer cared whether she visited her or not. She would care though if she lost her Commander-in-Chief. And by God, thought Sarah, if I have to endure much more insolence I shall insist on Marl giving up his command. If he were here now she would tell him so, but he was at this moment in Holland, fighting the Queen's battles while his wife at home was being insulted.

In the heat of her fury she did what she always found soothing to her rage. She sat down and wrote to the object of her anger – in this case the Queen rather than Abigail.

'Madam, upon Lord Marlborough's going into Holland I believe Your Majesty will neither be surprised nor displeased to hear that I am going into the country, since by your very hard and uncommon usage of me, you have convinced all sorts of people as well as myself that nothing would be so uneasy to you as my near attendance. Upon this account I thought it might not be improper at my going into the country to acquaint Your Majesty that even while Lord Marlborough continues in your service, as well as when he finds himself obliged to leave it, if Your Majesty thinks fit to dispose of my employments, according to the solemn assurances you have been pleased to give me, you shall meet with all the submissions and acknowledgements imaginable . . .'

There, she felt better. That would show Anne that if she did not wish to see Sarah, Sarah had no wish to be with her.

Anne read the letter and sighed. She was too preoccupied with poor dear George to give any attention to Sarah's tantrums. In fact when she read the letter she felt somewhat relieved because lately she had simply not cared that Sarah should be angry and was secretly pleased when she stayed away from Court.

For the first time since she had met Sarah she did not care what Sarah thought of her.

It was escape from a long bondage.

The Prince's health did not improve during that hot May and Anne discussed with Abigail the desirability of moving farther into the country. Windsor would be delightful but the castle was high and sudden winds, even in summer, could render it draughty. There was the little house in the forest close to the castle which Anne had acquired when her quarrel with her sister had made it impossible for her to reside in the castle.

It would be so much easier, said Abigail, to nurse the Prince in this small establishment; and there they would be free from formality.

Anne remembered an occasion when she had lived the simple country life with her boy in Twickenham and how happy they had all been.

She was sure Abigail was right and they set off, and taking few servants with them installed the dying Prince in the little house in the forest.

Here Anne was with him constantly, for he was uneasy if she was not in sight or within call.

'It breaks my heart to see him, Masham,' she said, and Abigail assured her that it was the most touching sight in the world to see them together.

Mr Harley was a frequent caller and he enlivened those days made sad by the Prince's illness, which they all knew was progressing towards the inevitable end.

Sarah, having received no reply to her letter, was very angry; she declared that the Queen had cruelly taken the dying Prince to this little hut which was as hot as an oven, because the chambermaid wished to invite her paramour, Harley, there.

Such malicious gossip did not reach the Queen's ears; her days were filled by looking after her husband and talking to Mr Harley, listening to Abigail's music and conversation.

Dr Arbuthnot and his wife were with them and she often told them what a comfort she found in the presence of the Mashams.

It was a simple life – strange and unreal to those who lived it because it was so remote from the Court.

Abigail, however, never ceased to think ahead; and one day when she was walking through the woods with Samuel she said to him: 'I doubt the Prince will see the end of the year.'

Samuel was silent; like most people who served the Prince, he was fond of him.

'Has it occurred to you to wonder what will become of you when the Prince dies?'

She looked at him with a slightly contemptuous tenderness. She would always have to think for him.

'No?' she answered for him. 'Well, there will be no place for you then. We will have to think, Samuel, my dear. Politics? The Army? Perhaps both. I will speak to the Queen. But not yet. I would not have her think that my mind ran on such practical matters. But when the Prince is dead, and that cannot be long, I will speak to her. But in the time that is left to us, Samuel, we should think. We should think very carefully indeed.'

'Do you think I would make a politician, Abigail?'

'Your tongue is scarcely ready enough.'

She thought of Harley, whose tongue was ever-ready. In time Harley would become the Queen's chief Minister. She was sure of it. There ought to be room in his government for a place for Abigail Masham's husband.

Then she thought of the great Duke and the power of commanding the Army. With Marlborough abroad and Sarah at home the Churchills could have ruled the country. But Sarah had been a fool as Abigail never would be. But on the other hand Marlborough was a military genius and Samuel would never be any sort of genius.

Abigail sighed and slipped her arm through that of her husband.

'One thing we have decided,' she said, 'and that is that it must either be politics or the Army.'

The quiet of the little house in Windsor was broken by the news of Marlborough's great victory at Oudenarde.

'The great Duke is a genius,' said Anne when she read the news and hastily wrote to him expressing her appreciation, but when she saw the lists of dead and wounded in the battle and understood the losses which had gone to make this victory she wept.

'Oh Lord,' she cried, 'when will all this dreadful bloodshed cease.'

Such a victory, whatever it had cost, must be celebrated. The nation would expect it; and Anne must therefore leave Windsor and travel to London for the thanksgiving service at St Paul's.

Marlborough's new feat had brought Sarah back to Court triumphantly, snapping her fingers with glee. Let them understand once and for all that they could not do without Marlborough.

She was back at her old duties at the wardrobe. She would ride with the Queen to St Paul's, and receive the cheers. And some people would realize that they must take her into account, for she was far more important than any dirty little chambermaid could ever be.

Anne, terribly anxious on account of George, was subdued when she considered all those who had fallen on the battlefield, asking herself how much longer this dreadful war would continue and whether the good which would come of victory was worth the price that was paid; and Sarah with customary blindness and concern with her own affairs mistook this for remorse for the manner in which Anne had treated her and a desire to return to the old relationship.

Very well, thought Sarah, she would take her back; but she must realize that if the friendship was to be put back on its old footing, there must be no more foolish tantrums.

She bustled into the royal apartments where the Queen was resting in preparation for the ordeal before her and busied herself with arranging the Queen's jewels. Mrs Danvers, recovered from her illness and no longer concerned with immediate death, fluttered sycophantishly round her, whispering of the further insolence of that upstart Masham, for in Sarah's presence it was impossible for some people to doubt that she was all she believed herself to be.

'The Queen will wear these rubies and these diamonds,' Sarah told Danvers. 'She must look . . . dazzling. The people will expect it.'

'Well, Your Grace, she will look magnificent.'

'And so she should, Danvers. To look anything less would be an insult to the Duke!'

Sarah was undoubtedly back. Mrs Danvers predicted to Mrs Abrahal that Mrs Masham would not be lording it much longer. It was only necessary for the Duchess to make an appearance and it was remembered how important she was. It would not be long, mark her words, before Madam Masham was sent away and things would be as they used to be in the old days.

Abigail was in attendance on the Queen, helping her prepare for the journey to St Paul's. She was uneasy. The attitude of the bedchamber women had changed towards her; they were faintly insolent. 'Her Grace has said that Her Majesty shall wear these . . .' As though Her Grace were the Queen. They did not know that the Queen had changed towards the Duchess in the last months. Abigail was certain that the moment could not be far off when there would be a final break between the Queen and her one-time friend. Yet Sarah had only to appear and everyone was ready to accept her as the invincible Duchess.

Well, it should not be so. Sarah was a fool, Abigail reminded herself, who could not control her anger, keep her mouth shut nor her fingers from a pen. Her anger when she was crossed was so fierce that it had to flow, but that was Sarah's undoing and Abigail was going to see that she was vanquished once and for all time.

'I am sorry this has to be,' Abigail was saying. 'Your Majesty is worn out.'

'My thoughts are with George. He will be needing us.'

'I have given Masham firm instructions. He will not fail us.'

Anne pressed Abigail's hand. 'But I shall be glad, my dear, when we are back with him.'

'It will be soon, Your Majesty.'

'I feel in little mood for thanksgiving. You saw the casualty lists. They haunt me. I think of those poor men dying on the battlefield and I wonder whether it is worth while. I wonder whether any fighting is worth while.'

'The Duke of Marlborough will explain that to you, Madam.'

'Ah, the Duke! A brilliant soldier, a genius.'

'And where would brilliant soldiers show their genius if not on the battlefield, Madam?'

'But the carnage! My subjects! I told you I think of them as my children, Masham.'

'Yes, Your Majesty. Your heart is too good.'

'I want the best for them, Masham. I want to see them in their homes, with plenty to eat, work to do, families to bring up . . . most of all families, for I feel that is the greatest blessing of all. If I had had children . . . If my boy had lived there would not be this tiresome matter of George of Hanover. You know, Masham, the Whigs wanted to bring him to visit England as the future heir to the throne. I will not have it. I will not.'

'Mr Harley told me of it. He thought it monstrous. But he said Your Majesty has only to refuse to receive him.'

'You know how insistent these people can be.'

'The Whigs at the moment have too much power. Since they turned out Mr Harley and Mr St John and the others, they have taken control and that could never be a good thing.'

Anne nodded.

'People are saying that the war is a Whig war, Madam. The Duke of Marlborough was a Tory until he needed the Whigs to support his war.'

'Sometimes I think, Masham, that Marlborough's great concern is to make war for its own sake.'

'And for his, Madam.' Abigail's face formed into an expression matching that of the Duke's, and Anne smiled appreciative of this amusing talent.

'I never liked George of Hanover,' went on Anne. 'He was most . . . uncouth. I met him in my youth.'

Yes, she thought, most uncouth. They had brought him to England as a possible bridegroom for her but he had declined

303

the match presumably. It was fortunate, for because of that they had brought her that other dear, good George who now, alas, lay so ill in the little house in Windsor Forest. But although she rejoiced that she had missed George of Hanover, she would never like him.

'If he came,' she went on, 'he might stay. He might set up a Court of his own. I should feel that there were some who were simply waiting for me to die. Oh, no, I will not have him here.'

'Even the Whigs will not dare, Madam, if you refuse to have him. It is a pity that there has been so much noise about his exploits on the battlefield of Oudenarde.'

'Ah! The battle!' sighed the Queen. 'How I wish that we could have done with battles.'

'And now, Madam, you must leave His Highness at Windsor to come here to take part in this celebration.'

'I never felt less like celebrating, Masham.'

'I know it.'

'I do not want my people to think that I glorify war.'

'I understand Your Majesty's deeply religious sentiments, and how you feel about going to St Paul's decked out in jewels. It would give the impression . . .'

'I know exactly what you mean, Masham.'

'It is a victory over the French, but in my opinion it would be better to give thanks humbly to God and to pray that soon there might be an end to this bloodshed.'

'You voice my feelings so admirably, Masham.'

'Then since Your Majesty is of this opinion why should you not act according to what is in your heart?'

'The Duchess has a grand occasion in mind. She has set out my most dazzling jewels.'

'But if it is not Your Majesty's wish . . .'

'You are right. It is my heart which I should obey . . . not the wishes of the Duchess of Marlborough.'

The cavalcade went on its brilliant way from St James's to St Paul's; the people of London lined the streets to watch it pass and to wait for the first glimpse of the Queen. They wanted to shout 'Long live Good Queen Anne.'

She *was* a good woman and a good Queen, they agreed. The

fact that she herself was nursing her sick husband won their regard more certainly than the fact that her Commander-in-Chief had scored up yet another victory against the French at Oudenarde. She touched for the Evil; she had set up her Bounty; and they sensed that she genuinely cared for her subjects. There was no scandal in her married life; the only strange aspect of her emotional life was her passionate friendship for Sarah Churchill and now it was said for Abigail Masham, her chambermaid. But she was Good Queen Anne and they cheered her heartily.

And in the coach with her rode the Duchess, the beautiful Sarah Churchill who was – not excepting the Queen the most famous woman in England and abroad.

Sarah was delighted. Another victory for dear Marl. *She* was the heroine of the occasion. All these people on the streets who were cheering the Queen were in reality cheering her and of course dear Marl. Who was responsible for the victory? Was it this fat woman with the rheumy eyes and the swollen limbs? No, it was her companion – handsome, though well advanced into her forties, with her rich hair, still golden and her fine glowing skin and her brilliant eyes – because after all, Marlborough's victories were hers. Genius that he was he owed his success to her.

A great occasion to be celebrated as such. Nothing should be spared to show the people how important was Marlborough's victory.

Sarah glanced at the Queen, and for the first time noticed that she was not wearing the jewels she had set out for her.

No jewels at all! On an occasion like this! Whatever had happened?

'Where are your jewels?' she snapped.

The Queen turned to her. There were tears in her eyes. She had been noticing that some of the subjects who cheered her were ill-clad and hungry looking. 'My jewels . . .?' she murmured absently.

'I put out what you were to wear. What does this mean?'

The Queen, her thoughts still not entirely on the jewels, said: 'Oh, we thought that because there had been such bloodshed it was a sad occasion as well as a great one.'

'We?' thundered Sarah.

'Masham agreed with me.'

Nothing the Queen could have said could have whipped Sarah's anger to greater fury. *She*, the wife of the hero of the hour, had set out the Queen's jewels, in accordance with her duties as Mistress of the Wardrobe, and Abigail Masham, the chambermaid-slut had said 'No jewels!' and no jewels there were.

This was too much to be borne and even on the ceremonial ride to St Paul's Sarah could not curb her anger.

'So Your Majesty would insult the Duke?'

'Insult the Duke? What do you mean, Mrs Freeman? How could I do aught but honour him?'

'It is hard to imagine that you could; but it seems that if that slut Masham orders you, you obey.'

'I would rather not discuss this matter.'

'But *I* would.'

'Mrs Freeman . . .'

'Oh, here is a nice state of affairs. The Duke risks his life for you. His one thought is your honour and that of his country. He brings you victories such as no Sovereign has ever been given before and you behave as though this victory is an occasion for mourning rather than rejoicing.'

'I rejoice, naturally, but at the same time I think of those of my subjects who have lost their lives. I think of those poor families who have lost a dear one . . .'

'Sentimental nonsense, Mrs Morley.'

'I do not think it is sentimental nonsense. It is true. Masham and I were very sad about it . . .'

'Don't give me Masham Madam. I am sick to death of that name. I wish most heartily that I had known what a snake I was sending you when I put her in your bedchamber.'

'I have had nothing but kindness and consideration from Masham. She has served me with greater care than any . . . yes *any* ever did before.'

'Since Mrs Morley is so enamoured of this dirty chambermaid . . .'

The carriage had stopped at St Paul's and the door was being opened for the Queen and the Duchess to alight.

The Queen walked painfully towards the Cathedral, Sarah beside her.

'God Save the Queen!' shouted the crowd. Anne smiled her shortsighted but most appealing smile and lifted one of her hands to wave to them.

'A dirty chambermaid!' continued Sarah. 'She has come into your bedchamber and poisoned your mind against all your best friends! It is a marvellous thing, and none would have thought you could be so duped. But it has happened!'

'I do not want to hear such things,' said Anne.

'But hear them you shall!' cried Sarah. 'I was ever one to speak my mind. In the past you always said that you preferred my frankness to the subterfuge of others. You knew that when I said something I meant it. But it seems that has changed. You prefer a mealy-mouthed chambermaid who has nothing to say but "Yes, Madam," "No, Madam" – whatever you wish to hear. And all she asks in return is your permission to bring her dear friend Harley into the bedchamber to pour his lies into your willing ears. And Marlborough, the Commander-in-Chief of your armies, is nothing to you.'

They had reached the top of the Cathedral steps. The Queen was exhausted by the effort. She cried in a loud and agitated voice: 'It is not true. It is not true.'

Several people looked startled and the Duchess being aware of this said in a voice which was heard by many standing close by: 'Be silent. Don't answer me now.'

There was a titter of astonishment as the Queen and the Duchess passed into the Cathedral.

Had they heard correctly? Had a subject actually given the Queen such a peremptory order and in public?

Surely not. But it *was* so. Many had heard it. It would have been incredible if the subject had not been the Duchess of Marlborough.

After the ceremony, Anne was exhausted; yet she could not shut out of her mind the peremptory voice of the Duchess of Marlborough telling her to be silent.

'This is too much,' she told herself. 'This really is too much. I should be happy never to see her again.'

307

Masham tended her and helped her to bed. She did not speak of the matter, even to Masham, who was so discreet though she must have heard of it, for all London would be talking of it.

Sarah had not come to St James's. Perhaps she too understood that she had gone too far.

Sarah did in fact realize that she had been somewhat outspoken; also that many people must have heard the manner in which she addressed the Queen on the steps of the Cathedral. But it was true, she excused herself. And I will have truth.

She had received a letter from the Duke, for he always wrote to her in detail as soon as was possible after one of his battles, in which he said that he was sorry that the Queen no longer favoured the Duchess and himself and was fonder of Mrs Masham than ever. He did not believe that there could be any happiness or quietness while this was so. It was not good for the country.

'There!' said Sarah to herself. 'Is that not exactly what I have repeatedly told her.'

She immediately took up her pen and wrote to the Queen:

'I cannot help sending Your Majesty this letter, to show how exactly Lord Marlborough agrees with me in my opinion that he has now no interest with you, though when I said so in the church on Thursday you were pleased to say it was untrue!

'And yet I think he will be surprised to hear that when I had taken so much pains to put your jewels in a way that I thought you would like, Mrs Masham could make you refuse to wear them in so unkind a manner, because that was a power she had not thought fit to exercise before.

'I will make no reflections on it, only that I must needs observe that Your Majesty chose a very wrong day to mortify me when you were just going to return thanks for a victory obtained by my lord Marlborough.'

Sarah never stopped to consider the effect her words might have – written or spoken – and immediately dispatched the letter to the Queen.

How tired I am of her perpetual quarrels! thought Anne. But since she asked for Marlborough's letter to be returned she wrote briefly:

'After the *commands* you gave me at the thanksgiving of not answering you, I should not have troubled you with these lines, but to return the Duke of Marlborough's letter safe into your hands; and for the same reason I do not say anything to that nor to yours which enclosed it.'

When Sarah received that letter she began to believe that she was indeed losing her power over the Queen. Never had Anne written to her in such a cool and regal manner.

She was disturbed. She wrote copiously to Marlborough telling him what was happening at home. She also could not refrain from writing to the Queen.

But Anne had no time for correspondence. She was eager to return to her husband and she set out with Abigail and a few attendants for the house in Windsor Forest, where Dr Arbuthnot greeted her with the idea that he thought a cure at Bath might be beneficial to the Prince.

Anything that would help him Anne was willing to do and immediately made arrangements to set out for the Spa which she herself loved to visit.

Bath welcomed the Queen and her consort, and it seemed as though Dr Arbuthnot was right, for the Prince's health certainly did seem to improve.

Anne's spirits rose. As she said to Abigail: 'It is long since I have felt so pleased with his state of health.'

Sarah in the Death Chamber

The Bath visit having proved such a success, the royal party returned to Kensington. The Duchess still kept in the shadows and Anne and her husband, with the Mashams in close attendance, settled into the ground floor apartments of the Palace.

Each October the Queen went to Newmarket for the racing and although Anne did not feel the Prince was quite well enough to accompany her she made preparations for the journey.

A few days before she was due to leave she noticed that George seemed unhappy and as, in spite of his sufferings, this was unusual with him, she noticed his mood immediately.

'What is it, George?' she asked. 'Are you anxious about something?'

He took her hand and said: 'I wish you were not leaving me.'

'You are not feeling so well?'

'I haf a feeling that I do not vish for you to go.'

'You do not care to be parted from me, is that it? We have been married for more than twenty-five years . . .'

'*Est-il possible?*' he asked.

310

'Yes, George, it is . . . and you still do not like to be parted from me.'

'My love,' he said, 'I haf this feeling . . .' He touched his heart. '. . . in here . . . that I vould not vish you to be away from me . . . at this time.'

Tears filled Anne's eyes. 'Then, my love, I shall remain.'

That night the Prince became very ill. Anne, alarmed, aroused the Mashams. Abigail helped her to hold up George to enable him to breathe while Samuel hurried for the doctors.

'He knew,' whispered Anne. 'Oh, my poor dear angel, he knew. He begged me not to leave him.'

This was a more virulent attack than usual and both women knew that the end was near.

'I thank God that I have you with me, Abigail my dear, to help me bear this trial,' said the Queen.

'I suffer with Your Majesty,' Abigail answered, as she expertly lifted the Prince and helped to maintain him in a more comfortable position.

'How . . . can so little a person . . . hold such a big one . . .' whispered George.

'Don't talk, my dearest. Masham is an angel. And I don't know what we should do without her. But don't talk, my love.'

The doctors arrived and eased him a little. But there was consternation throughout the Palace.

Prince George, old Est-il-Possible?, who had never been really unkind to anyone since he had come to England, was dying.

Sarah heard the news. The Prince dying and she not at the Palace! Others would be attending the Queen at this important moment. It was unthinkable. There had been that quarrel in the Cathedral when the Queen had been so bad tempered and there had been no reconciliation. But at a time like this, the Duchess of Marlborough must be at the Palace.

Could she present herself to the Queen? Scarcely when Anne had not answered her letters.

She sat down and wrote a letter to the Queen telling her that

311

in spite of the latter's ill treatment of her she was ready to let bygones be bygones and return to look after the Queen at this sad time. But she could not curb a word or two of reproach.

'Though the last time I had the honour to wait upon Your Majesty your usage of me was such as was scarce possible for me to imagine or anyone to believe . . .'

The angry pen raced on; the letter was written and sealed. Now to send it by a messenger.

But perhaps there was little time to waste. It might be that the Prince was already dead. Others would be there, taking over her duties. She could not allow that, so she would take the letter herself.

She arrived at Kensington, haughtily summoned a page and told him to take the letter to the Queen immediately.

'Her Majesty is with the Prince,' was the answer.

She looked amazed that anyone could question her orders. 'I have told you to take that letter to the Queen . . . and no matter where she is I expect you to obey me.'

The page, intimidated as everyone was accustomed to be by the great Duchess, immediately obeyed. But no sooner had he gone than it occurred to Sarah that when she read the letter the Queen might refuse to see her. So without waiting for a summons from the Queen she went to the bedchamber where the Prince lay dying and brushing aside those who were guarding the door strode into the room.

The Queen, blinded by tears, was not aware of her until she came close.

'Mrs Morley, I should be with you at such a time.'

The Queen did not seem to see her.

'Although,' went on Sarah, 'in view of your treatment of me when we last met I am sure you did not expect to see me . . .'

The Queen turned away from her, but Sarah caught her arm.

'But at such a time we must forget that unfortunate incident. I shall remain here with you. But naturally I must ask you to dismiss Masham. She will not be needed while I am here . . .'

Anne turned her tragic face to Sarah and in that moment

none could doubt that she was the Queen and Sarah the subject.

'Go away,' she said.

Sarah was deflated. Anne turned her back. There was nothing the Duchess could do but leave the bedchamber.

The Queen sat beside her husband's bed, unable to speak, stunned by her misery. The Duchess, who when told to go away had only left the bedchamber and was waiting in the adjoining room, immediately came back and ordered everyone from the room so that only she and the Queen remained at the bedside of the dead Prince.

Sarah knelt by the Queen and took one of her hands.

'My poor friend, this is a terrible blow. I suffer with you.'

The Queen looked at Sarah as though she did not see her.

'But,' went on Sarah, 'there is nothing you can do by weeping.'

Still the Queen did not answer and Sarah, continuing to kneel, allowed the silence to remain for some minutes; then she said gently: 'Your Majesty should not remain here. It is not good for you. Will you let me take you to St James's?'

'I will stay here,' said Anne.

'No, no,' said Sarah. 'You cannot stay in this dismal place.'

'Leave me,' whispered Anne.

'How could I leave you at such a time? You need your friend with you now as never before. My dear Mrs Morley, I suffer with you, but I repeat it would be well to leave this place.'

'I wish to stay at Kensington.'

Anger bubbled up in Sarah. Why was she so stubborn? Who ever heard of a widowed Queen refusing to leave the bedside of her husband? Masham was here, of course. Did she think that it was easier to have Masham with her constantly at Kensington than it would be at St James's?

With tremendous restraint Sarah prevented herself from mentioning Masham's name. Even she realized that one could not quarrel in the death chamber.

But she would not give up. 'Madam, no one in the world ever stayed in a place where a husband lay dead. Wherever you go in this place you cannot be far from that dismal body.'

'Do not speak of him so!'

'Dear Mrs Morley, I speak only for your welfare. It is my only concern. If you went to St James's you need not see anyone you did not wish to see. And you might see any person that is a comfort to you . . . there as anywhere else.'

Anne nodded slowly. 'It is true,' she said.

'I will take you in my coach. We will draw the curtains and none will be aware that it is you. You will feel better when you leave this place.'

'Leave me with him for a while,' said the Queen, 'and then send Masham to me.'

Sarah looked stricken for a moment and then the blood rushed into her face; but the Queen had turned from her and Sarah could do nothing but leave her.

Send for Masham. Never!

The Queen looked up as the door opened and her disappointment was obvious when she saw Sarah instead of Abigail.

'I did not send for Mrs Masham,' announced Sarah. 'There are bishops and ladies of the bedchamber waiting to see Your Majesty and I thought it would make a disagreeable noise if you kept them out on account of a chambermaid.'

'I asked for Masham . . .' began the Queen.

'Your Majesty can summon her to St James's . . . if you wish.'

'I need to prepare for the journey.'

'My dear Mrs Morley, it will be the pleasure of Mrs Freeman to wait on you. I will send for your travelling clothes and we will leave at once.'

To Sarah's dismay the maid who brought the Queen's travelling cloak and hood was Alice Hill, and Sarah in her jealous awareness saw that the Queen's expression lightened a little at the sight of Abigail's sister.

Anne bent towards her. 'Tell Masham that I need her. She is to come to me at once,' she whispered.

Alice, aware of the thunderous expression on Sarah's face, inclined her head and curtsied to show that she understood and would obey the Queen's order immediately; and Anne wrapped in her travelling cloak passed on with the Duchess behind her.

In the gallery along which she must pass, certain of her household were gathered – among them Dr Arbuthnot and, to Anne's delight, Abigail herself.

Anne smiled and as she passed leaned towards Abigail and pressed her hand.

Abigail understood. She was to follow the Queen without delay; and when Anne had left and Alice came breathlessly to her to give her the Queen's message, Abigail lost no time in setting out for St James's.

Sarah took the Queen triumphantly to her apartments.

'Dear Mrs Morley, I pray you leave everything to me. Friends should be together at a time like this.'

Anne did not answer.

'If Mrs Morley would like to go to the green closet I will take her there and have something warm and soothing sent to her.'

Anne nodded and together they went to the favourite room.

The green closet! There he had sat dozing in his chair while Masham played on the harpsichord, made bohea tea or produced something stronger which she served so daintily, moving noiselessly about the apartment. How she longed for the return of those days which were gone for ever. But Masham was still here.

She wanted Masham to come and Sarah to go and leave her alone. She never wanted to see Sarah again.

But Sarah was giving imperious orders. 'Bring broth for Her Majesty. Yes, Mrs Morley, it will do you good. You must *eat*. It will give you strength.'

The broth was brought, and Anne sipped it without tasting it.

'Now,' said Sarah, 'I will see about ordering you a really nourishing dish. You will feel so much better when you have had something really good to eat. It was well that I brought you from that dismal place. You could do no good by staying there.'

Sarah went out and after a few moments there was a light scratching at the door.

Anne gave the order to enter, and when she saw who was there she gave a cry of joy. Abigail ran to her and knelt at her feet, kissing her hands.

'Masham . . . dearest Masham!' said the Queen.

Abigail lifted her face to the Queen's; Abigail's was blotched with weeping. The Queen stretched out her hands. 'Such comfort to have you with me, my dear. Stay . . . stay here.'

Sarah came back and found them together.

The Prince lay in State at Kensington for fifteen days before his body was conveyed to the Painted Chamber of Westminster. During this time Anne kept Abigail with her, although Sarah refused to leave the Court. Her posts *demanded* that she stay, she declared.

The Queen spent her days planning the funeral and drawing comfort from Abigail. Sarah looked on with distaste. It was most unseemly, she told Danvers. Did the Queen care nothing for the Prince, and all for ceremonies!

As the Queen was clearly heartbroken this statement seemed strange, but no one dared disagree with the Duchess of Marlborough.

Anne, wanting the whole country to understand that this was indeed a period of mourning, ordered the closing of all theatres. She herself remained in the green closet, seeing only her ministers and a few of her servants. Abigail was in constant attendance and the Duchess remained at St. James's.

It was a shock to Sarah to see the change in Abigail, who, she told Godolphin, had become arrogant and completely forgetful that she was merely a chambermaid.

The funeral took place as Anne had wished with the utmost pomp – an impressive ceremony by torchlight attended by all the important ministers and officials.

But the main preoccupation of the Queen's ministers – Whig and Tory – was not the death of the Queen's husband but the shifting of the Queen's favour from the Duchess of Marlborough to Mrs Masham.

Marlborough's Request

The Duke was in England and Sarah had gone to St Albans to be with him. As usual there was great joy in being together, but they were both apprehensive for the future.

Marlborough was the great hero, but a war hero, and the people were tired of war. While Marlborough was abroad his enemies were undermining his position at home. He knew; but Sarah refused to accept it.

But the biggest disaster of all was the fact that Sarah had lost her place in the Queen's affections.

In spite of the evidence she could not believe that she had been put aside in favour of her insignificant poor relation.

'Abigail Hill!' she would murmur even in her sleep. The woman was becoming an obsession.

'To think that I took her from a broom!' she would say apropos of nothing. There was no rest from the subject.

Marlborough, more philosophical than his wife, tried to soothe her and at the same time warn her. He might have said that it was her overbearing behaviour which had brought about the rift, which would have been true, but he refrained. He knew his Sarah and he loved her for what she was; and in any case had always known it was useless to try and change her.

Therein lay the success of their relationship, although some said that Marlborough was so devoted to his Sarah because he was forced to spend so much time away from her.

'Do not distress yourself so,' he begged her. 'Give up struggling against the wind and the tide.'

'Give up everything to that chambermaid.'

'You are only distressing yourself and not making the Queen more fond of you. You'll never get her friendship back by railing against Masham.'

'I'll force her to be friends again!'

Dear Sarah. Such energy, and so little knowledge of human nature!

He was tired, feeling his age. There had been moments of grandeur in his life but to what were they leading? Blenheim, Ramillies, Oudenarde ... and others — and what was the result? Loss of favour at home; his enemies working to oust him from politics if not from the Army; the peace he had hoped to make had not been achieved. He had wanted to take the war right to the gates of Paris and then he would have been able to make demands which Louis would have had to accept. But the Dutch were uneasy allies. As soon as he had made their frontiers safe for them, they wanted to have done with war.

And he himself? One could not be young for ever. Strangely enough he cared more for Sarah's disappointments than for his own; but she would take no advice. She had listened to him more than to most, but she believed that she alone was capable of decision.

'It is no use hiding ourselves here,' she said, 'while Abigail Hill and her friend Harley plot against us. Tomorrow I shall go to the Queen.'

In vain did Marlborough beg her not to act rashly. Sarah believed that eventually she would wear down the Queen's resistance.

How peaceful it was without Sarah at Court! thought Anne. It had been an exhausting time, giving constant audiences to her ministers. It seemed that they now realized that George was not so insignificant as they had once believed him to be. He had always been so good natured and never a troublemaker, so that they had been apt to overlook his strength.

The Queen had always liked to listen to his advice on state matters, even if she had not taken it; and his presence at the interviews gave her confidence. Moreover, he had a way of cutting short an interview which had gone on too long by showing his impatience for his dinner; which might seem a frivolous excuse for cutting short a conference, but was effective.

'Dearest George! What shall I do without him?' sighed the Queen.

There was Masham, always ready to help, always eager to comfort.

'At least *you* are left to me, dear Masham,' she said.

Abigail replied with fervour that she hoped to serve the Queen as long as she lived; she would ask nothing more of life.

'It is at such grievous times as this that we know our friends,' said the Queen.

'The Prince was the kindest of masters,' murmured Abigail. 'Poor Masham is desolate.'

'Poor faithful Masham!' agreed the Queen. 'The Prince always relied on him. He is a good man and I am glad you chose him for your husband.'

'I do not know how to comfort him, Madam. He is without one whom he revered and he has nothing with which to occupy his mind. I tell him the sooner he finds something to do the better. The Prince would not have wished him to grieve.'

'No,' she said. 'Poor Masham! He has lost not only the kindest master in the world but his position.'

'I think he would like to join the Army, or to go into politics, Madam.'

'Well, he is following a noble example.'

'You mean the Duke's.'

'Mr Harley tells me that he wishes to govern the country as well as the Army.'

'Mr Harley is Your Majesty's most brilliant statesman and he is very likely right. But poor Masham is no Marlborough, Madam. He would, I suppose, be grateful for a humble post . . .

319

something to take his mind off this dreadful loss.'

'I understand, Masham. It is what the Prince would wish.'

'Your Majesty and the Prince were always in harmony. I declare it was a lesson for all married people merely to see you
together.'

The Queen put her hand to her eyes and Abigail brought the
handkerchief with which to wipe away the tears.

Marlborough returned to the Continent to open a new campaign, and Sarah came to Court. But she could not now walk
into the Queen's apartments and scatter all those who were in
attendance. She must ask for an audience and await the
Queen's pleasure.

She was constantly seeking openings to see the Queen, to
bully her into returning to the old relationship. She found an
opportunity to see her when she wanted her apartments to be
extended and sent in a request that a few small rooms adjoining this apartment might be assigned to her. The reply came
back that the Queen had already promised these rooms to one
of her women.

Sarah was furiously frustrated. How dare Anne send her
messages in this aloof fashion, as though she were some unknown person soliciting a favour!

She summoned Danvers whom she could still terrify.

'Is this true?' she demanded.

'Yes, Your Grace. The rooms are promised.'

'Which woman has them?' Sarah wanted to know, believing
that if she made her wishes known the rooms would be re-
linquished.

'Alice Hill, Your Grace.'

'Alice Hill!' screamed Sarah. 'Sister of the . . . chambermaid.'

'She is Mrs Masham's sister, Your Grace.'

'That's who I mean,' cried Sarah.

'She has been given these rooms, Your Grace. Mrs Masham
thought those she had before were unsuitable.'

'But I wanted them! I shall see the Queen. I refuse to be
treated in this way. Do you know, Danvers, that I took that
woman from a broom.'

'Your Grace has mentioned it.'

'And now she seeks to direct *me*.'

'That, Your Grace, would be quite impossible.'

'It is impossible!' cried Sarah.

At length she forced herself into the Queen's presence. Anne was clearly fretful, playing with her fan, her eyes on the door, wondering, thought Sarah grimly, whether she can ask me to summon Masham. Dear Masham! Kind Masham! Who coos in her ear and gets favours for her good-for-nothing brother and ninny of a husband and . . . Sarah could have screamed in her rage . . . for that sly toad, that monster, that traitor Robert Harley.

'It would seem that Mrs Morley sets out to frustrate me,' she cried.

The Queen closed her eyes and looked tired.

'Even a simple matter of rooms . . .'

'If Mrs Freeman has anything to say to me she may write it,' said the Queen.

'I have much to say to Your Majesty and I have been writing to you all through the years. It seems to me that Mrs Morley has allowed herself to be deceived by those whose greatest pleasure is in doing harm to Mrs Freeman.'

'If you have anything to say to me you may write it,' said the Queen.

She had her parrot cry and Sarah could see that she would not be tempted from it.

A pleasant state of affairs! What could she do with a woman like that? Her coolness was apparent and there were times when Anne could remind any subject – even Sarah – that she was the Queen.

So there was nothing Sarah could do but retire.

But she would not let the matter rest there. She had been told that if she had anything to say she could write it. If she had anything to say indeed! She had much to say to that ungrateful friend.

She therefore returned to her lodgings and set to work to write a long account of her twenty-six years' service to the Queen. She quoted passages from Jeremy Taylor on the subject of friendship. She accused the Queen of infidelity and ingratitude. She surpassed even herself in her invective.

The Queen's response to this missive was to express her grief. It was impossible for her to recover her former friendship towards Mrs Freeman and her chief complaint against her was her inveteracy towards Mrs Masham. She would however always treat Sarah with the respect due to the wife of the Duke of Marlborough. She would in time, read what Sarah had sent her, and give Sarah her reply.

That was all the answer Sarah could get. She waited for an answer to her accusations. None came.

And when she saw the Queen in church Anne smiled at her vaguely as she would towards any lady with whom she had a slight acquaintance.

That was an uneasy summer. It was being said that the war was being prolonged unnecessarily by a faction with Marlborough at its head; and that the sole reason was that the Duke might continue to indulge his love of war.

His brilliant victories had reduced the French to a great desire to put an end to the carnage; Louis would consider terms, but those put forward were not acceptable. He had agreed to banish the Pretender – and his protection of James Stuart was one of the main reasons for the war – to acknowledge the Protestant succession in England, to demolish Dunkirk as a fortress and grant a protective frontier to the Dutch. There was one demand he could not accept and that was to gather an army and send it to drive his grandson from the Spanish throne.

'If it is necessary to make war,' said Louis, 'I would prefer to fight my enemies than my children.'

This was a sentiment which all could understand and the war-weary English were more in sympathy with the old enemy than their own victorious Duke.

Then came the news of the victory of Malplaquet.

Marlborough had done it again. 'He is invincible!' cried Sarah when she heard the news. 'Now Mrs Morley will see that she cannot ignore the wife of the greatest commander on Earth.'

But when the Queen saw the results of the battle and the tremendous slaughter of her countrymen, for the allies, losses were 25,000 and although the French had lost the battle they had not lost nearly as many men.

'How long must this wicked slaughter go on!' cried the Queen; and although she took up her pen to write the usual congratulatory letter to the Duke she could not do so. How could she feel that this was a matter of congratulation when thousands of her subjects – her *children* – had died on the battlefield? For what? Had not Louis offered to banish the Pretender? Was he not suffering great stress in his own country through this war? Why could there not be peace, for it seemed that only with peace could there be the prosperity she wanted for her people!

Abigail brought Mr Harley to the green closet. Dear Abigail! She was pregnant and it made such a bond between them. It reminded Anne of those years of hopes . . . hopes which had come to nothing except in the case of her dearest boy who had lived a while to make the tragedy the greater. And Abigail's husband and her dear brother were soldiers too.

Such occasions for condolences; and Abigail agreed with her that the Duke was perhaps the only man who wholeheartedly wanted war.

Mr Harley kissed her hand. He sat beside her and Abigail brought them tea, which though perhaps not to Mr Harley's taste he always took.

'Malplaquet!' he said. 'A victory, they tell us, Madam. But a bloodstained victory. The Duke never loses a battle – but what he does lose is countless English lives. Madam, forgive me. I am carried away by this terrible carnage.'

'You voice my own thoughts, Mr Harley. I feel I can scarce attend a thanksgiving service for such slaughter. How long must this dreadful war continue?'

'For as long as it pleases His Grace of Marlborough, it would seem, Madam.'

'I shall not allow it.'

'Then, your Majesty, the war will end.'

'The Government, Mr Harley, seem so firmly *behind* the Duke.'

'Godolphin, Sunderland — family connections! A Marlborough junta Madam. That sort of thing can be very powerful.'

'I never liked the Whigs.'

'Nor did the Duke, Madam, until he needed their support for his war. I have been consulting with my friends . . .'

'Yes, Mr Harley.'

'If we could overthrow the present Government I believe I could present Your Majesty with a Tory Ministry which would be very much to your liking.'

A Tory Ministry! thought Anne. Peace abroad! The Church and State safe! And dear, amusing, *clever* Mr Harley at its head. That was a very desirable prospect.

Marlborough had returned from the campaign which had culminated at Malplaquet. He was very anxious; he had heard from Sarah that the reception of the victory had been less enthusiastic than that of Oudenarde and that the joy which followed the news of Blenheim was entirely lacking.

The Queen, Sarah pointed out, continued devoted to her dirty chambermaid, and Snake Harley with Slug St John was continually in her presence.

As for Sarah, she had written to the Queen reminding her of all she had done for her and how she had given her friendship over the years, and had had no reply.

Marlborough himself asked for an audience with Anne.

She received him with affection. He was such a charming man and had none of his wife's overbearing manners. Anne would always have a fondness for Mr Freeman however much his wife provoked her. He never forgot that she was the Queen and although he was the hero of so many great battles and his brilliant generalship had astonished Europe, he was far more modest than Sarah ever was.

'Dear Mr Freeman,' said Anne, 'I am pleased to see you home safe and well and I trust you will remain here with us for a long time.'

He knelt and kissed her hand.

Marlborough replied that there was nothing which would delight him more but that he had the Queen's interests to protect and he feared they would soon take him from home.

Anne sighed, remembering the casualty lists from Malplaquet.

'I wish,' said Marlborough, 'to make sure that Your Majesty and the country are safe for ever. And there is only one way in which I can be sure of bringing this about.'

'And that way, Mr Freeman?'

'If Your Majesty would make me Captain-General of your armies . . .'

'But you are that already.'

'I have my enemies, Madam. They could replace me at a moment's notice if they banded together and were sufficiently strong against me. If Your Majesty would make me Captain-General of your armies for *life* . . .'

He paused, aware of the magnitude of the demand he was making. Sarah had represented Anne to be a fool, a cipher in her hands; and although he knew that Sarah had exaggerated in her contempt for the Queen, he had accepted the fact that Anne was a simple woman.

This was not entirely true. She might love her cards and her chocolates, her gossip and her comforts, but she had a great sense of her responsibilities to her country; and she would not make a rash promise before she had first pondered the matter or consulted with those whose opinion she valued.

She understood what this would mean. The title of Captain-General for life would make Marlborough a military dictator whom none could shift.

She thought of Sarah grown more arrogant than ever, forcing her way into the royal apartments. Oh no! That would never do.

She lowered her eyes and studied her hands.

'I should need time to consider that, Mr Freeman,' she answered.

Disappointed, but not unhopeful, Marlborough talked of other matters and after a while took his leave.

Anne was thoughtful after the Duke had left. How right Mr Harley and Abigail had been! It was true that the Churchills were trying to reduce her to a mere cipher; and they had begun it by joining themselves through marriage with the most influential families so that the junta was formed; and now there they were – Marlborough, Godolphin and the hateful Sunderland – ready to rule the nation. All they needed was for Marlborough to become Captain-General of the Army for life – which would mean that no one would have the power to dislodge him – and there would be the military dictatorship for which they would all be working.

Relations with Sarah were very strained; they would soon be so with her husband, for Anne was certain that she was putting no such power into the hands of Marlborough.

But how to act in a manner so tactful that she could refuse Marlborough's demands without alienating him, for if he were to resign from his present position at this moment she could not imagine what evil might befall her armies abroad.

She considered her ministers and thought of Earl Cowper who was not of the Churchill faction, and was a man whom she trusted and who would not wish to see Marlborough supreme. She sent for him.

'My lord,' she said, 'if I were to ask you to draw up a commission to make the Duke of Marlborough Captain-General of the Army for life, how would you do it?'

Cowper was momentarily speechless at such a prospect.

'Your Majesty . . .' he stammered at length. 'Madam . . . I . . . I could not advise such an undertaking in any circumstances.'

'My Lord Marlborough has asked that his position should be made permanent,' she told him.

'Madam, it is an office which has never been bestowed, other than for the time of the Sovereign's pleasure.'

'I know it, my lord; but now His Grace would have it otherwise.'

'But, Madam . . .'

'You will know what to say to His Grace, I am sure, my lord,' said the Queen with her placid smile.

Cowper did know. He first went to his friends and told them what had taken place between him and the Queen. They were immediately apprehensive and angry. Marlborough was clearly aiming at military dictatorship. How disastrous if the Queen

326

had agreed to his request which, they believed, she might have done if the Duchess had been on the old terms with her.

In the circumstances, Cowper was able to go to the Duke, with the support of his friends, to tell him that the great seal of England would never be put to such commission.

There was consternation throughout the Ministry. Marlborough's preposterous suggestion was seen as a dangerous one.

Harley and St John talked of it to their political and literary friends.

Sarah had failed to keep her hold on the Queen, it was said; so Marlborough was going to rule instead of the Queen. Military men with big ambitions should be watched.

John went down to St Albans with Sarah. Restlessly and angrily they talked.

'Nothing goes as we could wish!' cried John; and he looked sadly at his wife, for none believed more than he did that if Sarah had retained her friendship with the Queen everything they desired would have come to them. But he never criticized her; all he would do was warn her gently. Sarah was far from gentle. She railed against Abigail Hill, for she was certain that all their troubles came from her.

'They have no gratitude,' she cried. 'The nation, the Queen ... nor Abigail Hill. You have won resounding victories for England; I have spent hours with the stupid woman when I would have preferred to be shut in a dungeon; I brought that whey-faced slut from a broom to a palace ... and where is the gratitude, I ask you. Those who have most reason to love us turn against us.'

It was soothing to go down to Woodstock and look at the progress of Blenheim; but even that was slow and not to Sarah's taste and she and John Vanbrugh had by now conceived a great dislike of each other.

Disgruntled and angry they returned to London. The Duke realized he had made a mistake in underestimating the Queen, and believing she would grant his request without consulting her ministers. Who would have thought that she would have called in Cowper before the commission was a *fait accompli*?

He was getting old; he was tired; and in spite of his brilliant victories he had not achieved what he set out to do.

The Duke of Argyle called on the Queen.

'Madam,' he said, 'the Duke of Marlborough is a danger to the peace of England. It is believed by some that he might attempt to seize that which has been denied him.'

'I do not believe that the Duke of Marlborough would ever turn traitor to his own country,' protested Anne.

'It is as well to be prepared, Your Majesty.'

'That is true,' agreed Anne.

'Your Majesty need have no fear. You have but to give me the alarm and I would seize Marlborough – even at the head of his troops, and bring him to you dead or alive.'

Oh dear! sighed Anne. How alarming. War was bad enough abroad, but civil war was something she could not bear to contemplate.

She thanked the Duke of Argyle and told him she would remember his promise although she trusted it would never be necessary for her to make use of the services he so kindly offered her.

Abigail found her deeply disturbed and she confided in her as she had come to in all things.

Abigail was sure that Mr Harley would have a better plan than the Duke of Argyle who, she suggested, could be as ambitious as the Duke of Marlborough; and where would the virtue be in replacing one ambitious man for another?

Mr Harley was brought to the green closet. He had a plan, he would bring together a secret council of men who would protect the Queen and in due course hope to be her Government, for it was possible that the Whigs would be defeated at the next election.

He agreed that at all costs the Duke of Marlborough must be watched and given no more power than he already had – which was far too much.

If the Queen would trust him he would in turn devote his life to serving her beloved Church and the Tory party.

How fortunate, Anne agreed with Abigail, that Mr Harley was at hand.

Wine for a Laundress

Abigail lay in her bed awaiting the birth of her child. She felt aloof from all that intrigue which for so long had formed part of her life. It had been so for the last weeks as the time for her confinement grew nearer and nearer. A child of her own – hers and Samuel's.

The pains had started and she had heard the women whispering in the chamber. They feared it would be a long labour, for she was small, thin, not built for child-bearing, so they said.

But she felt strong and capable of anything; and she was astonished by the softness of her feelings.

The Queen had been gracious; she knew that Anne was anxiously waiting for news. They had been pleasant, those last cosy weeks, seated at the Queen's feet, leaning against her, talking of the Queen's 'boy', laughing and crying together. Never had they been so close – friends, not sovereign and subject.

'You must let me share in your joy, my dearest Abigail,' said Anne.

The pains were more acute. It was Mrs Abrahal who was bending over her.

'Take it easy,' she was soothing her. 'It won't be long now.'

Mrs Danvers was there, with Mrs Abrahal and the others, and the Queen had sent for her own physician, for nothing was too good for Mrs Masham. Mrs Danvers would report to the Duchess of Marlborough that it had been royal attendance, if you please. But would she? Mrs Danvers had begun to wonder whether it was necessary to report everything to the Duchess, for what need was there now to seek her favour? Better perhaps to watch over Mrs Masham's comforts with the same assiduous care as one had once bestowed on the Duchess of Marlborough.

Mrs Abrahal seemed to have come to that conclusion too.

Mrs Abrahal curtsied to the Queen who cried: 'What news?'

'A little girl, Your Majesty.'

'And Mrs Masham is well?'

'As well as can be expected, Madam. It was a long and hard labour.'

'Poor Masham! And is Dr Arbuthnot with her now?'

'Yes, Your Majesty.'

'Help me up. I will go to her.'

Anne stood smiling at Abigail who looked so wan and yet triumphant. Lucky Abigail who held a child in her arms.

Anne quietly prayed that dearest Masham would have better luck than she had had. May this child live and be a comfort to her, she said to herself.

'You are well content,' she said tenderly.

'Yes, and shall be more so if Your Majesty will consent to this child's being named after you.'

'It would give me the greatest pleasure,' said the Queen, with tears in her eyes.

Anne delighted in the baby.

'My dear Masham,' she said, 'it brings back the old days to me so clearly. I think of my own little ones . . .'

And the baby had a fondness for the Queen. 'She's like her Mamma,' sneered Abigail's enemies. 'She knows how to please.'

It was such a pleasure to sit together and talk of Abigail's long labour and the antics of the child. It helped Anne to forget all the unfortunate tensions about her throne which had been caused by that alarming demand of the Duke of Marlborough. Mr Harley was determined to prevent the Duke's causing trouble; and as for Godolphin, she was getting tired of him; Sunderland she had never liked, although she had been forced into allowing him to take office. How pleasant then to talk of babies with Abigail. There had never been such cosy confidences with Sarah, although Sarah had had a large family. Sarah was unnatural. She had never been interested in the charming details of family life.

'Mrs Abrahal was a comfort,' said Abigail. 'I should like to reward her. And she is so fond of little Anne.'

'We must let her know how much we appreciate her goodness,' replied the Queen. 'I will raise her allowance. That will please her.'

'Shall I send her to Your Majesty later?'

'Please do. I do declare the enchanting creature is smiling at me.'

'She knows her Queen already. I'll swear she will be as good a servant to Your Majesty as her mother has always tried to be.'

Such pleasant hours! So far removed from the demands and schemes of ambitious men.

Mrs Abrahal curtsied to the Queen.

'Ah, Abrahal, Mrs Masham has been telling me how *good* you were to her during her trying confinement.'

'Your Majesty, it was my duty and I would say that Mrs Masham bore herself with courage for it was not an easy labour.'

'No. I understand that. And I know full well how trying such times can be.' The Queen looked sad but brightened as she remembered the Masham child who seemed so healthy – far more so than any of hers had been. 'Mr Masham must be delighted,' she added. Then she noticed that Mrs Abrahal was looking very pale.

'You do not look well yourself, Abrahal,' she said.

'Your Majesty is gracious to notice, Madam. But I am growing old.'

'You have been long in my service I know.'

'Yes, Your Majesty, it is twenty years since I started washing your Brussels lace-heads.'

'Is it possible?' sighed the Queen and was sad again, being reminded of George, who had used that phrase so often. 'Well, Abrahal, Mrs Masham has told me how kind you were to her and as a result I am going to have your allowance raised.'

'Your Majesty is so good,' said Mrs Abrahal, tears in her eyes.

'I like to see good service rewarded,' said Anne kindly. 'But what I do not like is to see you looking so pale. You should drink a little wine each day. I remember the dear Prince's saying that a little wine, taken regularly, was very good for the health.'

'Your Majesty . . .'

Anne held up a hand. 'I shall order a bottle of wine to be sent to you every day. I want you to go on washing my lace-heads for many years to come.'

Mrs Abrahal, murmuring her thanks, was ushered out of the apartment by Mrs Masham. When she had recovered from her surprise and pleasure a little, she remarked to Mrs Danvers that there was no doubt whom one had to please now if one hoped to advance one's fortunes at Court. The Duchess of Marlborough was on the way out; Abigail Masham was undoubtedly in.

Although the Queen had no wish to see Sarah, Sarah clung tenaciously to her duties. Always at the back of her mind was the thought that she could not fail eventually to win her way back to her old position at Court.

Looking through the accounts one day she saw that a bottle of wine was going to one of the laundresses. 'A bottle of wine a day!' cried Sarah. 'I did not order this. And what would a laundress want with a bottle of wine a day?'

She summoned Mrs Abrahal, the recipient of the wine, and demanded to know what was meant by it.

'It was ordered by Her Majesty,' said Mrs Abrahal.

'Ordered by Her Majesty . . . and no reference made to me! But did you not know, Abrahal, that such expenditure has to be sanctioned by me!'

'No, Your Grace, not when it was an order of Her Majesty.'

'Then you had better learn quickly to the contrary.'

'Your Grace, after I attended Mrs Masham's confinement . . .'

'Don't speak to me of that chambermaid who has nothing to do with this case.'

'Excuse me, Your Grace, but it was because I had nursed Mrs Masham that the Queen raised my allowance and ordered me to take a bottle of wine each day.'

Sarah turned pale with rage.

This was too much. Not only was Masham usurping her place in the Queen's affection, but taking her duties from her while they still belonged to her.

This was too much to be borne. Marl treated as though he were a common adventurer! Herself treated as though she were of no account!

She simply would not hear of it.

She stormed her way to the green closet.

'Her Majesty does not wish to be disturbed,' she was told.

'Get out of my way,' cried the Duchess. 'Whether she wishes it or not she is going to be disturbed.'

Abigail was seated at the Queen's feet and they were smiling together. Sarah threw a look of hatred at Abigail and then turned her gaze on the Queen.

'I did not hear you announced,' said Anne coldly.

'I was not announced,' retorted Sarah. 'I would speak with you alone.'

Abigail rose and looked to the Queen for orders. Anne bowed her head slightly, signing for Abigail to go. Abigail obeyed and went into the ante-room, out of sight but not out of earshot — and, as she thought later, it would not have been easy to do that for the back stairs pages must have heard Sarah's tirade.

'What have you to say?' asked Anne coldly.

'This, I have to say. I hold the Privy Purse under Your Majesty and I expect at least to be consulted on expenditure.'

333

The Queen sighed and looked at her fan.

Sarah went on: 'It now comes to my ears that a laundress has been given a rise in her allowance and, if you please, a bottle of wine every day!'

'It does please me,' said Anne.

'A bottle of wine . . . for a laundress! And without consulting me.'

'She shall have her wine,' said Anne.

'And I say this is a matter on which my opinion should be asked. Who ever heard of laundresses being given bottles of wine every day? We shall soon have them making merry in the laundries.'

'She shall have the wine,' said Anne, putting the fan to her lips.

'Madam, I shall not allow this to pass. I shall go to Lord Godolphin. He is your Lord Treasurer. We shall see what he will have to say.'

Dear me! thought Anne. How right Mr Harley was. These Churchills would rule us if they could. What a dangerous family! But Mr Harley and Mr St John need have no fear. I shall certainly do my best to see that no more power falls into their hands.

The Queen rose and made for the door. Sarah, her eyes blazing, did an unprecedented thing; she placed herself between the Queen and the door. It was difficult, Anne thought afterwards, to know how to act when confronted by a situation which had never occurred before and which one would never have thought possible. Here was she being harangued by a subject, being held captive in a room by a subject. How extraordinary — except when one reminded oneself that it was the coarse, overbearing, *vulgar* Duchess of Marlborough.

'Stand aside,' said Anne regally. 'I wish to leave.'

Sarah's eyes narrowed. 'You shall hear me out,' she cried. 'That's the least favour you can do me for my having set the crown on your head and kept it there.'

Anne was too astonished for speech.

'You are willing to forget all that I have done for you . . . merely because a sly chambermaid has come between us. Do not think that I care on *that* account. I do not want your *cloy-*

ing affection. But I will not be insulted by a chambermaid whom I took from a broom and kept as a servant in my own house . . . No, I will not be insulted by such a slut . . . nor will I allow the great Duke – who has won great glory for you abroad – to be so insulted. I do not care if I never see *you* again . . . but I'll have my rights.'

'I agree with you,' said Anne calmly, 'the seldomer we meet the better.'

'Do not think,' cried Sarah, 'that you have heard the last of this.'

Anne touched Sarah with her fan and in that moment she was a Stuart Queen, and the daughter of Kings. Sarah was momentarily overawed and stood aside, while Anne, as well as her swollen feet would allow, walked out of the room.

'Masham!' she called. 'Send Masham to me.'

Lord Godolphin did not like his mission; but the truth was he was afraid of Sarah Churchill. He admired her in a way; he was convinced that had she behaved differently all the hopes of the junta to which he belonged would have been realized. Secretly he believed that such a powerful personality must one day win her way back. So when she said that he must go to the Queen and tell her she could not allow Mrs Abrahal a bottle of wine every day, he weakly agreed to go. It was all very well to give way to Sarah, but when he thought of the triviality of his mission he felt ridiculous.

Anne received him in the green closet, with Mrs Masham in attendance. The spy, the snake in the grass, whom everyone knew now brought in Harley for secret conference with the Queen. That was how the rot had set in; and now it seemed that with Sarah leading them – they were all rushing downhill to complete and utter failure.

He kissed the Queen's hand. Her manner was cool to him. She could never receive him nowadays without being reminded of the Duke's arrogant demand and Sarah's rages.

He talked of political matters for a while, but she felt that he was coming to some point which was the reason for his visit.

At last it came. 'I have delayed sanctioning the rise in Mrs

Abrahal's allowance, and the bottle of wine she has asked to be delivered to her lodging each day.'

'For what reason?' asked Anne.

Godolphin looked uncomfortable. 'It is a little irregular, Your Majesty.'

'Irregular? In what way, pray? *I* have ordered it. Are you, my lord, telling me that the Queen may not raise a servant's allowance nor order her a bottle of wine without the consent of the Parliament?'

'Oh, no, Your Majesty.'

'Then,' said Anne, 'not without the consent of the Duchess of Marlborough?'

'N . . . no, Your Majesty, but . . .'

'There are no buts,' said Anne firmly. 'Pray sign the order without delay and let me hear no more of this ridiculous matter.'

'Yes, Your Majesty.'

Godolphin felt so foolish he could scarcely wait for the interview to be over; but after that he had the wrath of Sarah to face.

Dr Sacheverel

The light of a hundred bonfires made a glow in the November sky and the smell of their smoke penetrated St James's Palace. It was the usual fifth of November celebrations; and this date had become a very important one in the calendar.

On it the popish plot to blow up the King and his Parliament had been discovered, and, years later, on the same date, William of Orange had landed in England to rid the English of a popish King. So naturally the day must be celebrated.

> *'Remember, remember the Fifth of November*
> *The Gunpowder Treason and Plot,'*

chanted the people in the streets.

> *'I see no reason*
> *The Gunpowder treason*
> *Should ever be forgot.'*

In St Paul's Cathedral a sermon was preached before the

Lord Mayor of London by a Dr Sacheverel. He was an eloquent speaker and his sermon attracted a great deal of attention, for he spoke frankly of the coming of William of Orange to England and of the men who had helped him to his crown. From them he passed on to certain of those men who ruled them at the time and one especially he criticized, giving him the name of Volpone but speaking of him in such a manner that no one had any doubt that he referred to Lord Godolphin.

St Paul's was crowded, and although Dr Sacheverel spoke for three hours no one wanted to leave; and so impressed by the sermon was everyone who heard it, that the suggestion was made that it should be printed and circulated.

Unfortunately for Dr Sacheverel – and others – this was done, and it was not long before it was brought to the notice of Lord Godolphin who, reading it and recognizing Volpone as himself, fell into a violent rage and swore that he would be revenged on the rash prelate.

Godolphin stood before the Queen. Anne had not seen him so vital for a very long time. It was a pity, she reflected, that it took anger to make him so.

Had her Majesty read the pamphlet? he wanted to know.

She had read it. In fact she had found it very interesting and she was sure that Dr Sacheverel was a good and right-thinking man. But she did not say this to Lord Godolphin, for she had once been fond of him in the days when she had thought of him as Mr Montgomery. It was a pity that he had allowed the Marlboroughs to use him, for that, according to Mr Harley and Masham was what he had done; and she was sure they were right, for was it not so obvious?

'This man is contemptuous of the revolution and that can only mean that he is contemptuous of Your Majesty,' pointed out Godolphin.

'He speaks kindly of me and with respect and affection.'

'Madam, if he condemns the revolution and the accession of King William and Queen Mary he is condemning you, for it would seem that he is agitating for a return of the Pretender.'

Anne's eyes clouded. She often thought of her half-brother:

and sometimes when the gout was very painful and she thought of dear George now lost to her, it occurred to her that she had not many more years to live. Then if her half-brother came back it would be like righting the wrong she had done her father.

'Your Majesty,' went on Godolphin. 'In the circumstances I believe that Dr Sacheverel should be put under restraint until he can be brought to trial that it may be decided whether he be guilty of treason.'

'This seems harsh treatment for preaching a sermon.'

'Such a sermon! They are talking of it in the taverns and the coffee houses. As Your Majesty's chief minister I must ask you to leave this in my hands. If he is judged guiltless then he will be a free man. But this sermon has created a great deal of unrest and I believe that for the safety of the nation we must have Sacheverel in prison.'

Anne said she would like to consider the matter and that was all the satisfaction Godolphin could get; he went away very uneasily and would have been more so had he known that almost immediately after he had left, Abigail was bringing Robert Harley to the Queen.

Robert Harley was excited. He saw in the Sacheverel affair a possibility of overthrowing the Ministry of which Godolphin was the head. He had his ear to the ground. With St John he frequented the coffee houses and the taverns; at Albemarle House he entertained Swift, Addison, Steele and Defoe regularly; he liked to talk with them and the conversation was sparkling. It was illuminating too. These men had already given him some idea of how the people in the streets were reacting to this affair. They were with Sacheverel; they were devoted to the Queen but each day they were turning from Marlborough because they were heartily sick of the war which they were already calling Marlborough's war.

The country was ripe for change. This could be the occasion.

Robert Harley advised the Queen to agree to Dr Sacheverel's arrest. No harm would come to the man, he assured her; and she would see when he was brought to trial how firmly the people stood for her and the High Church.

'For you and the Church, Madam, should be our first concern,' he told her. 'Godolphin obeys Marlborough and Marlborough wants war, because, Your Majesty, Marlborough is brilliant at war. It is a sad state when one can only buy one's glory with the blood of others. Let the people see how this servant of the Church is treated. It could mean the overthrow of those who work against the Church.'

Anne trusted Mr Harley. So did Abigail. When he had gone they drank tea together – Anne's laced with brandy – and talked about the brilliance of Mr Harly and how they were sure that given the opportunity he would rid the Queen – and the Church – of those whose self interest made them the enemies of both.

Mr Harley was right. Mobs were parading the streets demanding the fall of the Government. Sacheverel was the hero of the day and the majority were behind his criticisms of Godolphin. Many a widow and orphan of the great war hated the very sound of Marlborough's name and did not hesitate to say so. He was the warmonger, who, because he liked playing soldiers, used men and deadly weapons to amuse himself. Not only that, he wanted to be the dictator. A fine state of affairs. There would be battles every day with such a man in power. This war had been costly enough in men and wealth. 'Have done with Marlborough!' cried the people. 'Have done with war! And down with the Government.'

When the Queen rode to the opening of Parliament that November the crowds cheered her frenziedly.

'Long live the Queen! God save Sacheverel!'

Anne smiled benignly and lovingly on her people; she was different, they noticed, sad and ill at ease. Why? Because she was on Sacheverel's side. Because she, like themselves, was heartily sick of the Whig Ministry.

When she made her speech she sounded listless.

'She is telling us,' said those who listened, 'that she is not with her Government in spirit and that she is merely performing a necessary duty.'

The writers were busy. They thrived on such occasions. All through the country people were alert, watchful of events. There was going to be change.

Mr Harley with Mr St John and others among them were ready for the moment for which they had long been waiting.

Abigail reviewed the situation. She was certain that the Government would soon fall and that Robert Harley would replace Lord Godolphin as the Chief Minister. What a triumph for her!

Everything was going well for her. Sometimes she would lie in bed nursing her baby and telling herself that her life was more satisfying than Sarah Churchill's. The fact was that Sarah would never be satisfied.

Samuel had come home from the war – different, more mature. She was not sure that this pleased her. Would he be less willing to be led? But temporarily it was a challenge. He was devoted to her and delighted by their child. They would have a boy, he said, next time.

Her brother Jack, quite a seasoned soldier now, was a friend of his; and she enjoyed seeing them together, particularly when Alice came too.

They were often in her apartments. Alice, of course, had been in attendance at the birth of little Anne. In attendance! Abigail mocked herself. I talk like a Queen.

But of course to be Queen's favourite was next best to being a Queen.

Queen's favourite! Little Abigail Hill – at the beck of and call of Lady Rivers, poor relation in the Churchill nursery – and now she could decide the fate of Sarah Churchill ... and perhaps the country.

People were now beginning to realize her importance. When Alice and Jack came to see the baby she could sense the difference in their attitude towards her. They were in awe of her. As for Samuel, he was frankly proud.

They stood round the child's cradle. Alice – getting even fatter – gurgled her pleasure; Jack was seated, for he had been wounded at the siege of Mons; and Samuel was beside Abigail, his hand on her shoulder.

'Such a little darling!' cooed Alice. 'I'll swear your mamma is planning a grand marriage for you.'

'What, already!' cried Samuel.

Abigail smiled at him. He was sentimental and the thought of losing a daughter so newly acquired even in marriage at some distant date appalled him.

'Oh come, Alice, there's time enough for that,' said Abigail.

'But she'll have a grand future I wouldn't mind swearing,' insisted Alice. She stood up and looked at her sister admiringly. 'You'll see to that. And the Queen won't deny you anything. I heard that said only yesterday.'

'It's not wise to be too sure of anything,' said Abigail sagely.

'And Abigail is the wisest woman in the world,' added Samuel.

Alice wanted to know whether Mrs Abrahal washed the baby's linen and what the Queen had said about the new tooth; the two men talked together of battles. They moved to a table, sat down, and picking up any small objects they could lay their hands on they used them to indicate their forces, and like a couple of generals fought out Malplaquet.

Watching them, Abigail said: 'Do you remember the day Lady Marlborough called and how alarmed we all were. The first time we saw her . . .?'

Alice nodded and her plump complacent expression was clouded. This life of plenty and excitement was far removed from those days.

'She brought us here,' said Alice. 'It's something I try to remind myself of now and then.'

'That she might use us,' retorted Abigail. 'Do you remember how she constantly reminded us of what she did for us?'

'And still does.'

'She does not remind me.'

'Oh, you, Abigail, you have become more important than she is. Abigail, I have heard it said . . .'

'Yes?'

'That you rule the Queen just as Sarah Churchill once did.'

'She listens to me.'

'Oh, Abby . . . Though it doesn't seem right to call you that now. My own sister. You, Abigail Hill, to be the friend of the Queen!'

'And others ...' murmured Abigail, thinking of Robert Harley. Her eyes went to Samuel – the general at the table. That was all he was capable of. He would never be a Marl-borough ... never a Harley. If she and Harley ... But that was a dream long ago abandoned. She must use what she had at her disposal and not reach out for the impossible as Sarah had done.

Alice was smiling at her with something like adoration. She would not forget that the present respect she enjoyed in the royal household was due to her sister.

Abigail savoured that adoration. Alice had sent her thoughts back to the past and she saw now a poorly furnished bedroom where she and Alice had tried on the cast-off dresses of the Churchill girls; she saw herself and her sister studying their reflections – Alice plump and gay, Abigail pale and thin. Then Alice had pitied Abigail, the plain one.

It was a different story now. She had shown them that a pale, plain face was no deterrent. She had an adoring husband; Alice had none; she had the Queen's love; and the admiration of a brilliant statesman.

She felt all powerful and she said on impulse, 'I must see what I can do for Jack. As soon as a Colonelcy falls vacant I shall speak to the Queen on his behalf.'

'Oh ... Abby!'

'Not a word yet. We'll wait, and it'll be a surprise for him.'

'What of Sam?'

'His turn will come,' answered Abigail serenely.

Those were trying weeks for the Queen. She wanted to be rid of her Government but could see no means of constitutionally doing so. It cheered her to know that her people were firmly behind her, but this in itself would not rid her of men whom she so heartily wished to dismiss.

She had not seen Sarah since the last outburst, but Sarah continued to write. It seemed that the woman must give in to her feelings somehow, and she could not rid herself of the desire to direct. The insolence of the woman was almost past belief; as Anne said to Abigail, if she had not the evidence before her eyes such behaviour would seem incredible.

Christmas had passed and the unsatisfactory state of affairs still persisted. Sacheverel was still waiting trial; and a great deal would depend on the outcome of that. But the new year, Anne told Abigail, would bring great changes.

They were sitting in the green closet when a messenger brought a package which by the writing on the outside Anne knew to come from Sarah.

She sighed and calling Abigail to her stool, asked her to open the package. This Abigail did and together they read Sarah's long letter of recrimination and advice.

'There is a copy here of Jeremy Taylor's Holy Living and Dying together with a prayer book,' said Abigail.

Anne read Sarah's letter and sighed. How could she ever have cared so deeply for such a woman. Sarah once more told her of her follies and how she should reform. The passages marked in the books were meant to convey a lesson to the Queen.

Sarah Churchill for all her vitality, for all her arrogance, thought the Queen, was a fool. She wants to return to her old place and everything she does makes me feel that I never want to see her again.

'What shall I do with the books, Madam?' asked Abigail.

'Put them in a drawer and let us forget them. These are very trying times, Abigail. I should like to get away for a short time to *think*.'

'Yes, Madam. Have you anywhere in mind?'

'I like the quiet of Hampton.'

'Shall I make preparations at once?'

Anne's fingers rested on the sandy hair. What a comfort! she thought. How *different*!

Hampton was delightful even in January. The Queen used a small chamber because of the cold, and it was very cosy to sit there with Abigail and talk of pleasant things like the virtues of Prince George and the brilliance of their boy; the future of Samuel Masham and the charms of his daughter Anne.

But there were other matters which could not be ignored.

'How I long to be rid of this Marlborough junta. But how? Only an election can dislodge them.'

'The people are eager to be rid of them too, Madam.'

'Yes, but the Ministry cannot be dismissed as easily as that. There is one drawback to Hampton, Masham. Mr Harley cannot visit me so secretly. If he came to Hampton he might be seen. And then there would be talk. From St James's it was easy for you to take a message; but if you left Hampton your absence would be noticed. You are being watched now, my dear.'

'Oh yes,' said Abigail. 'I am not simply the chambermaid now. But perhaps an idea will occur to us.'

'We will watch for it,' said the Queen.

It came when the Lieutenant of the Tower, the Earl of Essex, died. The Marlborough faction immediately chose one of their men to fill the vacant post, which was, naturally, in accordance with their policy.

'Your Majesty cannot allow them another victory,' warned Abigail. 'You should decide on the man for the post and insist.'

'You are right of course. How I wish it were possible for you to bring Mr Harley up to me by way of the back stairs so that I could discuss this matter with him.'

Abigail agreed on the wisdom of this. But how bring Mr Harley to Hampton without attracting attention?

'If we send someone with a message to him – someone who is so humble that his departure would not be noticed . . .' began Abigail.

'But it must be someone whom we could trust,' replied the Queen.

'Your Majesty is surrounded by servants who long to serve you.'

'We must select carefully, my dear,' replied Anne.

They chose one of the gardeners. He was astounded when Abigail approached him as he worked in the gardens and gave him a letter which she said the Queen wished him to take with all speed to Mr Harley in Albemarle Street. The man expressed his willingness to serve the Queen; and even the lowest servant knew that Mrs Masham came direct from the Queen – in fact they were saying in the household and in the streets that Mrs Masham was closer to the Queen than the mighty Duchess of Marlborough had ever been.

*   *   *

Knowing that he would come promptly in answer to the Queen's command, Abigail was watching for the arrival of Harley.

For a few moments, before he was conducted to the Queen, they were alone together.

'I thought this was the time to send for you,' Abigail told him.

He surveyed her from under his curiously hooded eyes, and as she smelt the strong smell of spirits, she was, for a moment, dismayed. She prayed he would not allow his love for drink to impair his talents; but need she have worried? He had always been a heavy drinker; he had once told her that he needed the stimulus of wine and was at his most brilliant when he was as near intoxication as such a hardened drinker could get.

'Wise Abigail,' he murmured, taking her hand and kissing it. His eyes were tender, but she knew that his caresses meant nothing; and she was too wise a woman to go on sighing for the impossible.

'The death of Essex is important,' she went on. 'Your man must have the Tower . . . not Marlborough's.'

He nodded.

'And Marlborough has already decided on the Duke of Northumberland.'

'Marlborough must be disappointed. We want the Tower for Rivers.'

'So I thought. The outcome of this will be the pointer we need. If we win . . . then . . .'

'The ultimate victory cannot be far off. My dear Abigail, you are my most able general.'

'An election now and Godolphin and Marlborough will be out. And you in . . . The Queen's first minister.'

Once more he kissed her hand. 'I shall not forget . . . Abigail.'

'Essex leaves a Colonelcy vacant as well as his office at the Tower. I would like that for my brother.'

'I am sure Her Majesty will be only too delighted to grant your request.'

He left her and went to the Queen's apartment.

*   *   *

Sarah was furious.

'Jack Hill . . . a colonel in your Army. Good God, Marl, now they have gone too far.'

'They're going to defeat us over this matter of the Tower, but I'll be damned if I'll give Abigail Hill's brother a regiment.'

'You should resign rather.'

John looked sadly at Sarah. She would never understand the importance of tact. He was determined that Jack Hill should not have the regiment, but the matter would have to be settled with diplomacy.

When Godolphin presented himself to Anne and she expressed her wishes that John Hill should become a colonel he assured her of the impossibility of this.

'My Lord Marlborough will explain to Your Majesty why this cannot be.'

'I see nothing but frustration,' cried Anne. 'It seems that you, sir, work continually against me.'

Godolphin with tears in his eyes protested, but the fact that she could not grant Abigail one of the few requests she had made, hurt Anne. A colonelcy in the army! It seemed such a small thing to ask – and it was so natural that Abigail should want it for her brother. Yet she, the Queen, was not allowed to make it.

Godolphin left in despair.

Marlborough called on the Queen, who regarded him coolly.

'Your Majesty,' he said, 'my enemies have distorted my action and I fear I have been greatly misrepresented in your eyes.'

Anne bowed her head and stared at her fan.

'I want to have a chance to clear myself of the calumnies of my enemies.'

'Pray proceed,' said the Queen.

'There is a charge against me that I made an attempt to become a military dictator of this country. That is false.'

The Queen did not answer. Had he not come to her himself and asked for the Captain-Generalcy for *life*? What else did that mean? Oh, she was weary of these Marlboroughs!

347

She put her fan to her mouth. It was a gesture implying that she wished to hear no more on that subject. In her opinion he had attempted what he denied and by great good fortune – and the services of good men like Mr Harley – he had been prevented.

Marlborough turned the subject to the proposed colonelcy for John Hill.

How much he wished to please Her Majesty she herself knew. The fact was that there were old soldiers in his Army who had served through many battles – deserving men. It was a commander's chief duty to keep his men happy. If favours were bestowed on men because of their charming relatives this was bad for the Army.

'Madam,' he said, 'we have won many great victories but we are not yet at peace. I cannot endanger the future of this country by making discord in the ranks. This would most certainly happen if a high command were given to an inexperienced soldier when veterans were overlooked.'

'So you will not give this colonelcy to Hill?'

'Madam, I would resign my post rather than do so.'

He bowed himself from her presence.

She was not a fool. At least on this point he spoke good sense. She would not give up, of course; but it seemed as though Abigail's brother might have to wait until he was a little more experienced before he received promotion.

Abigail was disconsolate because she had failed to give the colonelcy to her brother; but she believed that this was a small matter compared with the great victory which was just in reach.

She was certain that very soon the Godolphin–Churchill Ministry would be defeated and Robert Harley's set up in its place.

The Duke of Marlborough was preparing to leave for Flanders for the spring campaign and came once more to the Queen before he left.

Anne was gracious to him, for she had always had a fondness for him, and even when she felt him to be most dangerously arrogant he was always charming.

'I have come to speak to Your Majesty on behalf of the Duchess!' said Marlborough, and immediately noticed the stubborn set of the Queen's lips. 'She wishes to remain in the country a great deal and asks that her posts may be bestowed on her daughters.'

Anne was relieved. 'This should be so,' she said, and her relief was obvious. Anything, she was implying, to be rid of Sarah.

The Duke took his leave and Sarah arrived to thank the Queen for bestowing honours on her family.

Anne listened, in silence, and when Sarah asked if there had been some misunderstanding, she replied, 'There has been none. But I wish never to be troubled more on this subject.'

Sarah opened her mouth in protest. But Anne repeated that she did not wish to be troubled more on the subject.

Sarah knew that she was defeated.

For once she had nothing to say.

Marl was going away once more; and now everything depended on the outcome of the trial of Dr Sacheverel.

Abigail was alarmed. She realized now that she was in the forefront of the battle for power. At last her importance had been recognized. Not only was it known that she had ousted Sarah Churchill from her place in the Queen's affections, but she had allied herself with Robert Harley, making it possible for him to have many an intimate interview with the Queen, so that now there was consternation in the Whig Ministry – for the Queen had the power to dismiss Parliament – and it was realized that the trouble could be traced to one who had seemed to be nothing more than a humble chambermaid.

First it was a whisper, then a slogan; and after that it was a battle cry: 'Abigail Masham must go.'

The Earl of Sunderland, Marlborough's son-in-law, always inclined to rashness, declared that nothing must be spared to banish Abigail Masham from the scene of politics. His plan was that Marlborough should give the Queen an ultimatum: either Abigail Masham left the Queen's service or the Duke of Marlborough would.

There was a conference at Windsor Lodge, presided over by Sarah.

'It is too risky,' said Marlborough. 'What if she should choose Masham?'

'And disrupt the Army!' cried Sarah.

Marlborough looked tenderly at his wife; and even as he did so he thought how different everything might have been if she had not lost the Queen's favour by her own rash outspokenness, and her inability to see another point of view than her own. But how could he blame Sarah? He loved her as she was. Had she been sly like Abigail Masham she would not have been his dashing flamboyant Sarah.

'We have powerful enemies,' he reminded her.

'Harley. St John – that cabal . . . and of course whey-faced Masham.'

'The Queen cannot afford to lose you,' Sunderland reminded his father-in-law. 'She will have to give way.'

Godolphin, feeling tired and each day growing more and more weary of political strife, believed it was an odd state of affairs when a government must concern itself with the dismissal of a chambermaid. But he was too tired to allow himself to protest.

'At least,' said Sarah, 'we did not allow Masham's brother his colonelcy. It shows that we only have to take a firm stand.'

She laid her arm on her husband's shoulders. 'I will have Brandy Nan recognize your greatness however much she tries to shake her silly head while she gabbles her parrot phrases.'

Godolphin looked a little shocked to hear the Queen given such an epithet; but Sarah and Sunderland won the point and Marlborough was induced to write a letter to the Queen pointing out that she must either dismiss Mrs Masham or himself.

Robert Harley was a man who liked to work in the shadows and had spies concealed in all places where he believed they could serve him best. Even as Marlborough was writing his letter to the Queen news was brought to him of what it would contain.

Abigail or Marlborough. It would be a difficult choice; for although Marlborough would not be accepted as a military dictator of the state he must undoubtedly remain Commander-in-Chief in Europe until a satisfactory peace had been made.

Harley called on Abigail and as a result Abigail went to the Queen.

Anne knew at once that something was worrying her favourite as soon as she saw her.

'The baby is well?' she began.

Abigail knelt before Anne and buried her face in the Queen's voluminous skirts.

'They are trying to part me from Your Majesty,' she cried.

'What!' cried Anne, her mottled cheeks turning a shade less red, her dewlaps trembling.

'Yes, Madam. Marlborough is going to offer you a choice. Either I go or he does.'

'He cannot do this.'

'He will, Madam. I have heard that he has already written the letter and that it is only because Lord Godolphin is a little uncertain that it has not yet reached you. The Duchess and Lord Sunderland are in favour of it and . . . it will not be long before they have persuaded Godolphin.'

'I shall not let you go.'

'Madam, they may make it impossible for you to keep me.'

'Oh dear,' sighed Anne. 'What troublemakers they are! Why should they wish to part me from my friends!'

She was agitated. Lose Abigail! It was impossible. And yet these clever men and their devious ways were trying to drive her into a corner.

'There is no time to waste,' she said. 'I will send for Lord Somers at once and tell him how kindly I feel towards the Duke of Marlborough and how I hope that I shall soon have an opportunity of demonstrating my affection for him. At the same time I will tell him that I will never allow any of my ministers to part me from my friends.'

Abigail looked up into the Queen's face and seeing the obstinate set of the royal lips was reassured.

Godolphin paced up and down the chamber at Windsor Lodge.

'It's no use,' he said, 'she'll never give up Masham. You can be sure that our enemies abroad are getting the utmost amusement out of this situation. The Government versus a chambermaid. It is making us ridiculous.'

Marlborough saw the point as Sarah would not. It was for this reason that Godolphin had chosen a moment to speak to the Duke when he was alone.

Ridicule could be a strong weapon in an enemy's hand. In war an Army needed to have as many points in its favour as could be seized; and none was too small to be ignored.

Godolphin was right: Sarah and Sunderland were wrong. This battle between a Commander-in-Chief of an army and a chambermaid must not be allowed to become a major issue.

'I shall not offer the Queen the ultimatum,' said Marlborough. 'I shall write to her though and let her know how mortified I am to be exposed to the malice of a bedchamber woman.'

'This is better,' agreed Godolphin. 'For God's sake don't drive the Queen into a corner, for in such a position she could become the most obstinate woman alive.'

'We must find other means of dislodging Mrs Masham,' agreed the Duke sombrely.

'Better secretly than openly. You will go to visit the Queen.'

'I suppose it should be done.'

So Marlborough came to London to see the Queen who received him graciously, anxious to show him that her coolness towards his wife did not extend to him.

This is a victory for Marlborough, said Marlborough's friends.

But Robert Harley and his friends knew that the triumph was theirs. Marlborough had wanted to force the Queen to a choice between himself and Abigail; and had been afraid of the result. Triumph indeed.

The trial of Dr Sacheverel was causing a great deal of excitement throughout London. Anne, who had hoped to attend Westminster Hall incognito, had been recognized by the crowds who had shouted: 'God Save the Queen and Dr Sacheverel.'

Anne, acknowledging the royal greetings, knew that the people were with her and that the anger they obviously displayed was not directed against her but the Lord Treasurer,

Godolphin, who had brought the case against Sacheverel, and Godolphin was, of course, a member of that family which was seeking to take over the government of the country.

She believed then that if she dissolved the Whig Parliament the Tories would undoubtedly be returned to power at the next election. This was pleasing to contemplate, for she was heartily tired of Godolphin, and if he were dismissed his office he would take Sunderland with him ... and dear Mr Harley could form the government he had mentioned to her in their secret conversations. Then there would be no more threats of taking Abigail from her, for Abigail and Harley were very dear friends.

Therefore it was quite pleasant to hear the shouts of the people as she passed through the streets; knowing that although they were threatening to riot for the sake of Sacheverel, they had no quarrel with their Queen.

In the hall she made her way to the curtained box from which she would watch the trial, and she saw that one of the ladies in attendance was the Duchess of Marlborough. What a nuisance that woman was! She immediately disturbed Anne's peace of mind although, the Queen noticed, not without pleasure, she was a little more subdued on this occasion, no doubt being fully aware of the anger of the people against her party.

But it was not in Sarah's nature to be subdued for long. Very soon she was fussing as to whether the ladies should stand or sit and even went so far as to approach the Queen to remind her that the trial was likely to be long and that she had not given her ladies the required permission to sit.

'By all means, sit,' said Anne coolly, without glancing at the Duchess.

Sarah saw the glances which were exchanged between several of them, and the colour heightened in her cheeks. It was difficult to restrain her fury.

When she saw that the Duchess of Somerset did not however sit, but took up her stand behind the Queen's chair, Sarah approached her imperiously. 'And why, pray,' she demanded, 'do you not sit since Her Majesty has given the permission to do so?'

'I do not care to sit,' replied the Duchess of Somerset, and added: 'In her Majesty's presence.'

'Is Your Grace implying that I am ignorant of Court procedure?' Sarah's voice was high pitched and audible.

'I imply nothing,' answered the Duchess of Somerset. 'I merely say that I prefer to stand.'

Sarah sat down on her stool, glowering.

Oh dear, thought Anne, how pleasant it would be if I could be rid of that woman.

The trial lasted for several days and on each day the Hall was crowded. All the members of Parliament were present and as the Hall was full to overflowing those who could not obtain admittance filled the streets about the building.

With each day it became clearer with whom popular sympathy lay. The people who had taken the Queen to their hearts declared that she was with them on the side of Sacheverel against the Whig ministry led by Godolphin and supported by the Marlborough faction. This was more than the trial of Dr Sacheverel. The fate of the government was at stake.

When at last Sacheverel was found guilty of the charges brought against him, he was given such a light sentence that his supporters took this as a victory for them. He was simply forbidden to preach for three years and his sermon was to be burned before the Royal Exchange in the presence of the Lord Mayor and Sheriffs of London and Middlesex.

That night the bonfires were lighted and there was great rejoicing in the streets.

The Last Meeting

The sound of carousal could be heard in St James's Palace. Abigail smiled secretly as she administered to the needs of the Queen.

Dear Masham! thought Anne, I should like to honour her with a title, but if I did, could I expect a lady of rank to do the menial tasks she does for me? I do not want any change. I want everything to be as it is now between us.

'There is excitement in the streets tonight, Madam.'

'Yes, Masham. The people regard this as a victory for Dr Sacheverel.'

'And for Your Majesty. They have linked you with him. So often I have heard them shout, Long Live the Queen and Dr Sacheverel.'

'He stands for the Church and I do not believe my present Government has the good of the Church at heart.'

'Your Majesty will doubtless soon have a new Government.'

'I have had petitions from the people to dissolve the present Parliament.'

'Bringing Dr Sacheverel to trial has ruined them,' added Abigail.

'I shall seek an early opportunity of dissolving Parliament so that the people will have a chance of electing the Government they want.'

Abigail was exultant. This would be good news for Robert Harley and she would convey it to him at the earliest possible moment, although, of course, he knew, for the outcome was inevitable.

'Play to me for a while,' said the Queen. 'I have a fancy for a little music.'

So Abigail went to the harpsichord and played the Queen's favourite Purcell airs, but as she played there was such a sound of conversation from the ante-room that she stopped and, turning to the Queen, saw that she had fallen asleep.

Abigail went to the ante-room where she saw Lady Hyde and Lady Burlington laughing together.

Abigail said: 'The Queen is sleeping.'

A short while ago they would have resented the intrusion, now they knew that a word from Abigail to the Queen could do them much harm so they smiled ingratiatingly at her and asked her if she had heard of the Duchess of Marlborough's latest impertinence towards Her Majesty.

'I have not,' answered Abigail, 'and should like to hear it.'

'Well,' said Lady Hyde. 'Lady Marlborough was acting as sponsor at christening with the Duchess of Somerset and Lady Somerset suggested naming the child Anne. And what do you think Madam Sarah said to that? "There was never anyone good for much of that name. I'll not stand for a baby named Anne!"'

'How dare she!' cried Abigail.

'Sarah would dare anything. Did you not know that?'

Mrs Darcey, one of the palace ladies came into the room, just as Anne, awaking and missing Abigail, called to her.

'Masham,' said the Queen, when Abigail entered, 'you look disturbed. Is anything wrong?'

'I am just angered, Madam, by a further impertinence of the Duchess of Marlborough.'

'What is this?'

'It is just another rudeness, Madam. Scarcely worth the notice.'

356

'Nevertheless I would hear.'

Abigail told the Queen of the christening incident.

'That woman is continually showing her lack of respect and animosity towards me,' complained the Queen. 'I'll not endure much more of it.'

Mrs Darcey, who overheard the last remark, went to Sarah and told her what had been said.

'You see,' cried Sarah to John, 'there is continual tittle-tattle against me.'

'But what of this christening matter?'

'I was there,' admitted Sarah.

'And you made this remark?'

Sarah put her head on one side. 'I was joking about the occasion when the Duke of Hamilton christened his boy Anne – hoping for royal favour, of course – and I said since this was a girl, why not, after the fashion set by Hamilton, make a boy of her and call her George.'

'It might be a good plan if you could see the Queen and explain this.'

'My dear Marl, I am heartily sick of playing the humble supplicant to that woman.'

'But the Government is in danger of falling. If you could regain your old friendship with the Queen we could recover all that we have lost.'

'It seems ridiculous to have been pushed aside for that chamberwoman.' Sarah's eyes were glinting. 'She *shall* see me. She shall. I shall explain to her and she will have to take notice.'

Marlborough laid a restraining hand on his wife's arm. 'My love, be careful. You can do it . . . if you will. But you must curb your tongue.'

Sarahs lips were firmly set, but Marlborough's misgivings were great.

'Your Majesty is disturbed?' asked Abigail.

'A request for an audience from the Duchess of Marlborough.'

'And Your Majesty will grant it?'

'The woman holds all her appointments still and that gives her easy access to my apartments. I would be rid of her. Do you know, Masham, I never want to see her again. Does that surprise you when you consider the greatness of the friendship we once had for each other?'

'What surprises me, Madam, is Your Majesty's great patience with the Duchess.'

'My patience is fast running out. I do not wish to see her, Masham. She wearies me with her continual ranting.'

'Could Your Majesty write and tell her to put what she has to say in writing?'

'An excellent idea, Masham. I will do that.'

When she received the Queen's letter Sarah was furious. She immediately wrote that what she had to say could not be put into writing. Anne replied by giving her an appointment for the next day, but when the hour approached Anne called Abigail to her and told her that the thought of seeing Sarah gave her a headache and made her feet throb.

Abigail bathed the feet and afterwards massaged them while the Queen planned the letter she would write to tell Sarah that she preferred what she had to say to be written.

But Sarah was not easily diverted. Again she replied that it was not possible to write what she had to say and again she demanded a private interview.

'Shall I never throw her off?' Anne asked piteously. Then she had the idea of leaving for Kensington and wrote to Sarah telling her that she would be away for some days and if Sarah would care to put what she had to say in writing she, Anne, would consider it while she was away.

But there was no escape. Sarah's reply came back promptly:

'I am glad Your Majesty is going to Kensington to make use of the fresh air and take care of your health. I will follow you there and wait every day until it is convenient for you to see me, as what I have to say is of such a nature as to require no answer.'

Sarah arrived at Kensington Palace while the Queen was reading her note. She went straight to the royal apartments and told the Queen's page to announce her.

Anne, sitting at her writing desk, Sarah's letter before her, realized that she could not longer postpone the interview and gave permission for Sarah to enter.

When Sarah came into the room Anne remained at her desk, her pen in her hand.

She looked up as Sarah entered and said: 'I have just read your letter. I was going to write to you.'

As soon as she was in her presence, so many memories came rushing back to Sarah that she forgot the change in their relationship and replied to the Queen with all the old imperiousness: 'About what were you going to write, Madam?'

'I was going to write to you,' replied Anne, setting her lips into a line which should have warned Sarah.

'There was something in my letter, Madam, that you wished to answer?'

'There is nothing you have to say that you could not write,' insisted Anne.

Sarah was exasperated. The Queen was in what Sarah called the parrot mood. She would go on repeating her set phrases and it would be impossible to reason with her.

'I did not know that Your Majesty was ever so hard as to refuse to hear a person speak. Even the meanest have a right to be heard.'

'I tell people to put what they have to say in writing when I have a mind to.'

'I have nothing to say on the subject which is so upsetting to you, Madam. Mrs Masham is not concerned in what I would say, but I cannot be quiet until I have spoken to you.'

'You may put what you have to say in writing,' insisted the Queen.

'It has been brought to my notice,' burst out Sarah, 'that evil tales concerning me have been laid before you. It is said that I have spoken disrespectfully of Your Majesty. I would no more think of doing that than killing my own children.'

Anne's expression did not change, but she did not look at

Sarah's heated face. Sarah Churchill had often spoken disrespectfully to her in her own hearing, so how much more inclined she would be to do so behind her back! Sarah no longer moved her to affection and her greatest desire was never to look on her one-time friend's face again.

'There are many lies told always,' murmured Anne, turning her head and picking up her fan.

'I ask Your Majesty to let me know what calumnies you have heard against me. I know you will agree that I should have a chance of clearing myself.'

'In your note you said you required no answer,' said Anne. 'I will give you none.'

Sarah was furious. 'Do not think to thrust me aside in this way. Do not think that I will stand aside for a chambermaid. You *shall* hear me.'

'I will leave the room,' said the Queen, rising painfully from her chair.

Sarah strode to the door and stood against it, her arms outspread, her eyes flashing.

'You will stay here until you have heard what I have to say.'

Anne's meekness dropped from her; she drew herself to her full height and looked in cold amazement at the Duchess.

'I think Your Grace forgets she is in the presence of the Queen.'

The coldness in Anne's face alarmed Sarah. She knew in that moment that she had failed. The horror of the situation impressed itself upon her. Everything for which she had worked was slipping away from her. And not only had she lost what she ardently desired, she had failed Marl.

Angry tears came to her eyes and in a moment she was sobbing as she never had before. It was a display of frustration and anger; the acknowledgement of defeat; she turned away and opening the door stumbled into the gallery, where she sat down and gave way to her grief.

Anne looked at the door; she could feel nothing but relief. Sarah Churchill had gone too far, but perhaps even she at last understood that their friendship was at an end.

She went to her chair and sat down thoughtfully. She would

dissolve the Whig Ministry. There would be a Tory Government which would please her, for she was a Tory at heart. Mr Harley would be at the head of her new Government and there would be no further attempts to rob her of dearest Masham.

A scratching at the door. She sighed. There was Sarah again, her face blotched with weeping, but her eyes unusually meek.

She has learned her lesson, thought Anne. She knows that I never want to see her again.

'Well, Lady Marlborough?' said Anne haughtily.

'Madam, my posts demand that I am at times in attendance on Your Majesty.'

Anne inclined her head. Yes, she thought, but we must find a means to put an end to that.

'And,' went on Sarah, 'I hope that Your Majesty will have no objection to seeing me on state occasions.'

Anne inclined her head. No, she would not object to seeing Sarah on state occasions. What she would not tolerate was giving her another private interview.

'You may come to the Castle,' said the Queen coolly. 'That will not disturb me.'

Sarah bowed and the Queen turned away signifying dismissal; but Sarah had never learned to control her feelings and she could not do so now. Her rage took possession of her once more, suppressing common sense.

'This is cruel,' she cried. 'All our friendship forgotten for the sake of a woman whom I myself took from a broom. Everything I have done for you is thrust aside as though it had never been, and I am treated to scorn and indignity. Through the court they are whispering about me and talking of your ingratitude to me. Mrs Morley, have you forgotten the old days?' As the Queen was silent, Sarah went on: 'You will be sorry for this. You will suffer for your inhumanity.'

'That,' answered Anne, 'will be my affair. Your Grace is dismissed.'

Sarah gazed in astonishment at the regal figure so different from Mrs Morley of the past.

'I can only believe,' went on Anne, as Sarah did not move, 'that Your Grace is hard of hearing. You are dismissed.'

There was nothing Sarah could do but turn away.

Anne had made up her mind that it was the last time she would ever grant Sarah Churchill a private audience.

The Queen could be stubborn, but Sarah went away planning the next stage of the campaign.

It took her some time to accept the fact that she would never be permitted to speak to the Queen again.

The Fall of Godolphin

In his Chelsea lodgings Jonathan Swift was waiting for the arrival of an important visitor. He stared gloomily into the fire and took up his pen to write to Esther Johnson in Ireland. It was one of his pleasanter diversions. Stella, as he called her, was as devoted an admirer as his dear friend Miss Vanhomrigh, who was Vanessa to him. Irascible, gloomy, he was dissatisfied with life because a man of his genius must be forced to lend his talents to men of lesser stature for the reason that they, through birth, riches or their own personalities, had forced themselves into positions of power. He hated his poverty, his caution, his ill temper. What a comfort it would be if Stella were with him now – or perhaps Vanessa. Both adored him; both were ready to give him the adulation he desired. Neither was poor. Stella had her fifteen hundred pounds on which she had believed she could get a better return in Ireland than in England. Vanessa was closer at hand to administer comfort.

But he was born disgruntled. He would not marry because he believed he could not afford to; he could not write as he wished to write for fear of landing in the pillory as poor Defoe had. Perhaps he would not have escaped so lightly.

His great pleasure on cold nights when there was not enough fire in the grate to warm his bones and his Irish servant was more incompetent than usual, was to write to Stella. He pictured her eagerly opening his letters and reading news of the English Court which he was able to give her. All the latest gossip gleaned in the coffee houses; the fall of Viceroy Sarah; the rise of Abigail Masham. This was an excellent state of affairs, he told Stella, for he considered the Whigs to be malicious toads; and Robert Harley was his friend and therefore so was Abigail Masham. The great Duchess was in decline; the Duke might follow her. Jonathan Swift was on the side of his good friend Robert Harley for whom he now waited.

There was the knocking on the door. Swift laid down his pen while his servant let in the visitor.

He rose then to greet Robert Harley.

'Ah, my friend,' cried Robert Harley. 'Great news! At last we are on the way.'

He bade Swift sit and drew a chair for himself while from his pocket he took a bottle of wine and shouted to the servant to bring glasses. Robert Harley provided his own wine for he knew that his friend Swift could not afford the quality his palate demanded.

Swift watched his benefactor as he savoured the wine which he did with relish before he spoke.

'Sarah is dismissed,' he said. 'Finally. Irrevocably.'

'There remains the Duke.'

'My dear Swift, you are your gloomy self. Of course the Duke remains. The hero of Blenheim, Ramillies, Oudenarde and Malplaquet! Let us not forget Malplaquet where the losses were so great that it could scarcely be called a victory. There is still the Duke, but, my dear fellow, we must see that it is not long before he follows his good lady.'

'The Duchess invited dismissal. She is a virago who plays into the hands of her enemy. I have heard the Duke called one of the most charming men in England and the Queen is still fond of him in spite of his wife.'

'You are a pessimist, Jonathan. There are ways and means. There are two things Marlborough loves in this life besides his military glory – Sarah and money. He'll stand by Sarah; he'll refuse to see she brought this on herself. That will go against him. And money? He is a very rich man. How did he become so? Well, his wife was very clever in selling places, I'll swear. And in squeezing gifts from her loving mistress. Sarah is a rich woman in her own right. But Marlborough always knew how to feather his nest. I have my friends in every place and they have told me many interesting things. Do you know that during his office the Duke of Marlborough has put away some fifty thousand pounds. How Jonathan? How? As for my lady, she is some way behind her husband with all the royal favour she once enjoyed. Her pickings were a mere twenty-two thousand.'

'Is it possible then that they have filched this from public funds?'

'Where else?' laughed Harley.

'It's a scandal!'

'It is certainly so. Now, it is our task to see that it is not the secret scandal it has been until now. We will make it a public scandal.'

'I see,' said Swift, 'the reason for your visit here tonight.'

Marlborough, white lipped, came into the bedroom he shared with Sarah, and handed her the copy of *The Examiner*.

'That fellow Swift,' he said. 'By God, he dips his pen in poison.'

Sarah read Swift's article and, clenching the paper in her hand, gave vent to such a spate of fury that Marlborough was afraid for her.

'Calm yourself, my love,' he begged.

'Calm myself. When this sort of thing is being written about us. *You* can be calm!'

The Duke might be outwardly calm but he did not like what he read at all. He thought of the comfortable fortune he and Sarah had set aside; and it was disconcerting to see in cold print such accusations.

'We are surrounded by enemies, Sarah. We are among wolves and tigers.'

'That may be so,' retaliated Sarah, 'but these wolves and tigers will find they have to deal with a lion and his lioness.'

365

'Caution, Sarah. Caution.'

'You have been preaching caution for years.'

'And if you had listened to my sermons, my dearest, we might not have come to this pass.'

'I have had to contend with that tiresome woman until she drove me to show what I really felt for her.'

'If you had but remembered that she was the Queen.'

'Queen! That bundle of blubber! Nay, John, if you will accept these insults, I will not.'

'Sarah, where are you going?'

'I am going to *do* something, John Churchill. I am going to show our enemies – be they royal Queens or paid scribblers – that it is a mistake to cross swords with Sarah Churchill and attempt to taunt the victor of Blenheim.'

'Sarah . . . Sarah . . . I beg of you.'

But she flounced away from him. Sarah was listening to no one . . . not even John.

Sarah unlocked the drawer and took out the letters. There was a large packet of them and she selected one at random and read it through.

Oh damning letters! Letters betraying a deep and strange affection – careless letters, the kind of letters a lover would write; and the Queen had written these to Sarah Churchill in the days of the foolish fondness Mrs Morley had felt for Mrs Freeman.

She took another. It had been written in the days when the Princess Anne so turned against her own father that she plotted against him with her sister Mary and Mary's husband William. Not the sort of letters which a Queen would wish her subjects to read. And here was another – showing clearly her hatred of her own sister, then Queen Mary, and that 'Dutch Abortion' her husband.

Stupid Anne, fat and foolish Queen, who was so unwise as to alienate a woman who could reveal so much.

Sarah was not going to consult with John . . . dearest but oh so cautious John! Sarah had done with caution.

How many times, she asked herself, have I demeaned myself . . . waiting in ante-rooms like a Scotchwoman trying to present a petition! How many times have I been told that Her Majesty cannot see me . . . and she shut away with that whey-faced Abigail Masham, tittering together, laughing because they are insulting the Duchess of Marlborough!

Sarah knew what she was going to do, and she needed no advice from anybody.

She asked Sir David Hamilton, one of the Queen's physicians, to come to her, and when he came she greeted him graciously and bade him sit down for she wished to talk to him.

He was astonished to be thus summoned, and more so as he began to understand the reason for the invitation.

'I am at the end of my patience,' said Sarah imperiously. 'I have asked for audiences with the Queen and always I am refused. I know my enemies have succeeded in working against me, but I am not a woman to accept defeat. You are in attendance upon the Queen?'

'Yes. Her Majesty is in constant need of attention.'

'So you will have no difficulty in taking a message from me.'

'I do not think Her Majesty wishes to receive . . .'

'She will certainly not wish to hear this message. But nevertheless I am sure she will want to know what I intend doing . . . before I do it.'

'I am afraid I do not understand Your Grace's meaning.'

'It is simple. Her Majesty turns her back on me. If she continues in this attitude I shall publish all the letters she has written to me since the earliest days of our friendship. Tell her this. I think she will be prepared to go to great length to prevent this happening.'

'Your Grace cannot be serious.'

'I was never more so.'

'You are threatening the Queen.'

'No. Only threatening to publish her letters.'

Sir David Hamilton bade farewell to the Duchess and went at once to the Queen.

Anne was alarmed. She thought back over the years of foolish fondness, of absolute trust. How had she betrayed herself? Her intimate life would be exposed to her people. They would read of her wicked conduct towards her own family; and although she now recognized this as wickedness and knew that Sarah Churchill had largely been responsible for making her act as she did, that was no excuse.

How could she ever have been deceived by that woman! But what could she do now?

She sent for Sir David Hamilton and the Duke of Shrewsbury.

'At all costs,' she said firmly, 'the Duchess of Marlborough must be prevented from publishing the letters. You must find some way of stopping her.'

Sarah was now growing alarmed on her own account, for Swift's article was being discussed throughout the Court and in every tavern and coffee house. It would not have surprised her if charges were brought against her for bribery and peculation; and she could not see how, if this were so, she could defend herself. She remembered an occasion when John had been a prisoner in the Tower and how he had come near to losing his life during the reign of William.

When Shrewsbury and Hamilton came to talk to her about the Queen's letters this fear was uppermost in her mind.

In her blunt fashion she betrayed this to her visitors who immediately saw in her fear a means of gaining their desire.

'Grave charges have been made against Your Grace,' Shrewsbury pointed out.

'You have come to tell me this?' asked Sarah fearfully.

'There is no need, Your Grace, to tell you what you know already,' pointed out Hamilton.

'If such a charge were brought against me I should have no alternative but to publish the Queen's letters,' bartered Sarah.

She had made her conditions. No charges; no publication of letters.

Since there had been no intention of making a charge at this stage the two men were well pleased with their visit. They were able to return to the Queen and tell her that the Duchess of Marlborough would not publish the letters if no charge was brought against her for helping herself to public funds.

*   *   *

The people in the streets hated the imperious Duchess. On the other hand they loved the Queen. The stories of the Marlboroughs' riches were discussed and magnified. Marlborough was the war-monger and what good did war bring the poor? And did they know that since the Queen no longer favoured the Duchess the latter had threatened to publish her letters?

Crowds clustered outside Marlborough House. Sarah listened to their shouts. What was it they were saying?

She shuddered as she listened.

If the Duchess of Marlborough published anything to harm the Queen they would storm Marlborough House; they would drag her into the streets and there they would proceed to tear her to pieces.

Who would have believed, Sarah asked herself, that during the reign of Queen Anne she, who had done so much to put the Queen on the throne and keep her there, should find herself in such a position?

They were saying in the streets that this was the end of the Marlboroughs' glory. Some might think so. Not Sarah.

Harley was constantly with the Queen. The time was fast approaching when the Whig Parliament should be dissolved. Then it was in the hands of the people, but Harley was confident of a Tory victory. The trial of Dr Sacheverel had damaged the Whigs irrevocably and since the charges of dishonesty had been aimed at the Marlboroughs, it was certain that the Ministry would fall.

Anne had always disliked Sunderland and had been reluctant to appoint him; he was the first to be dismissed.

Sarah was frantic with rage. Her son-in-law dismissed office! Godolphin would be next – and after that would it be Marlborough?

How could she stand by and watch her schemes dissolving into nothing?

She sent for Godolphin and Sunderland; John was with her when they arrived.

'There is only one course open to us,' she declared, and when they looked at her expectantly she said: 'Anne must be forced to abdicate.'

'Abdicate!' stammered Godolphin.

'Don't look so startled,' retorted Sarah scornfully. 'Catholic James was forced to . . . why not his doltish daughter?'

'And in her place?' asked Sunderland.

'Marl can call on the Elector of Hanover . . . and sound him.'

They stared at her in astonishment; but she saw that her son-in-law Sunderland who was ever ready for rash adventure, was beginning to smile.

Godolphin knew that the end of his career was in sight. He was old and he had never been a man to take his duties lightly, but he had been timorous and had allowed Sarah Churchill to dominate him as she had never been able to dominate her own husband. Now Sarah herself was out of favour and the ministry which he had led was about to decline. The Queen who had once shown him favour was seeking an opportunity to be rid of him and this had been brought about by the high-handed conduct of Sarah.

Godolphin was melancholy, considering what a deep effect the quarrels of women could have on a country's affairs.

He was in this mood when he attended the Cabinet meeting at which the Queen would be present. He was fully aware of the antagonism of his enemies. They were as vultures hovering about his head . . . waiting for his fall.

Shrewsbury, one of the most powerful of them, opened the attack by making sarcastic comments which Godolphin could not allow to pass. He should, of course, have answered in the same vein, but he was tired and worried and he found himself attacking Shrewsbury in the querulous tones of the tired old man he was.

'My lord,' protested Anne, 'I beg of you to curb your anger. It is of no use to this Council.'

Godolphin turned to the Queen. 'Your Majesty, my task is becoming more difficult as the days pass. I am surrounded by those who seek to undermine me. What good can come when those in high places turn their backs on the legitimate ministers of the country and give ear to secret counsels.'

This was a direct attack upon the Queen, and Anne,

mortified, remained silent. But all present knew that this must be the end of Godolphin.

Anne sat in the oak-panelled closet at Kensington.

She was sad. In the past she had been truly fond of Godolphin – Mr Montgomery as she had affectionately called him. She had felt so secure with such a minister as her friend; and there was his family connexion with the Duke who had always been so thoughtful and charming. But Sarah had poisoned those relationships as she had poisoned everything she came near.

Wherever she looked she was brought back to Sarah. It was time she finished with everything connected with her. She took up her pen and wrote:

> 'The uneasiness that you have shown for some time has given me much trouble, though I have borne it, and had your behaviour continued the same as it was for a few years after my coming to the Crown, I could have no dispute with myself what to do. But the many unkind returns I have received since, especially what you have said to me personally before the Lords (in council) makes it impossible for me to continue you any longer in my service, but I will give you a pension of four thousand pounds a year, and I desire that instead of bringing the staff to me you will break it, which I believe will be easier for us both.'

Sunderland gone! Godolphin gone! The Whig administration was over. Now it remained to see what happened at the polls, though there could be little doubt of the result.

A Tory majority was returned to Parliament. Robert Harley was Chancellor of the Exchequer and virtually the Leader of the Government with his friend and protégé Henry St John a Privy Councillor and Secretary of State.

This was defeat for the Churchills; and they waited in trepidation for what would happen next.

The Golden Keys

There was no need now to show Harley up to the green closet in secret. As the Queen's chief minister he came openly. Did she imagine it, wondered Abigail, or was he in truth slightly less affectionate towards her? Sometimes when he passed her by she would smell the wine on his breath more strong than usual. He angered her by the change in his manner; and she asked herself again and again whether had she never acquired the Queen's favour he would have acknowledged their cousinly relationship.

He has used me, thought Abigail.

How far she had come! It was not really so many years ago when she had been almost grateful for one of the Churchill girls' cast off gowns. Now Samuel was a colonel. She would have a title for Samuel before long. She was carrying a child and if this child should be a boy she owed it to him to make him Lord Masham.

How ambitious one became when one moved in ambitious circles!

Robert Harley was with the Queen. She knew what he was saying. The Duchess of Marlborough had been dismissed from the Queen's friendship, but she still retained the keys of office. Until she gave them up they could not be bestowed elsewhere. And Anne was still afraid of the Duchess, for she put off commanding their return. It was as though she could not bear to think of Sarah and wanted to pretend the woman had never existed.

But Harley was in there explaining that the Duchess must be ordered to give up her keys. And when those keys were in Anne's possession, to whom would they be passed?

Abigail had little doubt.

The door to the Queen's chamber was opening and Harley came out. He was smiling. Mr Harley was very pleased with himself these days.

When Abigail approached him, he looked at her with that slightly glazed expression in his eyes. Too much drink ... or mere indifference? Surely he had not been to the Queen in a state of semi-intoxication? That was absurd. Harley would never be semi-intoxicated. He was too accustomed to drink.

'It was a successful meeting?' she asked.

'Very successful.'

'And . . .?'

He smiled at her in that manner which was almost mocking. He was not going to confide in her.

'I shall call on Her Majesty tomorrow,' said Harley, and bowing passed on.

She looked after him, resentment rising within her. He had his place and no longer needed her help. Had she not always known? Of course. Then why should she be so angry, so hurt?

Marlborough did not know which way to turn. He felt sick with worry and frustration. He had to speak to Sarah; he had to make her understand the position in which they were placed. Sarah would not accept the truth. It had always been so. She saw herself twice the size of others, twice as powerful, twice as brilliant; and even in the face of defeat she refused to admit it.

He, the most ambitious of men, had dreamed of ruling England. That had once seemed a not impossible dream for there had been military dictators before. On the Continent he had shown his genius and his enemies trembled at his name, yet here in his own country he was faced with disaster and defeat. And the reason . . .? It was no use blinking the truth. Sarah.

Sarah had brought him to this. Her overbearing manner, her bluntness, her arrogance, her belief that she could behave as pleased herself to anyone on earth including the Queen. Blind Sarah, who had brought herself and all those connected with her to disaster!

Sarah had lost the Queen's favour forever. She refused to believe it, but it was true. She was no longer wanted at Court, yet the country needed the great soldier. Even Harley, the chief of his enemies, realized that. It was for that reason that he had sent St John to advise him.

They wanted Marlborough . . . but not Marlborough's wife.

St John had been blunt. 'The only way in which Your Grace can hold your position in this country is by ridding yourself of your wife.'

Repudiate Sarah! Cut himself off from her! Let it be known that he was out of sympathy with her overbearing conduct.

He loved Sarah. He thought of passionate reunions after long absences, the days when they were alone together at St Albans or Windsor Park. The family . . . the daughters who meant so much to him; his grandchildren.

Give up Sarah! Choose between his wife and ambition!

There should be no problem. Did he not love Sarah? Was she not his dearest soul? Yet he was a commander of genius who had dreamed of ruling England. So he was being asked to choose between the two things he loved best.

Sarah came into the room – brisk, bustling, bellicose.

'Why, my dear Marl, what has happened? You look ill.'

'I'm getting old, Sarah.'

'What nonsense!'

'And everything I have hoped for has gone sour . . . has turned to nothing.'

'Nonsense again. Nothing can eliminate the glory of Blenheim.'

'They'll make peace with France. They will decide that it is impossible to turn Louis's grandson from the throne of Spain. They will say that the war was hopeless and need never have been fought. That is the way to make nothing of great victories, Sarah.'

'You *are* in a mood! Something has happened to upset you. That worm St John has been here, I believe.'

'Yes, Sarah, he has been here.'

'And what did he want?'

'He wants you to return the keys of office.'

'I shall do no such thing.'

'Sarah, for God's sake be reasonable. You cannot cling to an office when the Queen has decided to dismiss you.'

'Do you think I'll be dismissed like some frightened chambermaid caught stealing the tea!'

Caught stealing! What unfortunate phrases she used! When he looked at Sarah, her face distorted by rage, when he listened to her shrill voice denouncing everyone, refusing to see any point of view but her own, he wondered . . . He despised himself for this, but he even wavered.

So many pictures could come unbidden to the mind. He thought of himself – without Sarah – being taken into the new ministry. He had been a Tory at heart – until Sarah had given her allegiance to the Whigs and determined he should do the same. He saw himself continuing the war, finding fresh triumphs . . . without Sarah.

But there she stood before him – his Sarah, for whom he had braved his parents' wrath in the first place in order to marry her, Sarah who had had no fortune any more than he had, when of course an ambitious man should have made a rich marriage.

How could he live without Sarah? Yet it was said that his love could never have endured if he had been forced to live with her night and day. It was the long separations which had saved their marriage. It might be so, but he knew he could never be without her.

She was bold and rash; she was crashing them all to disaster, but she was still his beloved Sarah.

'You are smiling. *I* see nothing to smile about.'

'I was thinking of all the years we have been together.'

'A fine time to think of that!'

'No, a good time, Sarah.' He took her hands and looked into her face. 'You are still beautiful,' he said. 'Our girls are lovely, but they can't compare with you.'

'What is it, Marl?' she asked tenderly.

'If we are forced to live in obscurity . . . even in exile . . . I was thinking that at least we should be together.'

Her lips quivered and she threw herself into his arms.

'Dear Marl,' she said. 'Dearest Marl!'

He had known all along that there was no problem. They were together for the rest of their lives.

He put her from him and said: 'You will have to give up the keys.'

The tender mood had passed. 'You are too easily defeated, Marl. Leave this to me. I haven't finished with my fat friend yet . . . so I shan't allow her to finish with me.'

'Sarah, I tell you this is the end. She will not have you back.'

'I shall write to her,' said Sarah stubbornly.

'She'll read no letters from you.'

'She will if you take it to her.'

'Sarah, don't you know when you're beaten?'

'No, my brave general, I do not agree that I am beaten.'

'Sarah . . .'

But she put her arms about him and laughed. She would have her way as she always had, and there was one thing he knew, which was that it was better to suffer defeat with Sarah than to bask in success without her.

Sarah shut herself into her room and wrote to the Queen. I wouldn't do this, she thought, but for Marl. This is breaking him. He'll be ill if we go on like this.

Her pen had always been as violent as her tongue, but now she tried to use it to advantage. She remembered the cosy chats when Prince George had been alive and she and Anne had sat together like two goodies discussing their men. Mr Morley and Mr Freeman. What intimacy there had been in those days! And Anne had been fond of Mr Freeman. He had charmed her as he charmed everyone. Marl was a charming man.

Now she must soften the Queen; she must remind her of those days. Anne had always been sentimental and if she could touch that sentiment now who knows she might yet retain the keys of office. And she must retain them, for to lose them would mean to be cut off from Court, cut off from all hope of regaining power.

She wrote to the Queen in an unusually humble style and the theme of her letter was her concern for the Duke. She believed she wrote, that if he must continue in this state of anxiety, he would not live six months. If Anne would allow her to remain her servant she would, she promised, never do or say anything disagreeable to her.

There was submission. She was sure of success.

Having written the letter she went to the Duke who was lying on his couch and coming on him unawares she felt a twinge of anxiety. Perhaps she had not exaggerated in her letter to the Queen.

'Dearest Marl,' she said, 'you are not well.'

He rose and immediately looked more like his old self. 'I'll be well enough when this unpleasantness has passed away.'

'I have the letter here. Take it to the Queen and *insist* that she reads it.'

'I am in no position to command the Queen.'

'Oh, come, you know what I mean. Beg prettily as you so well know how to do, and she will do as you ask.'

'Sarah, she is firmly determined . . .'

'I know her better than you. She will read that letter and be touched. Once I get back to her, I'll see that I stay there.'

'I would rather not . . .'

'Now, my brave commander. We shall win yet.'

She was irresistible. He had to obey her. Godolphin had felt the same, even Sunderland.

'We have to do this,' she said earnestly. 'It would have been different if the Elector had listened to our plans.'

The Duke shook his head. 'He believes that he will get the crown handed to him in a few years time so he sees no reason to fight for it now.'

'He should not be so sure. There are Jacobites and to spare in this country. They'll have the Pretender back . . . and then

Master Hanover will wish that he had paid a little attention to his friends.'

'He is not prepared to risk war for the English crown, Sarah. I can't say that I blame him.'

'It seems I am beset by lily-livered cowards,' cried Sarah fiercely. 'Well, there's nothing to do but try to get back with Anne. She'll read that letter, Marl; and when she does she'll remember our friendship. She won't have the heart to dismiss me then.'

Marlborough was uncertain of that, but nevertheless he obeyed Sarah and presented himself at the palace to ask for an audience.

This was granted, but when he produced Sarah's letter the Queen said that she did not wish to read any communication from the Duchess.

'I beg of Your Majesty to read this letter,' said the Duke, kneeling and looking entreatingly up at her. Anne shook her head sadly. He was so handsome, and he at least had always been so modest, and in the old days she had thought Mr Freeman to be one of the most charming men she had ever met. Mr Morley had a high opinion of him too. What happy days they had been! But even then of course *Mrs* Freeman had been over-bearing; she had dictated the way they should go. Sometimes when she felt weakened by the gout and dropsy Anne would wake in the night from dreams about her father; she would imagine he upbraided her for her part in his downfall and in such dreams Sarah was always beside her, urging her on.

No, she did not want to think of the past; she would not read Sarah's letter.

'Madam,' said the Duke, 'if you will retain the Duchess until such a time as you will have no need of my services, this will save her much pain. I hope that the war will be over within the next year and then we could both retire together.'

'I cannot change my resolution,' said Anne firmly.

'The Duchess deeply regrets any uneasiness she caused Your Majesty and longs for a chance to revive that love you once had for her. She has sworn that if you will give her another chance she will serve you in all humility and endeavour to make up for any pain she may have caused you.'

Anne was silent.

'I beg you read the letter,' he implored.

She did so, but when she had finished it, she was silent.

'Your Majesty is moved to some tenderness I see. I know that you will wish to put an end to the anguish which the Duchess now suffers.'

'I cannot change my resolution,' repeated Anne.

The Duke sighed, exerting all his charm in his endeavours to move her, but she only said: 'The keys must be returned to me within three days.'

'Within three days, Your Majesty. I pray you give the Duchess ten days that the affair may be settled more discreetly.'

'No,' said the Queen, 'there has been too much delay. The keys must be returned to me within two days.'

'Two days . . . but Your Majesty said three.'

'Two days,' repeated Anne firmly. 'I cannot alter my resolution.'

There was nothing to be done but return to Sarah to tell her of his failure.

Marlborough faced his wife.

'Well?' she demanded, although his expression betrayed how the interview had gone and there was no need to ask.

'No use,' he said.

'She read my letter?'

'Yes, and remained adamant.'

'You should have talked to her.'

'I did.'

'Crawling at her feet, I doubt not.'

'Behaving in a manner best calculated to soften her, and at least I induced her to read the letter which she refused to do at first.'

'You allow her to treat you like a servant!'

'We are her servants.'

'Bah! That fat fool! If I could get back I would show her that I will not take such treatment from her.'

'That is precisely what you have done and why we are in this position now.'

'So I am to blame?'

'Can you suggest who else?'

'Yes, that disagreeable woman . . . with her filthy little dogs, her doting chambermaid, cards, her chocolates and her drivelling conversation. I cannot tell you what I endured from her. I was nearly driven mad by her inanities. And now . . . look at the way I am treated!'

'Sarah, for God's sake be calm. You have to give up the keys.'

Her eyes narrowed. 'If you had talked to her . . .'

'She could not be talked to. Her mind was made up. She kept repeating that she could not change her resolution.'

'The old parrot!'

'Sarah. Accept this. You have to give up the keys. She refuses to discuss any further business with me until those keys are in her hands. Unless you give them back I will have no position either.'

Sarah tore the keys from her waist, where she always wore them. Two golden keys, symbols of those coveted posts: Groom of the Stole and Mistress of the Privy Purse. She had held those offices for a long time and now they were lost.

She could have burst into tears.

To relieve her feelings she threw the keys at her husband and they struck his head before falling to the floor.

He picked them up quickly before Sarah could change her mind; and he lost no time in delivering them to the Queen.

Anne looked at the two golden keys – the symbol of release. Never would she allow herself to become the slave of another as she had with Sarah Churchill. Not even dearest Masham, although she knew full well that Abigail would never presume to rule her.

She was devoted to Masham more than to any other living person, but she was also fond of the Duchess of Somerset. There was a similarity between them; they both had the same colour hair. Some might call it carroty, but Anne found it delightful. She had also been fond of Lady Somerset ever since she had lent her Syon House when she had had nowhere to go during one of her quarrels with her brother-in-law William of

Orange; she recalled even now how William had tried to prevent Lady Somerset's lending her the house and how both the Duke and his wife had insisted that she had it. They had been true friends then – and she would never forget it.

But Abigail was more necessary to her than anyone on earth. She juggled the keys, smiling to herself at the pleasure she was going to bestow.

'Mrs Masham.'

Abigail started from her chair and stared at the man who had come into the room. He rocked a little uncertainly on his heels and his eyes were glazed.

'Mr Harley.'

She thought: He is getting careless. His coat was spotted; perhaps he had just come from carousing with the literary men who were glad to work for him in exchange for the chance to call themselves his friends.

He was breathing fumes of wine at her.

'Mr Harley,' she went on coolly, 'have you just come from the tavern?'

'Nay, Madam, from Her Majesty.'

He was smiling at her almost insolently, as though he were reminding her that although she might give herself airs with others she must not do so with him.

Resentment flared up in her. She found him attractive – this adventurer in the political jungle. Now she knew that when she had served the Marlboroughs in the house at St Albans she had envied Sarah, not so much her position but the adoration she had aroused in a man like Marlborough. That was what she had wanted. Samuel was no Marlborough; but Harley might have been. Harley was a brilliant politician . . . but a drinker. Together they could have been supreme – as the Marlboroughs had planned to be – for she would never have lost her place as Sarah had. She would have known how to lead her man along to greatness. But instead she had Samuel – pleasant, mild, unexciting Samuel; while Harley – the first minister – was merely amused that she – an insignificant nobody – had been of use to him. Now he no longer needed her, for he had reached his goal.

The thought occurred to her then that he would have to fight as hard to keep his place as he had to attain it, and therefore should curb his insolence.

'Mr Harley,' she said, 'you have been drinking.'

'Mrs Masham,' he replied, 'I have also been breathing.'

'The latter is necessary, the former scarcely so.'

'What! Do you understand me so little? The last is as necessary as the first.'

'It is even more necessary to hide the fact.'

'My guardian angel!' He laughed. 'And here I have a present for a good girl.' He held up a golden key.

She stared at it.

'The Privy Purse for you. The Stole goes to Carrots Somerset.'

'The Privy Purse!' echoed Abigail.

'By far the most important post. "Please tell Mrs Masham that I wish her to have it." So spake her Majesty.'

She held out her hand to take it, but he still retained it, mocking her with his eyes. Then he slipped it inside her bodice so that it rested between her breasts.

Yes, he was certainly slightly intoxicated.

She watched him turn and walk away. He was not as respectful as he had once been. Surely he was not the brilliant student of human nature she had believed him to be. Did he not realize that if he wished to hold his place he should be very careful to show the utmost respect to Abigail Masham – now Keeper of Her Majesty's Privy Purse.

Sarah was furious. Dismissed from offices which were now in the hands of her greatest enemies! Ordered to remove from her rooms at the Palace which would now belong to someone else!

Very well, she would remove herself.

She went to St James's Palace and took with her several of her servants.

'Dismantle those rooms,' she ordered. 'Take everything ... the mirrors from the walls and the locks from the doors.'

Her servants were bewildered by these orders but they knew better than disobey.

They took the locks from the doors and Sarah declared that she would have the chimney-pieces in time.

Back to Marlborough House went Sarah, laughing exultantly as she thought of those rooms, the doors that would not even shut, the walls denuded of their mirrors.

'Wait ... wait until I get the chimney-pieces,' she promised herself.

Marlborough seeing what she had done was aghast.

'This is folly, Sarah,' he warned.

'Folly! You think I should meekly stand aside and allow them to insult me. I am told to go ... so I will go ... and I will take what belongs to me with me. Do not think this is all. I shall send back and have the very chimney-pieces brought to me.'

'No, Sarah, no.'

'I tell you, I will.'

'Sarah, are you mad?'

'Mad I may be, but at least I am not a coward.'

'This was a foolish thing to do.'

'Foolish! To show the world how ill I have been used! I would have everyone know that the Duchess of Marlborough does not lightly take insults even if her husband does. I'll have those chimney-pieces.'

'You will not.'

Sarah stopped her tirade to stare at him.

'What?' she cried.

'I said you will take nothing more from the Palace.'

'I have sworn to have those chimney-pieces.'

'I have sworn that you will not.'

She was silent and he went on: 'Sarah, for your own sake ... for both our sakes ... be calm ... be dignified. We are on the edge of disaster. For God's sake don't send us hurtling down to utter destruction.'

She looked at him and saw the pain in his eyes, the weariness of anxiety.

Then she threw herself at him and burst into tempestuous weeping. He led her to a couch and they sat there together until he had calmed and comforted her.

Abigail came to the Queen to tell her that Lady Marlborough

had removed herself and her belongings from the palace.

'For ever,' declared Anne. 'She shall never come back.'

'Your Majesty is now rid of a nuisance.'

'Oh, Masham, how relieved I am! I cannot tell you what a threat that woman has been to me.'

'A fury, Madam, as they call her in the lampoons. She leaves much damage behind her.'

Abigail told the Queen of the dismantled apartments. 'The very locks have gone! She bade her servants remove them.'

'Oh, what a wild woman she is!' cried Anne.

'But she has gone, Your Majesty. You need never see her again.'

'Nor shall I. But to defame the palace! And when I think of all the money we are spending to build a palace for her and her husband. The cost of Blenheim is terrifying, Masham . . . quite terrifying.'

'It seems incongruous, Madam. You are supplying money to build her a palace while she is destroying yours.'

'It is quite incongruous. I have made up my mind. There shall be no more money for Blenheim. I shall build no house for the Duchess of Marlborough while she is pulling mine down.'

These were indeed dark days for the Marlboroughs. Sarah deprived of her offices; Marlborough uncertain of what support he would receive from the Government; and Blenheim Palace which was to have been presented to them by the Queen and a grateful nation unfinished and the work on it stopped by royal command.

Disgrace and Departure

The Queen was dozing in her chair when Abigail told her that the Abbé Guiscard was waiting to see her.

'I will see him, Masham,' said Anne, smiling. 'He is such a brave man, and we must show how pleased we are to receive those who desert Catholicism for our Faith.'

Abigail brought the Abbé to the Queen and retired into an ante-room where she could hear all that took place between the Queen and her visitor – a long standing habit of Abigail's.

Anne, peering myopically at her visitor, did not notice how wild his eyes were and how his lips twitched. She saw a brave Frenchman forced to leave his native country on account of his religion. He had impressed certain people and as a result had been given the command of one of the regiments abroad and had committed himself with valour – so rumour said – at Almanza.

Declaring that such men should receive encouragement in England Anne had arranged that he should receive a pension of four hundred pounds a year. Guiscard, in London, had been taken up by society and gave hair-raising accounts of military

385

adventures in which he was always the central figure. Many of these had been recounted to Anne and it was for this reason that she had been willing to grant the interview.

As soon as he was alone with the Queen, Guiscard became disrespectful.

'I am offered a pension of four hundred pounds a year,' he said in a loud voice. 'How do you think a man such as I can live on such a pittance?'

Having expected a display of gratitude for her beneficence Anne was astounded, but before she could answer, Guiscard continued that he had thought it would be worth his while to come to England where he had expected to receive better treatment than he had. He might have stayed in France and been paid better for his services.

'The interview is over,' Anne told him coolly. 'You may retire.'

'But I have not finished,' cried Guiscard. 'I tell you this: I'll not accept your miserable four hundred a year. I shall give my services to those who are prepared to pay what they are worth.' He rose and stood towering over the Queen who, her feet swathed in bandages, was unable to move.

'Pray call Mrs Masham,' said Anne imperiously.

'You shall hear me,' shouted Guiscard . . .

It was at this point that Abigail called the guards.

When they entered Guiscard was shouting and flinging his arms about as though at any moment he would attack the Queen. The guards seized him and hustled him away.

The next day Guiscard was arrested on suspicion of spying for France and was taken to The Cockpit where the Council was assembled.

Harley at its head rose, when the man was brought before them, and approached Guiscard, who lifted his right hand and struck; Harley reeled backwards, blood on his coat, as he fell fainting to the floor.

The whole nation was talking about the attempted assassination. Guiscard, the French adventurer, suspected of being a spy, had been arrested to answer charges before the

Council; Robert Harley had long suspected him and had been taking steps to reduce the pension which was being paid to him. Thus the villain decided to take his revenge.

Fortunately Harley had not been alone; his friends in the Council — Henry St John at the head of them — had immediately drawn their swords and falling upon the assailant, attacked him so severely that by the time he reached Newgate Prison he was dying.

But that was not the end of this dramatic incident. Robert Harley had been very slightly hurt for his assailant's weapon had merely been a penknife which had done little more than scratch his skin. But Harley was too wily to treat the matter lightly. He took to his bed while the crowds gathered outside his house, loud in their lamentations, declaring that England was threatened with the loss of her saviour. Harley revelled in the fuss. When at length he rose and went to the House of Commons his carriage was stopped in the streets while the crowds cheered him; women knelt in the streets and thanked God for his recovery; they wept to see him. The House of Commons was full to overflowing; he was embraced even by his enemies; flowery speeches were made. Harley had reason to be grateful to Guiscard's penknife.

When he went to the Queen she received him tearfully.

'Dear Mr Harley, *what* a great pleasure! I feel Providence has saved you for me and the country.'

'I trust Providence never regrets the action, Madam.'

Anne smiled. 'You were always a wit, dear Mr Harley. I have been talking to your friends and we feel that this occasion should be marked with a celebration. We want the whole country to know how grateful we are.'

Harley was alert. This was the very pinnacle of success. It was amusing to realize that Guiscard's penknife had given him the final push necessary to stand up there, savouring the rarified air.

'I am going to ask you to be my Lord Treasurer.'

That was good. He was virtually the head of the Government now, but in future he would be so in very fact.

'And it is ridiculous that you should continue plain *Mr* Harley. I suggest the peerage. Earl of Oxford and Earl Mortimer.'

Harley kissed the Queen's hands, tears of triumph in his eyes.

'Your Majesty is good to me.'

Abigail was in the ante-room as he went out. He smiled at her vaguely, scarcely seeing her.

The Earl of Oxford, Lord Treasurer, the most popular man in the country, no longer needed the services of Abigail Masham.

Robert Harley, Earl of Oxford, was closeted with the Queen. They were alone for he did not care to say what he had to in the presence of any other.

Abigail, delivered of a son after a long and arduous labour, was not in attendance, for Anne, delighted with the child, had been concerned for Abigail and had commanded that she rest from her duties until she had recovered.

Oxford was secretly excited although he wore an expression of consternation. There was one thing he wanted more than any other and that was to destroy Marlborough. The Duchess was dismissed but the Duke could not be thrust aside so easily. He was the leader of the armies still – the victorious armies; he was a power in Europe, and England still needed him. On the other hand, Marlborough was Oxford's enemy in chief for it was through the services of Abigail Masham, whom Sarah regarded as her evil genius, that he had been helped to power. There was not room in English politics for Marlborough and Oxford and the latter was awaiting the opportunity to rid himself of his enemy. While there was war in Europe, England needed Marlborough; it was for this reason that Oxford was secretly delighted as he came to the Queen.

'Grave news, Your Majesty. The death of the Emperor Joseph is going to colour the entire situation which is of such importance to us.'

'Poor man! It is so terrible and unexpected. The smallpox is a scourge, my dear Lord Oxford. A positive scourge. I remember how it struck my poor sister.'

'Your Majesty is right; and now that Charles of Austria has become the new Emperor we have lost our candidate for the Spanish throne, for the union of the Empire and Spain is impossible. Your Majesty will realize the trouble such a state of affairs would create, for it would completely upset the balance of power.'

'You are right, of course. And the main reason for continuing this dreadful war was to prevent Louis' grandson from keeping the throne of Spain and to set our candidate upon it.'

'Exactly.'

'What a menace Emperor Charles would be,' sighed Anne, 'if in addition to Austria, Italy and the Netherlands he ruled Spain as well.'

'Louis XIV himself would not be more formidable and it is impossible to remove his grandson from the throne. Louis is an old man now. He has offered to meet all our demands except that of fighting against his own grandson. I have to remind Your Majesty that he has not been unreasonable.'

'My dear Lord Oxford, you do not have to remind me. Nothing would please me more than to end this dreadful war. I have wept bitterly when I have seen the list of casualties. Too many of my subjects are losing their lives in this struggle.'

'How fortunate we are to have a sovereign so humane . . . so reasonable.'

'My dear Lord Oxford, *I* am the fortunate one, to have such ministers.'

Oxford kissed her hand. He could see that he was going to get his way with the utmost ease.

'I think we might sound the French as to peace terms, Your Majesty. But in the beginning we should not allow too many to share this secret. My Lord Marlborough for one . . . His great desire is to continue the war and win more glory. He is a brilliant soldier, Your Majesty. But we cannot allow him to buy his glory at the cost of so much English blood.'

'How I agree with you, my dear Lord,' sighed Anne fervently.

'Then we will work in secret for a while; and I think I can promise Your Majesty peace in a very short time.'

'Nothing could give me greater happiness than to see an end to this spilling of blood.'

Oxford bowed his head in assent. An end to the spilling of blood, he thought; and an end to Marlborough.

Abigail was back at Court after her brief convalescence. And the Queen was delighted to have her.

'Dear Masham, so you have a boy and a girl now. How fortunate you are.'

Abigail sat at the Queen's feet while they talked of children. Anne went sadly over the childhood of her boy, how precocious he had been, how precious. Abigail had heard all before and while she listened she was wondering when the Queen would reward her for her services and give her the title she needed that it might be passed on to her son.

If only Samuel were a little adventurous. He was a good soldier. Brigadier-General now, and Member for Ilchester. But he lacked all the qualities of a leader. As for my lord Oxford; he was growing farther and farther from her; but as he grew farther away, Henry St John came nearer.

St John was different from Oxford – less complicated. Something of a rake still, he had been notorious in his youth for his extravagance and dissipation. He had been a disciple of Oxford's, but was he just a little piqued now by Oxford's great and undeserved popularity over the Guiscard affair? Did he feel that Oxford was neglecting his old friends now he was secure in his position?

Abigail intended to discover – very discreetly. It might be that she and Henry St John could work in unison as once she had worked with Robert Harley.

It was St John who told her that Marlborough was sounding Hanover. The Queen was middle aged; she was constantly ill. Each year she became slightly more incapacitated. If she were to die and there was a Hanoverian succession which the Marlboroughs had helped to bring about, it would go ill with the Marlboroughs' enemies.

St John smiled roguishly at Abigail. 'And we all know whom the Marlboroughs consider their first enemy: You, my dear lady.'

Abigail was uneasy. To contemplate the death of the Queen was a nightmare. All blessings flowed from the royal invalid; and so far, she had nothing which she could pass on to her family.

'It is no use our looking to Hanover,' said St John.

390

'In that case we must look in the opposite direction,' replied Abigail.

'St Germains,' whispered St John.

The Queen was in tears. News had been brought to her that her uncle Lord Rochester was dead. She sent for Masham to comfort her.

'We were not on good terms, Masham, and that makes it so much more tragic. How I regret the quarrels and discords in my family!'

'Your Majesty has always acted with the greatest goodness,' Abigail replied.

'Oh, but the troubles, Masham ... the troubles! When I think of my poor father and what we did to him sometimes I think I shall die of shame.'

'Your Majesty did what you believed to be right. He was a Catholic and the people of England would not tolerate a Catholic on the throne.'

'It haunts me, Masham. It still does, and I know that it haunted my poor sister Mary. Why, when she died we were not on good terms.'

'I believe Lady Marlborough made great trouble between you.'

'She did. And my dear sister implored me to rid myself of her. If I had but listened! But I was blind then, Masham ... quite blind.'

'Your Majesty is free of her now.'

'Yes, and I thank God. But I think of the past, Masham. Now that I am getting old and am so often ill and infirm I think the more.'

'I understand, Your Majesty. That young man at St Germains is after all your half-brother.'

'I often think of him, Masham, and wish that I could put everything in order.'

'Your Majesty means by fixing the succession on him?'

The Queen caught her breath. 'I had not gone so far as that.'

'But it is on your mind and it would comfort Your Majesty if you considered this matter ... explored this matter ...'

'I should not wish him to be brought to England while I lived.'

'No, no, Your Majesty. I thought perhaps you meant you would prefer him to succeed you – which I pray and trust will not be for many years for I do not wish to be here to see it – rather than the Germans.'

'I have no great love of the Germans, Masham. And he is my brother.'

'Your Majesty should talk this over with ministers you trust.'

'Dear Lord Oxford! But the boy would have to change his religion. We cannot have papists in England, Masham. The people would not accept it . . . and I should not wish it. We should have to communicate with my brother. We should have to impress upon him the need to change his religion. My father would not change . . . although he saw disaster all about him. I wonder if his son is as obstinate.'

'It may be that Your Majesty may wish to find out.'

The Queen was thoughtful; so was Abigail. The Hanoverian succession must be prevented if she were to remain at Court after the Queen's death for it seemed that the Marlboroughs were taking their stand with the Germans.

It was not possible to live perpetually in the glory of a penknife wound and Lord Oxford was facing difficulties in the party. Among the Tories were many Jacobites and since the Queen's half-brother had intimated that he preferred his religion to the throne of England the plot to place him next in succession had foundered. Marlborough was still powerful and firmly set against peace; he had his adherents.

The Tory party lacked a majority in the Lords and the only way this could be remedied was by creating new peers. Here was where Abigail could be useful in persuading the Queen. She would do it, Oxford knew, for an adequate reward. It was time she ceased to be plain Mrs.

Samuel Masham was among the twelve peers created to swell the Tory Majority in the Lords. Abigail was secretly delighted.

Lady Masham now; she had come far from the backstairs quarters in Lady Rivers' house! She would like to see any of the Churchills look down on her now as the poor relation!

For a short while she was friendly with Oxford, but that passed. He was only interested in his own affairs; she noticed that since his elevation to rank and position he was becoming more and more careless in his dress and manners.

Let him. She would not warn him. Meanwhile her friendship with Henry St John was rapidly growing. Lightly they criticized their one-time friend; but there was a gleam of understanding in their eyes.

Oxford was a fool. He was growing careless.

Oxford sat with the Queen. She enjoyed these tête-à-têtes with her new minister as she had the old ones with dear Mr Montgomery and Mr Freeman.

He talked to her frankly and intelligently and as he was what she called so right-thinking on matters of Church and State, she was well pleased with her minister.

When he pointed out that there would never be an effective peace while the Duke of Marlborough was such a power in the country and on the Continent, she believed him, for the Duke, being such a brilliant soldier, had naturally hoped for war.

One day Oxford came to her in a state of excitement which he hid under an expression of gravity.

He had ill news, he told her. He had heard from reliable sources that the Duke of Marlborough had amassed a great fortune through ill practices.

'What practices?' asked Anne in alarm.

'Peculation, Madam. He made a fortune of sixty thousand pounds on bread contracts alone during his service in the Army. I have been questioning Sir Solomon Medina who controls the bread supplies to the Army and he reluctantly admitted that he paid the Duke six thousand pounds a year as a bribe to obtain the army contracts. This is not his only sin, Madam. In fact the Duke of Marlborough must be one of the richest men in the kingdom. We might ask ourselves how he became rich. Both he and his Duchess had means of filling the family coffers and these means, although highly successful, could be put under the unpleasant name of peculation.'

'I will not have the Duchess charged,' said Anne quickly,

remembering Sarah's threats to publish her letters.

'The Duchess's case is over,' said Oxford, 'but not that of the Duke.'

In Windsor Lodge Lord Godolphin was dying. Sarah had nursed him, ruling the sick room as imperiously as she had once ruled the Queen's Court.

Times had changed. They had too many enemies. And she knew that a Government intent in making peace was determined to disgrace one who would stand against that peace.

Poor Godolphin! But perhaps he was fortunate for he would not have to stay and fight his way back to power. There he lay on his bed oblivious to all that was happening about them – an old man now; yet it did not seem so long ago that they had all laid plans together.

She left the bedchamber, for she heard sounds of arrival. John had come to Windsor.

She ran into his embrace but she knew before he spoke, that the worst had happened. He had lost. He was disgraced. He was discredited.

They were silent as they clung together. She was thinking bitterly of her own violent nature which had brought them to this; he was blaming his avarice. He loved money for its own sake; he loved it as much as he loved fame and power – almost as much as he loved Sarah.

He had amassed great wealth – not always by fair means. He had founded his fortune on a gift of five thousand pounds given to him by an ageing woman whose lover he had been. He had never been particular as to how he found money. All that had mattered was that it came to him.

Now he was exposed. The man who had used the war to enrich himself! All the arrangements with suppliers, all the bribes and golden rewards – nothing could take away the glory of Blenheim and the rest. But none the less the Queen had dismissed him; he was a ruined man.

'There is nothing left for us in England while this Queen lives, Sarah,' he said.

She looked at him in fear. 'You are going away, John?'

He nodded, but she shook her head violently.

'You will be with me,' he assured her. Then his eyes brightened. 'As long as this Queen lives we shall be in exile . . . but she will not live forever.'

'And then!'

'George of Hanover will be George I of England. I fancy he will have a use for our services.'

'So, it is a game of patience,' she said.

'Never your greatest gift, my dearest.'

'But we shall be together.'

'Together,' he said, 'playing the waiting game.'

Lord Godolphin died soon afterwards and Marlborough immediately made plans to leave the country.

Sarah quickly joined him.

Queen Anne is Dead

Lady Masham waited for Lord Oxford to leave the Queen. She had seen him before he went into her presence; he had staggered a little and he had not bothered to change his coat on which were stains of snuff and wine.

Yet the Queen did not seem to notice the disgusting appearance of her first minister. Nor had she remarked that he was less respectful than he had once been. He must be drinking very heavily, thought Abigail.

It might be that wine dulled his perceptions. He had certainly grown very careless since taking office.

His head was full of financial schemes – so much more to his taste than war. His thoughts were mainly occupied with enlarging British Commerce and he was a governor of that great enterprise known as the 'Company of Merchants of Great Britain trading to the South Seas and other Parts of America'. People had rushed to invest their money believing that they would make a fortune in a very short time. He was also involved in the slave trade which he believed could bring a great source of revenue. The word *assiento* was on every lip. This meant the right to provide Spanish colonies with slaves.

Lord Oxford, nodding over his wine, sleeping the sleep of intoxication every night, dreamed dreams of doing for England through commerce what Marlborough had done through war.

Abigail was pregnant once more and this brought home to her the fact that she would soon have a growing family for which to provide. Samuel would never do very much and it rested with her. Her son would be Lord Masham in due course, but she wanted to give him something more than a title.

When Lord Oxford left the Queen and she met him as if by accident, he would have bowed and passed on. She was angry although she gave no sign of it, and there were more than one reason for her emotion. What a fool he was! With all his chances, to throw them away as surely as Sarah Churchill had thrown hers. Why was it that success corrupted? Why, when people achieved it, did they lose their sense of proportion? Why did they build an image of their importance which no one accepted but themselves? If he had been different ... if he had been a warm-hearted man, capable of loving a woman – capable of loving Abigail Hill as Marlborough had loved his wife – how different everything might have been!

She was angry now for frustrated hopes, for the reckless disregard for a career which together they could have made great.

'My lord ...'

'Why, 'tis Lady Masham.'

'You seem surprised. It is true we do not meet as frequently as we did once.'

'Lady Masham will understand that there are many duties to claim my attention now.'

Yes, thought Abigail; and so old friends who have helped you to your place can be forgotten.

She said: 'It is agreeable for your old friends to see your success.'

'I would not deprive them of their pleasure for the world.'

'I am sure you are not the man to forget old friends.'

'I regret I have little time for brooding on the past – an occupation not suited to my talents; and it is an astonishing thing how many are ready to claim old friendship now who were once on little more than nodding acquaintance with me.'

'You cannot count me among those,' retorted Abigail sharply. 'And for that reason I wished to ask you for a little advice regarding some investments. I am not a rich woman . . .'

Oxford waved his hand lightly. 'My dear Lady Masham, I am sure that one of my secretaries will give you all the advice you need.'

He bowed; she could scarcely hold her expression until he had passed.

How dared he! After all he owed to her! In all the vast profits he had made he was not ready to give one bit of recognition.

She was a woman with children, whose future she wished to make secure. Very well, Robert Harley – Lord Oxford as he had become through her good graces – would see that if he would not have her for his friend, he could have her for his enemy.

The Queen was enjoying a return to health. Peace was at last in sight; and the Marlboroughs were abroad. It was surprising what an effect these two facts had upon her. She never ceased to marvel with her two dearest friends Lady Masham and the Duchess of Somerset.

It was exciting to hunt at Windsor, riding furiously in the chaise she had used in the past which was drawn by one horse, so that she could follow the stag as though she were actually on horseback. It was long since she had been able to enjoy that form of relaxation.

How good it was to feel well again – or almost. Her feet were swollen and sore but her dear friend's ministrations soon soothed them; then they would settle down to gossip and cards. What pleasure! She was reminded of the old days in the green closet when Abigail Masham – who was Hill then – used to bring in Mr Harley for their secret conferences.

Mr Harley! There was a faintly disturbing thought. He was a little uncouth in his appearance. And last time he had come to her he had had the appearance of being intoxicated.

She would not have believed it, but she had seen the quick glance Masham had given him and then herself . . . as though she were wondering if she, Anne, had noticed.

Masham would be concerned, for she had always thought so highly of Lord Oxford and they were related, though obscurely.

Oh dear, Anne hoped there was not going to be trouble there, just as she had believed everything was going so well.

Such busy days! She even went to the Datchet races. These pleasures must not interfere with her state business of course; and she performed all the public duties which her rank demanded. She was seen at church; she received in her drawing room; and she ordered that an announcement should be put into the London Gazette reminding the people that she would touch people afflicted with the Evil in her palace at St James's; and as a result the people flocked there.

She sat benign, the mother of her people; and in the streets it was said that the bad days were over. No more war; prosperity was coming; and England was going to be merry under Good Queen Anne.

Abigail had dressed with special care to receive her visitor. She was excited. What transpired at this encounter could be very important to her. She must be wary; she must remember her rival's downfall and never make the mistake Sarah had made of believing herself to be superior to those about her. She must never lose sight of the astuteness of her enemies, but remember she was playing a dangerous game when she set herself to teach the head of the Government a lesson.

But she had a powerful friend.

He bowed over her hand. How different from Lord Oxford. He was younger and so much more handsome. Henry St John was a rake; he had had countless mistresses and would doubtless have countless more and could never contemplate a relationship with a woman which was not a sexual one. In his youth he had run naked through the park for a wager; and not long ago when he had become Secretary of State and had rode through the town in his carriage, the Madam of one of those establishments to which he was a frequent visitor, had amused the crowd by shouting to her girls, 'Five thousand a year, my beauties, and all for us!'

Now Henry St John had become Viscount Bolingbroke but he

was the same elegant, aristocratic man of pleasure who had delighted the madams of London by his extravagant patronage of their establishments.

He came to confer with Lady Masham.

He was disgruntled and made no effort to hide such an obvious fact, and as he bowed over Abigail's hand and lifted his eyes to her small pale face, he fully understood how they might work together; Abigail was pregnant yet even at such a time he was wondering when she would become his mistress – such a consideration being automatic with him.

'So, I greet Viscount Bolingbroke,' said Abigail.

'A Viscountcy! No Earldom! Our friend – should I say our one-time friend – wants no rivals. An Earldom for him, so therefore I must be a mere Viscount.'

'I think we have been somewhat mistaken in our one-time friend.'

'He sees himself as the mighty dragon breathing fire to destroy all his enemies.'

'Rather should they be overcome by the fumes of alchohol.'

They laughed together. 'Harley is a fool,' said Bolingbroke. Abigail nodded.

'He has used us and now believes he has no need of us.'

'He will be shown his mistake,' added Abigail.

'I see,' replied Bolingbroke, 'that you and I are of one mind.'

'On certain matters.'

He laid his hand on her arm. 'I hope we soon may be in unison in every way.'

'That we shall take time to discover.'

Bolingbroke was a rash man. He wanted to pursue politics and women at the same time, and he was excited by Abigail because she was different from any woman he had ever known. Many would call her plain, but a woman who had gone into the arena and beaten Sarah Churchill at her own game could not be insignificant. Abigail had worked for Harley; but for her, Harley would never have been able to worm his way into the Queen's good graces. What had she wanted from Harley? Something which he had failed to give? What a fool Harley was! He had warned him, Bolingbroke, against philandering

400

with women; how much more dangerous to philander with the bottle. If Harley had not been such a virtuous husband, such a family man, if he had taken off a little time from virtue to understand Abigail Hill, he might not now be in the danger in which he stood. For in peril he certainly was, since his one-time friend whom he still believed to stand beside him, and the woman who had helped to bring him to power and had grown dissatisfied with him, now stood together, to teach him a lesson – a grim lesson which would bring him tottering down from greatness.

Bolingbroke would make no such mistake. He would not underestimate the powers of the Queen's favourite woman. The Queen's support was necessary and Abigail could bring him that.

Well, he was always ready to take on a new mistress.

Abigail was watching him covertly, reading his thoughts. Did he imagine that he only had to beckon to her? What did he think he had to offer her? His charm, his elegance, his experience? None of these she wanted.

She knew now what she longed for: devotion, adoration, fidelity, that relationship which she had seen idealized in the St Albans house.

Was there no escaping from the Marlboroughs?

But in the meantime it would be amusing to join with Viscount Bolingbroke, for although he could never fit into her emotional life she needed his help in taking her revenge on the man who had failed her. In every way, she whispered to herself. Yes in every way!

She smiled at Bolingbroke, as she evaded his proximity.

'We have much to discuss, my lord.'

He agreed. Business first, he thought. Pleasure later. At least there was one point on which they were in immediate agreement: the downfall of Robert Harley, Earl of Oxford.

Bolingbroke planned to create a new party and place himself at its head; he was following the path which Harley had set when he had formed his party to defeat Godolphin. The Queen's brief return to health was over. Her little fling had resulted in a return of the gout and dropsy. Her hands were swollen – all trace of the beauty of which she had once been so proud, gone; her face was patchy with erysipelas; her legs and feet so distorted that she could not walk.

She needed Masham and her dear Duchess day and night and since Masham was expecting, it meant that the Duchess was in constant attendance. Dear Duchess! To whom Anne could talk so much more intimately of the past than she could to Masham, for the Duchess had been with her long before Masham had come.

One could not expect such a noble lady to do the menial tasks which Masham still performed but Anne often found it difficult to decide which was the more important to her. But when Abigail returned she was not really in any doubt, and she understood that she had imagined she might prefer the Duchess because a pregnant woman must think primarily of the child she was going to bear. No one could administer a poultice with the same care as Masham – so that the minimum of pain went hand in hand with the maximum of benefit.

'Dear Masham, when your child is born, you must be in constant attendance.'

'Nothing could delight me more than to obey Your Majesty's command,' answered Abigail.

Abigail often talked to her of her half-brother in France, for Abigail understood how worried she was at the part she had played in her father's downfall. When she talked to Abigail she believed that the best thing possible would be for her half-brother to come to the throne on her death.

'That, Madam, would make you happiest. I know full well,' Abigail told her; and when she was with Abigail it seemed that this was so.

Abigail brought Bolingbroke to her and he was of the same opinion.

But then the dear Duchess of Somerset would remind her of the perils of popery. Yes indeed, said the Duchess, she would be happy if she could bring back her half-brother; but she must not forget her duty to the Church. Her father had been driven out of England because he was a Catholic; would she not, by bringing back her brother – also a Catholic – plunge England into trouble again?

'For Madam,' insisted the Duchess, 'the people of this country would never accept a Catholic monarch.'

It was true and she must consider the Church. But when Masham and Bolingbroke talked to her, of keeping the crown to the Stuarts – her own family, her own brother to follow her – she could not help but sway towards their opinions.

Who were these Germans? The Electress Sophia – an overbearing woman – her son George Lewis who, it was said, could not speak a word of English and would not try to! His marriage was unfortunate. His wife was imprisoned on an accusation of adultery, and it was said that he had plenty of mistresses. Not quite the monarch to follow good Queen Anne!

How complicated it was; and there was Mr Harley – Lord Oxford who had once been able to answer all her problems so satisfactorily – now it seemed at loggerheads with Bolingbroke who was next in importance in her Government – and worst of all with Masham, who had once thought so highly of him.

He was disturbing her too, for often his speech was so slurred that she could scarcely understand him; and his clothes were becoming more and more untidy. It was not the happiest manner in which a first minister should present himself to his Sovereign.

She had seen Masham turn away in disgust.

And she was in such pain and often so tired. Oh dear, the happy days when she believed she had solved her difficulties by ridding herself of the Marlboroughs and enjoyed a brief return to better health, were over.

Abigail was lying in her bed. Her time would soon come, and she hoped this time it would be another boy.

It would not be long now, she was thinking . . . not that her child would be born, but that Oxford would go just a little too far.

The Queen had certainly been aware of his state of intoxication the last time she had seen them together. Fool! Fool! she thought; and tears came into her eyes.

She was a foolish romantic dreamer. She had allowed him to fascinate her in those days when she had been young and silly. Often now she thought of John and Sarah together. How was life with them? Did he still love his virago as tenderly now that they were together all the time in exile?

It came back to her so vividly. The house in St Albans. The return of John. The eager manner in which he looked about him for Sarah and then . . . that long hungry embrace. The scamper of impatient feet; the slamming of the bedroom door; the smiles of the servants.

'He cannot wait to take off his boots.'

The great General, who was first of all the impatient lover, had, by his love for Sarah set up an impossible ideal in the heart of Abigail Hill.

Had her hatred of her cousin stemmed from her envy? Had she become what she was because of the love the Duke of Marlborough bore for his wife?

It had never changed, that love, although Sarah had done little to cherish it. She had gone her wild and wilful way; she had crashed to disaster because of her own rash foolishness and she had taken him with her. Yet, he loved her still.

That was what Abigail wanted . . . a love such as that. Hers was a dream of romantic love and power. There had been only one man in her life who could give her that: Robert Harley. And he had denied it. Bolingbroke? Never! She could have been his mistress for a month or so. But that was not what she sought.

Someone had come into the room.

'Samuel!' she said; and he pulled a chair and sat by her bed.

'You are not feeling well?'

'A little tired. It is natural.'

'You do too much.'

She was impatient. 'If I did not where would we be?'

He sighed. He knew that he owed everything to her; he knew too that he failed to give her what she wanted.

'My clever Abigail.' He took her fingers and kissed them. They were limp and unresponsive.

'I'm sorry,' he said.

She turned her head away. For what was he apologizing? His inadequacy?

'I must go,' she said; 'the Queen needs me. I must not allow Carrots Somerset to take over all my duties.'

404

'Do not drive yourself too hard, my dear.'

'And if I did not . . . would you have your fine title? Would you have your position here at Court?'

'No,' he said. 'But there are other prizes.'

She shook him off impatiently. He looked so . . . how could she say? Complacent? Smug. Lord Masham – a man of title through his wife's endeavours.

It was not what she wanted.

'You are going to the Queen?' he asked. 'You should not walk across the courtyard in your condition. Take your chair.'

She shrugged him aside. It was years since she had taken advice from Samuel.

As she came out into the cold air, her eyes smarted with tears – tears of frustration. She was thinking of what might have been if the child she carried had been another man's, not Samuel's, the child of a brilliant politician, who loved her as Marlborough had loved his wife, with whom she could plan the future as Marlborough did with his wife.

Her vision blurred; she was not watchful of her step as one must be in the courtyard. She caught her foot in the cobbles; in a second it had twisted under her and she fell.

She lay bewildered and stunned. Then her pains began. The child was demanding to be born although its time had not yet come.

The news spread all over the Town. Lady Masham was dying. A fall in the courtyard; a premature birth; and the Queen's favourite was lying very near to death.

The Queen was in despair. She sent Dr Arbuthnot to attend to Abigail and commanded him not to leave her until he was sure she was out of danger; and she must have hourly messages as to Abigail's state.

Anne could not be comforted. She rocked herself to and fro in her chair and asked herself how she could live without dear Masham.

Alice Hill, sitting by Abigail's bed, listened to her rambling, and knew that she was living in the past, in those days of uncertainty and degradation when she had been as a servant in the house of the Marlboroughs.

She wept, and Mrs Abrahal who would always be grateful to Abigail for speaking well of her to the Queen sought to comfort her, and Mrs Danvers took time off from the Queen's bed-chamber to come to the invalid's bedside.

There were messages from important court personages. Viscount Bolingbroke called or sent his servant every day but Lord Oxford did not inquire once and it might have been that he was not even aware of the accident to his cousin.

Dr Arbuthnot, who knew Abigail well, and had always admired her, used all his skill, and by great good fortune saved the life of the child which was a boy.

'Don't fret,' he told Alice. 'This is the best thing that could have happened. The child is a boy and he'll live. Once I can get her to understand this, she'll start to recover. I promise you.'

He sat by her bed and took her hand.

'Abigail,' he said, 'can you hear me?'

She opened her pale green eyes and he thought how colour-less they were, how lifeless – almost the eyes of a dead woman.

'Ah, you hear me then. Ye've a fine boy. Do you understand me. A fine boy.'

'Robert . . .' she began.

The Doctor glanced at Alice. 'Is that the name she wants. Robert. Why . . .'

'Named for my lord Oxford,' suggested Alice.

'Ah, it may well be.'

Abigail's eyes were open and she appeared to be listening.

'The boy's a fine strong wee laddie,' said the doctor. 'Do you want to see him?'

But Abigail had already closed her eyes. They thought that she was not aware of what was going on but this was not so. She knew that she had had an accident and that her son was prematurely born. She had been close to death and for that reason life seemed doubly precious.

Her hand was taken and held gently. She knew by whom before she opened her eyes. She thought of Samuel who was gentle and unassuming and lacked the overwhelming ambition of men like Robert Harley, Henry St John and John Churchill. But perhaps for that reason he was capable of giving her greater devotion. Harley had failed her; St John she would never trust; but she could rely on Samuel. He would always be there to love and cherish her . . . as well as their children.

She had demanded too much of life; she had wanted a great leader to love her, but great leaders were not always successful, and there were times when they were sent to pine in exile.

She had been foolish not to accept life as a compromise. Was she a foolish romantic girl to ask for the impossible?

'Samuel,' she said. 'You are there?'

She heard Alice's voice, gruff, relieved. 'Is he there? He has not been far away for the last forty-eight hours.'

No, he would not be far away when she was in danger.

'Samuel,' she repeated.

He leaned towards her. 'A boy,' he said. 'Arbuthnot says he will live and he is healthy and strong. Listen. You can hear him crying.'

She nodded drowsily. The doctor said. 'Let her sleep now.'

'I'll get a message to Her Majesty,' said Alice. 'She asked that news be sent to her without delay. She'll be delighted.'

'There have been messages . . . ?' asked Abigail.

'The Queen had to be kept informed,' replied Alice excitedly. 'Viscount Bolingbroke sent his servant every day.'

'My lord Oxford . . .'

'Oh, come, you have a Queen demanding news of you. Is that not enough?'

So he had not asked for her. He cared nothing that she might have died.

'And,' went on Alice, 'a husband who has not slept or eaten since you fell.'

She smiled and closed her eyes.

Is that not enough? That phrase of Alice's kept ringing in her mind. If it was not enough it was as much as any reasonable woman could hope for. She was not going to be foolish. She had grown wise in the last hours. Life with its compromises had become very precious.

Samuel put his head close to hers. 'I hear that you wish the child to be called Robert,' he said.

'Robert!' Her voice sounded scornful. 'No . . . I want him to be called Samuel.'

He was pleased, she sensed it.

'Samuel Masham,' she repeated, 'after his father.'

Sarah was homesick. It was distressing to see poor Marl eagerly reading his letters from home, thinking as she did every day of the meadows about Holywell, the forests at Windsor, the greenness of England, the sound of English tongues.

She was not patient in exile. She was critical of weather, scenery and people.

'Oh,' she would continually cry, 'it is not as it is in England.'

It was comforting though to be with Marl for his health was not good and he needed attention; he was as homesick as she was, although not as bitter, yet, as she herself conceded having more reason to be.

It was she who ranted on about the ungrateful country which had benefited from his victories and then had turned its back on him.

Abroad they had more respect for Marlborough than they had had in England. They remembered him as the great commander here. Prince Eugene had visited them in Frankfurt for the express purpose of seeing the Duke and doing him honour which, declared Sarah grimly, was more than his Queen had done him.

There could not be enough news from home for Sarah. She laughed grimly when she heard how fond the Queen was of the Duchess of Somerset.

'I am pleased," she said, 'that she has a friend nearer her own rank than some I could name.'

Never did a day pass without her mentioning Abigail. She told everyone with whom she conversed how she had taken the wretched creature from a broom, and how ungrateful the whole family were.

There was John Hill, brother to the Creature, whom she had found as a ragged boy, clothed and fed and sent to school. And she had prevailed upon my lord Marlborough to give the lad a place in his Army which he had done, against his judgment. And how had John Hill repaid such benevolence? When wicked charges were brought against the Duke of Marlborough, he had risen from a sick bed in order to go and vote against him.

'There is gratitude for you!' cried Sarah. 'Did you ever hear the like?' She would talk of how she had devoted her life to an ungrateful monarch; how she had sat for hours listening to banalities which had nearly driven her mad – all this she had done and what was the result? She was thrown aside for a chambermaid. Lord Marlborough had won honour and glory for his country; he was the saviour of England and what was his reward? Exile! He had been promised a palace, which was to be built at Woodstock and to be named after the greatest victory of all time: Blenheim. And what had happened? A fool named Vanbrugh – with whom she would never agree – had been allowed to plan it; and the money which had been promised had not been supplied. On and on she raved about the ungrateful country to which she longed to return.

'Better a cottage in England,' she would say sometimes, 'than a palace anywhere else in the world.'

And her longing for home was like a physical pain.

She knew of the conflict which was raging there and longed to join in, partly because she liked to be at the heart of any conflict, partly because what happened after the death of Anne could be of such vital importance to her and her husband.

She had news of the efforts the Pretender's friends were making to bring him to the throne and she and John spent many anxious hours discussing whether it was possible to swerve their devotion which had up till that time been given to Hanover. In fact he was in communication with Hanover at that time and was making plans as to what action he should take, should the Queen die suddenly.

It was disconcerting. Abigail Masham was a Jacobite and she would have every opportunity, fumed Sarah, for pouring poison into that stupid ear. Moreover, the Queen was a sentimental fool and would doubtless believe that by naming her half brother as her successor she was expiating her sins.

'Our only hope is her passion for the Church,' declared Sarah. 'She will think very hard before she lets a papist in.'

In the meantime she and John must be content with moving from one place to another. They had stayed too long in Frankfurt and were growing restive, so they moved on to Antwerp. 'Like sick people,' grumbled Sarah, 'glad of any change.'

It was while they were in Antwerp that a terrible blow struck them.

Elizabeth, their third daughter, had died of the smallpox. When Sarah read the news she was stunned. Elizabeth had been well when they left England; and this blow, in addition to all their frustration and despair, was almost too great to be borne. Marlborough was even more deeply affected than Sarah. He had always been more devoted to his family than she had and when he received the news he collapsed with grief. Sarah found some solace in nursing him for in her hectoring way she was an efficient nurse, providing the patient obeyed her absolutely and John was too wretched to do anything else.

Sarah sat by his bed and they talked of her – their little Elizabeth – who now seemed to have been the most beautiful and accomplished of all their children.

'I remember,' said Sarah, 'how she would marry . . . and she only fifteen. I thought she was too young but she would have her way. She adored Scroop and he her . . . and no wonder. And of course it was a good marriage. That was only eleven years ago, Marl. Twenty-six . . . it is too young . . . too young. . . .'

Sarah covered her face with her hands and sobbed. John tried to comfort her; he felt ill and, like Sarah, he longed for home. To be with his family . . . to continue with his career . . . to wield power . . . to accumulate wealth. There was so much he desired, so much that could have helped to comfort him. These were indeed dark hours.

Seeing him so distraught Sarah cried angrily: 'She is happier, I doubt not, than in a world like this!'

But they continued to mourn their beautiful Elizabeth; and there was no news from home to comfort them.

In London a crisis was threatening. There was an open rupture between Oxford and Bolingbroke. The Queen's health deteriorated every day, and the Court was in a ferment of excitement. Letters were passing between Hanover and London on one hand and between St Germains and London on the other.

The Queen swayed between her two beloved women – Lady Masham and the Duchess of Somerset; but there were days when she was too ill to think of much but her own relief.

Oxford, who had always hated to make decisions and whose greatest weakness was his vacillation, was now uncertain how to act. He had gone over to the Whigs but still tried to placate the Tories. In view of the strength of his enemies he was doomed, and Bolingbroke was ready to destroy him. Oxford searched for the solution to his problems in the bottle, and it was not difficult to turn the Queen against a man who reeled in her presence, who now and then gave way to ribald and disrespectful comment and at the best mumbled so that she could not understand what he said.

'Our drunken dragon will soon be slain,' Abigail told Bolingbroke.

He agreed with her. They were allies, though not lovers, as Bolingbroke had expected. But that was a small matter to be shrugged aside. There were plenty of women ready to share his bed; there was only one Lady Masham to smooth his way to the Queen.

Oh, what a fool was Oxford! He had used Abigail to climb to favour, for what he owed to those *têtes-à-têtes* in the green closet he should have been in no doubt. And just as Abigail had given him a helping hand in the beginning now she was barring his way – more than that, she was forcing him down to disaster.

He understood; but it was too late to change. Bolingbroke had the support which had once been his. He was angry with himself . . . too late; and because his brain was so often fuddled by wine, he was unable to control his temper.

His good friend Jonathan Swift, appalled at what was happening, had made an attempt to reconcile him with Bolingbroke – to no avail. The rift was too wide; and Bolingbroke was too ambitious. He wanted the position Oxford now held and how could he achieve it until Oxford had lost it?

Oxford could see the end in sight. He had wanted to placate the two parties; he wanted the support of both Whigs and Tories, in the same way as he swayed between St Germains and Hanover. After the Peace of Utrecht he should have broken away from the Tories; he saw now that he should have boldly asserted his beliefs – instead of which he had wavered, he had procrastinated – and had won the approbation of neither.

Moreover he had neglected those who would have helped him; and Abigail Masham was the first, and most important of these.

Oxford was about to fall and Abigail Masham was the reason. The Court watched and waited. Why had Abigail who had once thought so highly of him, suddenly turned against him? No one was quite sure. He had not treated her with the deference she had expected and hoped for, perhaps. Was that it? He had not given her the shares she had desired in the South Seas Company. Could that be the reason? Had she been his mistress? Never. Oxford was an uncommonly virtuous man which was noticeable in a society of rakes. Had she transferred her affections to Bolingbroke? There was a rake if ever there was one! But there was no scandal of that nature attaching to Lady Masham.

No one was quite sure where that partnership had turned sour. No one could be really certain about the relationship between Lord Oxford and Lady Masham.

Abigail herself was not always sure. He had failed her, she knew; and it was not because of lack of shares in the South Seas Company, although that might have been part of it. She had dreamed a dream and he had destroyed it.

Oxford must go. Those words were being whispered throughout the Court. Bolingbroke was ready to leap into his place. It was the chance he had been waiting for.

The Queen had been persuaded by Abigail that she could no longer tolerate her Lord Treasurer. There was no doubt that he had come into her presence completely intoxicated.

'Your Majesty is disturbed and distressed by this conduct,' said Abigail. 'I know how it affects you. Your health is not good enough to allow you to endure it.'

Masham was right. Anne was so weary. Sometimes she heard the arguments of her ministers going round and round in her head. There was one matter which worried her more than any other. If only her half-brother would give up his religion; if only he would become a good member of the Church of England; then he would be accepted and she would be so happy. Then she could feel that she had righted a wrong; then she would be able to face her father if and when they came face to face in another life. She had tried so hard since she had become Queen to be a good and Christian woman; she had wanted above all things to right any wrong she had done. If her brother could come into his inheritance and be King of England and she could bring it about, she would have expiated that long-ago sin.

'Masham,' she said, 'I have written a letter which is to be opened after my death. I want to keep it under my pillow.'

'Yes, Your Majesty.'

The succession! thought Abigail. James Stuart will be King • when she dies and he will remember that I have worked for him.

'You will not forget, Masham.'

'I will remember, Your Majesty.'

Anne held her swollen hands, swathed in bandages on her lap.

'Are they painful, Madam?'

'I think fresh poultices might comfort them.'

Abigail set about preparing them. The Queen's health was rapidly declining and that saddened her. She would never have another mistress like her; but when James Stuart was James III • of England he would remember those who had worked for him; he would remember the one who had found the letter under the pillow.

She must not forget her enemies though – the chief of these was Oxford. He had at last realized that he could waver no longer on such an important point and had come down on the side of Hanover, and would do everything he could to bring the Germans over.

'Your Majesty is tired,' she said, 'and I know this is due to Lord Oxford's behaviour.'

The Queen sighed. 'Dear Masham, he was even more difficult than usual.'

'Your Majesty should put an end to the trouble he causes you, by dismissing him.'

'I really believe I should, Masham.'

'Bolingbroke will be so much easier to deal with. There, Madam. That is not too hot?'

'Just warm and soothing, Masham. You are always so good with the poultices. You soothe away the pain.'

'I wish I could soothe away Your Majesty's other afflictions as easily.'

Anne was thoughtful. The following day she told her Council that she would ask for Lord Oxford's resignation. Her reasons were that he neglected business and was seldom to be understood, and when he did explain himself she could not be sure that he spoke the truth. Above all, he often came into her presence drunk, which was obnoxious to her, and when he was in a state of intoxication he had behaved indecorously and disrespectfully. She could no longer tolerate such conduct from a minister in his position.

Oxford was dismissed. This was triumph for Bolingbroke . . . and Abigail.

In the Council chamber Oxford faced his enemy – Bolingbroke.

Bolingbroke was a traitor, declared Oxford. He had lied and cheated his way into the Queen's graces. He was ready to bring the Popish Pretender into the country; he had abused and misrepresented the man who had befriended him and who had made his way easy along the path of politics. Bolingbroke was a liar, a cheat and a traitor.

Anne sat in her chair trembling; her head ached; her limbs throbbed; and she longed for nothing so much as escape.

Bolingbroke, went on Oxford, the worse for drink, had been aided in all these wicked practices by a certain woman. . . .

Anne's swollen fingers twitched; she felt as though she would swoon. She looked appealingly at her ministers. They must not wrangle about Abigail; they must not attempt to probe the intimate secrets of her bedchamber.

She threw a look of dislike at the ranting Oxford. Was it meet and fitting that drunken men should give vent to their feelings so in her presence?

Bolingbroke had risen and drawn his sword. This silenced Oxford.

'You forget the presence of the Queen,' said Bolingbroke.

'I forget nothing,' retorted Oxford. 'Nor shall I. I will be revenged and leave some as low as I found them.'

Anne sat back in her chair, her eyes closed; she could hear their angry voices going on and on. How ill she felt! How she longed for the quiet of her bedchamber with Abigail's tender hands to massage poor swollen limbs, to provide hot poultices.

But she must do her duty. She must sit here while they wrangled.

It was late when she was taken to her room and they were saying that there must be another meeting the next day.

Abigail and the Duchess of Somerset put her to bed where she lay exhausted until Dr Arbuthnot came to her.

'These conflicts are killing me,' she said to him. 'Oh, how I long to be at peace!'

At last she did sleep and Dr Arbuthnot turning to Abigail shook his head gravely.

'You should get some rest yourself,' he said. 'Her Majesty will have need of your nursing in the next few days.'

Anne awoke from her uneasy sleep.

The voices of her ministers still jangled in her head. Lord Oxford, his eyes bloodshot, his voice slurred . . . she could not forget him; nor the venom she had seen in Bolingbroke's face. 'How tired I am . . .' she murmured. Then she remembered that she must attend yet another meeting today.

She rose from her bed and stood unsteadily. Where were her women? What time was it?

Time? she thought. It is time for the meeting . . . and I must go. I must do my duty. I am the Queen.

She moved unsteadily towards the mantelpiece and peered at the clock. Time! she thought. What time was it? She felt herself slipping back in time . . . living in The Cockpit . . . listening to Sarah Churchill's vituperations against the Dutch Monster . . . working so hard to drive her father from the throne. The warming-pan baby . . . that brother who was now waiting to take his inheritance. . . .

If she could go back. . . . Would it be different? She was afraid of time. It would soon be time for the Council meeting. . . . Time. . . .

She looked into the clock's face and thought she saw another face looking at her, calling her, giving her a summons that she could not disobey because it was not in the power of any – Queen or commoner – to do so.

'Your Majesty.'

She turned. Mrs Danvers was standing beside her, frightened.

'Danvers . . .'

'I wondered why Your Majesty was staring at the clock.'

'I saw . . .' she began; and Mrs Danvers caught her as she would have fallen.

Mrs Danvers called to the Queen's woman and together they carried her fainting body back to her bed.

'I saw death in her face,' said Mrs Danvers, her teeth chattering.

The Queen was dying. Outside the palace the people gathered waiting for news. This was more than the death of a Queen who had worked for the good of her subjects; this could be civil war; there was a choice of two Sovereigns; the German who could not speak a word of English and the Papist Pretender. People took sides, but half-heartedly. Who wanted the German? Who wanted the Papist? If James had been a good Churchman the country would have stood behind him. But his father had been driven away for his religion. Would it be the same trouble again?

Marlborough's war was over and the people wanted no more wars. For this reason they were more inclined to accept the German.

In the palace the conflicts raged more fiercely.

Abigail had been in constant attendance. Her thoughts were confused; she had scarcely slept for several nights and was exhausted; yet she knew that the Queen was uneasy when she was not close.

The Queen was dying, and Abigail now realized how much she loved the Queen. Her friendship had been calculated it was true, but she had received such kindness from her Sovereign, she had found such joy in serving her – what would her life be without Anne?

416

The Council had decided against Bolingbroke as Oxford's successor, and had chosen the Duke of Shrewsbury as Lord Treasurer.

Shrewsbury had declared that he would not accept office without the Queen's consent and as a result he had been brought to her bedside. Those about her had believed that she would not recognize him, but she did, for when she was asked if she knew to whom she had given the staff of office she whispered: 'To the Duke of Shrewsbury.'

More than that she took his hand and implored him to use his office for the good of her people.

Shrewsbury knelt at the bedside and assured her that he would do all in his power; and she seemed satisfied.

She closed her eyes, but shortly afterwards those about her bed heard her rambling about the past. She mentioned the warming pan, and there were tears on her cheeks.

'My brother . . .' she whispered. 'My poor brother.'

Glances were exchanged. Was she going to demand that her brother be her successor? And what would the reaction be towards a dying woman?

Those who had supported the House of Hanover were afraid; but they need not have worried on that score for Anne was too far gone to remain coherent.

Abigail, almost numb with tiredness, stood close to the bed; they were very near the end, she knew, and when the Queen died she must take the letter from under her pillow. That would let everyone know what the Queen's wishes were.

But in her heart she knew that there would be so many to oppose the Queen's wishes and that there was little chance of James Stuart's coming to England. He himself had refused to give up his religion and the English would not have a papist on the throne. Moreover she knew that he had no means of bringing an army with him to fight for his rights and the French were not in a position to supply him with what he would need.

Yet if the Queen's dying wishes were known . . .

But who would care for a dead Queen?

'They are going to bleed the Queen,' whispered Mrs Danvers in her ear.

'Yes, Lady Masham,' said Dr Arbuthnot. 'She is suffering from an excess of apoplexy.'

Abigail whispered: 'Dr Arbuthnot, what hope . . .'

But the doctor pretended not to hear her.

The apothecary was at the bed; and as the Queen lay back, her eyes closed, the room seemed to revolve round Abigail, and she fell swooning to the floor.

Anne was aware that something had happened and asked what it was.

'Lady Masham has fainted, Your Majesty,' said Dr Arbuthnot. 'Poor woman she has been with Your Majesty night and day and is worn out with exhaustion and her grief.'

'Poor Masham!' sighed Anne. 'Poor, poor Masham . . .' She was uneasy because they were taking Abigail from the sick-room; but she could not remember the cause of her uneasiness.

'My brother . . .' she whispered. 'My poor brother.'

The Queen was dying. She had lost consciousness and was fast slipping away.

Although there were services in which prayers were made for her recovery, the Council were making arrangements to send a message to Hanover the moment the Queen took her last breath.

It could not be long now.

Those watching heard the death rattle in her throat, they saw the film in her eyes.

As the doctors bent over the dead Queen they saw a paper protruding from under her pillow. It was taken out and handed to the Duke of Shrewsbury, who looked at it, nodded, and slipped it into his pocket.

'Lady Masham, wake up.'

It was Mrs Danvers standing over her.

'The Queen?'

'She has passed away.'

Abigail stood up, feeling sick with exhaustion and anxiety for the future mingling with an overwhelming sense of loss.

'I will go to her,' she said. Then her mouth twisted into a

wry smile. 'It's too late, though. She will never call me again.'

'Nor any of us,' said Mrs Danvers.

Abigail shook her head. 'What shall we do?' she whispered. 'What will become of us?'

She went to the bedside and looked down at the Queen and the tears blinded her eyes as she stooped to kiss that cold forehead and slip her hand under the pillow.

It was gone. She should have known.

This is the end, she thought.

Shrewsbury, seated at the Council table, held up the letter. 'My friends,' he said, addressing his fellow members, 'I think we can guess what this contains, but if we do not open it, we cannot be sure.'

'It may contain her last wish.'

Shrewsbury smiled at the speaker. 'We are in no position for civil war and the people would never accept a papist. If we do not know what her last wish was, we cannot go against it.' He turned to the fire which was burning in the grate and going towards it held the letter up so that all the members of the Council could see it. 'Gentlemen,' he went on, 'are you of my opinion for the sake of England it is better that this letter remains unread?'

There was a brief pause, then a voice said: 'I am of your opinion.'

'And I. And I.'

Shrewsbury smiled. 'Unanimous,' he said.

They watched the paper writhing in the flames.

Sarah saw the messenger approaching. News from England was always eagerly awaited and she had heard already that the state of the Queen's health was deteriorating.

This, she thought, as she hastened to greet the messenger, could be what we are waiting for.

She knew by the man's face that it was.

'The Queen . . .' she began.

'Is dead, Your Grace.'

She snatched the letters from him.

'Marl!' she cried. 'Where are you, Marl? The Queen is dead! This is the end of exile.'

The end of exile! How right she was! There was no longer need to remain abroad. Soon they would be back where the fields were greener, where everything she loved and cherished would be waiting for her.

Marlborough took the news more calmly. So much, he pointed out, depended on who was the next Sovereign of England. If it was the Pretender, their chances of returning to Court were small; but if the new King came from Hanover then he would have no reason to feel anything but gratitude towards Marlborough and his Duchess.

The next days were the most anxious Sarah had ever lived through.

'I should die,' she told John, 'if we could not go back now.'

They travelled to Calais to be ready to embark as soon as they knew who was to be the new King.

It was over, thought Abigail. Shrewsbury and his Council had caused the Queen's letter to be destroyed. They could guess its contents, and were not going to allow a papist monarch to mount the throne of England merely to salve a Queen's conscience.

Bolingbroke was not in a position to act. She had seen him and he told her there was nothing they could do. The people, he believed, would soon tire of the German King who in any case showed no eagerness to accept the throne, and then they would be only too glad to turn to James.

But a papist! thought Abigail. Never! If he would but change his religion. . . .

No, there was nothing which could save her now. Oxford had fallen – and she would not be long after him. The Queen's love alone had kept her in her place and now that was over.

George I had been proclaimed King of England; the people of London were behind him. Marlborough was coming home.

Abigail sent her maid to tell Lord Masham that she wished to see him.

Samuel came at once and she went to him and put her arm through his.

'This is the end, Samuel,' she said. 'There will be nothing more for us here.'

'I know,' he answered.

'So we will take the children and go away from Court.'

'It will be a different life for you, Abigail.'

'I know it is the end.'

'Or,' he said, 'the beginning.'

She laughed and she was surprised by the warmth in that laughter. 'It would depend on the way one looked at it.'

'Do you remember when we first met?' he asked her.

She nodded. 'We were watching the Duke of Gloucester drill his boy soldiers in the Park.'

'Neither of us was very important then, Abigail.'

'We were not. And now it's Lord and Lady Masham, with a family to keep.'

'We'll go to the country. We'll buy a manor there.'

'The thought of being a country squire is not distasteful to my lord?'

'I can imagine in some circumstances it would be very pleasant.'

'Yes, Samuel,' she said. 'So could I!'

She wondered then whether she meant it. She thought of the joys of Court life, the intrigues and triumphs.

She would never forget the days when it had been necessary to be on good terms with Abigail Hill in order to get a hearing with the Queen. She would always remember the first time Robert Harley had leaned towards her, endearingly, affectionately and said: 'We are cousins.'

She would never forget him; she would until she died ask herself with a touch of pain whether in other circumstances it might have been so different.

Revenged she had been, but there was little satisfaction in revenge. She had her sons; her daughter. They would have more children. Perhaps in them she could find the fulfilment she had failed to find in her own life.

It was over. There remained the country. There was no other choice.

The Marlboroughs landed at Dover to a salute of guns.

'Long live the great Duke of Marlborough!' went up the cry.

Sarah sniffed the air. Oh, how good it was to be back!

And there was Marl. The great Duke once more! The friend of the new King! The people were strewing flowers in their path; they were to ride through London in their glass coach.

'This is how it was after Blenheim!' cried Sarah.

And as the Marlboroughs rode into London, in search of fresh glories, Lord and Lady Masham, with their children, rode out seeking obscurity.

The Exiles Return

The Marlboroughs might be back in favour but it was not as it had once been, and Sarah continued to sigh for the old days, when those who craved royal favour knew they must first seek her help.

The new King was quite unlike the last Sovereign. George had little love for England; he made no concessions to his new people and he lacked the Stuart charm – so strong in Charles II and present even in his brother James and in his nieces Mary and Anne. George was a solid German, who could not speak English, who had imprisoned his wife on suspected adultery and brought his German ministers and mistresses with him. That one mistress should be excessively fat and the other extremely thin was characteristic of him. He was indifferent to ridicule; he was crude and a boor. But the country was behind him for the simple reason that the alternative was a Catholic.

In his Court there was no place for Sarah. The King's German mistresses were quite unimpressed by this blustering quarrelsome woman. Marlborough was useful, of course, but Sarah could not shut her eyes to the fact that the war had had a disastrous effect upon his health.

But when he rode through the City he was cheered; in fact it was noticed that he received a more enthusiastic welcome than the King; but that was a temporary triumph, and nothing was the same, mourned Sarah.

The new King delighted her by offering Marlborough his old post as Captain-General of the Army; and when John said that he thought it would be wise to refuse she was overcome with rage.

'Why! Why! in God's name! Are you mad, Marl?' she demanded.

'My dearest Sarah, I am not the man I was,' he explained. 'I am too old for this most exacting role.'

'Too old! I never heard such nonsense. You'll take it. Have we come back to tell the world we are too old! What have we been waiting for all this time?'

He embraced her and tried to stroke her lovely hair, which always delighted him, but she tore herself away.

'Marl, what nonsense is this that has got into you?'

'To be a success, a Captain-General must be strong ... alert ... capable ...'

'Oh, be silent. There are times when I could take a stick to you.'

'I am the best judge of my capabilities ...'

'So you want to rot in the country?' Her eyes were flashing; her hair had fallen loose about her shoulders. He thought how young she looked, and that her hair had lost scarcely any of the bright gold it had had in her youth.

She followed his thoughts and shook her head angrily so that the golden strands waved about her head.

'You don't age, Sarah,' he said. 'Your hair is the same as when we were first married.'

'Sentimental nonsense!' she cried. 'You are offered the post of Captain-General and you talk about *hair*. Now, Marl, of course you will take it.'

'Listen, Sarah, I am no longer young. I am ten years older than you. I am not fit for the post.'

'You will take it,' she said.

'I will not.'

When he spoke like that he meant it. There had been oc-

424

casions during their married life when she had had to bow to his wishes.

'So you have decided this?'

'I cannot take a post which I know I am not fit for. Sarah, for God's sake, accept the truth. We are no longer young. We must adjust ourselves to this new phase of our lives. We have each other. . . .'

Again the golden strands were shaken. Then she turned and left him.

She shut herself in her bedroom and looked at her angry reflection. He would rather stroke her hair than command an army, would he? In a sudden fury she picked up a pair of scissors and cut off strands of her hair so that instead of falling to her waist it scarcely reached her shoulders. Then gathering it up she she went with it to his study and threw it all onto his desk.

Back in her room she looked at her reflection. She seemed different – older.

Grimly she smirked. 'We shall see how my lord Marlborough likes that!' she cried.

But when they next met he made no comment; and when she went into his study she could find no trace of the hair.

He told her the next day that, as she so wished it, he had decided to accept the King's offer.

Marlborough was once more Captain-General of the Army.

It soon became clear that the new King, although he had decided to make use of Marlborough's services, had no great liking for him; and although some court posts were allotted to the family, none came the way of Sarah.

Mary, now Duchess of Montague, became a Lady of the Bedchamber to the Princess of Wales, and her husband was given a regiment. The Earl of Bridgewater, husband of Elizabeth who had died recently, was made Chamberlain to the Prince of Wales, while Henrietta's husband, Lord Godolphin, was given the offices he had possessed before the fall of his father and the Churchill faction, and Lord Sunderland, Anne's husband, was made Lord Lieutenant of Ireland.

An indication, commented Sarah, that the *family* was back in favour; and although Sunderland might be furious to be sent to Ireland, at least he had a little more recognition than herself.

But, she declared, they would soon find they could not do without the Marlboroughs.

Bolingbroke, realizing the danger of his position on the accession of George, had fled to France and there went into the service of James whom he had tried so hard to bring to the throne. As a result, James made an attempt to gain it in 1715; and then Marlborough as Captain-General, was called in to serve the King.

Alas, he was showing his age and it was clear even to him that he was no longer fit for the field. Although he directed operations he took no active part, and this more than anything brought home to him the fact that his days of glory were over.

When the rebellion was at an end, Sarah took him to St Albans there to nurse him back to health.

It was at this time that a further blow struck the household. A letter came to the house addressed to the Duke and the Duchess from the Earl of Sunderland to tell them that his wife, their daughter Anne, had been taken ill with pleuritic fever and he thought it advisable if they would come to her bedside without delay.

When John read the letter he sank down onto a chair and trembled violently so that Sarah, desperately anxious for her daughter, was equally so for her husband. He was in his sixty-sixth year and his had been a life of stress and tension. The death of her daughter, Elizabeth, had shaken him severely, and had put years on him; and now it seemed that Anne, the favourite of all her children, was in danger.

'I will go to her,' she said, 'and you will remain here, you are unfit to travel.'

John protested. He would go to his daughter and nothing would keep him away.

While they were arguing, there was a further letter. Anne, Lady Sunderland, was dead.

*   *   *

Sarah had wept until those about her thought she would lose her reason, and when Sarah wept the whole household knew it; hers was no secret grief.

'Why has this ill fortune come to us!' she demanded. 'What have we done to deserve it? I thought I had endured all the ill fortune in the world when I lost my only son. And now . . . two daughters . . . my best daughters . . .'

She stormed through the house, one moment harrying her servants for incompetence, the next shutting herself into her room to throw herself onto her bed and give way to her grief.

Anne had been the sweetest member of the household; she had been the peacemaker – and in that family they had needed one. Sarah had loved her dearly because she never argued as her eldest Henrietta and her youngest Mary did; Anne would smile when she disagreed and bow her head, while she kept firmly to her opinions. She had been lovely – a daughter to be proud of. Marl had been against her marriage with Charles Spencer. Dear Marl, the most ambitious man alive and the most sentimental. He had feared that Charles Spencer, who had become Lord Sunderland on his father's death, was not good enough for their Anne although he was one of the richest men in the country. But she, Sarah, had had her way and the marriage had taken place. Not that she had ever liked Sunderland. Dearest Anne! She had been one of the beauties of the Court – for she surpassed her sisters, and Marl used to say that she and Elizabeth were the ones who rivalled their mother for beauty, although even they could not quite equal her. The Little Whig they called her and the Whigs had toasted her in their coffee houses. And now she was dead.

'My only son, my two daughters!' moaned Sarah. 'Why should I have to suffer like this.'

Marl had tried to comfort her. 'We still have Henrietta and Mary.'

A hollow comfort! Henrietta and Mary had always gone their own way. Their wills were almost as strong as Sarah's and they could not be together for long without quarrelling. Those two left out of her family of five! It was heartbreaking.

There seemed nothing to live for. Even the days when they were wandering about the Continent were better than this.

Sarah stormed into the bedroom she shared with John and found him sitting in his chair. He did not look up when she entered and she cried: 'We'll have to go to Court. We can't stay here grieving for the rest of our lives. German George will have to be made to understand what he owes to you. What's the matter. Are you struck dumb? Marl. *Marl!*'

She went to him and the thought came to her in that moment: Why did I think I had reached the ultimate suffering. Then I had Marl, and while I have him I still have what I need to make life worth living.

'John,' she cried. 'Dearest. . . .'

But he did not answer; he could only look at her with dull, bewildered eyes.

She ran screaming from the room, summoning the servants. 'Send for doctors. At once! At once! My lord Marlborough is taken ill.'

It was said that the shock of Lady Sunderland's death, following so close on that of Lady Bridgewater, had brought on the Duke of Marlborough's stroke.

When she realized that although he had lost the power of speech and it was obvious that he could not clearly grasp what was going on about him, he could still recover, Sarah threw off her grief for her daughters and set about nursing him, giving to the task all that energy which she had previously squandered on quarrels.

Nothing in that household was allowed to interfere with the Duke's recovery. Sarah was supreme in the sickroom. She insisted that Dr Garth – a local doctor – take up residence in the house that he might be called to attend the Duke at any time of the night and day.

The Duke must be kept alive, and it seemed that none dared disobey Sarah – not even the Duke, for he clung to life with a tenacity which surprised everyone, including the doctors.

'You will recover, John,' Sarah told her husband. 'My dearest, you must recover. We have been together so long. How could we be separated now?'

That was one thing he seemed to understand and each day there was an improvement. His powers of speech began to return and Dr Garth said his recovery was a near-miracle.

While Sarah was nursing John she received a letter from the Earl of Sunderland in which he said his wife had written to him when she knew she was dying and he enclosed the letter, for it concerned Sarah.

'Pray get my mother, the Duchess of Marlborough, to take care of the children, for to be left to servants is very bad for them and a man can't take care of little children as a woman can. For the love she has for me and the duty I shall ever show her, I hope she will do it and be very kind to you who was dearer to me than my life.'

When Sarah read this letter she took it to her private sitting room and wept over it.

Then she took it to John and sitting by his chair told him what it contained. He understood and nodded his head.

'It will be good for you, Sarah,' he said in his slow and painful way.

And she wept afresh – quiet tears unlike those she usually shed.

'I shall write at once to Sunderland,' she said. 'We will have the children here as soon as it can be arranged. There is Elizabeth's girl, too. Perhaps I should bring her here. As my poor darling Anne has said: It is not good for children to be left to the care of servants.'

John understood. He seemed happier than he had for a long time.

This was Sarah's new life – far from Court intrigues; a sick husband to nurse; a houseful of grandchildren to care for.

At Langley Marsh

In the Manor of Langley Marsh Lady Masham had become the gracious chatelaine. Samuel was an ideal lord of the manor; gentle, kindly, he quickly became popular with his tenants, who knew in the neighbourhood that they must not be deceived by the quiet manner of Lady Masham; she it was who ruled the household.

She entertained frequently, yet she appeared to enjoy the simpler pursuits of the country. Her still room occupied some part of her time, and there was also the governing of the servants, the planning of dinner parties and of course, the bringing up of her children. When her son George died she was stricken with grief but she still had her Samuel, named after his father, and there was another son Francis to replace the one she had lost. She had her daughter Anne and looked forward to having more children.

She was avidly interested in the news from Court but she saw it all from a long distance and with each passing month her nostalgia grew less, and there were days when she never thought for a moment of the intimacies of the green closet; she sometimes poured the bohea tea without hearing the echo of a

430

beautiful voice murmuring: 'Dear Hill . . . or dear Masham . . . you always make it just as I like it.'

Those days were over but they had led to the present, and she must never allow the glory of Court power to obscure the degrading beginning. Abigail, Lady Masham, had come a long way from poverty and indignity and she was not the sort to forget it.

Samuel understood, perhaps more than she had believed he could; he was gentle and unobtrusive.

There came a time when she was restless; this was when she heard that Robert Harley, Lord Oxford was to be impeached for high treason and other crimes and misdemeanours.

Unlike Bolingbroke he had not fled the country. He had stood firm and she was glad that he had. Yet she hoped that he would not be found guilty. What had he done?

She waited for news with trepidation. Samuel knew it. He was watchful of her during that time – watchful and full of tact.

'They cannot call him a criminal for pursuing a policy of which they don't approve,' pointed out Samuel.

'They will have other charges to bring,' answered Abigail.

And so they had. They accused him of helping the Pretender to which he replied that everything he had done had been sanctioned by the Queen.

But with the fears of rebellion and so much political activity, the Harley affair seemed unimportant. It was shelved and he was left a prisoner in the Tower for two years.

Often Abigail in her comfortable bed would think of him in his prison in the Tower. Then she became pregnant again and his image grew faint.

'You need not think,' Samuel told her, 'that you could be involved in his affairs.'

'I am not afraid,' she answered.

And strangely enough she believed Samuel understood that her preoccupation with Harley's affairs was not due to a fear of being accused with him. It was some subtle connection, some vague relationship between them which she was striving to forget.

The End of the Favourites

Sarah was making a busy life. The houses at St Albans and Windsor as well as Marlborough House in London were always full of young people, and she was already planning grand marriages for her grandchildren. John's health was a continual anxiety, for shortly after the first stroke he had another which was even more severe than the first, and yet Sarah nursed him through it. He found it difficult now to speak but he still clung to life. He must, Sarah told him, for what would she do without him?

He would sit in his chair and listen to the talk of his grandchildren whom he loved as devotedly as they did him. Sarah never had their affection. They were afraid of her. The only one to whom she showed real tenderness was Anne's youngest Diana, whom she called Lady Dye. Lady Dye was her favourite and reminded Sarah frequently of her mother; moreover, the child had her mother's temperament which made it so much easier for them to get on together. This was particularly noticeable because Lady Dye's elder sister, Anne, had a touch of Sarah's temper. This was certain to make for trouble and it was not possible to have such a temper duplicated in one household, so Lady Anne Spencer was sent away when her father married again.

This was another source of fury to Sarah. Only a year and a half after the death of her beloved Anne, Sunderland took another wife! He had left his Irish post and become Secretary of State which was all the more reason, Sarah believed, why he should have consulted her. She quarrelled violently with him over his marriage – to a nonentity, she declared. She could not bear it when any of the family escaped from her orbit; and she considered even son-in-laws, of whom she was not particularly fond, as part of her family.

In addition to these family troubles, she was involved in a series of quarrels with Sir John Vanbrugh over the building of Blenheim. She was a fury, said Vanbrugh, and an impossible woman. No one could hope to work with her or for her and enjoy any harmony. She was suing the Earl of Cadogan, who had been a great friend of John's and his comrade-in-arms through many campaigns, for misappropriation of funds which John had entrusted to him; Vanbrugh had written to her that he could no longer continue to work on Blenheim for her accusations were far-fetched, mistaken and her inferences wrong. He would give up, he wrote, unless the Duke recovered in health sufficiently to shield him from her intolerable treatment.

Blenheim was not yet completed although vast sums had been spent on it; it was going to cost £300,000 before it was finished and although the country supplied four fifths of this sum the remaining fifth had to come from the Marlboroughs. This gave Sarah the firm belief that she had every right to dictate what should and what should not be done.

So quarrelling with Vanbrugh, Cadogan, Sunderland and her grandchildren Sarah found her days lively. John had no idea of all the strife which was going on about them; as for Sarah, she constantly assured him that all was well; she would not have him disturbed in any way and on the occasions when he suffered relapses she remained in the sick room day and night.

Nor did she neglect her grandchildren. They were now growing up and much entertainment took place at her various

433

houses. It was amusing to act plays – for the Duke loved to watch his grandchildren performing, and they played for his benefit *All for Love* and *Tamerlane*.

Even so she must expurgate the plays before she allowed the children to perform them.

'I will allow no bawdy words to be spoken in my house,' she warned them. 'And I shall have no unseemly fondling and embracing in my house even though you tell me it comes in the play.'

So they argued together and often the sound of high words would come to the Duke's ears as he sat in his chair. There must be these quarrels wherever Sarah was, and he had to accept this. It was part of her nature. And he would rather hear her voice raised in anger than not hear it at all.

She was alternately triumphant because of some conquest over an enemy or wildly vituperative. She would not have a friend left in the world, he feared, when he was dead. She quarrelled incessantly; her two daughters were on bad terms with her; this upset her but she could not curb her violent tongue – and nor could they; moreover they were not of an age now to fear her. She had her favourites among her grandchildren but there was trouble with them too – and there would be more as they grew up.

She was as fond of money as he was. He wondered if he had taught her that. They were rich and growing richer. When the South Sea Bubble exploded Sarah was one of the few who sold out in time. While others lamented that ruin had come upon them Sarah was boasting that out of her adventure in speculation she had made £100,000. Yes, they were rich now, but that could not make Sarah happy.

She lived in constant anxiety for John and although her assiduous care for him was such a comfort to him, even he, who loved her devotedly, was made uncomfortable by her. If she disagreed with doctors she would threaten to pull off their wigs and drive them from the apartment. They were incompetent ninnies, she told them, when she fancied that John did not respond to their medicines.

Her daughters Henrietta, Lady Godolphin, and Mary, Duchess of Montague – neither of them having the sweet tempers of Elizabeth and Anne – decided that they would no longer allow her to bully them and made a point of visiting their father when Sarah was not at home.

John reasoned with them; their mother would be hurt, he pointed out.

'Dearest father,' replied Henrietta, 'it is no use. We are not children any longer and we will not be treated as such.'

'Your mother has nothing but your good at heart.'

Mary kissed him. 'You are the sweetest man on earth and where she is concerned the blindest. She makes it so unpleasant for us that frankly we have no wish to be with her.'

But seeing how such remarks distressed him they allowed him to tell them how good their mother was, while they promised that they would try to understand her.

But even for his sake they could not tolerate her interference in their lives and whenever they were with her flew into rages almost as violent as hers.

The Duke was aware of the atmosphere of his home and thought how characteristic of his life it had become. He had married the woman he loved and his love for her had been like a thread of gold running through the dark web of his life; she was with him now at the end which he knew could not be far off and her devotion and care for him was all he could have asked; and yet there must be this continual strife in his home – and not only in his home but in all his affairs. The building of Blenheim, the dismissal of Vanbrugh, the trouble with Cadogan ... the quarrels with Sunderland ... But these belonged to Sarah and wherever she was there would be tempest.

As he sat in his chair he would hear the sound of family quarrels. Sarah's shrill voice arguing with her daughters or expressing her contempt for her grandchildren. Lady Dye seemed the only one who was not at some time or other in the cloud of Sarah's displeasure.

As the spring of the year 1722 passed into summer John felt himself growing weaker and tried to keep this from Sarah. His tenderness for her was as great as it had been in the days of their courtship and his greatest concern now that he knew death to be near was for her future. He knew that he had held her back from even greater recklessness; he admired her; she was in his eyes brilliant, but he could not be blind to the fact that she made trouble for herself and everyone around her.

Without him to restrain her what would become of her? Her daughters could help her – if they would. But she would never accept help from them; nor did they love her sufficiently to give it.

Whenever they came to see him he would turn the conversation to their mother; he tried hard to make them see her virtues.

'You have the best mother in the world,' he told them.

Mary, the franker of the two, replied that they had the best of fathers and that was all they could expect.

Their love for him pleased him but he would have transferred that devotion to Sarah if he could have done so.

He sighed. His daughters were as strong-willed as their mother – or almost; and he knew that he was too tired and sick to attempt to bring peace between them.

He would lie in his chair listening to Sarah discussing his case with Sir Samuel Garth, a doctor whom she respected, or sneering at Dr Mead, whose methods she described as useless; he knew that there was trouble about a rumour concerning Sarah's support of the Pretender; she would always have her enemies. It was very troubling and, most of all, the knowledge that he could do nothing about it.

It was June and from his window in Windsor Lodge he could see the green of the forest and hear the bird song. Everything fresh and renewed, and he so old and tired! He was seventy-two. A good age for a man who had lived such a life as his; and something told him that the end was very close.

Sarah found him lying on his bed and she knew the worst.

'John, my dearest love,' she whispered.

And he looked at her unable to speak but the devotion of a lifetime was in his eyes.

'What shall I do without him?' she murmured.

Then she was all briskness. Send for Garth. Where was that fool Mead? The Duke had had another stroke.

Henrietta and Mary came and waited in an ante-room, and Sarah left the sickroom while they were there.

'We want no quarrels over his death-bed,' said Sarah.

It was too late for him now to plead with them; he was failing fast. His daughters took their last farewell of him and Sarah came to be with him to the very end, which was what he would wish.

On the 16th June in the year 1722 the great Duke of Marlborough died.

He lay in state at Marlborough House and was later buried with military honours in Westminster Abbey.

Sarah gratified at the honours done him, for none, as she repeated frequently, deserved them more, faced the world with a defiant glare, but inwardly she felt that her life was over, for what could it mean to her without him?

The news of Marlborough's death came to Langley Marsh bringing back old memories.

The affairs of the Marlboroughs were often discussed at the table when guests were invited. Abigail would amuse the company with stories of Sarah's antics; but as the years passed they seemed more like her imaginings of some fictitious creature than truth. But when news of Sarah's latest adventures came, Abigail realized that she had not exaggerated.

Now the Duke was dead, and Sarah would no longer be supported by that wonderful devotion on which Abigail had built an ideal. Sarah had lost her most precious possession, and Abigail could even feel sorry for her.

She ceased to think of Harley now who, when he had been taken from his prison in the Tower and faced his judges, had been acquitted, though forbidden to come to Court or to go to the House of Lords. This meant that he was cut off from any hope of continuing his political career and passed into obscurity.

She occasionally heard stories of Bolingbroke, how he had married his French mistress, after the death of his wife and continued to live in France.

So they, who had been so close once, were widely separated to live lives of their own.

She was content with hers.

It was two years after the death of Marlborough when news

reached her of Robert Harley's death. He was at his house in Albemarle Street when he had been taken ill.

Memories came flooding back as they did when such events occurred. John, her brother, who had been a constant visitor to them since they had lived at Langley Marsh, kept talking of the past.

'It brings it all back,' he said. 'It's odd how you forget . . . until something like this happens.'

But John forgot more easily; he went off riding with young Samuel who was a favourite with him and was doubtless telling him stories of the old days when he had a command in the Army, and how he had lost it when the Germans came. Abigail remembered how she had fought for John against Marlborough – and lost. It was natural that when Anne was dead and Marlborough high in favour that John should lose his command.

But he was reconciled. He was not rich but he had a comfortable income and that would go to young Samuel in due course.

But as Abigail went about her duties she was thinking of the house in Albemarle Street and how she had gone there in secret to warn, to advise . . . and to hope.

She thought of Harley often during the months that followed, asking herself whether she would ever be completely rid of this nostalgia for the past which was like a physical pain. But when in October of that year her youngest daughter Elizabeth, who was only fifteen, was taken ill, she nursed her night and day and all past longings were obliterated in fear for the present.

Elizabeth died; and Abigail's grief overwhelmed her; but it taught her one thing: her life, her emotions, her loyalties were there in Langley Marsh.

Sarah had not realized, until she lost him, how deeply she had loved her husband. He had been the one to show affection; she had accepted it as her right; she had stood fiercely by him, she had schemed for his sake; but only now did she know how much she needed him.

There was no one in the world who could take his place. The Earl of Coningsby tried. He was a man she and John had known for many years and six months after the funeral he wrote to Sarah offering her marriage.

Sarah read his letters through with astonishment. That anyone could think to take the place of Marl – and so soon! But she wrote to him gently, declining.

It was shortly afterwards that she received another proposal. This amused her because it came from the Duke of Somerset, whose wife had been that lady who had shared the Queen's favour with Abigail Hill. Moreover, the Duke was a man obsessed by his nobility; he was known as the Proud Duke and some of the court wits had said that his pride in his birth amounted almost to mental derangement. Of course he was one of the premier dukes, sharing that honour with Norfolk; but it was rumoured that even his own children had to stand in his presence and one of them who thought he was asleep, daring to sit, was immediately 'fined' £20,000 which was cut out of her inheritance.

Sarah, therefore, reading his dignified offer, was flattered; he must have a very high opinion of her, for one thing she had to admit she lacked was noble birth. Of course as Duchess of Marlborough she stood as high as any, and she would have everyone know it; but such a man as Somerset would certainly consider the Jennings's and Churchills very humble folk.

Sarah took some pleasure in her reply. 'If I were young and handsome as I was, instead of old and faded as I am, and you could lay the empire of the world at my feet, you should never have the heart and hand that once belonged to John, Duke of Marlborough.'

Having despatched this reply she went to John's study; her thoughts were back to the past and the terrible sense of loss was as strong with her as it had ever been.

She decided that she could no longer delay sorting out his belongings and as she went through the treasures he kept in his cabinet she came upon a package; and when she opened this her own golden hair fell out.

She stared in astonishment. Her hair! Then she remembered that occasion when in a fury she had cut it off and thrown it on his desk. So he had gathered it up and preserved it.

She discovered that she was crying – not the tempestuous

sobbing which was characteristic of her – but quietly, heart-brokenly.

She put the hair back into the packet and went to her room. There she lay on her bed, quietly weeping.

'Marl,' she murmured, 'why was it so? You should never have left me. We should have gone together. For of what use is life to me without you?'

She continued to battle her way through life – but much of the old zest was gone. Life had little meaning without Marl. But she was the same Sarah – bellicose, furious, quarrelsome, impulsively going to battle. She had a new name now. 'Old Marlborough'. And she was old; she had been sixty-two when the Duke died.

She might have found some contentment in those last years. She was an extremely rich woman – and she had always loved money. She had only two daughters it was true but many grandchildren. But she could never live in harmony with them. She could never resist meddling – neither in the affairs of the country nor those of the family.

She would not be excluded from the country's affairs and since she had always sought for her opponents in the highest quarters chose the Prime Minister Robert Walpole as her number one enemy and Queen Caroline, wife of George II – who had now succeeded his father – as the second. Nor did she neglect her own family. Mary, who was perhaps more like herself than any of the others, could never forget how her mother had prevented her marrying the man she believed she had loved. It was true she had been little more than a child at the time, but the memory of that romance remained with her and all through her unsatisfactory marriage she thought of what might have been and blamed her mother.

'You are an ill wife, a cruel daughter and a bad mother,' Sarah screamed at her daughter. 'I married you to the chief match in England and if it hadn't been for me you might have married a country gentleman with nothing more than two thousand a year.'

Mary turned on her mother and cried: 'You are an interfering old harridan. You interfered in our lives when we were

440

unable to stop you. You shall not do so now.'

Mary stalked out of her mother's house and declared she would never enter again.

And Sarah went about the house complaining to everyone who listened – and none dared do otherwise – that she had the most ungrateful daughter in the world. 'And as to Montague her husband, he's a fine specimen of man, I declare!' she shouted. 'He behaves as though he's fifteen although he's all of fifty-two. He thinks it fun to invite people to his house and into his garden where he squirts them with water. And in his country house he puts vermin in his guests' beds to make them itch. There's the Duke of Montague – my daughter Mary's husband!'

No one pointed out to her that shortly before she had been boasting of marrying Mary to the chief match in England; no one had ever dared point out anything to Sarah, except her daughters, and she quarrelled with them, or her husband, and he was dead.

Nor were her relations any better wiith Henrietta, who had become the Duchess of Marlborough on the death of her father, for it had been agreed that since the Duke had no sons the title should go to his daughter.

Henrietta was causing quite a scandal. She had always been fond of play-acting and play-actors and had long ago formed a very close friendship with William Congreve, the playwright. She took him into her house, for her husband, Lord Godolphin, gave way to her in all things and when Henrietta went to Bath, Congreve went with her. Henrietta was brought to bed of a girl and it was rumoured that she was Congreve's daughter.

'A pleasant scandal,' commented Sarah, 'for one who bears the proud title of Duchess of Marlborough.'

But there was little she could do about that, for when she called on her daughter she was informed that she was not at home, although Sarah was certain that she was.

She had tried to make Henrietta's son William, now Lord Blandford, her favourite; and for a time succeeded in doing so. He was affectionately known as Willigo and Sarah fancied she saw a resemblance in him to his grandfather. But only in features. Willigo quickly became known as Lord Worthless, for he loved gay company and was too fond of the bottle. His mother disliked him, although she doted on her youngest daughter – Congreve's! said Sarah – and consequently Sarah sought to win the affection which he might have given to his mother. But there was little comfort from Willigo. He met a burgomaster's daughter when he was on the Continent and married her before Sarah could forbid the match.

Still eager not to lose him, Sarah met the girl and even found her charming.

But a year after the marriage Sarah was overcome with grief when Willigo died in a drunken fit. As usual her emotions were manifested in rage.

'I hope the Devil is picking the bones of the man who taught him to drink!' she cried.

She was growing more and more aware of loneliness.

To be old and lonely – it was a sad fate. There was only one member of a large family who had any real regard for her; and was it due to pity on Lady Dye's part? Sarah never stopped to consider. She was always right, she believed; and any who disagreed with her were wrong. She told Dye she would call her Cordelia for that was a name most fitting, because she saw herself as a Lear who was driven near to madness by the ingratitude and cruelty of those about her. She could not forbear to meddle, and occupied herself with matchmaking for her grandchildren; and with some difficulty married off Harriet Godolphin to the Duke of Newcastle. She produced Dukes for six of her granddaughters, though for her darling Lady Dye she had looked higher and had selected none less than the Prince of Wales. This was an amazing feat and she almost succeeded in bringing the affair to a successful climax. There were so many points in her favour. Frederick was unpopular and hated his parents, and Sarah and he had this hatred in common for she was at this time deep in her quarrel with Walpole who was supported by the Queen. It was a daring plan. Lady Dye to become a Princess and the royal family to be discountenanced all in one stroke. Frederick had many debts and Sarah was reputed to be the richest woman in England, so there was much to recommend such a marriage.

Such a victory, Sarah believed, would have equalled that of Blenheim. What would Marl think if he could look down from Heaven and see his granddaughter Princess of Wales?

Alas for Sarah! Robert Walpole, the enemy, heard of Sarah's plans and put an end to them. And Sarah had to be content with the Duke of Bedford for Dye.

And when Dye was married she could not stop herself interfering, telling her granddaughter what was wrong with her town house, what improvements should be made, and quarrelling fiercely with her husband.

It was twelve years after the death of Marlborough when death came again to Langley Marsh.

Abigail lay in her bed, her family about her and her mind drifted back and forth from past to present. Her son Samuel knelt by her bed. Her husband was there too with her brother John and her sister Alice.

She knew she was dying; and as she looked at her sister and her brother she was reminded of the day Sarah Churchill had called and how they had received her, trembling with awe and expectation.

Alice was plump and unmarried still; she had lived well and contentedly during the years; John was an old man, his life behind him, and for her and Samuel there were the children.

If Sarah Churchill had not come to them, if she had not given them a helping hand, where would they all be now? No one had had a greater effect upon her life than Sarah – or perhaps than she on Sarah's.

She saw her coming into the shabby house – resplendent in her power and beauty.

'The beginning . . .' she whispered.

And those about the bed looked at each other significantly.

Abigail had left them forever.

Sarah lived on for another ten years. Eighty and as vigorous as ever in mind if not in body, she continued to harry those about her.

Lady Dye had died when she was only twenty-five after only

four years of marriage; next to the death of Marlborough that was the greatest blow of Sarah's life.

It occurred to her then that she was living too long; that too many of those she loved were going on before her.

She thought little of the past; she did however write her memoirs which was an account of how she had first governed the Queen and then been ousted from her favour by Abigail Hill.

Momentarily she recalled all the venom she had felt for that whey-faced creature whom she had taken from a broom.

If I had never taken pity on her, if I had never found a place for her in the Queen's bedchamber ... everything might have been so different. She was the true enemy. She with her quiet ways, her respectful curtsies and her 'Yes, Your Grace!' 'No, Your Grace!' Who would have thought that one so plain, so insignificant ... such a nothing ... such an insect ... could have made so much mischief in the life of people such as herself and the great Duke of Marlborough!

That gave her pause for thought ... for a while. But she was never one to brood on the past.

Occasionally she took out John's letters to her and read them through and wept over them.

'I should destroy them,' she said. 'They can give me nothing but pain now.'

But she could not destroy them. She took out the coil of golden hair which he had kept and which she had discovered in his cabinet and she wept into it.

Then resolutely she put away these souvenirs of the past which so bitterly recalled his love for her; and went once more into battle.

But she was old; and even she could not live for ever.

She was in her bed and the doctors were there, whispering ... waiting for her to die.

'She must be blistered or she will die,' they murmured.

But she lifted herself from her pillows and shouted: 'I won't be blistered and I won't die.'

Nor did she ... just then.

But even she could not stave off death for ever; nor did she wish to.

There was nothing in her life now to make her cling to it even if she was the richest woman in England.

Deliberately she made plans for her burial. She would be buried in Blenheim chapel where she had had John's body brought from Westminster Abbey.

'It is meet and fitting that we should lie together,' she said.

'Old Marlborough is dying.' The news spread through the Court. No one cared. She was a tiresome old woman who was amusing because she was continually making trouble, nothing more.

And on an October day in the year 1744, twenty-two years after the death of the Duke, Sarah died.

She was buried as she had wished; and although the members of her family attended her funeral, there was no one to mourn her.

Jean Plaidy

THE ROAD TO COMPIEGNE	35p
THE SIXTH WIFE	30p
ST THOMAS'S EVE	30p
ROYAL ROAD TO FOTHERINGAY	35p
DAUGHTER OF SATAN	30p
THE THISTLE AND THE ROSE	35p
HERE LIES OUR SOVEREIGN LORD	30p
THE SPANISH BRIDEGROOM	30p
THE WANDERING PRINCE	30p
A HEALTH UNTO HIS MAJESTY	30p
GAY LORD ROBERT	30p
THE MURDER IN THE TOWER	30p
MADAME SERPENT	30p
MURDER MOST ROYAL	35p
THE CAPTIVE QUEEN OF SCOTS	35p
THE ITALIAN WOMAN	30p
LOUIS THE WELL-BELOVED	30p

Georgette Heyer

FARO'S DAUGHTER	25p
BEAUVALLET	25p
THE CORINTHIAN	25p
POWDER AND PATCH	25p
COUSIN KATE	30p
ARABELLA	30p
SPRIG MUSLIN	30p
THE MASQUERADERS	30p
THE TALISMAN RING	30p
THE CONVENIENT MARRIAGE	30p
REGENCY BUCK	35p
THESE OLD SHADES	35p
THE UNKNOWN AJAX	35p
THE RELUCTANT WIDOW	35p
COTILLION	35p
THE GRAND SOPHY	35p
FRIDAY'S CHILD	35p
SYLVESTER	35p
ROYAL ESCAPE	35p
THE TOLL-GATE	35p
DEVIL'S CUB	35p
VENETIA	35p
THE BLACK MOTH	35p
THE QUIET GENTLEMAN	35p
CHARITY GIRL	35p

Juliette Benzoni

CATHERINE   35p

CATHERINE AND A TIME FOR
LOVE   35p

ONE LOVE IS ENOUGH   35p

BELLE CATHERINE   35p

CATHERINE AND ARNAUD   35p

MARIANNE Book I:
The Bride of Selton Hall   35p

MARIANNE Book II:
The Eagle and the Nightingale   30p